PRIVATIZING CHINA

PRIVATIZING CHINA

The Stock Markets and their Role in Corporate Reform

Carl E. Walter

and

Fraser J. T. Howie

John Wiley & Sons (Asia) Pte Ltd

Other Wiley Editorial Offices

John Wiley & Sons, Inc., 111 River Street, Hoboken, NJ 07030, USA
John Wiley & Sons Ltd, The Atrium, Southern Gate, Chichester PO19 1UD, England
John Wiley & Sons (Canada) Ltd, 22 Worcester Road, Rexdale, Ontario M9W 1L1, Canada
John Wiley & Sons Australia Ltd, 33 Park Road (PO Box 1226), Milton, Queensland 4064, Australia
Wiley-VCH, Pappelallee 3, 69469 Weinheim, Germany

Library of Congress Cataloging-in-Publication Data

0-470-82120-5 (Paperback)

Typeset in 10/12 points, Usherwood by Cepha Imaging Pvt Ltd
Saik Wah Press Pte Ltd
10 9 8 7 6 5 4 3 2 1

Once again, for our families and friends

Contents

Preface

More than three years have gone by since we completed the research for *To Get Rich is Glorious!*, the book that provides the starting point for *Privatizing China*. Looking back at 1999 it seems like an entirely different era. In fact, it was the end of an era, the era of the state's "experimentation" with stocks and markets. After seven years of debate, the National People's Congress passed the Securities Law in late December 1999 and it went into effect on July 1, 2000. This marked the party's and state's complete acceptance of state enterprise reform through initial public offerings. No longer was this just an experiment founded on "provisional" measures and decrees. It is now (and has been for the past 12 years) the fundamental direction of government policy affecting the entire corporate – and now the financial – sectors of the economy. For anyone who has studied the first 40 years of China's post-Liberation history, who would ever have thought this could happen? As someone put it, "In the '60s we stood in line for pork, in the '90s we stood in line for stocks." Now, at the turn of the new century, people are standing in line to buy controlling stakes in state-owned enterprises outright. So much for theory.

Beginning in 2000, the year they raised US$20 billion with overseas public offerings and nearly another US$20 billion domestically, China's corporations and stock markets have entered a new phase. The pace of change has become faster than anyone might have imagined, driven by the country's entry into the World Trade Organization in December 2001. The one common theme shared with the 1990s remains the unceasing demand for capital. With underdeveloped debt markets and increasingly conservative banks, the only way to raise significant amounts of new capital is through domestic and international stock offerings. This in itself is astounding. In the early days during the 1980s, the People's Bank of China was supportive of share offerings because they relieved pressure on the banking system to make loans. This was also the principal reason for continued state support of the experiment in the days after June 4, 1989, the last time strident leftist politics came to the fore. The financings had the people's support: share fever, after all, built momentum in late 1989 and early 1990. Now, 20 years later, the banks are relying on the stock markets to strengthen their own balance sheets, preparing to fight for global market share. Major industrial companies, China's potential national champions, have formed and accessed the international markets for billions of dollars in new capital in a single offering. All told, international stock offerings since 1992 have contributed over US$60 billion to China's corporate reform effort and the domestic markets another US$85 billion. Add this US$145 billion to the over US$400 billion of foreign direct investment and you have a good explanation for why talk of China's economic dynamism is as widespread now as it was about Japan in the 1980s. In sum, the shareholding "experiment" has defined the state's financial policy process now for over a decade.

Agreement on the Securities Law, however, came just in time. During the 1990s, a weak market regulator faced a hugely political process aimed at sourcing capital for state enterprises. The China Securities Regulatory Commission had the final signoff authority over which companies could list and raise funding and which could not. But there was little it could do if a provincial governor or industry minister got support for his pet company at the State Council level or above. It faced a similar problem with the securities companies, especially the large national ones that had access to the very top of the system. Consequently, China's own stock markets listed politically connected companies, not companies with fundamentally sound economic prospects. At the same time, the retail investors, whose wild enthusiasm had catalyzed the formation of the exchanges, were driven largely to the sidelines by the institutionalized corruption of the brokerages and other professional market participants. These problems were compounded by a growing overhang of non-tradable state-owned shares. This overhang has distorted the operations of the market, as well as its valuation function.

For this paperback edition, we decided to rewrite our first book completely, not because the Securities Law created on paper a single, strong industry regulator, but because the regulator has actually begun to regulate. Over the past three years, the true picture of domestic development has become clear as the CSRC attempts to reverse the damage done in the 1990s. At the same time, we have been able to draw on new data that enabled us to develop a better grasp of the underlying trends in the corporate sector. The obscure categories of Chinese shares defined in law in 1992 to prevent the privatization of state enterprises have, it turns out, created the conditions leading in the end to something resembling privatization. The ceaseless demand for capital has created what we call parallel markets in the different shares. Valued at different prices, with different participants, and even different regulators, China's public and private markets veil what might be called "privatization with Chinese characteristics."

Although the just completed 16th Congress of the Chinese Communist Party has affirmed the "legal" rights of the "non-public economic sector," what has been legally obtained and what has not continues to be a matter of political judgment. There are no laws protecting private property in China yet, and there are many burdens for the non-state sector. In these circumstances, can privatization be carried out in any way other than behind the guise of the status quo? To those engaged in the process, it makes no difference. There is no question, and it is an open secret here, that China is carrying out one of the greatest redistributions of wealth in history. The state is spinning off its possessions first into the hands of lesser state entities, and the latter, due to their own need for capital, are spinning them into the hands of the private sector. Many believe this may be the last great chance to strike it rich in China. This process can be seen through the lens of the stock markets. We previously claimed that enterprise reform in China was corporatization and not privatization, and that, for the most part, is true today as well. Corporatization is the first step. Next has come an obscure and legally tenuous form of something akin to ownership that brings with it outright control, but not clear ownership, of companies. We never thought things would move so fast.

This time, we sincerely want to thank Zhou Tao, regional sales manager at Wind Information Company, Beijing. We used Wind intensively for the first go around, but never appreciated it as much as we do now. Tao gave us complete access to the system without cost during the period of research and writing. We plumbed its depths, and what depths! The only thing that Wind didn't have about the stock markets was full details on the ownership of China's brokerages. This information was "private," we were told! We are deeply in his debt and acknowledge this with gratitude. This book could not have been written without Wind.

One of us has also been spending time at China M&A Management, run by Wang Wei, one of the people in at the beginning of China's stock markets. We have learned much about the private markets from work being done by his group. Professor Chen Zhiwu of the Yale School of Management has been kind enough to provide us a copy of a recent paper on illiquid stock discounts; his comment was: "I didn't know anyone here would be interested in these things." Thanks also to Liu Xu of the Shenzhen Stock Exchange, Beijing Liaison Office, who allowed us to rummage through the office and take whatever we wanted for free. The Shanghai Exchange has no such office in Beijing.

Nick Wallwork at John Wiley & Sons happily undertook this edition and we are indebted to him. Robyn Flemming, our editor, ripped through the book's arcane details and obscure sentences with a sharp pen, making it much more readable. Many thanks are due to both. Once again, our families have borne the brunt of this work. It has taken over all of our evenings, weekends, and holidays when both of us could have been taking care of them instead of feeding our obsession. Since they saw us through this once before, they were willing to see us through it again, and we are grateful to them for their understanding and support. We promise not to do it again!

Last time we were sure when we had finished that we had made mistakes or omissions. We did. We caught some of them, and have probably made more this time. They are our responsibility, as are any errors of misunderstanding. We also wish to point out that the contents and views herein represent only our own opinions and not those of the firms with which we are now associated. Within the very near future, there will be many professionals looking at the domestic stock and bond markets of China. With QFII, asset management joint ventures, and maybe a new foreign-invested securities company or so, China's securities markets are now opening for all to see.

Carl E. Walter
Fraser J. T. Howie
Beijing
March 2003

List of Figures

List of Tables

List of Boxes

List of Abbreviations

ABC	Agricultural Bank of China
ADR	American Depository Receipt
AWSJ	*Asian Wall Street Journal*
BOC	Bank of China
BoComm	Bank of Communications
CAAC	Civil Aviation Administration of China
CAS	China Appraisal Society
CB	convertible bonds
CCB	China Construction Bank
CCP	Chinese Communist Party
CDR	Chinese Depository Receipt
CEA	China Eastern Airlines
CGB	Chinese government bond
CICC	China International Capital Corporation
CICPA	Chinese Institute of Certified Public Accountants
CIRC	Chinese Insurance Regulatory Commission
COFCO	China National Oil, Grain and Food Products
CPA	certified public accountant
CSDCC	China Securities Depository and Clearing Corporation
CSRC	China Securities Regulatory Commission
CSTS	China Securities Trading System Corp. Ltd.
ECM	equity capital markets
EPS	earnings per share
FDI	foreign direct investment
FMC	fund management company
GDP	gross domestic product
GEM	Growth Enterprise Market
HSCCI	Hang Seng China-Affiliated Corporations Index
IAS	International Accounting Standards
ICBC	Industrial and Commercial Bank of China
IOSCO	International Organization of Securities Regulatory Commissions
IPO	initial public offering
ITIC	international trust and investment company
JV	joint venture
LP	legal person (shares)
M&A	mergers and acquisitions
MBO	management buy-out
MOF	Ministry of Finance
MOFERT	Ministry of Foreign Economic Relations and Trade

MOFTEC	Ministry of Foreign Trade and Economic Cooperation
NASD	National Association of Securities Dealers
NAV	net asset value
NETS	National Electronic Trading System
NPC	National People's Congress
NYSE	New York Stock Exchange
OTC	over the counter
PBOC	People's Bank of China
P/E	price/earnings ratio
PICC	People's Insurance Company of China
PRC	People's Republic of China
PT	particular treatment (shares)
QDII	Qualified Domestic Institutional Investor
QFII	Qualified Foreign Institutional Investor
RMB	Renminbi
SAC	Securities Association of China
SAEC	State Administration of Exchange Control
SAFE	State Administration of Foreign Exchange
SAIC	State Administration of Industry and Commerce
SAMB	State Asset Management Bureau
SC	State Council
SCMP	*South China Morning Post*
SCRES	State Committee for the Restructuring of the Economic System
SCSC	State Council Securities Committee
SDB	Shenzhen Development Bank
SEC	Securities and Exchange Commission
SEEC	Stock Exchange Executive Council
SEHK	Stock Exchange of Hong Kong
SETC	State Economic and Trade Commission
SEZ	Special Economic Zone
SIF	securities investment fund
SISCO	Shanghai International Securities Company
SLMB	State Land Management Bureau
SOE	state-owned enterprise
SOET	State Office of Economics and Trade
SPC	State Planning Commission
SPDC	State Planning and Development Commission
SPCB	State Price Control Bureau
SSCCRC	Shanghai Securities Central Clearing and Registration Company
SSE	Shanghai Stock Exchange
ST	special transfer (shares)
STAQ	Securities Trading Automated Quotation System
SZSE	Shenzhen Stock Exchange
TVE	township and village enterprise
WTO	World Trade Organization

Chronology

Historical Performance, Shanghai and Shenzhen Stock Exchanges

1882	China's first share trading organization, Shanghai Pinghuai Stock Co., founded in October
1891	Shanghai Stock Exchange founded to broker foreign stocks
1905	Shanghai People's Exchange founded in Hong Kong
1914	Shanghai Stock Commercial Association founded: China's first formal stock trading association; Northern Government issues "Stock Exchange Law"
1918	Beijing Securities Trading Exchange founded
1920	Shanghai Securities and Commodities Exchange founded and becomes the largest trading center in China; Shanghai Stock Commercial Association changes name to Shanghai Huashang Securities Trading Exchange
1921	Tianjin Securities Trading Exchange founded
1949	Tianjin Military Command decides to establish a securities exchange. It opens on June 1, four months before Liberation, with five listed stocks

1950   Beijing Securities Exchange opens on February 1

1952   Government closes Tianjin and Beijing exchanges in
            February and July, respectively

1978

December 22   Third Plenum of 11th Party Congress focuses party work
            from 1979 on economic construction, marking a formal
            end to the Cultural Revolution and the return of
            Deng Xiaoping

1979

July 3   State Council issues "Decision on Several Problems on the
            Development of Commune and Brigade Enterprises"
            suggesting that rural enterprises could self-finance through
            selling shares. The shareholding experiment finds its origin
            in the countryside

October 20   Liaoning Fushun No. 1 Brick Factory gets party approval for
            a share issue

1980

January 1   Fushun Brick Factory issues its shares. This appears to be the
            first stock issue in post-1949 China

July   Chengdu Shudu Office Building Co. Ltd. issues shares. Idea
            sprang from a movie; also has a claim to be the first offering

1981   Ministry of Finance revives issuance of treasury bonds

1983

July   Shenzhen Baoan County United Investment Co. Ltd. issues
            shares. Often cited as the first share offering

1984

July   Shanghai "Eight Articles" released: first formal regulations
            for the nascent securities market

September   ICBC Shanghai Trust and Investment Company, Jingan Office,
            establishes first OTC counter for treasury securities

            Beijing Tianqiao Department Store Co. Ltd. is established
            and issues shares. Often cited as first share offering

October   Third Plenum of 12th Party Congress passes "Decision on
            Reform of the Economic System" – partially resolves the family
            name game: do shares belong to Mr. Capitalism's family only,
            or can they also belong to Comrade Socialism's family?

November 14   Shanghai Feile Acoustics offers shares to the public: first "relatively standardized" public share offering. Feile is seen as the first IPO of the New Era

December   Shanghai has recorded 1,700 share issues raising RMB240 million; Shenyang 502, including 14 public issues, raising RMB400 million

1985

September 27   First specialized securities company established. PBOC Beijing approves Shenzhen Special Economic Zone Securities Company. Opening delayed for two more years due to ideological disputes

1986

January 7   State Council announces "Provisional Regulations on the Administration of Banks" giving PBOC authority over the financial sector, including, as an afterthought, securities

August 5   China's first securities exchange opens. The Shenyang Securities Exchange opens sponsored by the Shenyang City Trust Company, owned by PBOC Shenyang Branch

September 26   Shanghai ICBC, Jingan Office, starts OTC share trading

October 15   Shenzhen Provisions released. These were the first comprehensive attempt to define and regulate the corporatization and listing process

November 11   Deng Xiaoping receives the chairman of the NYSE in the Great Hall of the People. The gift presented – a single (fake!) share in Feile Acoustics – caused a great tizzy

1987

March 28   State Council formally makes PBOC the regulator and supervisory agency for the corporatization and securities listing experiment

May   Sales begin of Shenzhen Development Bank IPO shares, including 170,000 shares denominated in Hong Kong dollars

September   Shenzhen Special Economic Zone Securities Company at last established

1988   To facilitate sales and transfer of treasury securities, the PBOC sets up 34 securities companies; by year-end, there were over 100 trading counters in operation across the country

March   Gao Xiqing, Wang Boming, and Wang Wei submit to senior party leadership "Policy Suggestions for Promoting the

Legalization and Standardization of China's Securities Markets (preliminary draft)"

April 11   Shenzhen Development Bank IPO shares begin trading on the counters of the Shenzhen SEZ Securities Co. These counters were Shenzhen's first formal securities exchange

April 13   NPC passes the Enterprise Law. The law recognized the reality of enterprise management autonomy and transformed SOEs into legal persons

May 1   Zhu Rongji becomes Shanghai mayor

July   PBOC convenes conference on securities markets; decision taken to establish a working group to produce a White Paper

November 9   Completed White Paper is received by top party leadership, who decide that further research is needed by a non-state entity, leading to the creation of the Stock Exchange Executive Council (SEEC)

1989

March   "Share fever" ignited for the first time. Shenzhen Development Bank announces 1988 dividend. The generous dividend policy sets off "stock fever" in Shenzhen and southern China; in Shanghai, the third share issue by Shanghai Vacuum Electronic Device fails

March 15   SEEC formally established with the mission of setting up a Beijing exchange with ultimately 600 listed companies

June 4   Direction of the country called into question, particularly the suitability of creating capital markets

December 2   Zhu Rongji becomes Shanghai Party secretary and convenes conference on financial reforms in Shanghai. A working group was set up to begin work on a securities exchange proposal

1990

March   Shenzhen Yuanye IPO two times oversubscribed: "share fever" continues

Spring   Zhu Rongji in Hong Kong returning from trip to U.S. announces that Shanghai will establish a stock exchange within one year

Late May   State Council and SCRES issue report restricting the market to Shanghai and Shenzhen only and to SOEs only; Shenzhen shares rocket ahead on the news. Regional trading centers continue to thrive

June 2	The government approves Shanghai's request to establish a stock exchange in Pudong
August 8	Shenzhen attempts trial operation of stock exchange, but is not approved
October 12	PBOC issues "Provisional Measures for Management of Securities Companies"
October 13	Shenzhen exchange again seeks to start trial operations, but again is not approved
November	Government intervention cools the Shenzhen and Shanghai markets, but share fever has given birth to an equity investor mentality
November 22	Shenzhen hears Shanghai about to begin stock exchange operations
November 26	PBOC with State Council authorization approves establishment of the Shanghai Stock Exchange and establishment ceremony is held
December 1	Shenzhen begins "trial operations" without formal approval and with only one stock trading
December 5	Securities Trading Automated Quotations System (STAQ) is established
December 19	Shanghai Stock Exchange begins operations. PBOC announces that all public stock issues and listings can only be done on the Shanghai and Shenzhen exchanges: opens the primary market again

1991

January	National Electronic Trading System (NETS) formally established
July 3	Shenzhen Stock Exchange is formally approved and opened after seven months of "trial operation"
August 1	First convertible bond issued; Hainan Xinneng Power
August 28	Securities Association of China established
November	Shanghai Vacuum Electronic Device begins first B-share IPO; shares begin trading in February 1992
December	SCRES working group travels to Hong Kong to explore idea of listing Chinese companies on overseas markets
December 31	*People's Daily* on first page publishes major article, "Exploring a socialist stock market with Chinese characteristics." Article

confirmed that the government had not given up support of securities markets despite June 4

1992

January	Deng Xiaoping undertakes the "Southern Excursion," affirms China can try out stock markets; his comments unleash a fury of energy
January 13	Xingye Real Estate completes the first listing of new shares since the opening of the Shanghai exchange
April	Charles Y. K. Lee, chairman of the SEHK, meets Vice Premier Zhu Rongji and proposes listing SOEs on the SEHK; Zhu agrees and suggests 10 companies
May 7	PBOC with State Council approval sets up a Securities Market Office (*Zhengguanban*) to supervise all aspects of the securities industry. The Office was a forerunner of the SCSC and CSRC
May 15	SCRES announces passage of the "Standard Opinion," the first systematic national approach to corporatization and share listing. The Opinion introduced tradable and non-tradable share types
May 21	Stop trading limits removed; stock prices could now rise and fall freely for first time since founding of exchanges
June	PBOC Securities Market Office transferred to State Council
July	Joint China–Hong Kong working groups seek to establish the regulatory basis for SEHK listings of Chinese companies
July 7	Trading in Shenzhen Yuanye shares is halted. First market fraud scandal and first actual de-listing of a listed company
August 10	"810 Incident" – Shenzhen crowds riot over PBOC mismanagement of IPO application process. This led directly to the establishment of the CSRC
October	PBOC sponsors the opening in Beijing, Shanghai, and Shenzhen of three national securities firms: Huaxia, Guotai, and Nanfang. This led to local governments following suit, establishing a large number of illegal financial institutions. The clean-up of these entities continues until today
October 7	Brilliance China Automotive lists on NYSE, raising US$80 million. This was China's first ever overseas IPO
October 25	CSRC established; shortly after announces nine candidate companies for Hong Kong listing, known as the "First Batch"
December 17	State Council Document 68 clarifies roles in the securities industry

1993

July	MOF announces new accounting principles for SOEs based on International Accounting Standards
July 7	CSRC authorized to appoint senior managers of Shanghai and Shenzhen exchanges: the first step in the central government takeover of the exchanges
July 19	Formal Memorandum of Understanding signed with SEHK
July 29	Tsingtao Beer completes the first SEHK IPO by a Chinese company, raising US$115 million
August	Bear market begins; will last for three years
August 20	First closed-end securities investment fund lists on the Shanghai exchange; previously such funds had been listed only on the regional trading centers
November 4	State Council authorizes SCSC and CSRC to supervise the commodities and futures exchanges
December	State Council issues "Decision on Reform of the Economic System" initiating clean-up of the financial markets, including separating the banking and securities industries. PBOC approves the licenses of new brokerages and restructuring of bank brokerage operations. Total brokerages consequently stand at 91
December 4	Shanghai exchange institutes repo trading of CGBs
December 29	National People's Congress passes the Company Law

1994

January	Second Batch of 22 listing candidates announced by CSRC: investment bankers go wild
July 1	Zhu Rongji signs Company Law into effect permitting Shandong Huaneng to proceed with its NYSE listing, the first direct listing of a Chinese company on the NYSE
July 29	Shanghai market hits record low, 326
August 1	CSRC announces the "Three Major Policies to Save the Market"
August 10	First direct listing of a Chinese company on the NYSE, Shandong Huaneng Power Generation, raising US$333 million
September	Due to intense lobbying, CSRC revises Second Batch list to include seven additional candidates

December	Inflation peaks at nearly 22%
1995	PBOC restructures bank securities operations creating seven new brokerages. Nationwide total reaches 97, of which 63 were in some way related to the PBOC
February 23	"327 Incident" – Treasury futures scandal breaks out with March 27 CGB future trades accounting for 80% of total market trading as SISCO corners the market. All futures trading halted
March 7	Treasury futures resume trading except for 327 contract
March 25	Liu Hongru removed from chairmanship of CSRC. He remains highly regarded as one of the market's pioneers
March 31	Zhou Daojiong appointed chairman of CSRC
April 21	SC and SCRES issue decree forbidding the trading of listed company shares outside the two formally constituted exchanges
May 17	CSRC with State Council approval "temporarily" halts treasury futures trading
August 9	First foreign companies to become largest shareholder in a listed company. Isuzu and Itochu acquire LP shares in Beijing Bus. This practice is not permitted again until 2002
August 26	First time a listed company posts operating loss
1996	
May 1	PBOC reduces deposit and loan interest rates: reflects end of anti-inflation struggle; full-year inflation falls to 6.8%
June 14	Shenzhen index tops 2,000, marking the start of the second bull market
July 17	Shenyin Securities merged with Wanguo Securities (SISCO) to form Shenyin Wanguo Securities: the first major merger due to scandal in the securities sector, but not the last
July 30	PBOC announces measures forcing the four state banks (and its own branches) to divest their trust banks of all securities operations by year-end
August 23	PBOC again reduces deposit and loan interest rates
October	PBOC requires all commercial banks, insurance companies, urban credit cooperatives, enterprise groups, leasing

	companies, and other financial entities to spin off a total of 763 securities operations. This was largely completed in 2000
October	CSRC begins release of the "Twelve Gold Shields" policies aimed at regularizing the markets
October 23	Shanghai Index tops 1,000
December	Third Batch of 39 listing candidates announced by CSRC; the largest group to date; bankers go back to work after two down years
December 16	*People's Daily* "Special Correspondent" editorializes "On correctly understanding the current stock market" and warns against the highly speculative nature of the current market
December 16	Shanghai and Shenzhen reinstitute a 10% daily trading range for all listed products
1997	PBOC forced to spin off 43 brokerage firms owned by branches in its own system; these represented half the entire number of legally approved brokerages
January 4	"Basic" completion of trust and investment company restructurings by the four state banks. Of 186 trust companies, 148 are closed and ownership transferred for 33. "Basic" meant "not yet completed"
February 3	Former head of SISCO, Guan Jinsheng, sentenced to 15 years for leading the 327 treasury futures scandal
February 18	Deng Xiaoping passes away
April 18	LP shares auctioned off for the first time.
April 24	Shenzhen Index breaks 5,000
May 12	Shenzhen Index breaks 6,000
May 16	Shenzhen and Shanghai indexes crash: Shenzhen to 5,100
May 22	Shenzhen and Shanghai indexes crash again; Shenzhen to 4,789
May 27	State forbids SOEs to use state funds or bank loans to buy shares
July 1	Hong Kong returns to Chinese sovereignty
July 12	Zhou Zhengqing, vice chairman of SCSC, also named temporary CSRC chairman: State Council dismisses Zhou Daojiong: another one bites the dust

July 29	MOF announces start of accounting industry restructuring
August 15	State Council announces that the Shenzhen and Shanghai exchanges are under CSRC control: central government completes its takeover of the exchanges
September 23	Shanghai and Shenzhen reach new lows
September 24	The three major securities papers print editorials expressing greatest confidence in the market's development
October	Asia Financial Crisis breaks out just after China Telecom's IPO, the first industry-wide restructuring
October 23	PBOC again reduces deposit and loan interest rates to spur market
November	PBOC approves Junan Securities' plan to increase capital: start of yet another scandal
November 15	Efforts begin to restructure the funds management industry. CSRC announces new regulations for securities investment funds
December 19	Shanghai exchange moves into its new building
1998	SCSC dissolved and CSRC elevated to full ministry status; SAMB eliminated and asset appraisal industry clean-up instituted
March 25	PBOC again reduces deposit and loan interest rates
April	Unapproved MBO of Junan Securities revealed and fails; recapitalization halted and company nearly bankrupt
April 7	First two new securities investment funds listed in Shanghai and Shenzhen
April 18	Zhou Zhengqing confirmed as CSRC chairman
April 28	First ST share is born: Shenyang Materials Development
June	CSRC takes over responsibility for licensing securities firms from PBOC
July 1	PBOC again reduces deposit and loan interest rates
July 24	CSRC announces merger of Junan Securities with Guotai Securities, forming Guotai Junan
September 12	ST Jiangsu Sanshan Industries is de-listed: first de-listing since Yuanye Industries stopped trading in July 1992

November 18	Chinese Insurance Regulatory Commission established
November 20	CSRC reveals Chengdu Hongguang Industries had fraudulently used its 1997 IPO proceeds to invest directly and through a gray market consultant in the stock market
December 2	PBOC emphasizes that trust company securities operations must be completely separated from banking operations; such securities entities totaled 960. January 4, 1997, announcement of "basic" completion of this effort was, in fact, premature
	CSRC forbids issuance of internal employee shares
December 7	PBOC again reduces deposit and loan interest rates
December 29	National People's Congress at last passes Securities Law

1999

January 16	Guangdong International Trust and Investment Corp. (GITIC) declared bankrupt
February 10	Shenyang Materials Development returns to profitability, loses "ST" designation, the first such case in market history
May 19	"519 Event" – Driven by the craze for hi-tech companies, Shenzhen and Shanghai reach record highs as well as record trading volumes
June 10	PBOC again reduces deposit and loan interest rates
June 15	*People's Daily* "Special Correspondent" for the third time intervenes directly in the market, stating that the buoyant stock markets reflected the reality of a strong economy and that the 519 Affair was "healthy." The market roars ahead
June 22	Shenzhen and Shanghai reach post-1993 record highs: third bull market begins
	CSRC chairman Zhou Zhengqing affirms that the 519 Affair is a healthy reflection of the economy; adds jet fuel to the blazing fire
June 30	All regional trading centers to be closed by this date
July	First minority shareholder lawsuit ever rejected by court. Suit against management fraud in Chengdu Hongguang Industries
July 1	Securities Law goes into effect; CSRC begins preparing regional offices that would give it a national presence for first time

	Shenzhen and Shanghai markets record significant fall: third bull market sputters out following Hong Kong handover
July 9	"PT" share designation instituted by both exchanges: for companies with three consecutive years of losses
July 29	Placement of shares to "strategic" corporate investors combined with online share issuance method instituted
September 3	First successful restructuring of old non-standard investment funds. Three non-standard Hunan investment funds de-list from Southern Regional Trading Center and list on the Shanghai and Shenzhen exchanges
September 9	CSRC announces regulations once again permitting SOEs to open securities accounts and trade shares
September 10	Capital Steel becomes first A-share issue to be supported by "strategic" investors
September 19	For the first time, the CCP refers to stocks and the shareholding system in its public report. The affirmation of strong support indicates end of "experimental" stage of the reform
September 23	First IPO of a commercial bank since 1987 – Shanghai Pudong Development Bank
October 25	Insurance companies allowed to buy securities investment funds
October 27	Sale of state shares through inclusion in public offerings announced
November 1	Tax placed on interest earned from bank deposits in effort to stimulate the stock markets
	Insurance companies invest for first time in a securities investment fund listing
November 4	Konka completes successful secondary offering using strategic and retail investors
November 13	Hong Kong Growth Enterprise Market (GEM) established
December 13	Only a bit more than 3% of Sheneng Energy shareholders pass resolution to buy back RMB1 billion in state shares from parent
December 16	Sheneng successfully buys back state shares; first example of a state share buy-back – market sees parent company pay off
	Fourth and final batch of nine listing candidates announced by CSRC

2000

January 6	Securities firms and investment funds permitted to trade in the inter-bank bond market
February 17	Daily trading volume in both exchanges exceeds US$1 billion for first time
February 24	Zhou Xiaochuan becomes CSRC chairman; CSRC begins period of activism
March 3	First loan collateralized by stock. CCB and Xiangcai Securities sign loan agreement
March 14	CSRC approves listing and trading of leftover rights offering shares (*zhuanpeigu*) beginning in April. A start to getting rid of residual "non-tradable" shares
March 17	To comply with the Securities Law, CSRC releases regulations defining the new review method (*hezhunzhi*) for listing applications, and eliminates old quota and administrative pricing mechanisms
March 27	Shanghai and Shenzhen set new records exceeding 519 rally highs – Shanghai hits 1,771; Hong Kong Hang Seng Index also hits high
April 3	*Zhuanpeigu* begin listing and trading
May 18	CSRC forbids selling new share offerings only to securities investment funds
June 1	Shanghai hits 1,900, a new high: fourth bull market off and running
June 13	Open accounts exceed 50 million
July 6	Listed companies exceed 1,000
July 19	Shanghai breaks 2,000 mark before falling back to 1,998
July 26	Shanghai breaks and remains above 2,000 at 2,012
August 21	Shanghai breaks 2,100
August 29	CSRC warns investors against illegal trading activities; announces that Shenzhen has uncovered an illegal trading scheme: the Mr. K case begins to break
September 20	The first brokerage stock concept is born. CSRC approves the restructuring of listed Hongyuan Trust into Hongyuan Securities.

October 8	The Black Funds Scandal – *Caijing* magazine reveals pervasive stock manipulation by fund management industry
October 12	CSRC approves regulations permitting open-ended funds
October 16	Ten fund management companies publish denial of any illegal trading activities, promise retribution
October 18	Draft Shenzhen Growth Market regulations and articles of incorporation posted on CSRC website to seek public input
October 25	Zhou Xiaochuan comments that foreign investment in brokerages and fund management companies will be permitted in the near future and that foreign companies will be allowed to list domestically. Expectations for the B-share market go up
October 29	Wu Jinglian on CCTV strongly criticizes the fund management industry and casts doubt on quality of regulation. Wu claims that China's stock markets are a "casino." The CSRC responds at once, claiming it is actively investigating the Black Fund Scandal. The casino remark sparks a major public debate
October 30	Zhengzhou Baiwen Department Store scandal bursts into public exposed by Xinhua News. State Council sends investigation team
November 20	State Council passes measures permitting asset management firms to underwrite shares
December 1	Zhengzhou Baiwen submits reorganization plan
December 14	First court judgment against a listed company. Chengdu Intermediate Courts finds Hongguang Industries guilty of fraud
December 19	BaoSteel does jumbo A-share IPO, raising US$900 million

2001

January 4	In 2000 for first time, total funds raised in one year exceed RMB100 billion
February	First major stock-market manipulator, Mr. K, arrested
February 12	State Council appoints Laura Cha as a vice chairman of CSRC
February 14	CCTV does one-hour program revealing the "Black Story of Lanzhou's Securities Markets"
February 19	Domestic investors permitted to buy B shares

March 2	CIRC permits three insurance companies to invest up to 100 % of certain types of insurance premium in securities investment funds
March 6	Zhou Xiaochuan states that opening B shares to domestic investors does not imply a possible merging of B shares into the A-share market
March 7	First parent bankruptcy to impact a listed company. Parent of listed company Monkey King declares bankruptcy on February 27, resulting in Monkey King being declared an ST share
March 17	Formal implementation of CSRC review and approval system
March 23	CSRC releases report on investigation of the Black Funds Scandal absolving the industry and indirectly impugning Shanghai exchange research
April 5	All *zhuanpeigu* completely listed and trading as A shares
April 23	Shanghai Narcissus becomes first company to be de-listed
April 30	CSRC regional offices formally open
May 17	Shanghai breaks through 2,200
June 18	First major corporate domestic bond issue. China Mobile via its Guangdong subsidiary issues RMB5 billion corporate bond
June 22	First major overseas listed company to list domestically. Sinopec announces plans to issue A shares
June 30	PBOC releases results of its investigation of gray market money managers, concludes private funds under management may total RMB900 billion – more than half of the market free float
July 3	Mid-year results show 40 % of securities investment funds are losing money. First widespread losses in industry
July 16	Third Board begins trading. Two stocks previously listed on STAQ begin OTC trading among brokerages
July 23	First time pension funds enter A-share market. Pension funds participate in Sinopec's A-share IPO, subscribing to 300 million shares
July 24	First domestic offering to include state shares, representing 10 % of total shares. State and A shares offered at same price
July 27	PBOC announces four banks in Shenyang have provided loans used for share purchases. Responsible officials dismissed and banks placed under restructuring

July 30	"Black Monday." Fear of state shares flooding market causes Shanghai to drop for six days, losing 10.2%, 5.3% on July 30 alone, breaking through the 2,000 level for first time since February 2001
August 3	*Caijing* magazine reveals listed company Yinguangxia fabricated RMB745 million operating results to achieve listing
August 6	"Black Monday II." Shanghai drops 9.8% in one day, breaking through 1,900 level. Largest single-day drop in market history. Shenzhen drops 7.2%
	Fund with large holdings of Yinguangxia trades below RMB1 face value. First time since the June 1999 rally any fund has done so
August 8	Sinopec jumbo offering begins trading. Shares open at RMB4.60, higher than offering price (RMB4.22), but fall back to RMB4.36 with turnover nearly twice issued amount. Pension fund investors "very unhappy" with pricing decision: no upside
August 9	Yinguangxia admits to falsifying results, announces halt in trading for 30 days to investigate
August 16	CSRC announces requirements for independent company directors
August 22	Sinopec shares fall below offering price: calls into question new pricing methodology
August 25	MOF announces plans to conduct a "severe inspection" of all listed companies' finances, responding to Yinguangxia incident
August 27	"Black Monday III." Both markets drop over 3%
August 30	MOF takes punitive action against 13 accounting firms and 21 CPAs, as well as 16 listed companies and 42 accounting personnel
September 4	Hua-an Innovation Fund lists, first standardized open-ended fund
September 6	CSRC spokesman announces that persons responsible for falsifying Yinguangxia results have been turned over to police pending trial
September 8	MOF announces it has canceled all licenses of Yinguangxia's auditor and is pursuing legal action against two of the firm's partners. First time auditors have ever been implicated

September 13   CSRC releases regulations on "green shoe" share over-allotments

September 19   Shanghai falls below 1,600 level

September 23   CSRC announces a halt to state share sales; markets respond by actively trading up

November 12   China joins World Trade Organization

November 14   MOFTEC and CSRC announce regulations permitting foreign companies to list domestically

November 21   Shanghai falls through 1,400 points

December 10   Shenyin Wanguo begins making market in de-listed shares of Shanghai Narcissus. First de-listed shares to be traded on the Third Board

December 11   CSRC announces details of WTO commitment: foreign firms can hold up to 33% of brokerages and FMCs, the latter growing to 49% after three years

December 13   CITIC Securities announces its IPO; first IPO of a brokerage

December 28   CSRC severely punishes Zhejiang Securities for using investor funds totaling RMB630 million and for providing margin financing totaling RMB460 million. The firm loses its proprietary trading license and persons responsible are held by police pending trial

2002

January 14   "Black Monday IV." Shanghai breaks through 1,500; Shenzhen sets new lows

January 15   Supreme People's Court issues ruling allowing investors to file suit in securities cases once CSRC has determined that illegal activity has taken place

January 21   "Black Monday V." Shanghai falls below 1,400; 200 stocks hit price limits going down

January 29   CSRC issues convertible bond regulations

February 21   PBOC decreases interest rates on loans and deposits

June 4   CSRC issues regulations on foreign investment in brokerages and fund management companies

June 24   State Council announces cancellation of plans to reduce holdings of state shares except in the case of overseas issues. Both markets surge upward by over 9%; 900 stocks trade to their ceiling level

July 18   Zhou Xiaochuan announces that China is prepared to imple-
                 ment a QFII system

July 27   CSRC circulates draft of "Listed Company Merger Measures"
                 for public comment

August 9   CSRC cancels Anshan Securities license; Anshan is the first
                 brokerage ever to have its license canceled

September 7   CSRC, Liaoning provincial government, and Dalian municipal
                 government form team to close down Dalian Securities

                 CSRC revokes Tonghai Hi-tech IPO approval; forces firm to
                 disgorge IPO proceeds and return them to investors

September 20   China Unicom lists domestically in largest IPO to date

October 8   CSRC releases final Listed Companies Merger Measures

November 27   Sichuan Intermediate Court finds in favor of 11 plaintiffs
                 against Chengdu Hongguang. First court finding for minority
                 shareholder lawsuit

December 1   QFII becomes effective; qualified foreign institutional funds
                 can enter the domestic securities markets for first time

December 27   First JV fund management company is established by ING
                 Group and China Merchants Securities; ING holds 30%,
                 China Merchants 40%, the remaining 30% is held by three
                 domestic firms

December 30   Zhou Xiaochuan leaves the CSRC, becoming governor of the
                 PBOC; replaced by Shang Fulin, former chairman of the
                 Agricultural Bank of China

2003

January 2   The year starts badly with Shanghai and Shenzhen hitting $3\frac{1}{2}$-
                 year lows: Shanghai closes at 1,320.63, Shenzhen at 2,689.49

January 3   Citigroup buys an initial 5% stake (legal person shares) in
                 Shanghai Pudong Development Bank for RMB600 million

January 6   CITIC Securities lists on the Shanghai exchange, raising
                 RMB1.8 billion; the stock performs poorly, closing up only
                 11%. This is the first IPO and listing of a securities company

January 8   New CSRC chairman, Shang Fulin, visits the Shanghai Stock
                 Exchange and leading brokerage firms in Shanghai. The
                 market jumps 10% within a week of his visit

January 9   Supreme People's Court permits "joint" action suits once
                 CSRC determines that fraudulent activity has taken place

January 21	Shenzhen Vice Mayor Song Hai dismissed suggestions that the Shenzhen and Shanghai exchanges would merge He states that Shenzhen was fully prepared to start the Second Board, but was still awaiting central government approval
January 23	Domestic media reports that domestic social security and welfare funds will start to invest directly in the A-share market in 2003
February 1	Supreme People's Court guidelines on investor lawsuits become effective
February 21	Zhengzhou Baiwen applies to resume normal trading
February 26	Former CSRC vice chairman Gao Xiqing becomes head of the National Council for the Social Security Fund
February 27	ABN Amro announces plans to buy a 33% stake in Xiangcai Hefeng FMC
	JF Asset Management announces that plans to take a stake in Hua-an FMC are on hold

"You're None of Those!"

Securities and stock markets, are these things good or bad, are they dangerous, are they things that only capitalism has and socialism cannot use? It is permitted to try them out, but it must be done with determination. If they work out, if they are tried out for a year or two and work out right, then we will open up; if they are mistakes, then just correct them or close the markets. If they are closed, they can be closed quickly, or they can be closed slowly, or we can leave a little bit of a tail.

Deng Xiaoping, Southern Excursion, January 22, 1992[1]

Shanghai in 1984 was not the Shanghai of 2002, the year the city enjoyed its "coming out party" on the international stage, regaining its position as the most exciting city in Asia. In the early 1980s, it had just emerged from being the fortress of the far left during the Cultural Revolution. The place was rundown and gray. The leadership consisted of the mayor, Jiang Zemin, Huang Ju, the first party secretary, and Wu Bangguo, a vice mayor – all very careful people. But over on Wuyi Street, a small audio equipment maker decided to raise "capital" by issuing "shares" to the public! These words, let alone the ideas they convey, had been among the most vilified in China during the 1960s and 1970s. Yet, in December 1984, here was a company, Feile Acoustics, openly selling its shares to the public!

Each time the chairman of the company visited the city party committee's offices to report on progress, he was terrified that he would be accused of stirring up capitalism.[2] After all, this was Shanghai, the leftist capital of the Cultural Revolution. In fact, the whole thing went smoothly and Feile sold 10,000 shares at RMB50 a piece. That didn't mean it was over, though. When the chairman applied to the State Administration of Industry and Commerce (SAIC) for a revised business license and was asked what system the company operated under – state ownership, collective, or private ownership – he simply didn't know how to respond. When he referred the matter to Wu Bangguo, he was told, "You're none of those! (*Nimen shenme dou bushi!*) You're the shareholding system." Feile was the first such company to be registered in Shanghai.

BOX 1 **"Shanghai Feile Acoustics Company on the 18th starts accepting individual and collective purchases of stock" Issue: 10,000 shares   Each share: RMB50**

This city has produced a new type of company that accepts voluntary share purchases from individuals and collectives – Shanghai Feile Acoustics Company. The company is issuing to the public 10,000 shares at RMB50 per share.

This afternoon this reporter visited the chairman and main plant factory manager of Wuyi Street's Feile Acoustics, Qin Qibin. He revealed that on the 18th of this month, to open Feile, he would make use of individual and collective voluntary stock purchases to raise capital. For all individuals, the shares would use special terms of a "guarantee of principal and interest" and a principle of voluntary purchase – that is, "voluntarily purchase, return the shares at any time." The company has entrusted ICBC Shanghai branch to issue the shares. After individuals or collectives purchase shares, no matter how small the purchase, each is a shareholder of the company and will enjoy equal rights, has the right to attend shareholder (or shareholder representative) meetings, to make propositions before the shareholder meeting, to propose projects to the chairman, or to participate in other activities organized by the company. At the end of each year, based on the company's after-tax profit, the chairman will declare a dividend that will be paid on a pro rata basis in proportion to how many shares the shareholder bought.

It is understood that Shanghai Feile Acoustics Company's duty is to produce complete sets of audio equipment, as well as contracting for the design, installation, and management of audio equipment for hotels, movie theaters, sports facilities, and so on.

Source: Xinmin wanbao, November 18, 1984, p. 1, cited in Wang An, pp. 69–70.

Shortly thereafter, a Western reporter asked the chairman whether he realized that his company was going down the "capitalist road." He replied that Deng Xiaoping himself had said that China should now look to the West and adopt concepts and technologies that could assist China's growth. Since Deng's return to power in 1978, the mood in China had changed and people were no longer frightened to experiment with Western methods. Nevertheless, old habits die hard and Feile's chairman had periods of doubt about what he was attempting to achieve. He Gaosheng, then director of the Shanghai Economic Restructuring Office, comforted him, saying: "Everyone always talks about the shareholding system, but let's not talk. Whether stocks are called capitalist or not, my position is to let practice speak for itself. I'll be happy when I see Feile's shares listed on the New York Stock Exchange (NYSE)."[3] Feile never made it as far as New York, but eight years later another company did.

In October 1992, Jinbei Light Passenger Vehicle completed an initial public offering (IPO) of its shares on the NYSE and became the first Chinese company to list on an international market. This small transaction, worth only US$80 million, was wholly unexpected and wildly received by investors. Just as Feile came to signify the start of active domestic interest in shares, Jinbei marked the emergence of China on the global capital markets.[4] Its domestic impact was even larger, since it highlighted changes in China's economy that had been gathering momentum since the early 1980s. Enterprises and projects had begun to seek financing outside of traditional state channels, which in any event had dried up. Informal social associations most likely provided such funds, but with a difference: the obligations were called "shares" and not "loans." The genie was out of the lamp. If an enterprise could provide "lenders" with a piece of paper called a "share" that did not require repayment of principal, why should it ever borrow again?

By the mid-1980s, over-the-counter (OTC) markets had sprung up in major cities, although trading in treasury securities was more common than trading in the very few publicly available stocks. Local and provincial governments, unable to provide funding to enterprises directly, supported the "experiment" by drafting basic rules and regulations.[5] This all took place at the local level with the full support of branches of the People's Bank of China (PBOC). The national records of the PBOC, the financial market regulator and nominal central bank, are bare of references to local branch activities during this time.[6] By late in the decade, thousands of enterprises had issued shares to internal staff and associated entities, and some had sold stock to the public at large. In 1988, the new mayor of Shanghai, Zhu Rongji, was in active pursuit of approval to build a stock exchange, egged on by a group of students who had returned from the United States and supported in the background by Deng Xiaoping. Then came June 4, 1989. The debate over who belonged to Mr. Capitalism's family and who to Comrade Socialism's began to rage anew.

If Deng Xiaoping had not gone to see Guangdong himself in early 1992, China's experiment with corporatization and shares might have stopped right there, an interesting side bar to a story that would have been quite different. But, Deng *did* go. He went to see for himself what large dollops of capital could accomplish. The booming towns of southern China contrasted sharply with Beijing's post-June 4 paralysis, and Deng took a position that provided cover to those promoting equity shares and stock markets. His open-minded comment on securities and stock markets is still cited repeatedly and reverently (if only partially) in all manner of books. In response to a question raised in Shenzhen, he said: "Are such things as securities and stock markets good or not? Are they dangerous? Do these things exist only in capitalist systems or can socialist ones use them too? It is permitted to try them out, but it must be done in a determined fashion."[7]

This part of his comment was clearly heard throughout the emerging securities industry, by the hard-strapped local governments and those parts of the bureaucracy (and Party) with a stake in the "shareholding system."[8] Deng's positive attitude touched off an explosion of activity, not just domestically, but internationally as well, as the world's investors suddenly "discovered" China. "China fever" extended beyond the private markets, from which direct investment poured in as if there were no limit; it also included the international equity and debt capital markets. For the first time, international money managers had the opportunity to buy the shares and fixed income securities of China's state-owned enterprises (SOEs). They liked what they saw and grabbed the opportunity with both hands: whatever piece of China they grabbed seemed pure gold. In short, against the background of the collapse of the Soviet Union and the technological triumph of the Gulf War, there was a nearly universal belief that Deng had now removed the final barrier to capitalism in China. Everyone, Chinese and foreigners alike, was going to get rich by participating in the development of the country's vast, untapped market. Across China, ordinary Chinese took to heart Deng's assertion that "To get rich is glorious."[9] Without question, China had changed overnight.

Perhaps if he had remained in vigorous health for a few more years, Deng would have taken this promise to its expected conclusion – large-scale privatization – much more directly. For example, he might have forced a more determined execution of the "grab the big and release the small" policy. Instead, and despite great progress, early in the new century China remains mired in deflation amid overproduction of virtually ever consumer good, including fake DVDs. There is a crisis of confidence in what is equivocally called a "socialist market economy," but which is most assuredly neither. Caught in the transition to something resembling Western capitalism and on its way to the 2008 Olympic Games, the country appears confident. Its government, however, is gridlocked and its leaders, old and "new," are seeking a way out in the World Trade Organization (WTO) as if from a *deus ex machina*. There has been a failure to attack head-on the problems of its own making, and these most especially relate to the stock markets. On the other hand, anything other than tinkering at the margins may be too much to expect from a country as complex, fearful of social instability, and with such deep-rooted traditions as China.

China's stocks and stock markets fully reflect this tinkering approach. These are what might be called equity markets "with Chinese characteristics." Securities markets in any other country in the world evolved in market economies in support of, and benefiting from, the capital-raising efforts of privately owned companies. In such markets, equity securities from an investor's viewpoint represent a right, both of ownership and economic benefit, in a company and, from the company's viewpoint, an obligation. In China, the stated objective of securities markets at the start, at least, was to promote greater operating efficiencies in SOEs still controlled absolutely by the state. It is, therefore, entirely unclear just what securities did, in fact, represent, other than the opportunity perhaps to profit from trading and to receive a dividend.

For the companies, there still seems to be no sense of obligation to minority shareholders; only to the state, if at all. In China, the markets are operated by the state, regulated by the state, legislated by the state, and raise funds for the benefit of the state by selling shares in enterprises owned by the state. In the entire system, the only things that do not belong to the state are the actual money, or capital, put up by presumably individual investors, and the market itself. These two things, however, represent the heart of a system that, without question, has driven the political process before it. As a recent editorial commented, "Each time there are rumors in China's stock markets it influences policy…"[10]

Despite rapid growth over the last decade, in the overall context of China's economy the securities markets remain relatively small. The primary, or IPO, market, even at its peak of nearly US$20 billion in 2000, is a fraction of total bank deposits of nearly US$900 billion or of annual state fixed asset investment of US$450 billion.[11] More interestingly, the primary market is also only a fraction of foreign direct investment (FDI), which has been running at around US$40 billion per year. On the other hand, the total market capitalization of A-share companies, at US$500 billion, is rather larger. This figure is compared to other Asian markets in Figure 1.1. The only problem is that this figure is at best only notional. Some 70% of the equity market capitalization of China is represented by the value of legally non-tradable shares owned by the state. The remaining 30% represents what might in other circumstances be called "publicly" owned shares freely tradable in the secondary market.

The approximately US$150 billion market value of these shares, however, is based on the expectation that the other 70% will remain non-tradable in the long term, if not in perpetuity. This expectation is founded on the state's declaration at the outset of the market experiment that it must maintain absolute majority ownership in the companies listed. Should this position alter, or be perceived to alter, the possibility of huge volumes of new shares coming on to the market could destroy current market values, as has been shown by the failed state share selloff of 2001. Poorly managed, this could lead to a crash with its apparently unforeseeable consequences, both economic and otherwise. But this is only one consequence of the way China's stock markets have evolved.

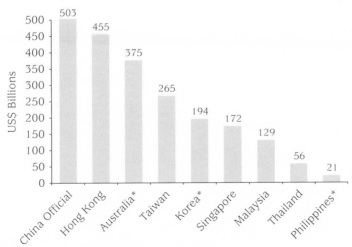

FIGURE 1.1 Comparative Market Capitalizations, Non-Japan Asia.
Note: October 2002 figures; *year-end 2001 figure.

How did this all start? After all, China had just emerged from 10 years of extreme ideological warfare, followed by a half-hearted attempt to restore Stalinism. Between 1978 and 1983, far away from the cities, the agricultural enterprises out of necessity began to raise funds and pay interest on things called "shares" but which more closely resembled fixed income securities. On July 3, 1979, the State Council affirmed this spontaneous practice in a notice. The notice listed the following as one way to solve agricultural brigade financial difficulties: "It is permitted to take an appropriate amount of funds from the brigade or production group's common accumulated funds to put in as (start-up) equity (*gu*)."[12] This is a very early example of the broader political environment being relaxed enough to permit experimentation with previously toxic ideas. The Chinese know well that when the door opens slightly, it is best to rush through and not hesitate.

During the period from 1978 to 1983, the number of collective stock enterprises (*gufen hezuo qiye*) in the countryside grew. The central government generally approved of the practice and began to call it formally the "agricultural stock cooperative system (*nongcun gufen hezuozhi*)." Then there were the early local pioneers. In October 1979, the Liaoning Fushun No. 1 Red Brick Factory began to organize a share offering to raise funds that, in January 1980, was supported by the subscription of over 200 enterprises.[13] In Chengdu at the exact same time, city officials were searching for ways to finance an exhibition center. One of them remembered people selling shares in a movie he had seen and the idea took life. The Chengdu Shudu Building, the Fushun No. 1 Red Brick Factory, 1983's Shenzhen Baoan Joint Stock Investment Co., and 1984's Beijing Tianqiao Department Store are all pretenders to the claim of being the first to issue shares. Most commentators, however, give the honor to Shanghai Feile Acoustics, also in 1984, because of its relatively standardized offering procedures. In short, the answer to the question "How did it start?" is: spontaneously all across the country, wherever people needed money ... and no longer feared political repercussions. By late 1986, the number of enterprises issuing shares had reached 6,000 to 7,000 nationwide, raising altogether around RMB6 billion.[14] These were no longer pioneers.

Shenzhen has played the role of catalyst at several critical points in the creation of active stock markets. In 1986, the Shenzhen government was the first to produce regulations standardizing the process by which enterprises could be reorganized as shareholding companies. This led directly to the first major public offering of shares by the Shenzhen Development Bank (SDB) in 1987. This offering, however, attracted orders for less than 50% of the planned subscription amount from 7,276 "investors" despite strong local government support and, in fact, direct party participation.[15] Shenzhen Vanke's smaller offering in December of the same year suffered the same fate. Quite clearly, no one knew what stocks were at this point and a market did not yet exist.

The fact is that after more than 30 years of central planning, society-wide political struggle, and state ownership, there was no understanding of what exactly an equity share was. The issuers treated them like debt without principal repayment. Consequently, investors thought of them as valuable only for the "dividends" paid, and people bought them to hold for the cash flow. There was no awareness that they might appreciate (or, for that matter, depreciate) in value, and so yield up a capital gain (or loss). All this changed, however, in early 1989 when the SDB announced its dividend plan for the 1988 financial year.

This simple dividend payment marked a major turning point in China's experiment with stocks. The bank was exceptionally generous to its investors, awarding them a cash dividend of RMB7 per share and a two-for-one stock dividend. In the blink of an eye, investors who had bought the bank's shares in 1988 for about RMB20 per share now enjoyed a profit several times their original investment. Even so, a small number of shareholders failed to claim their stock dividends and the bank moved to sell them publicly. In an instant, one individual appeared, offered RMB120 per share and bought the whole lot in what may have been the first effort to manipulate the new market.[16] Once this news had spread in Shenzhen, the fire began to blaze. Shenzhen investors got the point – there was more to shares than a simple dividend – and the rush was on. The bank's shares, as well as the few other stocks available, skyrocketed in value in wild street trading. They jumped from a year-end price of RMB40 to RMB120 just before June 4, 1989 and ended the year at RMB90, the June interruption notwithstanding. In the late 1980s, this was very big money.

Armed with this new insight, China's investors set off a period of "share fever" centered on Shenzhen and gradually extending during 1990 to Shanghai, where the local populace were still in the dark. In the end, government authorities were forced to take steps to cool the markets, even posting billboards reading "Investors Beware! Shares Can Lose Value!" More serious measures included daily price movement limits, increased transaction taxes, and ownership transfer stamp duties. These restrictions eventually took hold, leading to a market collapse in late 1990. But never mind, investors had learned the lesson of equity investing: stocks can appreciate – and with this, they acquired the speculative habit.

These early years were the heyday of retail investors in China. Their enthusiasm for making a quick buck compelled the government to develop regulatory controls in a bid to impose order. In turn, this much-needed infrastructure created the conditions in which the market could further develop. There was a flurry of activity by the State Committee for the Restructuring of the Economic System (SCRES) in late 1988 and early 1989, aimed first at documenting the extent of the market and then developing appropriate regulations. Final drafts had even been submitted in the spring of 1989 to the State Council for approval, but were shelved due to the political fallout from the events in Tiananmen Square. What did emerge came in May 1990 with a State Council announcement of restrictions on the shareholding experiment. These included limiting the opportunity to the state sector and the designation of Shenzhen and Shanghai as the only officially recognized

OTC trading markets. The limitation of the corporatization effort to the state sector alone marked a major reversal of 1980s' practice and was a defining event in the development of the market.

The focus of OTC trading in Shenzhen and Shanghai was the public part of a formal decision made at about the same time to proceed with the establishment of the Shanghai and Shenzhen securities exchanges.[17] Taken during the wild market conditions in the first half of 1990, the intent was to provide a controlled venue for securities trading in two administrative areas presumably well under the thumb of the central government. The prospect of having potentially disruptive securities exchanges located throughout the country, much less in Beijing, was unacceptable to the government in the post-Tiananmen period, even though there were many regional exchanges operating at this time. In the event, the Shanghai exchange opened in December 1990 and Shenzhen shortly after in 1991.[18] This great advance, however, was by no means the government's stamp of approval on the experiment; it was an effort to clamp down on street markets – June 4 was barely a year in the past. There continued to be a significant amount of tinkering with the markets, and even the creation of new ones during the 1990s, all of which is reviewed in Chapter 2. Despite these new experiments, the major focus of policy has been on the Shanghai and Shenzhen exchanges which, combined or not, represent the future.

The early 1980s' period of spontaneous experimentation with corporate forms and securities was entirely unregulated, promoted by local governments and largely unnoticed by Beijing. Almost as an afterthought, the People's Bank of China was given responsibility for securities in 1986 as part of more elaborate regulations governing the commercial banking sector. From that point on, until its displacement in 1992 by the China Securities Regulatory Commission (CSRC), the PBOC or, more properly, its local branches, played an active role in promoting developments, even to the extent of establishing its own brokerages. From its initial involvement, therefore, the PBOC was entirely self-conflicted, acting more as a market player than a regulator. This culminated in the 1992 NYSE listing of the automaker noted at the outset: the PBOC was the ultimate sponsor of the transaction.

It was in the regulatory area that Shenzhen inadvertently made its second major contribution to market development. In August 1992, tens of thousands of would-be investors had lined up overnight to obtain the forms necessary to subscribe to a share offering, only to discover that the PBOC had already fully distributed them "internally." Major riots ensued. What is popularly called the 810 Incident led directly to the replacement of the PBOC as market regulator by a new, specialized body, the China Securities Regulatory Commission.

The need for such a specialized body had always been a topic of dispute, since the objective of the corporatization process was primarily to reorganize SOEs, a matter internal to the state itself. It is in this context that this 1989 statement from an official at SCRES should be understood: "The purpose of the share system is the share system and not to issue shares to the public."[19] Practical reality dictated otherwise. Enterprises needed financing which the state could not fully provide, and the state needed to manage the process so that investors stayed quiet. Practicality won out over the original objective. The 810 Incident fully demonstrated that the PBOC was incapable of acting as regulator. The State Council decided almost immediately to establish the CSRC as the specialized securities market regulatory body reporting to a policy and coordinating commission in the State Council. This new player in the bureaucracy provided a much-needed focus for both the corporatization and securities market effort. Moreover, it created a regulator whose self-interest lay in further market development.

The decision had a second, and perhaps even more important, ramification. Together with the CSRC announcement, the State Council made public the designation of nine enterprises as candidates for listing on the Stock Exchange of Hong Kong (SEHK). These two announcements came less than a week after the surprise PBOC-sponsored first overseas listing. Together, these events put China on the map of international financial investors and gave rise to a "China fever" in the international capital markets, putting events in Shenzhen and Shanghai in the shade.

This necessarily meant that the CSRC spent an inordinate amount of time at its inception dealing with the issues of listing Chinese SOEs overseas. The commission's original staff was well prepared to do so, since it consisted of a body of professionals many of whom had been educated, trained, and lived in Hong Kong and the United States. Moreover, its chairman, Liu Hongru, had long been associated with the stock-market effort and had been the leader of the team that had negotiated the Chinese listings with the Hong Kong exchange. This association with overseas listings, however, tainted the CSRC and made its institutionalization even more difficult. Within the central government, the PBOC and other bureaucracies that stood to lose power continued to resist the new agency notwithstanding an extraordinary effort by the State Council to clarify the scope of authority of all the entities involved. At the local level, the two stock exchanges, controlled by their respective municipal governments, kept up a continuous criticism of the CSRC for supporting the overseas listings of presumably the best companies in China. They wanted such companies listed locally in order to support their own development. In retrospect, they may have been correct. This constant negative lobbying, plus a massive bond futures scandal, eventually led to Liu Hongru's resignation in late 1995. Most of the commission's international staff dispersed over the following year. The CSRC thus became a traditional Chinese bureaucratic organ.

Despite this, or perhaps because of it, the CSRC gradually gained authority over the markets. This accretion of power was marked by three stages. During 1992–93, with Liu Hongru as chairman, the CSRC gradually found staff, consolidated its influence over the securities and futures markets, and was given extended powers of investigation and enforcement. The next major step came with its assumption of full control over the two securities exchanges in 1996. From 1997, local governments, which had lobbied for and created the exchanges, were locked out of direct participation in their management. With the passage of the Securities Law in sight, the CSRC in 1998 became a full ministry-level organization reporting directly to the State Council. Along the way, many of the "historical remnants" of the earlier period of market experimentation were eliminated. The best examples of this were a variety of securities exchanges operated by the PBOC, local governments, and other bodies. Their closure left Shanghai and Shenzhen as the focus of continued reform effort. The background to the birth of the CSRC, the development of a regulatory regime for the markets, and the CSRC's empowerment by the 1999 Securities Law are described in Chapter 3.

The greatest challenge faced by the CSRC was created by the approach the state had taken in the late 1980s to defining the shareholding system. On looking back, what was hopeful about the early 1980s period, and particularly the events in Shenzhen, was its freedom from state planning and political jargon. State-owned and other enterprises reorganized and issued shares to investors to raise funds with little government restriction. Although investor categories were largely different arms of the state and enterprise employees, there was nothing dogmatic about which companies could or could not restructure and sell shares, there were no investor restrictions, and shares could be freely transferred.

Beijing's involvement, however, brought immediate restrictions, although without doubt enterprise restructuring activities and stock trading needed clear guidelines. First came the limitation of corporate restructuring and eventual share offerings to state enterprises alone. In the long run, this preference for helping SOEs would not have created problems for the market's development. What was harmful was the approach the state adopted to define equity shares. The state's psychology was different from that of Shenzhen (and Hong Kong, from which Shenzhen liberally borrowed) and its spirit was infused with fear and distrust. First of all, the central government and, no doubt, most local governments feared outright privatization of state enterprises. If nothing else, it would detract from their power base.

The government had no confidence in any state entity to which it might entrust the holding of shares representing its ownership rights in a company: given the chance, they would sell out. To mitigate these concerns, the government devised a system that defined shares in terms of the relationship of the holder to the state and then made any state-related shares non-tradable. Only shares representing the investment of non-state investors could freely trade on the public markets and, in certain cases, not even all of these. Nearly all of the problems now plaguing China's stock markets can be traced back directly to this decision.

The June 1989 events, however, prevented the issuance of formal laws and regulations elaborating this decision. With Deng's 1992 approving comments on the socialist utility of stock markets, there poured forth all the provisional measures and regulations drafted in 1989, including, most importantly, China's first stab at a corporate law, the Standard Opinion. It has since been superseded by the 1994 Company Law and by the 1999 Securities Law, but neither has truly eclipsed its importance. The Standard Opinion gave the market its framework and obscure categories of shares that continue to this day. The Opinion defined shares based on the relationship to the state of the entity that owned them, rather than on the particular rights they might represent. Thus, if an agency of the government, say a ministry, owned the shares, they were state shares; if a state enterprise with legal person status owned them, they were legal person shares. It is amazing how many permutations of the state–shareholder relationship came to light over the years as the economy grew more sophisticated.

This treatment may have resolved the state's fears over loss of control, but not the needs of market participants. After all, the shareholding experiment had arisen from the need to raise capital. This unquenchable demand also existed on the part of state promoters of listed companies. Many enterprises had restructured themselves into shareholding companies without issuing shares to third parties. The shares held by the promoters of the restructuring were always defined as non-tradable, since the promoters were, after all, arms of the state. Promoters need capital as well, and this has continually conflicted with their regulatory inability to monetize their holdings. To respond to their clamor, the state experimented with private markets limited to qualified "state" participants on which the "transfer," not sale, of such "non-tradable" shares was possible. As a consequence, over time, a number of independent parallel markets grew up alongside the Shanghai and Shenzhen exchanges. A description of the design of China's share classes and how they grew out of the state planning system is provided in Chapter 4. This discussion is an important part of understanding how China's markets have become increasingly distorted over the past decade and what the consequences have been.

The Standard Opinion also laid out the way a state-owned enterprise could restructure itself as a company limited by shares. This process of corporatization refers to the reorganization of a haphazard body of state assets held by an SOE into a distinct corporate legal entity. Under state planning and "ownership by the whole people," enterprises and factories had no independent legal existence; they were part and parcel of the state, from which they were virtually indivisible. Enterprise reform efforts in the 1980s were based on the state's belief that greater autonomy for enterprise management would increase productivity. This culminated in the 1988 Enterprise Law, now long since forgotten. The Law enhanced enterprise management powers and for the first time gave independent legal person status to the enterprises themselves. But in contrast to the requirements of corporatization, the Law did not envision the complete restructuring of an enterprise into an independent legal entity in the form of a corporation.

The reorganization of SOEs into companies limited by shares is a monumental task. It involves not simply the creation of the requisite legal, accounting, and financial framework, but also instilling in the minds of management an entirely new way of thinking about enterprise operations. The aim, at least in theory, is not simply expanded production, but higher-quality production and improved financial performance to enhance shareholder value. Then there is the social issue. Enterprises then and now continue to act on behalf of the state as providers of education, medical insurance, and social security services for workers, both active and retired, and their families. Given the reality of nearly 75 million currently active employees of SOEs, the inclusion of retirees and dependents makes the number larger than the population of the United States. Gradualism, the social burden, and a focus on the state-owned sector alone have to date meant that the shareholding system and the markets have had only a superficial impact on the way the corporatized enterprises perform. The reasons for this become clear when the restructuring process itself is understood.

To attract outside investors to an SOE, the entire collateral social security system has to be deconstructed. At the core of an SOE's galaxy of services and related entities is a presumably productive manufacturing entity or service provider. The cash flow from this operation is what supports everything and everyone else. How, then, does one go about separating the state from the enterprise to form a profitable and competitive company that can survive market competition and grow? More to the point, how does one create a company that would be an attractive investment opportunity if shares are offered internationally? And if this can be done, what about the remainder of the original enterprise which is not included?

From a technical point of view, enterprise restructuring is relatively straight-forward. Although the work is challenging, it is not conceptually difficult and relies highly on judgment. The key is the first step: to identify a company in a sector which may have a competitive edge and which investors, therefore, might view positively. Although the sector may be attractive, it is nonetheless critical that the final company as restructured be profitable and have strong growth prospects. But, of course, this is impossible to know at the outset, since no proper financial statements exist for any SOE and the company as such does not yet exist. This is where judgment is called for, both of the potential company's prospects as well as of investor interests and appetite. After this first step, what might be called the boundaries of the new company are defined – in other words, what assets are in and what are out. Obviously, all the social support and other non-productive assets are excluded. With this pre-liminary definition of the company, accountants come in to conduct a full audit. Lawyers begin to prepare the required documents and formally define the relationship between the new company and what is left outside of it – that is, the former SOE, now called the parent. In short, what has been done is to carve out the heart of the SOE. This is formed into a new company distinct from what has been excluded and remains an SOE. The difficulty is that the parent SOE now has no direct access to the cash flow of the productive part, which was its life's blood. A technical triumph, if the international offering of shares is successful, but a looming social disaster for those left behind. This is the true problem in the government's effort to separate itself from its enterprises (*zhengqi fenkai*). It can be done, but it does not solve all the problems.

Having created a company limited by shares, the next step becomes listing a certain portion of those shares on a stock exchange to raise capital. This is not a first step toward privatization, at least in the Western sense. Privatization refers to the selling off of state assets to non-state owners. This has never been what China's equity markets have been about, although this was not necessarily clear during the 1980s.[20] What they *are* about is raising capital to finance the growth and, it is hoped, improved management and productivity of Chinese companies which remain Chinese state companies. Over the course of the 1990s, the government and companies experimented with a variety of different structures to achieve successful overseas listings. The evolution of both listing and company structures clearly demonstrates a learning process. This reflects the growing sophistication and understanding of the CSRC and other government agencies of the interests and expectations of the international fund managers who are the principal investors in their stock offerings. How companies are reorganized according to Chinese law, and typical examples of how they are structured to achieve a successful IPO internationally, are shown in Chapter 5.

Of course, Chinese companies do not just decide to list shares on the NYSE; there is a selection and approval process. In the early years of the experiment, 1993–98, the state was heavily involved even to the extent of including the expected proceeds in the State Plan. Once the Plan had set a financing quota, the CSRC distributed it to government agencies and provincial governments. There ensued fierce lobbying as SOEs competed for the right to restructure and list. Once the quota had been filled, the CSRC would make public the list of approved listing candidates and the bankers, lawyers, and accountants would begin furious marketing efforts.

Given how the lists were compiled, it is not surprising that of the 86 overseas listing candidate enterprises selected through 1999, only 44 managed to complete their full restructuring and list. This success rate is somewhat smaller when the composition of the listing candidates is considered. Of the 86 candidates, only 71 can be considered true SOEs; the remaining 15 were jerry-rigged highway, property, and agricultural companies added in to the most recent two groups of candidates. In fact, the last formal group consisted entirely of highway, port, and agricultural assets: many local governments by this time did not have suitable candidates. Of the 71 SOE candidates, only 38 successfully restructured and listed shares; of this number, 21 did so before 1995, during the early surge of international interest in Chinese shares.

There are two explanations for these results. First, as noted previously, although the process is technical, its consequences are social. Many SOEs, despite the attraction of new financing, chose not to proceed when the social costs became clear. Many other SOEs found that they could not proceed since their profitability and prospects were not sufficiently attractive. And still other SOEs decided not even to begin the process due to its expense, the amount of work involved, the social problems eventuating, and the ready alternative of the domestic markets. This, and the reality that China does not have large numbers of attractive enterprises, accounts for the growth in infrastructure companies and Red Chip conglomerates. Such companies, being entirely artificial, have none of the social problems of a true SOE. The second, and equally critical, reason for these results has been that investors have mostly lost money placed in Chinese shares.

In contrast, the domestic markets have consistently welcomed SOE issuers in the primary market, almost regardless of whether or not they are rationally structured. This response has to a great extent been due to government-set pricing policies calibrated to assure both issue success and investor profit. Because SOEs need not drastically restructure their operations, it is a much simpler matter to list. Moreover, there is the traditional Chinese flexibility in applying rules and regulations. The result is that most domestically listed companies are what might kindly be called conglomerates, although conglomeration is probably a more accurate description. Outside of perhaps 20 large companies, the remaining 1,000-plus listed companies have small market capitalizations, high price valuations, and high share ownership concentration. In fact, some 60% of domestic listed companies have under 50,000 shareholders, and even the most widely held companies have less than 500,000.

The small size of the companies and their concentrated ownership create the conditions in which professional market manipulators, whether individual or institutional, can flourish. To a large extent, manipulators have driven the typical retail investor out of the secondary market. A detailed discussion of internationally and domestically listed companies and their characteristics is contained in Chapter 6.

The reason for such different market responses to Chinese companies lies ultimately with the investors. International markets and investors are mature, and investors as a category represent an extremely diverse group with differing levels of expertise and investment strategies. Moreover, significant amounts of capital have been committed to the markets over time, so that such markets can be described as having both breadth and depth. International investors, therefore, deal in mature markets, in large amounts, and have a global selection of investment choices. They are not a topic of discussion in this book. In contrast, even 10 years ago in China the word "capital (*ziben*)" was still a dirty word and the perhaps 100,000 or so equity investors of the time did so for largely speculative reasons. Now, early in the new century, there are over 66 million investor accounts, the overwhelming majority of which have been opened by individuals, and 70% of which are located in the relatively rich coastal provinces and cities. Even for these provinces, account penetration rates, with the exception of Shanghai, remain for the most part in single-digit numbers. Beyond the retail sector, work has only just begun to broaden the market beyond the existing perhaps 300,000 institutional investors. Currently, such investors are mostly corporates, but there is also a growing number of both open- and closed-end funds, gray market money managers, insurance companies, and pension funds.

China's stock markets are often characterized by reference to the huge and rapidly growing number of retail investor accounts. This conclusion is superficial and extremely misleading. To arrive at a more accurate picture, Chapter 7 analyzes investor data from a variety of different angles. It looks at stock exchange data on active investor accounts, IPO participation numbers, the number of domestic participants in the recently liberalized B-share market, the physical constraints of brokerage offices, and, finally, data on daily account openings nationwide. The information gathered demonstrates that the number of active investors in the markets may be as few as two million in the primary market and fewer than five million in the secondary markets. This is an astounding result, which seems to be well known, though certainly not publicized in China. The policy consequences for the government are significant.

The characteristics of each investor type also reveal much about the market's nature. An estimation of funds available for stock investment by each type of investor illustrates who has market clout and how it is used. Securities companies, investment funds, corporates, and gray market money managers each have the power and the incentive to manipulate the primary and secondary markets to their own advantage, and examples are provided to show how they do this. All this leads to the conclusion that the domestic markets are not only *not* retail in character, but that the small retail investor has largely been forced to the sidelines except, perhaps, in the primary market. In his place are professional speculators in the guise of institutions creating opportunities for their own benefit.

China's population is rapidly aging: by 2010, there will be more than 100 million people aged 65 years and older; by 2030 this figure will exceed 200 million. The government's effort to create a viable social insurance system and its support of the growing insurance industry is severely hindered by the same dearth of investment opportunities faced by a typical retail stock investor. Without a broad reform of the stock markets, the investment vehicle required to allow pension funds and insurance companies to meet their increasing obligations to an aging society will not exist. Claiming that there are 66 million investor accounts, that the markets are a success, and that cases of illegal trading or fraudulent behavior are few in number is a charade.

Reform needs especially to come to what Chapter 8 refers to as the parallel markets. The original and fundamental regulatory and legal distinction between tradable and non-tradable shares and within non-tradable shares between state and legal person shares has given rise over time to three independent stock markets in China. To these three, the inconvertibility of the Renminbi has added a fourth, the overseas markets. Each market is subject to different regulations, has different participants, makes use of very different valuation standards, and trades independently of the others. Yet, the shares in each market represent the equity of one company, so they are fundamentally linked. Just *how* linked was demonstrated by the state's effort in 2001 to monetize a small portion of its own "non-tradable" holdings to begin financing the pension system. This led to a 40% collapse of the tradable market and a rapid retreat by the state.

All of this demonstrates the fact that China's public – that is, tradable – stock markets do not play the role of markets elsewhere in the world. They do not value listed companies. Yet, the official market capitalization figures assume the methodology of markets elsewhere. The traded price of a company's shares is applied to value the 70% of its shares that are by regulation non-tradable. At the same time, however, prices for legal person and state shares are traded in OTC markets or through negotiations at discounts to the market of 70–80%! Based on the official market capitalization figures, China's combined stock markets are larger than any other Asian market except Japan. If, however, market capitalization is calculated using the prices prevalent in the mergers and acquisitions (M&A) market in China, China's markets are only as large as Malaysia's. Big difference.

There have been various tentative efforts in recent years to reduce the massive overhang of state shares. The size of the problem depends on how the overhang is valued. If it is valued at the market price, the shares are worth US$252 billion, but at net asset value (NAV) they are worth far less, only US$89 billion. Assuming the state wants only to sell down 50%, it would still require US$45 billion at NAV prices. By way of comparison, US$18 billion was raised in 2000, the best year ever for capital raising on the two exchanges. This makes it clear that either there is a massive amount of new capital brought to the market to absorb the state's position, or the market must take a heavy valuation impact. This discussion also shows why it is critical to understand exactly just how many and what kinds of investors are at risk.

A second major consequence of the development of these parallel markets might be called "privatization with Chinese characteristics." This is hard to see by looking only at the publicly traded markets. The structure of the market capitalization of the Shanghai and Shenzhen exchanges has been remarkably stable since 1995, with state shares (including legal person shares) representing around 70%. This hides the reality that the markets have dramatically increased in size. In 1995, there were only 323 listed companies and at the end of 2002, 1,318. In addition, there have been constant secondary offerings, rights offerings, and other financings over the years.

The share structure of new listings is heavily weighted with shares held by the state promoters. Companies typically sell a stake amounting to about 25–30% of their post-offering share capital. For companies listed for a number of years, however, additional financings have gradually diluted down the state's position. These two trends offset each other and this accounts for the stability in the capital structure of the overall market. What is interesting, however, is the dilution effect in the older listed companies. At the end of 1995, there were 184 companies listed on the Shanghai exchange. Between 1995 and October 2002, 123 of these companies experienced a significant decrease in the ratio of tradable to non-tradable shares. In 1995, the ratio stood at 31 to 69, about the same as the overall market structure, but after seven years it stood at 44 to 56. The state's share had not changed, but it had been diluted in importance by new share issuance. As a second example, changes in shareholdings were traced for 449 companies over the 1999–2002 period. Of these, 318 saw an increase in tradable shares. For these companies, the ratio of the two share classes stood at 35 to 65 in 1999. By 2002, tradable shares had increased to 41.2%. In addition, companies in this group with a free float greater than 50% had increased from 44 to 97.

This does not necessarily mean that the state is losing control. From available data, the state, or something that appears to be related to the state, remains the largest shareholder in all of these companies. In addition, A-share investors have yet to unite against a single company's management. Changes in company control, therefore, can only take place in the negotiated markets for state or legal person shares. This is the realm of the Chinese M&A market, where thousands of transactions have taken place in the past few years. It is a market that has been little noticed and poorly regulated. The deals being completed include transfers of company control, backdoor listings, and management buy-outs (MBOs).

Transfer of control usually involves legal person shares. It is a simple administrative process for a private individual to create a company, register it with the relevant state agency, and thereby become a legal person. Acting through the new legal person, there is nothing prohibiting the acquisition of the holdings of other legal persons. Transfer of a controlling position in a listed (or unlisted) company to private hands in this way is impossible for the state to detect without a thorough investigation. Estimates suggest that nearly 11% of all listed companies are now privately controlled.[21]

These deals are completed without reference to the public market prices for shares in the same company. Nor has there been, until recently, a regulatory requirement for either disclosure or shareholder approval.[22] This kind of asset reshuffling may promote the development of true, if hidden, private owner-ship in China. It is, however, far from solving the share structure problems of companies or promoting the development of the market. The proud new pri-vate owners face the same problems of illiquid shares as the old state owner. In an environment where no laws exist to protect private property and private takeovers of state companies are not yet generally accepted, Chinese-style pri-vatization can only take place in the gray areas created by the parallel markets. It is highly ironic that the means used by the state to prevent privatization have, in the end, been quite conducive to it.

The public A-share markets have now completed their first full decade of trading. Chinese commentators have described their performance as the

"Ten-year Bull Market" and not without reason, as can be seen in Figure 1.2. In spite of the scandals and many difficulties the A-share markets face, they have at times been bullish. Chinese investors have few other investment choices. The bulls have run for A shares in 1992, 1996, and, more recently, from 1999 to 2001. In the early years through 1995, the number of companies listed was quite small. In 1992, there were only 40 listed stocks, so it was easy to make the market roar. Deng's positive remarks and the removal in May of trading limits account for the first early peak in mid-1992. This was brought low by the 810 riots in Shenzhen. Even positive words at the 14th Party Congress could not move the market up. But the Ministry of Finance (MOF) could. The second surge that year, which carried into 1993, is more representative of later things. Caizheng Securities (MOF backed) went on a buying spree that ignited interest again. This is a picture of how the A-share markets move: they are highly sensitive to government policies, the overall political situation, and last but not least, a good market play.

This hardly means that money cannot be made. For example, an early investment in the rightly famous Shenzhen Development Bank held all these 10 years would have yielded a large fortune in China. If an individual had bought RMB10,000 worth of SDB's shares at its 1987 IPO and had participated in all the rights offerings along the way, the value of his initial RMB10,000 would have peaked at RMB58 million in May 1997. If he did not sell out, in late 2002 his fortune would still be over RMB14 million. Enough to retire on in China.

The government has directly intervened in the markets three times by placing editorials on the highly sensitive front page of *People's Daily*. The first such editorial, that of December 31, 1991, came immediately after the official opening of the Shanghai exchange. Titled "Exploring a socialist stock market with Chinese characteristics," the editorial confirmed that the government had not given up support of corporatization and securities markets despite June 4.

FIGURE 1.2 Historical Performance, Shanghai and Shenzhen Stock Exchanges.

This was a hugely positive sign and, together with Deng's remarks, sparked the rally in 1992.

The second appearance by the "Special Correspondent" came on December 19, 1996, and was titled "On correctly understanding the current market." This time the paper warned of the market's highly speculative nature. The year 1996 witnessed an enormous bull market driven by speculation in SDB shares by the bank itself, as well as a major securities company in a last desperate throw of the dice to avoid bankruptcy. In 1996, people still read, and understood how to read between the lines of, *People's Daily* and the market commenced to collapse.

On May 19, 1999, the Shanghai market opened near an intra-day low of 1,057, but then commenced to climb. Fueled by interest rate cuts and slashed stamp duties, the market pretended that the Internet and telecom bubble was in China and not the U.S. The economy was still emerging from the inflation bender of the mid-1990s and, in fact, there was much noise about the "new economy." The "Special Correspondent" intruded into this situation with a hugely positive editorial, "Strengthen confidence, normal development," which concluded with the statement, "A good situation in the securities markets is not easy to come by; all sides should double its value."[23] This was a far cry from calling for class struggle, but the market knew how to take it. Shanghai broke through 1,500 and continued on up to 1,700 by June month-end.

It is an interesting fact that the "Special Correspondent" has not made his appearance during the steep decline beginning in late 2001. The fear of dilution by continued state share sales, despite government denials, plus the results of determined enforcement by the CSRC, which have revealed the market's true face, created a bear market early in the new century.[24] And this is in spite of very strong economic performance. There is concern that the government's policy is to let the market drift lower so as to decrease the valuation gaps between the tradable and non-tradable shares and between domestic markets and those overseas. A staged undoing of the currency's non-convertibility may be more possible in such an environment.

Despite this bear market, the Shanghai A-share index over the past seven years has turned in a better performance than the Dow Jones Industrials. Say what can be said about all the differences, but a US$100 bet on both markets in December 1995 (to eliminate Shanghai's early swings) gives you US$250 in Shanghai and only US$175 in New York by the end of 2002.

The still young fund management industry in China has also done well recently, following the "Black Funds" scandal of 2000–01. Comparing the performance of the funds index versus the Shanghai Index from May 2000, when such data begins, shows the funds breaking even while the A-share Index was down nearly 21%. This is good news for the government, which is trying hard to develop alternative investment paths and products for the market. The B shares, however, remain bad news. Even after allowing domestic investors to buy B shares legally, there has not been much interest. There is no primary market and no arbitrage tools to make the A- and B-share markets converge.

This is a product marching toward the end of the road: a merger with A shares. The markets' performance is discussed in Chapter 9.

If Deng were still alive, he might ask for a report card on the tenth anniversary of the corporatization and listing experiment. If so, then, without a doubt, the biggest achievement of this effort has been the amount of capital it has raised for China's SOEs. Over these 10 years, the issuance of A, B, H, and Red Chip shares has raised US$129 billion for over 1,400 companies. This compares to about US$400 billion in FDI over the same period. Moreover, China's combined market capitalization calculated on the basis of total shares now stands at slightly over US$500 billion, making it the second-largest equity market in Asia after Japan. As the markets have grown, so has trading volume, or liquidity. From a combined level of around US$30 million daily in 1992, over the past few years, daily volumes are normally around US$1 billion. Despite their reputation, which has carried over from the early 1990s, China's markets are in fact no more volatile than, for example, the Stock Exchange of Hong Kong. In comparison to the SEHK's Hang Seng Index, Shanghai's A-share market has turned in a far more impressive performance since 1995. More to the point, Shanghai's A shares have even performed better than the overseas-listed H shares. The overall report card, therefore, is quite impressive for what is still very much an emerging market isolated by currency inconvertibility from the global markets.

In December 2001, China joined the World Trade Organization and its domestic securities markets will witness increasing foreign participation. This will come first through joint venture insurance companies, asset management companies, securities companies similar to China International Capital Corporation (CICC) and a qualified foreign institutional investor program. After 2006, the end of the five-year implementation period, foreign financial companies will be able to participate directly. At the same time, these years will continue to witness dramatic market changes in China. Such changes will not simply be limited to the types of companies listed and how they are listed and regulated, but will also include a much-reduced state ownership role and all that that entails. Without question, China's stock markets, with only 10 years of "determined" development, are on track to become the largest and most dynamic in Asia.

CHAPTER 2

How China's Stock Markets Came to Be

The purpose of the share system is the share system and not to issue shares to the public.

State Committee for the Restructuring of the Economic System, 1989[1]

Shanghai's modernistic stock exchange building in Pudong houses one of the most advanced electronic trading centers in the world and is a matched set with that of Shenzhen. Both give the appearance of established markets that have just completed a full upgrade in preparation for the next millennium. This appearance is somewhat deceiving. It is a fact that China's experience with securities markets extends back to 1891 when the Shanghai Stock Exchange was established and grew to be the largest domestic securities exchange with 140 listed companies.[2] Beijing and Tianjin also had active exchanges during the late 1940s and early 1950s.[3] But here history paused for nearly 40 years until the 1979 policy of opening up and reform created an environment for positive change. Even so, who would have thought that in a country with no private property, securities, much less stock, exchanges could come to exist?

The more relaxed political environment of the 1980s, combined with the pressure of economic development and the need to finance it, before long led to experimentation with different forms of ownership at the fringes of the economy. In fact, it is a common point among Chinese historians of the market that the shareholding experiment began in the countryside.[4] This, in turn, gave rise to the spontaneous creation of various types of equity-like securities as early as 1980. Before the decade was over, shareholding companies had been established throughout the country and shares were being traded actively on an OTC basis in several major cities. Had June 4 not intervened and the country's direction become a subject of political dispute, China's national securities exchanges might have been (re)established much earlier than, in fact, they eventually were. Moreover, their character might have been substantially different. But this is only a part of the story.

FIGURE 2.1 Evolution of China's Securities Markets.

The formal exchanges in Shanghai and Shenzhen represent the future of China's equity markets. But there have been other market experiments along the way. These markets – the regional trading centers, the National Electronic Trading System (NETS), the Securities Trading Automated Quotation System (STAQ), the auction houses and now the so-called Third Board – suggest that developments were far from smooth and were not stage managed by the central government. Their ancestry in most cases can be traced back to the freewheeling 1980s. Today, housed in soccer stadiums or seedy office buildings, these lesser-known exchanges may be moribund, but they played important roles in driving China's experiment with securities markets forward.

This chapter reviews the emergence of the securities markets during the 1980s, the establishment of the Shanghai and Shenzhen exchanges in the early 1990s, and the parallel development of two electronic markets, NETS and STAQ (see Figure 2.1). The China Securities Regulatory Commission's effort to centralize trading in the two formal exchanges during the 1990s led to the closure of the regional markets, NETS, and STAQ in the late 1990s, and there are proposals to merge the Shanghai and Shenzhen exchanges. Economic pressures early in the new century, however, have given rise to other OTC markets. The picture, therefore, remains somewhat disjointed: will there be a merger, will Shenzhen open a NASDAQ-type market with looser listing requirements, and how will the Third Board develop? Nevertheless, the broader trend is one of centralization in a single national market located in Shanghai.

THE EVOLUTION OF THE SHENZHEN AND SHANGHAI SECURITIES MARKETS

China's securities markets developed in fits and starts during the 1980s. Shanghai got started first, but drew back, uncertain if stocks and markets were politically accepted. Shenzhen then picked up the baton and drove market developments forward at a rapid pace. Despite Shanghai's early experiments, Shenzhen was actually the mother to China's stock markets in an economy where no private property existed.

1979–84: The *"Batiao"*: Shanghai Gets Hot First

During the early years of China's experiment with equity, investors acquired securities paying a fixed dividend based on the bank deposit rate. They tended to hold, not trade, such securities, having invested to obtain the steady dividend cash flow, just like a fixed bank deposit or a bond. The ownership of these securities, however, was transferable since the market was almost entirely open and unregulated, but, given the original investment objective, little trading took place. From the mid-1980s, equity issuance, overwhelmingly to company employees, became increasingly frequent. During these early years, Shanghai was extremely active. By 1984, Shanghai had already recorded around 1,700 issues raising RMB240 million.[5]

The political environment at the time was, nonetheless, ideologically inhospitable: "spiritual pollution" was the watchword. This caused the city government to proceed with extreme caution; after all, shareholding was a capitalist concept. How sensitive these ideas were is conveyed in a story told by the head of Shanghai Feile Acoustics: "When we first began talking about stocks, the Shanghai leadership supported us. Wu Bangguo and Huang Ju often visited the factory, but they were careful about what they said. I also went to the party committee and was fearful that others would bring up capitalism."[6]

This caution was memorialized in the brief "Provisional Management Measures" released by the Shanghai Branch of the PBOC in July 1984. The so-called Eight Articles (*Batiao*) were the first formal government regulation developed for China's emerging stock markets.[7] They succinctly illustrate China's primitive understanding of equity at the time. The Eight Articles read:

1. Newly established collective enterprises can issue shares.
2. Shares issued can be collective shares or individual shares.
3. Collective shares issued to enterprises wholly owned by the people, township and village enterprises (TVEs), and agricultural production brigades pay dividends equal to the bank one-year deposit rate.
4. City and township employees, residents, commune members, and overseas Chinese can purchase individual shares with dividends equal to the one-year savings account rate.
5. Shares are classed as either fixed date repurchases or open-end buy-backs. The fixed date buy-back has a maturity date and can be bought back in installments or at one time by the issuing unit repaying the principal; for the open-end buy-back, the investor has share ownership and the issuing unit will not buy back the share.

6. At the end of each year, the issuing unit, based on its after-tax profit situation, can take a portion of its profit and pay dividends to shareholders on a pro rata basis. The annual dividend rate in general can be calculated as 3–5% of the face value of the share.
7. If the shareholder wishes to transfer share ownership, he can entrust a bank trust department to act as agent in the sale and transfer or apply to a bank for a secured loan.
8. Shares are limited to physical trading only.

The caution shows in limiting the scope of the experiment to new collective enterprises only – excluding SOEs and the party members running them to protect them politically. The summer's caution was followed by boldness in the fall when the Party proclaimed in its momentous "Decision on the Reform of the Economic System" that cooperative and private enterprises were to be promoted. With the support of the "*Batiao*" and the Party, Shanghai Feile Acoustics and Yanzhong Industries carried out the city's first equity placements with the public late in the year.[8] The public reception was cold, however, so cold that party cadres had to demonstrate their support by lining up to buy shares in an effort to stir up interest!

1985–88: The 1986 Provisions: Shenzhen Heats up

If 1984 was a year of "spiritual pollution," events continued to build up to 1986, which took reform's first major victim: Party Secretary Hu Yaobang was accused, among other things, of "bourgeois liberalism." During the same period, however, China created its first true inter-bank market. And Shenzhen, caring little about pollution or liberals, established the country's first specialized securities company, the Shenzhen Special Economic Zone Securities Company[9] and issued the first systematic regulations on corporatization and shares, the 1986 Provisions.[10] Up and down the country, the shareholding experiment also proceeded apace. Shenyang by now had 502 companies issuing shares, 14 publicly for a total of RMB400 million. By the end of 1987, there were reportedly 6,000 shareholding enterprises across China and a further 3,800 sprang up in 1988 alone.[11] Events were advancing independently of individual party bosses. A major factor influencing Shenzhen's continuing development as a center of equities was its proximity to Hong Kong. The city government, as it began to plan the establishment of an exchange, consulted closely the Hong Kong model and experience, as can be seen in the 1986 Provisions. As for local investors, the Hong Kong retail investor mentality (and hot money) seeped easily across the border.

Like Shanghai in 1984, corporate activity in Shenzhen forced the city government into action in 1986. The resulting 1986 Shenzhen Provisions[12] were directed primarily at the restructuring of its own SOEs. The local government, however, welcomed all to use them as a guide: "Other SOEs, cooperative enterprises implementing restructuring, and newly established internally capitalized companies limited by shares can also proceed based on these regulations." This was a very refreshing approach that, in fact, has yet to be equaled. The municipal finance bureau and the local branch of the PBOC oversaw the corporatization process and the market itself. At the same time, the city government, assisted by the PBOC, approved the formal establishment of OTC trading counters at various financial institutions. Five Shenzhen SOEs consequently offered shares to the public in 1987, led off in May by the Shenzhen Development Bank, China's first financial institution limited by shares, and followed in December by Vanke, a property developer. In contrast to Shanghai, Shenzhen led off with SOEs; there was no fiddling about with the non-state sector. By the end of the decade, there were nine financial institutions conducting OTC trades in 11 business offices across the city and one institution providing share registry services.[13]

SDB was the match that set fire to the previously quiet market.[14] Its IPO had been a complete dud – undersubscribed and drawing no interest, little different from Shanghai Feile Acoustics. In fact, as in Shanghai, the Shenzhen party organization was mobilized to buy shares as a good example. Even with such support, the issue was only 50% subscribed.[15] A year and a half later, in March 1989, the bank announced its dividend for 1988.

What happened next was an entirely different story from the IPO and marked a major turning point in China's equity markets. As described in Chapter 1, the bank was exceedingly generous to its investors, creating a market for its shares almost instantaneously. After this experience, investors did not need market professionals to tell them that shares were worth (potentially) more than their face value suggested. The bank's shares soared in OTC trading igniting "share fever" throughout southern China. Think of the now rich party members who had originally bought in under orders!

Shortly afterward, the Shenzhen Jintian IPO placed one million shares in three days. In December, Shekou Anda sold the same number in one day, and Shenzhen Yuanye in March 1990 beat them all with a 100% oversubscription for 16.5 million shares, raising RMB32 million. As shown in Table 2.1, through the summer of 1990, prices for the five publicly traded Shenzhen companies snowballed, with funds pouring in from all across China. In addition to raising

TABLE 2.1 Market Price of the Five Publicly Traded Shenzhen Shares, 1990

	SZ Development Bank	Vanke	Jintian	Anda	Yuanye
Face Value	1	1	10	1	10
May 1990	11.99	2.00	28.58	2.60	17.26
June 1990	18.18	5.80	50.91	3.59	30.63
Percent Change[16]	**52%**	**190%**	**78%**	**38%**	**78%**

Source: Cao Er-jie, p. 141.

TABLE 2.2 Shenzhen Shares OTC Market Peak Trading Volumes, 4Q 1989–2Q 1990

	SZ Development Bank %	Vanke %	Jintian %	Anda %	Yuanye %	Total CGB Volume
4Q1989	2.4	0.8	4.5	Not issued	Not issued	7.7
1Q1990	6.1	12.3	7.9	Not issued	Not issued	26.3
2Q1990	13.7%	18.0%	25.9%	40.9%	20.6%	119.1 Mn

Source: Cao Er-jie, p. 142.

investors' understanding of the long-term value of investing in shares, this experience had a second, and equally strong, effect of orienting investors toward a quick short-term capital gain: the market expanded and became speculative in nature.

Just how hot shares became can be seen in the significantly increased trading volumes of the five shares as a percentage of total trading volume in Shenzhen's OTC market, as shown in Table 2.2. Annual trading volume (stocks and bonds) expanded from only RMB4 million in 1988 to over RMB1.8 billion in 1990 on a year-end market capitalization of RMB7 billion.[17] Share trading has virtually eclipsed bond trading in Shenzhen ever since.

This frenetic activity, and the birth of an active black market, did not pass unnoticed by the Shenzhen government, which imposed a variety of measures beginning in May 1990 to bring the market under control.[18] These measures included ceilings on daily share price movement.

As shares became expensive in Shenzhen, money from the south began to buy up the relatively cheap Shanghai shares. The Industrial and Commercial Bank of China (ICBC) Jingan Index on March 19, 1990, for example, stood at 90.6; by June, it had reached 100 and in August 200. By mid-October, the index broke past the 300 level.[19] All this was more than enough to excite even the careful Shanghainese and caused PBOC Shanghai Branch to halt approvals for the establishment of new OTC trading offices by banks at this time.[20]

In the short term, shares continued to trade up against their price ceilings each day and the black market flourished. Even worse, many companies took advantage of the craze to issue shares illegally. By November 1990, the speculative frenzy had died down due to the accumulation of government control measures, which led to a market crash in Shenzhen.[21] But the experience had taught investors, actual and potential alike, that shares had value over and above the dividends paid. The equity investor mentality was born in Shenzhen. In addition, Shenzhen appeared on the edge of seemingly real privatization, as suggested in Table 2.3.[22]

These limited data suggest that the Shenzhen "experiment," had it not been interrupted by the political events of 1989, might have had untold consequences for Chinese companies and the Chinese economy.

TABLE 2.3 Shareholding Structure of National versus Shenzhen Samples, December 31, 1991

Type of Share	National Sample %	State %	Shenzhen Sample %	State %
State Share	47		23	
Legal Person Share	29	**76**	13	**36**
Individual Share	14		27	
Foreign Share	9		37	

Sources: *Renmin Ribao*, June 23, 1992, p. 5; and Gao Shangquan, p. 88.

1988–91: Zhu Rongji Becomes Mayor: Shanghai Steps up

On May 1, 1988, Zhu Rongji assumed the position of mayor of Shanghai and discovered, like other mayors throughout China, that the city treasury was empty. Shanghai then was not the Shanghai of the new millennium: it was poor, the central government skimming off all the cream and leaving little behind. While he pushed for more funds from the MOF, Zhu also sought to reform Shanghai's own financial sector.

Prior to his appointment, the Shanghai securities market had developed in a more cautious direction than Shenzhen, with an emphasis on government debt securities.[23] From January 1987 to March 1988, the budding market began to attract the attention of trust and investment companies. The trust companies sought PBOC Shanghai approval to establish OTC trading operations with a primary focus on treasury bonds (*guoku*). The first such office had been opened by the Shanghai branch of the ICBC on September 26, 1986. At that time, there were only two tradable shares – Feile and Yanzhong – and the market was slow no matter what the security. In the fourth quarter of 1986, only 30 shares of the two companies traded on average each day over the ICBC counter. A year later, over two months in the fall the office recorded only two treasury bond transactions.[24] Much of the action, if there was any, took place in the black market.

Zhu continued to push during 1988 and eight new trading offices were established.[25] From April 1988 to the opening of the Shanghai Stock Exchange (SSE) in late 1990, a specialized securities industry slowly began to develop. The Shanghai Branch of the PBOC approved the establishment of a number of securities companies, including Shanghai Wanguo Securities, Shanghai Shenyin Securities, Shanghai Haitong Securities, and Shanghai Caizheng Securities, all of which became major industry powers during the 1990s. But, like Shenzhen, share issues in Shanghai met with a yawn: the third issue by Shanghai Vacuum Electronic Device in March 1989 failed, forcing the underwriting syndicate to underwrite 80% of the offering. At this time, the shares of eight Shanghai companies were trading over the counter.

In late 1989, Zhu also assumed the position of Shanghai party secretary and shortly thereafter, in December, convened a conference on financial reforms.[26] PBOC Vice Governor Liu Hongru attended from Beijing. Zhu told him that although he had focused on finances since becoming mayor, the results had been small. Zhu felt that more financial reform was required and that he wanted to establish a securities exchange and bring in foreign banks. Zhu asked the opinions of two other senior attendees of the conference and received cautioning answers: it was politically dangerous. Zhu replied, "You two don't need to be afraid; if something goes wrong, Liu Hongru and I will be responsible. You two are not on the front line."[27] At this meeting, a three-person working group spearheading the preparatory work for an exchange was set up, staffed by the chairman of the Bank of Communications (BoComm), the governor of the PBOC Shanghai Branch, and the director of the Shanghai Committee for the Reform of the Economic System.

But only six months after June 4, the future of stocks and exchanges did not, in fact, look politically feasible. The Shanghai PBOC governor summarized the political objections in four points. First, he said, SOEs issuing shares or debt might lead to privatization. Second, selling shares or fixed income securities, especially to individuals, might reduce bank deposits and harm the banking system; moreover, trading would lead to speculation and social unrest. Finally, opening a stock exchange might result in the creation of a new class of capitalists.[28] So, Shanghai took the slow approach over the next year – sticking a reference to an exchange deep into a report on the planned development of Pudong and holding two international conferences on securities markets. But Zhu continued to push and he had some backing. Prior to setting up a stock-market preparatory team,[29] he had visited Deng Xiaoping who told him to go ahead.[30] A year later, the exchange was born.

Treasury bond trading, however, was the driving force behind the rapid developments that led to the establishment of the SSE. After the bright flash in 1984, Shanghai increasingly took on the nature of a central government-sponsored market for debt securities, while Shenzhen remained the Wild West of equity shares.[31]

1989–91: The Effort to Pull Back

Beginning in 1989, the state initiated efforts to impose order on enterprise experiments with the shareholding structure, as well as share issuance and trading. This was driven by the old political criticism that stocks and stock markets were capitalist manifestations that led to privatization and created social unrest and, therefore, should be eliminated. Many measures prepared to promote market development did not go through in the aftermath of the June 4 Incident. But in May 1990, the State Council did approve a report submitted by the pro-market SCRES. On its face, this report appeared to limit the equity experiment. It proposed: (1) experiments wherein only enterprises participated in the share capital of other enterprises; (2) restrictions on the further sale of shares to employees; (3) limiting the development of OTC markets to Shanghai and Shenzhen alone; and (4) no more public listings.[32] In reality, however, the SCRES report, together with Shenzhen's "share fever," drove the market forward.

On June 2, only a month later, the State Council gave the go ahead to the establishment of formal securities exchanges.[33] The motivation for this seemingly brave political decision, however, was fear. "Share fever" in Shenzhen and Shanghai was nearing its peak in the summer months and there was concern lest it get out of control. Far better to manage the situation and limit its scale inside the walls of formal exchanges.

The opening of the Shanghai Securities Exchange on December 19, 1990, followed shortly thereafter by the formal opening of the Shenzhen Stock Exchange (SZSE) in July 1991, were highly symbolic historical events. Elsewhere in the country, however, and regardless of regulation, OTC trading continued,

---

BOX 2   Which Came First: Shanghai or Shenzhen?

The winners always write the history. The reality is that Shenzhen issued shares to the public first. In the same way, the Shenzhen exchange opened earlier than Shanghai; it is just that Shenzhen's official approval document somehow got hung up in Beijing. But then again, on December 12, 1990, neither had the formal approval for Shanghai appeared ... but mayor and first party secretary Zhu Rongji did, and was not averse to forging ahead.

How much earlier (or later) was Shenzhen? City leaders were calling for trial operation on August 8, 1990, and failed to gain approval; they tried again on October 13 and failed again. No one was sure where the difficulty was: in Beijing or somewhere in the city government. When on November 22, Shenzhen heard that Shanghai would soon open, the city party secretary, the mayor, and the deputy mayor went to the exchange floor and said, "Today is your first day." Shenzhen began (trial) trading on December 1, 1990.

But there was no senior government member present from Beijing at the opening ceremony. Into the New Year there was still no approval, but the exchange continued trading. Finally, in May, the exchange president traveled to PBOC Beijing to ask for approval. He was told by the PBOC that the word "exchange" was too sensitive ... why not call it a market or trading center instead? So the legal name of the Shenzhen exchange went through a number of variations until on July 3, 1991, it was at last formally approved. Attendees at the formal ceremony this time included Chen Muhua, ex-PBOC governor and at the time the vice director of the National People's Congress Standing Committee; Zhu Senlin, governor, Guangdong Province; Liu Hongru, vice director, SCRES; and Li Hao, mayor of Shenzhen. This was formal support enough. From today's vantage point, most people in the Chinese securities industry recognize that the Shenzhen exchange was established on December 1, 1990. For that matter, the exchange in its brochures also claims this date outright.

The real truth, however, is that neither exchange was the first to be established in post-Liberation China. On June 1, 1949, the Tianjin Military Commission established a stock exchange and five companies were listed. Then on February 7, 1950, the Beijing Securities Exchange was established. Although both were closed shortly thereafter, these were new China's first stock exchanges.

Source: See Wang An, pp. 88–91, 105–7; and Cai Jianwen, pp. 45–50.

particularly in the major cities of Shenyang, Wuhan, Tianjin, and Beijing. Each of these cities had lobbied to establish a recognized exchange but lacked the political clout. Or, in the case of Beijing, political events absolutely precluded such an experiment.

It is difficult now to imagine the force of the market events of early 1991, even though the scale of the markets was in fact quite small. Unruly crowds of would-be investors teamed to open share accounts with securities houses. The trading floors of the SSE made the Chicago Mercantile Exchange seem like a public library by comparison. This was a period when the whole character of China seemed on the verge of changing overnight. It was the heyday of the masses as investor.[34]

The 810 Incident

The beginning of the end of local control over the hard-won exchanges started with the Shenzhen riots of August 10, 1992, or the 810 Incident. Some 700,000 would-be investors from within and outside Shenzhen packed into the town to subscribe to a new issue.[35] As the date grew closer, hundreds of thousands of people lined up for over three days and nights at the 303 subscription points to obtain a form giving them the right to subscribe to shares. But on the day the forms were handed out, August 10, the prescribed five million forms had been used up in less than four hours. That afternoon and evening, Shenzhen was the scene of violent rioting as the populace vented its anger against a process that was clearly corrupted by the managing PBOC officials. The next day, the government distributed a further 500,000 forms and order was restored. This event led directly to the establishment in October 1992 of the CSRC and the start of the central government's effort to exert control over the development of the securities industry in general and the stock exchanges in particular. Looking back, it is fair to say that this process is now over, as symbolized by the adoption of the Securities Law in 1999.

The Merger of the Shenzhen Market with Shanghai

Shortly after the passage of the Securities Law, talks began about merging the Shenzhen market with Shanghai. As Xu Kuangdi, then Shanghai's popular can-do mayor, stated in November 2000, "During the first quarter, or at least during the first half of next year [2001] the settlement of all the main boards will be done in Shanghai."[36] This did not happen; the central settlement company was located in Beijing (tax revenues).[37] Nor have the exchanges merged yet. Shortly before his comments, however, in September 2000, new listings on the Shenzhen exchange were halted and preparatory work began for establishing a Second Board for hi-tech companies, following in the footsteps of Hong Kong's Growth Enterprise Market (GEM). The Second Board was expected to be in operation by the end of 2000 but has yet to materialize. The Shenzhen exchange's organization chart, as well as discussions with exchange representatives, however, indicate that all internal work has been completed.[38] Given the hi-tech crash of 2001, the need for a Second Board seems debatable. But until the central government can find a suitable means to compensate the Shenzhen government for the loss of a major source of revenue and prestige, any merger with Shanghai seems unlikely in the near term. Equally unlikely to materialize is the rumored share listing of the SSE overseas, following the acquisition of the SZSE.[39]

ORIGINAL STRUCTURE OF THE SHANGHAI AND SHENZHEN EXCHANGES

From their establishment, both the SSE and the SZSE shared a similar organizational structure as non-profit organizations run by members through a general meeting which elects a standing executive committee, or Council.[40] The Council is headed by a director with a separate general manager selected as the legal representative for the exchange. In addition, a Supervisory Committee responsible to the members' general meeting was also established.

The degree of independence of the two exchanges differed significantly, however, as summarized in Table 2.4. While both exchanges were subject to the supervision of their respective local branches of the PBOC, the Shenzhen

TABLE 2.4 Comparison of Exchange Structure, Shanghai versus Shenzhen

Position	SSE Required Approval	SZSE Required Approval
Membership	Exchange followed by PBOC Shanghai Branch review, PBOC Beijing review if a non-Shanghai entity	Exchange followed by PBOC Shenzhen Branch review
Council	Nominated by Council followed by PBOC Shanghai Branch approval	Director nominated by PBOC Shenzhen Branch
General Manager	Nominated by PBOC Shanghai Branch and approved by PBOC Beijing	Nominated by Council director and approved by Council followed by PBOC Shenzhen Branch approval
Deputy General Manager	Nominated by PBOC Shanghai Branch and approved by PBOC Beijing	Nominated by Council director and approved by Council followed by PBOC Shenzhen Branch approval
Supervisory Committee	Director and deputy director appointed by PBOC Shanghai Branch	Director and deputy director elected by the Committee followed by PBOC Shenzhen approval

exchange had relatively more independence. For example, the designation of the general manager for the Shanghai exchange was subject to the approval of PBOC Beijing, while for Shenzhen this remained a local matter. The exchanges worked closely with their respective municipal Securities Commissions to which the city government appointed representatives from each of the agencies or bureaus responsible for certain aspects of the corporatization and listing process.[41] In practice, this meant nearly every government agency was represented. The commissions, in turn, operated through an executive body, a Securities Administration Office, which was devoted to the administration of the markets, approval of listings, supervision of listed companies, and oversight of dispute resolution. The two exchanges were thus well integrated into their local governments, which at the outset managed them for the benefit of companies domiciled in their own jurisdictions. As described in Chapter 3, over the course of the 1990s the local governments lost control over the exchanges to the CSRC, with the result that they became national rather than local in character and control.

The Growth of Exchange Membership

The development of the exchanges can be seen in the dramatic increase in the number of members (see Table 2.5). Originally there were three categories of members, including local Shanghai or Shenzhen brokerages, brokerages domiciled outside of Shanghai or Shenzhen, and trading centers, which are discussed in a later section of this chapter.

The sharp drop of membership in both exchanges beginning in 1997 has been largely due to stagnant trading volumes as retail investors seem to have left the market. Lower volumes drove a consolidation of the brokerage industry,

TABLE 2.5 Shanghai and Shenzhen Exchange Membership Trends

Year	Shanghai			Shenzhen			Trading Centers	
	Local	Non-local	Total	Local	Non-local	Total	SSE	SZSE
1991			26			15		
1992			101			177		
1993	46	330	376	28	398	426	2	
1994	49	501	550	30	466	496	19	15
1995	49	504	553	34	498	532	24	23
1996	45	478	523	34	508	542	24	27
1997	43	424	467	24	349	373	26	28
1998	12	305	317	15	314	329		28
1999	11	298	309	14	304	318		
2000	12	293	305	16	310	326		
2001	10	245	255	16	268	284		
7/2002	14	210	224	17	243	260		

Sources: Shanghai and Shenzhen Stock Exchange statistics annuals.

TABLE 2.6 Trends in Number of Seats, Shanghai and Shenzhen

Year	Shanghai Total No. of Seats	Visible	Invisible	Shenzhen Total No. of Seats
1991	37			
1992	284			
1993	1,647			
1994	4,315			782
1995	4,900			887
1996	5,233			1,125
1997	5,700	3,711	1,989	1,343
1998	5,394	3,037	2,357	1,505
1999	5,391	3,001	2,390	1,555
2000	5,316	2,841	2,475	1,697
2001	5,312	2,755	2,557	3,230*
7/2002	4,908	2,416	2,492	3,369

Sources: Shanghai and Shenzhen Stock Exchange statistics annuals.
Note: *The Shenzhen exchange, when asked, could offer no clear explanation for the doubling of seats.

which continues through the present. The decline in number of members is also reflected in the number of seats or trading positions at the Shanghai exchange shown in Table 2.6. Despite lower trading volumes during these years, the number of open accounts grew substantially to around 66 million equally divided between the two exchanges (see Figure 2.2). As discussed in Chapter 7, however, active accounts were dramatically less.

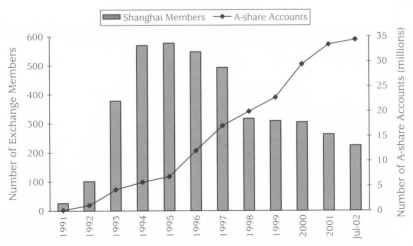

FIGURE 2.2 Growth of Shanghai A-share Accounts and Exchange Members.
Source: Shanghai Stock Exchange as of July 2002.

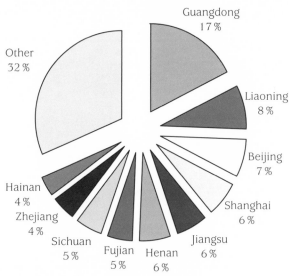

FIGURE 2.3 Geographic Representation of Shanghai Stock Exchange Members.
Source: Shanghai Stock Exchange, as of July 2002.

By mid-2002, there was a broad geographic distribution among exchange members but significant concentration as well. Ten provinces and cities accounted for approximately 68% of the total Shanghai membership, as shown in Figure 2.3. The Shenzhen exchange shows a similar distribution. Of the 10, seven represent the prosperous coastal regions, including Guangdong, Liaoning, Beijing, Shanghai, Jiangsu, and Henan, together accounting for 50.4% of the total membership. The relatively strong representation of Liaoning is accounted for by the fact that Shenyang was a leader from the very beginning in the experiment with shareholding companies and until the end of 1998 was the location of one of the three major regional trading centers. The strong representation of Henan, one of China's poorest provinces, is due to the presence in Zhengzhou, its capital, of a major commodity exchange.

Exchange-traded Products

Unsurprisingly, the exchanges share a similar product mix, although Shanghai continues to be the principal market for Chinese government bonds (CGBs), while Shenzhen is dominated by A-share trading. The exchanges trade A shares, B shares, CGBs, securities funds, corporate bonds, convertible bonds, and CGB repos. Dual listings – that is, the listing of a company's shares on both exchanges – are not permitted. As Table 2.7 illustrates, A shares dominate the trading volumes of both exchanges, while Shanghai dominates bond trading.

Because Shanghai dominates bonds, it also leads in CGB repo trading, which is directly linked to the equity market. A repo involves the use of a CGB as collateral for a cash loan.[42] Such loans are then used by securities firms to

TABLE 2.7 Exchange-traded Products and Trading Volumes, Shanghai and Shenzhen

Product	Shanghai		Shenzhen	
(RMB)	Products	Volume (Bn)	Products	Volume (Bn)
A shares	674	1,162.2	489	766.7
B shares	54	42.4	56	26.7
Securities Funds	24	41.4	27	48.4
CGBs	13	374.9	12	14.8
CGB Repo	8	1,197.6	9	0.00
Corporate and Convertible Bonds	13	4.6	6	3.5
Total Products	786	2,823.1	599	860.1
US$Bn		**341.0**		**103.9**

Sources: Shanghai and Shenzhen market statistics, YTD July 2002.

purchase shares for outright trading purposes or to acquire shares at the time of an A-share IPO. When new A-share issuance is heavy, there is a corresponding increase in repo volume and interest charged (the repo rate).

THE STOCK EXCHANGE EXECUTIVE COUNCIL AND THE ELECTRONIC MARKETS (STAQ AND NETS)

The Stock Exchange Executive Council (SEEC) (*Lianban*)

The story of how the Shanghai and Shenzhen exchanges became established is intimately wound up in the personal efforts of three students – Wang Boming, Gao Xiqing, and Wang Wei. In early 1988, these friends returned from their studies and jobs in the United States with the ambitious idea of promoting a stock market in China.[43] They achieved their dream – securities exchanges in China were established – but not as they expected. As Wang Boming put it:

> Write books, set up conferences, research markets, help our brothers in Shanghai and Shenzhen set up exchanges, talk at international conferences, busy in front, busy in back, busy up in the mountains and busy overseas ... then suddenly find both hands empty, fidgeting not knowing what to do next ... maybe we ought to give up and go repair bikes or sell steamed buns.[44]

Despite setbacks, they did not fix bikes or sell buns. On their return to China, the three had written a report entitled "Policy Suggestions for Promoting the Legalization and Standardization of China's Securities Markets (Preliminary Draft)."[45] Their principal recommendations included:

1. Build up a complete legal basis for the securities and finance systems.
2. Establish a Chinese Securities Trading Commission to regulate the markets.

3. Create a centralized trading structure in order to standardize securities operations.
4. Promote financial education as well as accounting, audit, and credit rating skills in order to meet the needs of the securities markets.

All these suggestions were, of course, spot on. In fact, many people at the time talked about setting up exchanges, if only to bring the black market under control. But none of them had ever worked in one for five years, as Wang Boming had done in the NYSE. This report, plus a bit of persistence, gave the three friends a voice in the process.

In July 1988, the PBOC held a conference on securities markets in Beijing.[46] The conference was attended by the most powerful financial organizations in China – the central finance leadership group, the State Planning Commission (SPC), SCRES, PBOC, MOF, and Ministry of Foreign Economic Relations and Trade (MOFERT). In addition, the most positive proponents also were there – the state-sponsored, but very capitalistic (for the time), companies China Venturetech, China Agricultural Trust, and the Kanghua Group. The decision taken at the conference was for the PBOC to lead the establishment of a small working group to produce a White Paper, "Thoughts on the Establishment and Management of the Securities Markets of China." Wang and Gao joined this eight-person working team and from then on became part of the official push for securities and exchanges.[47]

The final draft of the White Paper included such chapters as "Feasibility Study on the Establishment of a Beijing Securities Exchange," "Basic Thoughts on Establishing a Law on Securities Management," and a recommendation that an independent market regulator similar to the U.S. Securities and Exchange Commission (SEC) be established. On November 9, 1988, this report was received at the highest party and government levels. The meeting was chaired by Yao Yilin, a vice premier, Central Committee member, and a deputy director of the Central Committee finance leadership group, and by Zhang Jingfu, an advisor to the Central Committee and the secretary of the Central Committee finance leadership group. After a three-hour discussion, Yao expressed his support. Even so, little concrete action resulted from this meeting. There emerged, however, an important consensus (*shuofa*): "[C]onditions to establish a securities exchange are not yet ripe. But, given the overall trends, exchanges are necessary; and if necessary, research is needed and this requires an organization to do the research, but the state won't do it." Zhang Jingfu suggested letting a non-state entity promote the work with state support and this idea was adopted.

Four months later, on March 15, 1989, the SEEC was established with a stated goal of eventually creating a Beijing securities exchange with 600 listed companies.[48] Although a non-state entity, the Stock Exchange Executive Council had strong indirect state backing from nine companies: Sinochem, China Foreign Trade Trust, China Everbright Group, China Economic Development Trust, China Village Development Trust, CITIC, China

Information Trust, China Kanghua Development, and China Venturetech. Each company contributed RMB500,000 in capital, a huge amount at the time. The timing, however, was not propitious: June 4. The SEEC was stillborn. Depression set in until Wang Qishan, then head of China Agricultural Trust, said that work could still be done, while warning that the SEEC's organizational status did not provide a "formal direct route to the top."

Wang's meaning was that the *Lianban*'s informal status rendered it politically vulnerable given the times. The SEEC had no state unit that it directly reported to, nor did it have a formal business license. Once anyone began asking questions, there would certainly be trouble. The first thought was to ask the PBOC to provide cover, but this did not work out. Finally, with the help of Li Qingyuan, the SEEC on Christmas Day 1991 was attached to SCRES.[49] But of the four remaining personal supporters – Wang Qishan, Zhou Xiaochuan, Gong Zhuming, and Zhang Xiaobin – the latter two had left government. Gong joined the SEEC as director general, and Zhang was more or less forcibly retired from a shortly to be disbanded Venturetech. So, who was the patron who would stand up and support the *Lianban*? And besides that, what was the *Lianban*'s "mission statement"? Post-June 4, there would be no consideration of a Beijing exchange and, furthermore, the Shanghai and Shenzhen exchanges were just being formally established.

The Securities Trading Automated Quotations Systems: 1990–99

On March 8, 1990, Gong Zhuming came up with an idea: in the West, he said, there were two types of securities exchanges. The first type, like the NYSE, provides a specific forum where securities are traded "within the walls." In the second type of exchange, like NASDAQ, securities trading takes place electronically between members, but not in a specific place – that is, "outside the walls." Considering the Chinese situation, Gong commented that the first type of exchange existed in Shanghai and Shenzhen, so why not establish a NASDAQ-like exchange in Beijing to provide a secondary market for government treasury bonds? The idea behind STAQ was born.[50] Preparation work proceeded quickly during the spring and summer months of 1990. The trading system was based on infrastructure owned by Civil Aviation Administration of China (CAAC).

By October, the SEEC had produced a draft document calling for the formation of a preparatory team for STAQ that was to be issued in the names of its presumed sponsors – the SPC, MOF, PBOC, and SCRES. But the PBOC was uncooperative. An official commented that, while such a system would fall under its regulation, it was inappropriate for the *Lianban* to seek PBOC sponsorship for an automated trading system, for the simple reason that the PBOC was already in the process of establishing one: the National Electronic Trading System.

In the end, other ministries did cooperate so that, although it was never brought under the control and regulation of the PBOC, STAQ was formally established in a December 5, 1990 ceremony in Beijing's Great Hall of the People.[51] Attending were Zhang Jingfu, Central Committee advisor, Xiang Huaicheng, MOF vice minister, He Guanghui and Liu Hongru, both vice directors of SCRES, and Lu Ning, vice mayor of Beijing. SCRES became the formal supervisory entity (*zhuguan bumen*) for STAQ, as it had for the SEEC. On its opening day, the STAQ system linked Beijing, Shanghai, Guangzhou, Haikou, Wuhan, and Shenyang and comprised 17 member securities companies. The first trade was completed between CITIC and China Venturetech.

So, December 1990 saw the birth of three securities exchanges in China: Shenzhen and Shanghai exchanges trading equities; and two automated systems – STAQ and, in January 1991, NETS – trading treasury securities. Each of these four markets pitted different state agencies against the other. Local governments sponsored the Shanghai and Shenzhen exchanges against PBOC, the promoter of NETS and the formal regulator of the securities markets, while the Beijing government and SCRES promoted STAQ. Each promoter had a different agenda.

STAQ began repo trading of treasuries in September 1991. It is not surprising that this business grew rapidly, since it is essentially a financing mechanism. In 1994, over RMB60 billion in repos were completed over the STAQ system, accounting for about 33% of all repos transacted on the major exchanges specializing in government securities – Shanghai, the Wuhan Securities Trading Center, and STAQ.[52] On STAQ alone, repos accounted for 90% of total treasury trading volume. Then, on February 23, 1995, Wanguo Securities (SISCO) attempted to corner the CGB market. Its trades in the March 27 CGB futures contract accounted for 80% of total market trading that day and paralyzed the entire settlement system. All futures trading was halted at once by what came to be called the 327 Incident.[53] By August, with the state still tangled up trying to unravel a mass of obligations, STAQ treasury trading halted completely.

By this time, STAQ had the beginnings of a second product: legal person (LP) shares. The opportunity stemmed from the prohibition of LP share trading. In 1992, tradable shares accounted for only 15% of the total capital of the 40 listed companies in Shanghai and Shenzhen. But there were far more unlisted companies, which had raised funds through placements of shares with other state entities. This inevitably resulted in their capitalization being predominantly non-tradable LP shares. By July 1994, when the Company Law took effect, there were some 6,000 such shareholding companies. The problem was that if the shares could not be traded, how would the original investors be able to realize a return on their investment or, more simply, how would they sell out if they wanted to? The pressure to sell all these "untradable" shares began to build.

Earlier, in 1992, the State Council had approved a report entitled "1992 Summary of Economic System Reforms." This report noted that experiments with the internal transfer of LP shares had begun on July 1.[54] As part of this experiment, SCRES had approved a pilot program of LP share trading, or better put, "transferring," through STAQ. Even at this time, the government wanted to release some pressure arising from the LP share build-up. By now, STAQ had been in operation for nearly two years and its system covered 37 cities and had 108 members. The first STAQ LP share purchase – 30 million shares of Zhuhai Hengtong – was completed on July 6 through a syndicate of 17 STAQ members in 10 provinces raising RMB120 million.[55] On July 8, these shares began actively trading throughout the STAQ system. By the end of 1992, 10 different LP share issues were being traded among over 200 members.[56] At its height, April–May 1993, over 6,000 legal persons – that is, companies – had opened accounts and were participating in LP share trading on STAQ. At least, the *presumption* was that these account holders were companies. It was a fact, however, that many individual investors had simply set up shell companies in order to participate in the market. In this way, individuals came to control a significant amount of LP shares.

The Shanghai and Shenzhen exchanges were trading at their lows during this period. In contrast, a frenzy built up on the STAQ as security companies across China began promoting the LP share market to individual account holders. Prices and trading volumes increased dramatically during May, although only a few companies had shares on the market. At the end of April, the STAQ Index was around 100, but by May 10 it had jumped to 241, with all shares hitting record highs.[57] Beginning May 12, however, the market began its fall against the backdrop of Zhu Rongji's pending announcement of measures to bring the finance system under control. On May 20, the CSRC announced that it would slow the approval of new LP share listings. This was followed on June 21 with the CSRC announcing a halt to all LP share listings. Although market participants expected the CSRC to come out with a formal regulation permitting LP share ownership transfers, it never happened. STAQ, now with no new tradable products, gradually stagnated and by 1997 had ceased to function as securities trading was increasingly concentrated in the two national exchanges. It was closed at last on September 9, 1999. Three years later, shares that had been listed on STAQ began to be transferred to the Third Board.

The National Electronic Trading System, 1991–97

The only difference between the NETS story and that of STAQ is that the former was supported directly by major state entities, primarily the PBOC, which had taken the idea from the founders of the latter. No matter, the outcome for both was much the same. NETS was established in January 1991 with the direct sponsorship of the PBOC and was operated by its majority-controlled company, China Securities Trading System Corp. Ltd. (CSTS). Other promoters included banks – PBOC, ICBC, Agricultural Bank of China (ABC), Bank of China (BOC), China Construction Bank (CCB), and BoComm; insurance companies – People's Insurance Company of China (PICC); and the three national securities companies – Huaxia, Guotai, and Nanfang.

The founding purpose of NETS was to provide a unified national electronic market for all securities, including "government bonds, municipal bonds, state bank bonds, corporate bonds, shares, investment fund bonds and other securities."[58] In other words, NETS shared the same business scope as the two main boards in Shenzhen and Shanghai. The timing was not accidental, coming immediately after the opening of the SSE, SZE, and STAQ. The political environment seemed to be right, and the PBOC aggressively sought to seize the opening to create its own system to strengthen its power base. Until 1993, NETS primarily carried out government bond trading, but it was not a significant player. In early 1993, the pressure to sell LP shares presented the chance to expand and on April 28, nine months after STAQ, NETS began LP share trading.

Given the formal position of the PBOC in the state hierarchy, it is not surprising that NETS received greater attention than STAQ. In June 1993, just before the slowdown and halt of LP share listings, Jiang Zemin as well as Liu Hongru, at this time chairman of the CSRC, both paid "inspection" visits. Their visits gave rise to false hopes for the market's development. Thinking that the events of the summer had cooled sufficiently, NETS listed six shares in October as a trial balloon. But after trading for only one day, the CSRC put its hand in and stopped the market.

Despite Zhu Rongji's efforts at the time to eliminate conflicts of interest in the banking system, the PBOC successfully retained CSTS, the direct holding company of NETS. The company was restructured and its operations focused on a small number of major cities.[59] In addition, "share trading" was removed from its Articles of Incorporation. Later the same year, as a part of the effort to bring the two national exchanges under tighter central control, the State Council compelled the PBOC to divest the company. It was thereupon merged with the Shanghai securities settlement company. NETS, however, remained, although it was largely moribund. In 1997, NETS was folded into and became a part of the PBOC's Central Government Debt Registration and Settlement Company, the back office for the inter-bank bond market. NETS should be seen as the PBOC's last-ditch effort to be involved as a player in the lucrative securities markets. Like STAQ, NETS was a remnant of the early days of the market that had outlived its usefulness.

THE REGIONAL TRADING CENTERS

The regional trading centers, like the major exchanges, evolved out of corporatization and share placement activity in various localities during the 1980s. Among the many centers, three stood out – Shenyang, Tianjin, and Wuhan. In addition to trading shares, these three, unlike other trading centers, had their own local products – funds and local enterprise debt securities. In 1986, Shenyang – the first regional center – had 502 companies with shares issued and 14 listed on the trading center with a total issue value of RMB300 million.[60] Trading centers suited the ambitions of local governments, which, like Shanghai, hoped to establish securities exchanges of their own. In the mean time, the centers were important sources of revenue for local budgets.

Following the formal establishment of the two national exchanges, the regional centers continued to play a role. In Shanghai's early years, the trading centers functioned as satellites for the exchange. Shanghai lagged Shenzhen in technology, since it did not at first have direct computer links with securities companies (the "invisible seat"[61]). As a result, securities firms had to buy actual physical seats on the exchange in order to trade. As order volume grew, the number of seats also grew, reaching more than 5,000 at one time. The exchange was forced to break up into several locations as no one building could hold so much activity. At the same time, orders coming in from securities firms nationwide jammed the Shanghai telephone system. If the Shanghai exchange was to continue to grow, it needed a solution to these physical limitations. The trading centers provided it. Local brokers could buy seats at the local trading center and transact business on the Shanghai exchange through the trading center's communications links. By late 1997, it had instituted its invisible seat system and in 1998 it settled into its new building, which had the telecommunications capacity to support invisible seats. With this the reason for the trading centers disappeared, at least from Shanghai's point of view.

Data on the trading centers are sparse, but are available for the Shenzhen exchange through 1997. Surprisingly, they played a significant role for Shenzhen, not by solving a technical deficiency, but by dramatically increasing trading turnover. As shown in Table 2.8, in 1997, trading centers accounted for five of the top 10 volume-generating exchange members. The centers are ranked by volume out of a total for 1997 of 1,343 exchange seats.

TABLE 2.8 Shenzhen Regional Trading Center Members Ranked by Trading Volume

No.	Trading Center	Ranking	No.	Trading Center	Ranking
1	Fujian	3	15	Harbin	84
2	Qingdao	5	16	Dalian	101
3	Jiangsu	7	17	Guangxi	155
4	Henan	6	18	Jilin	168
5	Sichuan	9	19	Jiangxi	186
6	Zhejiang	15	20	Shanxi	198
7	Chongqing	13	21	Xinjiang	271
8	Hunan	16	22	Ningbo	507
9	Shandong	17	23	Southern (Nanfang)	649
10	Xi'an	18	24	Shantou SEZ	583
11	Beijing	19	25	STAQ	644
12	Shenyang	25	26	Yunnan	768
13	Anhui	58	27	Hainan	1,104
14	Heilongjiang	65			

Source: Shenzhen Stock Exchange Fact Book 1997.

TABLE 2.9 Shenzhen Exchange Trading Center
Membership, 1993–99

Year	No. of Trading Centers
1993	0
1994	15
1995	23
1996	27
1997	28
1998	28
1999	0

Source: Shenzhen Stock Exchange Fact Book 1998.

As Table 2.9 shows, the exchange membership of regional centers increased during the mid-1990s until in 1999 they were closed. The 33% drop in Shenzhen trading volumes in 1998, at least in part, is due to the CSRC's preparations to close them (see Table 9.5 in Chapter 9).

Financial scandal, as usual, provided the reason for the central government to close down the regional exchanges. For a customer transacting with a trading center, the associated fees and share prices were the same as if he or she were transacting directly with the SSE itself.[62] There was one important difference, however: customer funds remained with the trading center. At its height, for example, the Beijing Trading Center contributed 12% of the SSE trading volume. Clearly, the amount of customer funds was enormous. It is easy to see how problems might occur as they did most spectacularly in Wuhan, where such funds were "lent" in support of investments promoted by the local government. In addition, Wuhan at this time was a major player in the government security repo markets, as noted previously. Between the misuse of customer funds and a tangled skein of irreversible repos, significant sums of money were lost.

At the end of 1998, as part of the larger picture of strengthening market regulation, the government told the centers either to return all customer funds or to deposit them with the two exchange-affiliated depository companies.[63] At the same time, the trading centers were given until June 30, 1999 to close. Most merged with local securities firms – for example, the Beijing center became a local brokerage, Beijing Securities.

THE AUCTION HOUSES

The auction houses (*chanquan jiaoyi zhongxin*) were first established in major cities across China in 1996 to regularize small-scale sales and purchases of real assets. At present, there are about 22 such houses operating under the regulation of the State Asset Management Bureau (SAMB).[64] Auction agents representing sellers or buyers are licensed by and operate under the joint scrutiny of the State Bureau of Industry and Commerce and the SAMB. The purpose of the houses is

TABLE 2.10 Shanghai Auction House Legal Person Share Trades,
August 2000–June 2001

Year/Month	No. of Auction Participants	No. of Auctions	No. of Shares Traded (000)	Total Value (RMB 000)
2000				
August	2	2	162	652
September	NA	–	–	–
October	14	31	8,474	23,533
November	14	34	2,652	8,910
December	5	15	1,360	4,584
2001				
January	56	145	23,455	78,326
February	69	288	53,720	158,348
March	110	346	118,660	353,989
April	113	460	113,453	349,834
May	132	835	114,688	384,562
June	103	422	51,778	163,373
July	NA	–	–	–

Source: Chen Zhiwu, p. 31; August 2000–June 2001.

to provide a legal framework for the sale and transfer of ownership of certain types of assets between legal persons, natural persons, or other organizations. The approved asset categories include equity rights and equity shares.[65] For all asset sales, the auction or negotiation is required to take place physically within the auction house. Regulations required an asset appraisal for the property to be sold, which establishes the base price. The sale price must be above this base price, but there are exceptions. For example, if the agreed-on price is 90% of the base price, the sale can go through with state agency approval.

The auction houses continue to exist, but in recent years they came to be used as an organized market to trade non-tradable shares – both state and LP shares – in much the same way that STAQ had performed previously. This illustrates once again the strong pressure to monetize these share types. Systematic data on trading is difficult to come by, but one complete run does exist for the Shanghai auction house, as shown in Table 2.10. During this one-year period, trading levels reached US$50 million equivalent for one month – a fraction of the daily trading on the Shanghai and Shenzhen exchanges. On September 30, 2001, the CSRC stopped LP share trading through the auction houses, although trade is still possible, as was previously true, with appropriate approvals.[66]

THE THIRD BOARD

Just as one crack in the system is closed, another pops open. On June 11, 2001, the Securities Association of China (SAC) announced the formal establishment of the Agency Stock Transfer System; commonly know as the Third Board (*sanban*). The purpose of the Third Board was, originally, to provide a new trading platform for the LP shares that had long been stranded on the defunct STAQ and NETS systems. More recently, it has become a trading platform for companies that have been de-listed due to irremediable performance from the Shenzhen and Shanghai exchanges.

The SAC oversees the Third Board, which functions as a purely electronic market operated by participating brokers. In fact, it differs little from how STAQ and NETS were organized. The SAC has approved six securities houses – Shenyin Wanguo, Guotai Junan, Guosen, Great Eagle, Minfa, and Liaoning Securities – to provide Third Board stock "transfer" services. Investors, individuals and legal persons, must open trading accounts at outlets of one of the six sponsoring brokerages.[67] Existing A-share holders of de-listed companies and shareholders of companies previously listed on STAQ and NETS must open new accounts to trade their holdings on the Third Board. At the outset, trading was limited to two hours in the morning and afternoon every other day. At the end of a trading day, a computer matches trades and sets the price to execute the various orders. Trading times were expanded on August 29, 2002 to full daily trading for stocks that met certain requirements.

As shown in Table 2.11, by the end of November 2002, the Third Board had 12 listed companies of which only three were exchange de-listed

TABLE 2.11   Third Board Listed Stocks

Code	Stock	Original Listing	Price (RMB)	Total Turnover to November 2002 (RMB)
400001	Nature Opto-Electronic Tech. Co.	STAQ	8.51	453,801,494
400002	Chang Bai Computer	STAQ	6.3	225,086,625
400003	Qingyuan Jianbei Group Co.	NETS	7.28	699,988,934
400005	Hai Guo Tou Industry Co.	STAQ	1.75	427,525,940
400006	China Development (Hainan) Co.	NETS	3.59	327,379,335
400007	Hainan Huakai Enterprise Co.	STAQ	2.27	237,507,538
400008	Shanghai Narcissus A	Shanghai	3.79	48,565,862
420008	Shanghai Narcissus B*	Shanghai	0.198	123,064,064
400009	Guangdong Guangjian Group Co.	NETS	2.75	201,106,019
400010	Beijing Jiufeng Science & Tech.	NETS	5.88	61,549,342
400011	Zhonghao A	Shenzhen	2.57	6,011,537
420011	Zhonghao B*	Shenzhen	0.164	5,649,948
400012	Guangdong Kingman Group	Shenzhen	1.99	15,453,397
400013	Gangyue Yongchang Group	STAQ	3.9	37,296,281
Total Turnover (RMB)				2,869,986,314
Total Turnover (US$)				346,616,705

Source: Wind Information, November 30, 2002.
*Price in US$.

companies[68] – Shanghai Narcissus, Guangdong Kingman, and Zhonghao Enterprise – the rest being former STAQ or NET LP shares. Over 95,000 investors have opened accounts. Since its inception, the Third Board has traded in excess of RMB3 billion.

Already commentators are talking about developing this market, perhaps by allowing private companies to list on it, rather than on the main exchanges.[69] It is hard to imagine that this sort of idea can become reality, since it goes against the trend of the past decade and more. But it does show that the economic pressure to uncover financing channels has not abated. Until all trading of all share types is brought into the recognized, formal Shanghai and Shenzhen exchanges and financing becomes a regularized corporate activity, marginal special-purpose markets will always be susceptible to manipulation.

CHAPTER 3

Who Minds the Fox: The Regulators

The CSRC's work is the most sensitive work. It's like sitting on the edge of a volcano; everyone should be mentally prepared. Simply put, if share prices rise explosively, those at the top will complain, worrying that something will happen. If share prices drop like a rock, those on the bottom will complain; the common people won't invest. If prices don't change at all, everybody will be unhappy since what you are doing is not market economics.

Liu Hongru, Chairman, CSRC[1]

The creation of an effective regulatory structure for the securities industry was an afterthought of the stock-market experiment. A senior SCRES official said that the purpose of the shareholding system was not to issue shares to the public. He meant that the purpose was to develop an ownership structure that would result in enhanced enterprise autonomy and, therefore, production efficiencies. This was the elusive goal of separation of government and enterprise (*zhengqi fenkai*). That being the case, the whole administrative side of the matter was simply one of the usual inter-governmental planning and coordination. There would be no new industry and no need for a special regulator. In fact, accountants and asset appraisers should be enough and they belonged to the MOF system.

From this, it is no surprise that the government's approach to securities markets regulation in the 1980s was haphazard and driven by local developments. As discussed previously, Shenzhen and its wide-open political and economic environment was the cradle of China's equity markets. But Shenzhen was also the catalyst for China's effort to create a relatively workable regulatory structure as well. This stemmed from necessity, given that a securities market had come into being there, even if not elsewhere. The Shenzhen market – in particular, the stock craze of 1989 and 1990, and the riots in August 1992 – forced the People's Bank from the scene and gave birth to the CSRC.

The PBOC and other agencies did not fade away easily, however. It took a fight and further market scandals. Through October 1992, the PBOC was the emerging regulatory power in the equity and debt markets. It was responsible for all aspects of the regulation and administration of China's securities industry. What's more, it was a player, sponsoring the establishment of securities companies across China and even China's first international IPO in October 1992.[2]

Although it has always been called China's central bank, the PBOC for most of its existence has served an entirely different function – that of cashier for the MOF. Under Soviet-style central planning, the People's Bank functioned as the country's sole banking institution from the late 1950s until the early 1980s when financial reform began. In addition to handing out working capital loans to SOEs, its attractiveness to all levels of the state as a financial partner was enhanced by its control of China's mints. The PBOC organization was enormous, with a branch in every provincial capital and a deposit-taking office on nearly every street corner. Its staff numbered in the millions. Until the 1994 passage of the Central Bank Law, the PBOC was the balancer of last resort for the national and many local budgets. So close was its "cooperation" with the MOF that the two were housed in the same building from the start of the Cultural Revolution until after its end in 1978.

So, although it was called a "central" bank, the People's Bank was, in fact, a very decentralized entity with principal staffing and functions at the provincial level and a staff of a few hundred in Beijing. Its close relationship with local governments became, at points during its history, entirely intimate, since the local party had the right to nominate senior branch staff. Local branches, in short, although reporting on a direct line to Beijing, had strong links to local governments and were active proponents of the corporatization wave that swept across China in the 1980s. After all, if an SOE could get money elsewhere, it meant less pressure on the bank itself. Against this background, it is clear that the PBOC was hardly an appropriate candidate to act as the national regulator of a rapidly evolving market-based experiment. On the other hand, there was, in fact, no other suitable entity to fill this role and the government did not foresee such a rapid pace of change. In fact, given the marginal nature of the shareholding experiment at the start, the government never conceived of the need for a more independent regulator until much, much later. By that time it had become clear just how sensitive the job would be, as Chairman Liu notes at the start of this chapter.

The establishment of a new bureaucratic entity in China is not easy and the China Securities Regulatory Commission is a case in point. In what is perceived and played as a zero sum game, there is resistance from all sides, particularly if the new organization is designed to supplant the roles of established players. At times, even the strongest political back-up will wilt in the face of a difficult decision. The PBOC was not happy. Nor were other agencies, including the MOF and its panoply of subordinate bureaus, such as the State Asset Management and State Land Management bureaus. Finally, the securities exchanges and their sponsoring local governments were not happy. Although the CSRC was established in late 1992, its position in the ministerial hierarchy was not solid until 1998. It victory was memorialized by the 1999 Securities Law, itself, like the CSRC, six years in the making and for mostly the same reasons. The story of the CSRC's emergence is a story of how market forces unleashed compelled the government to continue, rather than halt, the stock-market experiment and its required institutional development.

THE PBOC: MARKET PLAYER OR MARKET REGULATOR?

The Chinese government from the beginning of its experimentation with shares categorized them as a part of the financial (*jinrong*) or banking sector.[3] How else could securities be categorized: bonds and equities had been, in effect, "non-persons" since at least 1952. The PBOC's jurisdiction over the securities markets, therefore, was a consequence of historical reality. Added to this was the fact that it was the sole administrator and supervisor of the financial sector, meaning banks and non-bank financial institutions conducting traditional loan and deposit-taking businesses. By the mid-1980s, experimentation with securities, and debt securities in particular, had grown sufficiently widespread that some sort of regulation was necessary.

At the same time, the banking system itself was undergoing a radical restructuring as the government sought to reform the sector after nearly 25 years of nominally Soviet-style central planning. As a part of this, banks, which had been closed since the 1950s – for example, the Agricultural Bank of China and the Bank of Communications – were being re-established. In addition, the PBOC spun off its lending businesses into the new Industrial and Commercial Bank of China, eliminating a conflict of interest with its new role as a Western-style central bank.

Through 1994, the PBOC's authority was founded in the January 1986 State Council document, "PRC Provisional Regulations on the Administration of Banks" (the Provisional Banking Regulations).[4] These regulations were the predecessors of the Central Bank Law and the Commercial Bank Law, which came into effect eight years later in 1994. The 1986 Provisional Banking Regulations laid out the basis for a national commercial banking system including, almost as an afterthought, the nascent securities industry.

The regulations defined the PBOC's role as follows: "The PBOC is the State Council's organ leading and administering national financial undertakings and is the state's central bank…" For the most part, its responsibilities were most directly applicable to commercial banking institutions. But the provisions clearly defined financial organizations as those that could provide agented financing through the issuance of securities (*daimu zhengquan*). The PBOC's authority vis-à-vis financial institutions was spelled out in three points:

- review and approve the establishment, closure, and merger of specialized banks and other financial institutions;
- lead, administer, coordinate, supervise, and audit the operations of the specialized banks and other financial institutions; and
- oversee negotiable securities, including enterprise shares and bonds, etc., and administer the financial market.

In short, the PBOC was authorized to approve the establishment of "other financial institutions," specify how the ownership of securities should be registered and transferred, set the price for such transfer, collect data as to market trends, and so on. Local governments made use of this authority, with the acquiescence of local PBOC branches in 1988 moving ahead to establish 34 securities companies and 100 trading counters across the country.[5]

In response to a rapidly changing financial market, the PBOC was forced to re-state its authorities in 1988.[6] The State Council duly confirmed that the PBOC "… is responsible for the administration of stocks, debt securities and so on, and for the administration of the financial markets (including the securities markets, the issuance of government bonds, and the circulating markets), and the administration of all credit instruments." Local governments continued to pursue their own best interests together with the local branches of the PBOC, which began to establish their own brokerages. Eight years later, in 1996, PBOC was the controlling shareholder in 43 of the nationwide total of 96 brokerages, all of which it had approved itself. It was long since clear that the PBOC was at odds with itself.

What the PBOC was not involved in during these early days was the restructuring of enterprises into shareholding companies and the process leading to the issuance of shares. In later years, this was the sphere of SCRES, the institution responsible for defining policy for the shareholding experiment. In the beginning, however, it fell to the local governments with a process typically led by the Bureau of Finance.

The first step toward greater central government involvement came in March 1987, as a result of a State Council notice defining the scope of the corporatization experiment. The notice declared that all securities issuance must first be reviewed and approved by the PBOC.[7]

In this notice, the State Council explicitly halted the public issue of securities by SOEs, limiting a "very few" issues to collective enterprises only. Corporatization could proceed, but shares could be issued only to other legal persons. Hence, the SCRES official's comment about the purpose of the experiment. This exclusion ran directly in the face of the late 1986 Shenzhen provisional regulations governing equity issuance, including public issuance, and trading of shares.

It is clear that Shenzhen and other localities – for example, Shenyang – continued their experimentation with the full support of local People's Bank branches. For example, at an unspecified date in 1989, the PBOC Shenzhen branch, basing its authority on the Provisional Banking Regulations, took the lead in specifying approval procedures for share issuance.[8] This marked the first time that procedures had been formally established aimed at standardizing enterprise restructuring into shareholding companies. These regulations appear to have been issued late in the year in response to the stock-market craze that was taking hold at that time. However, the fact that only the year and not a specific date is referenced suggests that the regulations may never have been officially enacted.[9]

BOX 3   PBOC's Children: Anshan Securities, 1988–August 2002

Founded on May 4, 1988, with paid-in capital of RMB10 million, Anshan Securities was one of China's first brokerages. Anshan was approved by PBOC Liaoning Branch and its major equity holder was PBOC Anshan City Branch. Its headquarters offices were located on the sixth and seventh floors of the PBOC Anshan Branch. Its three-story brokerage office shared the same building as the PBOC Anshan Branch. The original chairman of Anshan Securities described the relationship with PBOC: "At that time Anshan Securities was equivalent to a division of PBOC Anshan and, like other divisions, reported directly to the PBOC leadership and attended the governor's business development meetings." The brokerage's principal management also came from PBOC. In reality, its capital was financed through PBOC Anshan private staff contributions of RMB138,000, with the rest made up by the branch itself. From its founding to 1998, PBOC Anshan was the brokerage's controlling equity holder, manager, and regulator all rolled into one.

From October 1998 and in response to the PBOC's 1997 notice on divesting its system of all invested securities firms, Anshan Securities began to separate itself from the Anshan branch. From that point on, it would fall under CSRC scrutiny as the security industry's regulator. The CSRC, however, from the very beginning would not accept Anshan Securities, due to its weak financial situation. In June 1998, in a meeting between the PBOC and CSRC to arrange the transfer of all former PBOC-invested brokerages, there were some 20 firms in a similar condition. The CSRC insisted that PBOC clean up its own mess in accordance with a Central Committee notice which stated: "… whoever approved [a firm] should regulate it, whoever issued debt should repay it, whoever issued a guarantee should be responsible, and whichever family's child it is should look after it."

From 1998, Anshan Securities existed virtually without regulation despite PBOC efforts to resolve its financial difficulties. By the end of the year 2000, most of the 20 hard cases had been cleaned up leaving, in the words of a CSRC staff member, "only those bones that are really tough to chew." Anshan Securities was one of these "tough bones." With debt of many times over PBOC's forecast audit result of RMB1.5 billion and each of its brokerage offices having fraudulently used retail investor account deposits, there was no way to resolve the problems. After a series of meetings during the summer months, it was decided to liquidate the company. Anshan Securities became China's first case of a bankrupt securities broker.

Source: Yu Ning and Ling Huawei, pp. 34–48.

It took the Shenzhen 1989–90 share frenzy plus the June 4 Incident to alter the central government's *laissez-faire* attitude. Political debate thereafter raged over whether shareholding belonged to the family of Mr. Capitalism or of Comrade Socialism.[10] This slowed developments temporarily, but events in Shenzhen ended any temporizing over what, after all, had become a practical reality. The awakening of Shenzhen investors to the capital gain potential of equity securities gave impetus to the discussion: rein in the experiment.

The May 1990 State Council circular referenced in Chapter 2 initiated the control effort by limiting the legal bounds of the trading experiment to Shenzhen and Shanghai and again emphasized inter-company investment by legal persons only.[11] The second half of 1990 marked the true start of the central government's attempt to impose control with a variety of measures issued in preparation for the opening of the Shanghai exchange.

This began with the People's Bank August 1990 prohibition of all banking institutions from directly trading or otherwise participating in the securities markets via branches or subsidiaries.[12] Henceforth, separate entities independent of the banking system would be required. This was largely ignored.[13] It was not until 1994, as part of Zhu Rongji's strenuous effort to reform the financial system, that a regulatory wall was built between the banking and securities sectors.[14] In October 1990, the PBOC issued the first national regulations governing the establishment of securities companies.[15] Of course, the regulations permitted its own local branches to retain ownership of securities companies they had capitalized and established. Thus, the PBOC continued, as before, to be both regulator of and active participant in (and beneficiary of) the securities markets. The tradeoff was that new securities companies could only be established with the approval of PBOC Beijing. PBOC branch and local government signoff was no longer sufficient. In addition, the scope of security company operations was limited to the administrative area of the sponsoring local government. Thus, at this very early stage, securities companies operating on a nationwide basis were prohibited. And not only that.

In recognition that the securities industry was creating a national as well as a local market, the PBOC attempted to regulate trading between regions.[16] Its measures called for local governments and PBOC branches to control securities trading between local securities entities and those elsewhere in the country. The securities defined included government, enterprise, and bank debt securities, as well as shares. Securities companies had to receive PBOC approval to establish trading links with counterparts (and, by extension, exchanges) elsewhere in the country. To ensure that prices between regions were standardized, the bank also initiated a national reference price list to be published by PBOC Beijing at the start and in the middle of each month. This list enabled local branches to "carry out inspection of and appropriate intervention in local securities prices." Trades made without reference to this price were deemed illegal.

Clearly, the PBOC had yet to emerge from the days of a planned economy. This approach shows that the bank, and perhaps the State Council as well, had absolutely no understanding that markets do not stop to wait for bi-weekly price quotes. Had these measures been effectively implemented over a long period, China's securities markets would never have grown to today's scale.

Shortly afterward, in December 1990, the Shanghai and Shenzhen exchanges were, if not fully approved, at least up and running.[17] The articles of incorporation of both exchanges clearly specify the role of the PBOC as overall market regulator. At this time, the exchanges themselves were purely local, not national in character. But at least China now had the basic infrastructure that would support the development of a securities industry. Moreover, as part of a series of documents leading up to the opening of the exchanges, public offerings were once again allowed, but limited to the exchanges only.[18]

So, China's stock markets came into being against an unfavorable political background and without the hope of listing significant amounts of new securities product. Their existence was based on the argument that centralized trading locations would give the state greater control over an experimental activity. This activity, the development of shareholding companies, might not be one that the state chose to further develop. Even if it did, the public listing of shares was not seen as the final objective, since such trading had a demonstrated capacity to produce serious social unrest. This was the reality in late 1990. What was important was that the exchanges existed ... new listings would come.

The state's effort then moved on to controlling the results of 1980s' experiments. In early 1991, the State Council required all companies which local governments had approved to issue shares publicly, to resubmit applications for formal issuance approval by the central government.[19] Without this new approval, the issuances would be deemed illegal and invalid. SCRES and the SAMB led the process. After the receipt of this approval, the company then applied to the local branch of the PBOC and, after receiving that approval, applied to PBOC Beijing for approval. If it received all four approvals, the company's previous issuance of shares was deemed legal. The involvement of the three ministries indicated the seriousness of the state's intent and, indirectly, its lack of faith in the integrity of the PBOC.

This reapproval process, however, was a one-off situation and did not apply going forward. In April 1991, PBOC Beijing recognized this as an opportunity and proposed to the State Council that it take the lead in establishing a specialized Securities Market Office to ensure coordinated central control over the industry.[20] This was approved and the PBOC created a coordinating body including all key organs of the planning bureaucracy. The list of representatives is a "Who's Who" of state planning and worth noting in full to illustrate how cumbersome and, therefore, how little changed the nature of the regulatory process was likely to be. Entities represented included the State Planning Commission, the Ministry of Finance, the State Administration of Exchange Control (SAEC), the State Tax Bureau, the State Asset Management Bureau, the State Council Office for the Economy and Trade, the Ministry of Foreign Economic Relations and Trade, and the State Bureau of Industry and Commerce. With no clearly designated senior leader, and there was none as most participating entities were bureaucratic peers, this gathering of interested parties did not represent much of an improvement over the previous situation.

In recognition of this, the Office established a smaller, more manageable working team. This group would be responsible for actual day-to-day operations. Its work included the review of enterprise listing applications, oversight of the operation of the two stock exchanges, as well as the coordination of the various bureaucracies whose approvals would be needed to get things done. Before this regulatory structure could be institutionalized, Deng Xiaoping's early 1992 Southern Excursion blew the doors wide open. During 1992, 40 companies listed shares on the two exchanges, nearly seven times as many as in 1991. An additional 3,800 issued shares through private placements.

In response to this, the State Council enhanced PBOC's authority in June 1992, giving it sole oversight of China's securities markets. At the same time, the State Council moved the just created Securities Market Office to its own jurisdiction, recognizing that such a group needed a firmer hand than PBOC could provide, as well as direction by a senior level. The Office became the immediate predecessor to the State Council Securities Committee (SCSC). The State Council's Securities Market Office thus was responsible for inter-agency cooperation, leaving the PBOC with the day-to-day operational responsibility.

Social unrest, in the end, abruptly terminated the PBOC's role as market regulator and led directly to the formation of the SCSC and the CSRC in October 1992.[21] The Shenzhen riots in August 1992 and memories of June 4 unleashed a fury of bureaucratic effort, and much of the critical national legislation on the markets came out in 1992 and 1993, having been pending since 1989. The complicity of the PBOC Shenzhen branch in catalyzing the riots finally brought home to the central government the reality that the bank as an institution was unsuitable to act as market regulator. There was simply too large an internal contradiction between controlling and participating in the market.[22]

BUILDING THE CSRC

The State Council's decision to establish the China Securities Regulatory Commission did not create the clear-cut regulatory structure the outside world might have thought at first sight. And the Securities Law, which eventually did create the strong regulator the industry needed, was delayed for years until its passage by the National People's Congress in December 1998, going into effect in July 1999. This delay was due in large part to the continued struggle over control of the industry.[23] It was not in the self-interest of other government agencies or of local governments to see the lucrative securities sector controlled by any single entity.

It was not immediately clear at the outset, therefore, that the CSRC would emerge as the dominant regulatory body. Given past practice, there was a higher probability that little would change. The combined SCSC/CSRC would likely perform in ways similar to the PBOC, given the conflicting goals of market participants and the overwhelming search by local governments and enterprises for access to financing. In fact, the CSRC and its limited initial staff of 80 faced severe opposition as they sought to establish themselves in the competitive bureaucracy of China.

First of all, and unlike the PBOC, the CSRC was merely a vice-ministerial non-governmental entity with offices only in Beijing.[24] Its lowly status was reflected in the poor office space its budget afforded, on the sixth floor of Beijing's oddly designed Poly Plaza, which was accessible by only one trundling elevator. Its governing agency, the SCSC, was similar to the Securities Market Office and consisted of a chairman, three vice chairmen, and 13 representatives from every potentially securities-related bureaucracy in China.[25] Vice Premier Zhu Rongji was the SCSC's chairman and Liu Hongru, the first chairman of the CSRC, one of the three vice chairmen. The other original vice chairmen, Zhou Daojiong and Zhou Zhenqing, became the CSRC's second and third chairmen, respectively, after Liu was ousted in March 1995.

The SCSC remained a smorgasbord of government agencies – SCRES, the PBOC, the SPC, the State Council Office of Trade and the Economy, the MOF, the SAMB, the State Bureau of Industry and Commerce, the State Tax Bureau, MOFERT, the SAEC, the Ministry of Supervision, the Supreme Court, and the Supreme People's Inspectorate. The group was given the sole policy authority for the industry. It drafted laws and regulations based on appropriate research, put together a development plan for the industry, and coordinated central and local governmental bodies with regard to the securities markets and managed the CSRC. But the SCSC was not an executory body.

This left the CSRC to be the implementing apparatus for the SCSC. Since it was established as a quasi-governmental organization (*shiye danwei*),[26] the CSRC could not formally be an executory body either. On paper, the CSRC was responsible for drafting detailed regulatory measures, supervising entities involved in the securities business, overseeing companies issuing securities both domestically and internationally, and compiling statistics and market analyses to advise the SCSC on policy matters. The first group of department directors under the pioneering chairman Liu Hongru was internationally educated and highly professional.[27]

Confusion, understandably, was rampant in the CSRC's early days. The government, for once, acted quickly. In its famous Document 68 of late 1992, the State Council delineated the functions of all agencies involved in the corporatization process in a deliberate effort to clarify the status of the two new entities.[28] This first ever effort by the central government to impose coordination among the various agencies indicates how critical market control appeared to be to the government. For example, Document 68 confirmed that the SPC was responsible for preparing a comprehensive Securities Plan setting the amount of securities financing for a given five-year period. It also confirmed that the PBOC continued to be responsible for the licensing of all financial sector participants (see Table 3.1).

This may have improved the situation, but it did not entirely eliminate the confusion.[29] What, for example, could the CSRC do if it determined that a particular firm or people within a firm were violating a particular securities regulation or market practice? It had no jurisdiction. The same problem existed with regard to lawyers, accountants, and asset appraisal companies,

TABLE 3.1   State Council Document 68: Distribution of Inter-agency Responsibility

Entity	Responsibility
SPC	■ Formulation of a securities fund-raising plan ■ Formulation of securities industry development plans based on recommendations of the SCSC
PBOC	■ Licensing of and administrative jurisdiction over securities institutions
MOF	■ Administrative jurisdiction over accountants and accounting firms with review by the CSRC of those engaged in securities-related work
SCRES	■ Formulation of regulations concerning shareholding pilot projects and coordination of the implementation of the shareholder system
SSE and SZSE	■ Under the administrative jurisdiction of the local governments but subject to supervision by the CSRC; any new exchange subject to the review of the SCSC and approval of the SC
Local shareholding companies	■ Conversion of locally owned enterprises into shareholding companies subject to the joint review of the CSRC and the local government
Central shareholding companies	■ Conversion of centrally owned enterprises into shareholding companies subject to the joint review of the industry regulator and SCRES

which were licensed respectively by the Ministry of Law, the MOF, and the SAMB. As another example, SCRES remained responsible for policies and regulations governing the structure of corporatization and the selection of the specific companies and industrial sectors involved in corporatization, and the Shanghai and Shenzhen municipal governments controlled their stock exchanges. Therefore, even though its own scope of authority was defined, the CSRC continued to be unable to exercise authority unilaterally without the acceptance of other agencies.

Even more important, as the later situation attests, Document 68 did not seek to extend the jurisdiction of the CSRC over local governments. Beginning in 1993, each provincial government established a securities office which coordinated securities-related matters within the province – for example, the selection of listing candidates, frontline supervision of futures brokerages and markets, training, and the transmission of important notices. Although such offices became in some ways correspondents of the CSRC, they were a part of the respective provincial government's staff and in no way were under the CSRC's control.[30] The CSRC was, therefore, isolated in Beijing with no organizational way to extend its authority other than through negotiations with other bureaucracies and local governments or through the intermediation of the SCSC. In short, it had little practical enforcement authority.

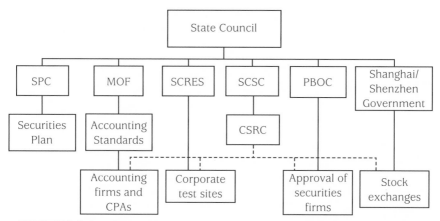

FIGURE 3.1 Chinese Securities Industry Regulatory Framework to July 1999.

To make matters more difficult, the CSRC's own position as a quasi-governmental vice-ministerial entity made it impossible to communicate directly with these other ministry-level organizations other than through the SCSC. Consequently, and entirely similar to previous experience, real regulatory action out of this galaxy of bureaucracies required a disaster which could not be shuffled away. One appeared and it was a beauty: the US$37 billion February 1995 Shanghai International Securities (SISCO) bond futures scandal.[31]

THE INTERNATIONALIZATION OF THE CSRC

Given this complex bureaucratic environment, it is understandable that the CSRC from the outset tended to focus its efforts on overseas listings and the organizations and institutions involved with them: here it had real influence and could extend it single-handedly. This international emphasis stemmed naturally from the selection of candidates for the first Hong Kong listings, which occurred simultaneously with the CSRC's creation. The logic behind this experiment was that China's own markets were too undeveloped to influence the behavior of the major SOEs. The government believed that exposing them to a strict regulatory environment would hasten management reform. The hope was that stricter regulation would promote better corporate governance and with it productivity and profitability. In fact, Chairman Liu had been working on a plan for overseas listing in 1992 while he was still at SCRES and prior to his assignment to the CSRC.[32] But it was also, in the short term, a good strategy to make the SOEs comply with its own regulations: no CSRC approval, no overseas listing, no money. The alliances struck up with the international exchanges and investment banks assured that its word would stick.[33] In the meantime, on the domestic front, the CSRC could wait for events to develop.

The idea of internationalizing the corporatization experiment on overseas markets turned out not to be that hard a sell. In the wake of June 4 and the 810 Incident, the idea began to make sense to the Chinese government: export potential social unrest by listing Chinese companies elsewhere. At the same time, there was money to be made. Moreover, it was an idea that the Stock Exchange of Hong Kong had long promoted. In 1991, the SEHK suggested to the Chinese government that it consider listing Chinese enterprises in Hong Kong. Coming so early in China's experiment with corporate equity listings, the government gave little consideration to the merits of such a proposal. It did, however, decide to follow up with an unofficial study group.

Consequently, in December 1991 a small team of "specialists" went to Hong Kong as guests of China's unofficial embassy, Xinhua News Agency.[34] This group included four members, all from SCRES, and was led by Liu Hongru, then senior deputy director. The purpose of their visit was to gather facts and then to report to the State Council concerning the feasibility of the SEHK's proposal. As might be expected after the inevitable wining and dining, the report concluded positively. It stated that listing Chinese companies in Hong Kong would: (1) support Hong Kong's economic stability and development (a nice point in consideration of the then long-awaited handover scheduled for 1997); (2) be of great assistance in raising much-needed capital for Chinese companies; and (3) promote the internationalization of Chinese companies. The report also noted some negative points. These included: (1) the existing joint venture (JV) strategy provided Chinese companies with advanced technologies that listed companies would have to procure directly and at a potentially higher price; (2) companies to be listed would have to be profitable and have a solid profit outlook, but that listing would mean giving up a piece of this profit to foreign investors; and (3) listing in Hong Kong might conflict with the state's effort to support the development of the Shanghai and Shenzhen exchanges. Overall, however, the report concluded that the benefits of listing in Hong Kong outweighed the negatives and proposed that the practical aspects be further explored. The State Council, however, decided to continue to prioritize the development of the two domestic exchanges. The idea appeared to have been effectively stonewalled.

THE STOCK EXCHANGE OF HONG KONG GOES TO THE TOP

But stonewalls can be jumped in China. Having won over the working team to the idea, the SEHK focused its strategy on the key decision-maker, Vice Premier Zhu Rongji, then responsible for overseeing the Chinese financial sector. In April 1992, the chairman of the SEHK, Charles Y. K. Lee, visited Beijing and met with Vice Premier Zhu. During the meeting, Lee brought up the idea of Hong Kong listings and actively pushed their positive aspects. Premier Zhu, having heard Lee out, suggested the selection of up to 10 companies as experimental listing candidates and agreed to the idea of establishing a formal working group to establish the basis for such listings. Premier Zhu's proposal was approved by the State Council. A working group was again established, this time with 12 members from the two sides. The Chinese team was composed of Liu Hongru (SCRES), Sun Xiaoliang (SCRES), Jin Jiandong (PBOC), Chen Baoying (State Council Office on Hong Kong Macao Affairs), Li Qingyuan (SCRES), and Nie Qingping (SCRES) as the secretary. All of these people would later play significant roles in the corporatization process. The Hong Kong side was represented by senior staff from the SEHK.

The first meeting of the working group was held in mid-July 1992 at the State Guest House in Beijing. Over the next eight months, the group met eight times, alternating in Hong Kong and Beijing, and established the basis for settling the legal, accounting, and technical listing methodology for Chinese companies seeking a direct listing on the SEHK. In the meantime, the CSRC was established, with Liu becoming its first chairman. With this, there was no doubt that Hong Kong would turn out to be a well-promoted "experiment."

The work of the two groups became public in mid-October 1992 when a list of nine Chinese SOEs designated to list in Hong Kong was announced. Listing details were formalized by a Memorandum of Understanding that the SEHK signed on June 19, 1993. The first trial run of the new process came on June 29, 1993, when Tsingtao Beer became the first Chinese state enterprise to list directly on the SEHK, raising approximately US$115 million. This deal was a blow-out, since even most Americans (and the fund managers, in particular) had had at least one bottle of Tsingtao beer at their local Chinese eatery and, therefore, were well acquainted with the brand name. Things got off to a strong start on the international side of the CSRC's equation.

THE CSRC'S DOMESTIC STRUGGLE

The CSRC's accretion of power domestically was a more extended process and came in three stages. The first stage, from 1992–93, marked the establishment and initial consolidation of authority over the securities and futures markets, as well as the extension of investigatory and enforcement powers. The second stage, from 1996–97, marked the CSRC's assumption of full control over the two securities exchanges and the PBOC's divestiture of all self-invested securities firms. This was followed by the dissolution of the SCSC in 1998. The CSRC thereupon became a full ministry-level organization empowered by the 1999 Securities Law with responsibility for all aspects of the securities industry.

1992–93: Initial Consolidation of Authority

In 1993, the CSRC assumed significant supervisory control over the two securities exchanges via the direct appointment of senior managers.[35] This marked the start of the central government's takeover of the exchanges. In addition, the CSRC assumed a larger part of the PBOC's supervisory authority over financial institutions, including securities exchanges and regional trading centers. This move terminated the PBOC's involvement in the securities sector with the exception of its licensing power, which would only be removed after passage of the Securities Law.

The exchanges were compelled to revise their articles of incorporation accordingly, but only the Shenzhen exchange explicitly recognized the CSRC's new powers.[36] In contrast, the Shanghai exchange made only a general reference to the securities regulator and no direct reference by name to the CSRC.[37] It appears that Shanghai was either not supportive of the national effort to establish an integrated regulatory regime or perhaps believed that the CSRC would not succeed. In fact, the first years of the CSRC's existence were marked by serious disputes between the Shanghai exchange and the CSRC over the latter's focus on listing Chinese companies on international markets and a variety of other issues.[38] Among other things, the Shanghai government wanted to know why China's best companies were not being listed in Shanghai and believed that if they were, the market would develop more quickly. Looking back, this judgment was probably right.

The CSRC's enforcement authority was also clarified in 1993. The SCSC authorized the CSRC to investigate and enforce regulations relating to the issuance and trading of shares.[39] This authorization gave the CSRC broad scope to enforce securities laws and regulations, as shown in Table 3.2. The CSRC was authorized to impose fines or other penalties on the violators unilaterally unless the revocation of the given violator's securities license was at issue, in which case the CSRC had still to obtain the PBOC's agreement.

Although the CSRC was given great authority, the reality was that, with limited staff in one office in Beijing, it could enforce very little. In an effort to increase its reach, during the course of 1993 the CSRC signed cooperative pacts with other government agencies directly involved in the share market. These included, for example, the Ministry of Justice, the SAMB, the MOF, the State Tax Bureau, the Office of the Audit, and so on.[40] In each case, these agreements indicated that the relevant license or approval would be jointly extended. These pacts, at a minimum, improved the coordination among the various departments. But as any SOE management will testify, obtaining listing approval is a story of chasing down elusive bureaucrats to chop documents. The CSRC no doubt experienced similar frustration when seeking to coordinate enforcement action.

At the end of the year, the State Council placed the SCSC and CSRC in charge of the futures markets and their participants, replacing the Ministry of Internal Trade and the State Bureau of Industry and Commerce.[41] In short, 1993 was a year during which the government significantly strengthened the central securities regulators – at least on paper.

1996–97: Full Control over the Securities Exchanges and Securities Firms

By 1996, the dispute with the Shanghai exchange had been solidly resolved in favor of the SCSC and the CSRC, and the 1993 Provisional Regulations were

TABLE 3.2 Acts Violating Securities Issuance and Trading

Violating Entity	Type of Violation
Shareholding company	■ Issuing shares without approval ■ Illegally obtaining approval to issue and trade shares ■ Issuing shares in an unregulated manner or outside the proper scope of issuance (e.g., selling state shares to individuals)
Securities company	■ Issuing shares at an unapproved time, by an unapproved manner ■ Unapproved distribution of share purchase applications ■ Lending of client shares to third parties or the use of client shares as collateral ■ Charging unreasonable fees ■ Use of client names to conduct own trading ■ Misuse of client guarantee deposits ■ Sharing of gains/losses with clients or guaranteeing clients against trading loss ■ Providing financing for share trading
Insiders	■ Insider trading or provision of insider information to third parties
Any organization or individual	■ Trading securities outside of established exchanges ■ Release of false information or rumors during the issuance or trading of shares ■ Conspiring to manipulate share prices at issuance or during trading ■ Short selling ■ Unapproved share or index options or commodities trading ■ Providing false regulatory required reports ■ Falsifying stock issuance and trading records

replaced by a final version, the 1996 Regulations, which came into effect a year later.[42] The proximate causes were the late 1995 Shanghai International Securities Company (SISCO) bond market fiasco and the explosive jump in the market early in the year that revealed numerous problems.[43] This victory was not without its losses, however: Liu Hongru, the CSRC's dynamic founding chairman, was forced to resign on March 31, 1995. He commented, "Nobody can keep going on with this sort of talk; you can only go on for a while."[44] He was replaced by a pleasant, but colorless, bureaucrat. Nonetheless, the 1996 Regulations removed all uncertainties as to who was the boss of the national exchanges, delegating the authority to the CSRC alone to supervise and administer (*jiandu guanli*) them and their related securities settlement companies.[45] And so the direct involvement of the Shenzhen and Shanghai municipal governments in the exchanges they had fought for, promoted, and finally established was brought to an end.[46]

The PBOC, however, went down stubbornly resisting. In 1997, the PBOC was forced to disgorge its investments in 43 brokerage firms and transfer supervisory personnel to the CSRC.[47] This was accomplished over several years, so that by 2001 the task was complete with few exceptions.[48] From 1998 on, the CSRC assumed full licensing authority and regulatory control over the brokerages. There continued to be redundant regulation of non-Shanghai or Shenzhen brokers and trading centers. The PBOC claimed jurisdiction over "cross region linkages" based on the old 1990 regulation and the CSRC counterattacked based on the 1996 exchange law. The 1999 Securities Law brought this dispute to a final close.

1998: CSRC Assumes Full Ministry Status

The dissolution of the SCSC in mid-1998 and the elevation of the CSRC as a ministry-level organization presaged the passage of the long-awaited Securities Law in late 1998. The Securities Law signified an end to the bureaucratic turf war in the securities industry, with the CSRC emerging as the sole winner.[49] The CSRC replaced the PBOC as the sole regulator for securities firms with the power to approve the establishment of new firms and the expansion plans of existing firms.

In addition to its function of approving the issue and listing of securities, the CSRC's oversight has been strengthened over all professional entities engaged in the securities business, including law firms and accounting firms. To crack the whip, the second half of 1999 marked a major relicensing effort for all securities companies operating across the country. In addition, the CSRC formulated specific qualification and conduct standards applicable to persons and firms engaged in securities business. It is responsible for investigating and sanctioning conduct violating the Securities Law. It now has the unilateral authority to enter into places to investigate illegal activities, conduct interviews, examine trading records, and review individual securities accounts and can apply to the courts to freeze such accounts. In the event that illegal activities are discovered, the CSRC can transfer the case to the judicial system. Despite this strengthened authority, intermediary organizations such as lawyers, accountants, asset and land appraisal companies, and so on, continue to be licensed and regulated in their non-securities business by their original approving government agencies.

The most significant organizational change has eliminated the CSRC's isolation in Beijing. In mid-1999, the CSRC took over the functions of all provincial Securities Regulatory Offices from the provincial governments (see Figure 3.2). The CSRC has since established 10 regional branches located in the cities of Tianjin, Shenyang, Shanghai, Jinan, Wuhan, Shenzhen, Chengdu, Xian, Beijing, and Chongqing. This will result in the CSRC having a central/regional organizational structure similar to the PBOC, both with the same objective – the reduction of provincial government influence. At the same time, this new structure should enable the CSRC to control implementation of central government policy over the markets and market participants (see Figure 3.3).

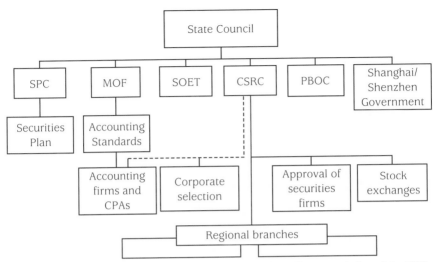

FIGURE 3.2   Chinese Securities Industry Regulatory Framework from July 1999.

REGULATORY PHILOSOPHY

Although the CSRC has emerged as the sole regulator of the securities indus-try, the Securities Law marked a shift in the philosophy of the regulatory process. For example, the Law makes no mention, as in the past, of any listing candidate quota system,[50] implying that the CSRC will review each application when it is submitted. This, in itself, marks a dramatic shift in the entire listing process from being a component part of a state plan to one more market-oriented and driven by companies and investment banks, as described in the next chapter.

In a second major break with past practice, before the Securities Law the CSRC had complete discretion over the approval of share issuance and listing. This discretion was justified largely on the need to protect the state's interests in the midst of a complex and, in many ways, incomplete legal and regulatory environment. The Securities Law, by limiting the CSRC's approval power, indicates that the government is now more comfortable with a process it may feel is well documented in regulations and laws which are final and not "provisional." At the same time, there has been a clarification of risk and respon-sibilities that shifts to the issuing enterprise the accountability for the results of its operations and to the investor the full risk of the investment decision.[51] The Securities Law represents an important step toward distancing the government, and the CSRC in particular, from potential investor discontent as the result of scandal, a market crash, or even the poor performance of a listed company.

This can be seen in the language describing the CSRC's role. In all past documents, public offerings are described as requiring the CSRC's approval (*pizhun*). The Securities Law has introduced three slightly different terms

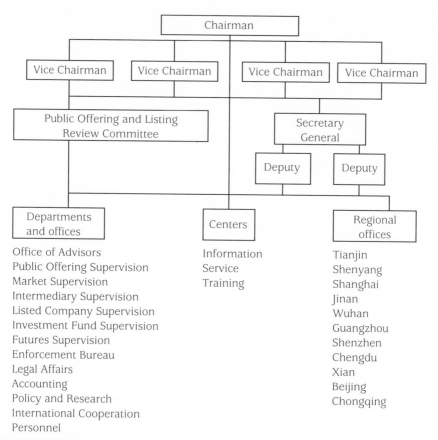

FIGURE 3.3 Organizational Structure of the CSRC, 1999 to present.
Source: CSRC.

signifying approval in reference to share issuance: verification and approval (*hezhun*), examination and approval (*shenpi*), and approval (*pizhun*).[52] The Securities Law requires that all domestic public issues conform to the Company Law and receive the "verification and approval" of the CSRC. The CSRC's role in the listing process has, therefore, been changed significantly, with the implication that the Securities Law's intent is for domestic share issues to be approved if they meet the required conditions.[53] As a further example, domestic corporate bond issues must satisfy the requirements not only of the Company Law, but also a number of PBOC regulations. In this case, the Securities Law describes the CSRC's approval as "examination and approval." In contrast, for overseas share issues, the CSRC continues to have full authority to approve (*pizhun*) such issues.

In 1993, the CSRC began to make use of a Public Offering and Listing Review Committee (*faxing weiyuanhui*) that has now been confirmed and required by the Securities Law. The Committee is composed of CSRC staff and, at times, outside experts who do not have voting rights.[54] The Committee has two working groups, each of which must be composed of at least seven members. After hearing the case for a particular listing, the Committee reaches a final decision through a secret ballot, with decisions based on a simple majority. The greater transparency of this process is to be welcomed.

On July 1, 1999, the Securities Law came into force, marking the end of a seven-year process and establishing the most definitive regulatory structure China's securities markets have had to date. The history of trial and error and bureaucratic turf battles which delayed the enactment of the Law have left many past compromises yet to be brought into line. Nonetheless, 1999 marked a major development and very positive progress for the industry as a whole. All that remains is for the regulator to decide how it will proceed to regulate now that it is empowered at last to do so.

THE CSRC TAKES THE INITIATIVE

This question has now been answered, primarily by the appointment in April 2000 of Zhou Xiaochuan as the fourth CSRC chairman. Dr. Zhou was the perfect candidate for the CSRC, given his long history in the securities industry combined with significant international contact as a result of his chairmanship of China International Capital Corporation, the Morgan Stanley joint venture. Under his leadership, the CSRC once again attracted bright, internationally educated staff, including most of the original group who had worked for Liu Hongru. Beginning in 2000, the CSRC's hand could be seen in such areas as minority investor rights, greater company disclosure, de-listing of poorly performing companies, enforcement of laws against management fraud, the pursuit of market manipulators, and the active development of the role of the Securities Association of China.

Minority Shareholder Rights

There has been significant progress in the last few years in the ability of minority investors to sue companies in order to protect their rights. One of the first instances, if not the first, of an individual investor suing a listed company, Chengdu Hongguang Industries, in court for fraud occurred in July 1999.[55] There appears to have been merit to this widely reported case, since the company's chairman and chief financial officer were both sentenced to terms in prison and the firm's auditors were barred from practicing. The court, however, told the plaintiff that it declined to hear his suit, since it was the CSRC's responsibility to address illegal acts by listed companies. This court's ruling may have been the last of the old pre-Securities Law era, since it came just after the law became effective.

It does, however, reflect the reality that even the 1999 Securities Law does not explicitly grant individual shareholders the right to take action against issuers. Moreover, the law suggests that any compensation for damages is owed the state, not the individual investor.

Then, on January 15, 2002, the People's Supreme Court of China ruled that investors could sue companies and company management as long as the CSRC in its investigations had determined fraudulent activity. The court, however, disallowed the possibility of class action suits. Across China, hundreds of lawsuits alleging company fraud are pending and the CSRC is publishing lists of companies that have falsified disclosure information.[56] Vice chairman of the CSRC, Laura Cha, has provided active support for legal redress, saying, "The current laws did not anticipate the kind of economic crimes that are being committed in the modern-day stock markets. We encourage investors to go through the legal system to seek remedies and redress."[57] And Zhou Xiaochuan was giving speeches before the International Organization of Securities Regulatory Commissions (IOSCO) stating that regulators had two objectives: (1) the maintenance of fair, transparent, and effective markets; and (2) the protection of investor interests.[58]

Given that the courts do not permit class action lawsuits, it appears that they may be on the verge of being overwhelmed. Thousands of shareholders have filed some 893 lawsuits against nine listed companies since the Supreme Court decision in January 2002. The first such suit, filed against Chengdu Hongguang Enterprises in 1999, was finally closed on November 25, 2002. The CSRC had found the company guilty of fraudulent disclosure in its listing prospectus. With a go-ahead from the Supreme Court decision, the Chengdu Intermediate Court found in favor of 11 plaintiffs, awarding them RMB224,000, 90% of the amount claimed.[59] Into the fray jumped a senior CSRC official calling for the introduction of class action suits.[60] Here is yet another example of how the market, as distorted as it is, has been a prime mover of change in China.

Corporate Governance

The CSRC has established the requirement that each listed company should have independent directors on its board. Laura Cha, the CSRC vice chairman and formerly a senior Hong Kong market regulator, has made a major contribution in this area.[61] Listed companies are now required to have at least two independent directors, rising to a minimum of three in 2003.[62] The hope is that with independent directors, the level of a listed company's corporate governance will improve. The CSRC is not ignorant of the many possibilities of twisting this new requirement by placing related parties on company boards. The CSRC has also instituted training classes for would-be independent directors. While not solving all the problems of corporate governance, truly independent directors would be a major step in the right direction.

De-listing

Over the years, there have been many listed companies that have failed to perform. On the other hand, local government and powerful ministries back most of these companies and the stock exchanges have been reluctant to lose listings. To compromise away dispute, the CSRC responded to this situation by defining money-losing company shares as either "PT (particular transfer, three years' consecutive losses)" or "ST (special treatment, two years' consecutive losses)." Thus, an ST company would be referred to as "ST XYZ company" on the exchange, in the media, and in the settlement system so as to alert investors. The time when such shares could be traded was also strictly limited. There are now over 80 ST and PT shares, approaching 10% of listed companies. In reality, there are many more, given the flexible nature of Chinese accounting.

In late 2000, the CSRC began preparations at last to de-list loss-making companies. On February 22, 2001, the CSRC published de-listing procedures.[63] The rumored top candidate was Zhengzhou Baiwen Department Store (ZDS). On April 18, 1996, ZDS had become the first company to list shares from Zhengzhou, the capital of Henan Province. In the ensuing five years, ZDS ran up debts of RMB2.5 billion versus assets of less than RMB600 million. The fact that it had not already declared bankruptcy is a consequence of the poorly drawn bankruptcy law and the reluctance of the various state agencies to press hard.[64] In the event, the company was saved by a buy-out and on April 23, 2001, PT Narcissus, a Shanghai-listed company with four consecutive years of losses, became the first company in history to be formally de-listed from an exchange.[65] The remaining ST and PT share companies are now in line for the same treatment.

This now makes it possible for the market to rid itself of the worst listed companies, which have often served as the basis of speculation. However, the stake has not yet been driven home. With an acceptable restructuring plan, de-listed company shares can be listed on the Third Board, as has already occurred (see Chapter 2). In theory, if the restructurings work out, these companies can apply to be re-listed on the main boards.

Enforcement and Disclosure

The CSRC has begun to enforce regulations much more vigorously than it has in the past. In 2000, inspection departments were established and staffed in the CSRC's major regional offices.[66] Companies or their managers and directors that have violated the law or committed fraud are now being punished and news of their punishment is being made public. For example, virtually the entire senior management, including the chairman, of the well-known company Triple Nine Pharmaceutical were found to have provided inaccurate disclosure and to have misused IPO proceeds.[67] A routine annual CSRC investigation discovered that senior management had appropriated for its own use more than RMB250 million, or about 96% of the company's total NAV! The CSRC used the findings of the investigation as the basis for a civil suit filed against the company and its management. In addition, public suits were also signaled as permitted.

In a major breakthrough, the CSRC in September 2002 for the first time ordered a listed company to disgorge its IPO proceeds. A CSRC investigation found that Jilin Tonghai Hi-Technology had fraudulently misrepresented its financial performance and prospects in its listing prospectus.[68] What is strange is that the CSRC did not proceed against the company's lead underwriter and auditors for obvious lapses in due diligence. In an effort to improve financial disclosure, the CSRC announced in April 2001 that it will require all loss-making listed companies to provide quarterly reports beginning with the first quarter of 2002. In the past, this requirement could easily have been gotten around: after all, China's auditors have shown extraordinary flexibility in handling clients' accounting problems.

The Yinguangxia (YGX) scandal has put at least a hint of rigor back into the auditing profession.[69] Due to the flagrancy of this case, for the first time a major intermediary organization, the firm's auditors, has been implicated and brought to court. During 2000, YGX's shares had jumped 440% on the Shenzhen exchange, reflecting a massive jump in reported net profit. This pattern exhibited all the features of being a manipulated share (*zhuanggu*). At the end of 1999, YGX had 51,800 shareholders – about average. A year later, it had only 17,500 who, on average, held 16,026 shares, showing already the high degree of concentration typical of manipulated stocks. Moreover, after announcing a 10-for-10 stock dividend, the shares reached new highs at year-end 2000. As of that time, Yinguangxia's shares had recorded the biggest annual increase of all save one. Its unqualified audited accounts, moreover, showed that net income for the year had jumped over four times compared to 1999. Then, in March 2001, the company announced that it had concluded a three-year US$300 million supply contract with a German company that would triple its earnings per share (EPS). Market professionals were beginning to doubt the story. As a fund manager commented, "Sure, Yinguangxia is good, but it defies common sense."

In August 2001, *Caijing* published an exposé. The CSRC immediately sent an investigating team. More importantly, however, the MOF, acting through its Audit Bureau, also investigated. By early September, the Bureau had canceled the license of Yinguangxia's auditor, Zhong Tian Qin Accounting. It was also in the process of bringing legal suits against the two partners, who had issued unqualified opinions for both 1999 and 2000.[70] This was the first time that any "intermediary" organization has suffered the consequences of its actions. This is no doubt a strategy of "killing the chicken to scare the monkey" and says all that needs to be said about the domestic accounting industry.

Market Manipulation

At the turn of the century, the Chinese securities markets were rocked by two major scandals. Both were broken in public by the financial magazine, *Caijing*, but like its other exposés came very likely at the instigation of the CSRC. The first involved fund management companies manipulating the market to their own advantage.[71] This was not in itself shocking, since it was something of a public secret. What *was* shocking was that the Shanghai exchange had produced statistical research proving it was fairly pervasive. The research also revealed the lack of independence of the fund management companies from their principal shareholders, the securities companies (and their clients).[72] A market participant was quoted as saying, "Fund management companies are little more than the second treasury department (*xiaojinku*) of securities firms." Of course, many in the industry shrugged, but with the exchange report made public, it was a substantiated open secret.

This was worrying enough – the fund management industry had just been "restructured" in 1997 – but the second exposé was even wilder. It exposed for the first time one of China's previously "hidden" individual market manipulators (*zhuangjia*) by the name of Lu Liang, a.k.a. Mr. K.[73] Of course, it was not news that China's markets are moved by manipulators. But it was news that one had been exposed and indicted for stock-market fraud. Lu was called a "Super Manipulator." He was an expert in company takeovers and restructurings, share manipulation, and, as the disguised market expert, "Mr. K," frequently published articles in support of his schemes in China's financial press. At the time of his arrest, he controlled four listed companies – China Venture Capital (000048), China-West Pharmaceuticals (600842), Suibao Thermal Power (600864), and Laizhou Steel (600102). A look at the trading performance of these shares in 1999 and 2000 shows each doubling, or even tripling, their price before crashing as Mr. K exited. A year later, in June 2002, Lu's case – by now involving nine defendants – was brought to court in an evidentiary hearing.[74] The evidence was startling, involving over RMB5.4 billion, the active cooperation with Lu of 125 securities brokerage offices, and the fact that Lu alone had used 1,575 individual investor accounts. If each of his co-defendants controlled a similar number of "ghost" accounts, then Lu's gang made use of over 14,000 accounts![75]

The Securities Association of China

The SAC was established at a very early stage, August 28, 1991, and was the first non-governmental national industry association.[76] Despite high hopes, the association in the years since served as little more than a scorekeeper for the industry – producing security company rankings in its annual industry yearbook. Nominally an independent organization based on the U.S. National Association of Securities Dealers (NASD), its members have failed to use it either to lobby the government or to discipline violations of industry practice. Now, the 1999 Securities Law provides the Association with the legal basis for a much broader role, including supervisory, training, and disciplinary functions.[77]

The CSRC from July 2002 has moved to activate the Association and has begun transferring to it certain of its own functions, including the training and certification of industry professionals. To date, the most important role the

SAC has assumed is that of supervising the operations of the Third Board (see Chapter 2). Whether or not the SAC will succeed in operating as a non-governmental association will depend on the support of the CSRC. For its part, the CSRC does not have the staff to fulfill every aspect of its mandate, so it makes sense to transfer some roles to the Association. In addition, distancing itself from certain of the more sensitive areas of the industry makes good bureaucratic sense.

Over the past few years, the CSRC has played an increasingly active role. It is perhaps China's only ministry dealing directly with a true marketplace and is extremely business-oriented. It is hard to say the same of the PBOC. Because of historical and ideological sensitivities, the potential for significant political scandal and the creation of social unrest, the CSRC's position remains extremely difficult. But a strong and well-led CSRC is exceptionally important if China is to develop effective solutions for its securities markets and to continue to drive its economy forward.

CHAPTER 4

Defining Ownership: Share Types

We will steadfastly continue to promote the shareholding system and I once again emphasize, the shareholding system is not privatization.

Liu Hongru, Vice Director, SCRES, March 1992[1]

China has taken an exceptionally awkward, and in the end dysfunctional, approach to defining equity shares. In the West, equity shares are defined in terms of the specific rights attributed to a holder in the ownership of a company. Different voting or economic rights, for example, give rise to different share classes. In contrast, China has spent little time defining the rights attached to shares; they are by law defined as all being equal. On the other hand, the government has spent an inordinate amount of time and energy defining a multitude of shareholder classes. The touchstone of this effort, however, is straightforward: the shareholder's relation to the state. For example, if the investor is the state itself, then the shares are called state shares. The second step in the definition was that all state-related shares were declared untradable.

In the early 1990s, when the economy remained relatively undiversified, this approach created few problems and supported the state's objective of maintaining its position as absolute majority shareholder. As more and more companies listed on the exchanges, however, the markets themselves took on the characteristics of the companies' capital structure. A huge overhang of state shares has created significant difficulties, not least for the state as a shareholder. Because these definitions have strongly influenced the direction of market development, it is important to understand their legal and regulatory underpinning.

How did the government come up with this set of definitions? The government took what it knew best, state planning and state ownership, and applied it to the task. The effort to define the legal status of enterprises and the shares they issued began in the late 1980s and was partially set out in the Enterprise Law of 1988.[2] At the same time, a number of provincial governments seeking to standardize local corporate restructurings drew up some very thorough and systematic policies and regulations. Among them, Fujian Province developed the concepts later adopted nationally.[3] Although work began in late 1988 to codify systematically all aspects of the corporatization and share issuance process, the events of June 4, 1989 stalled further reform for a time. It was not until early 1992, after Deng's Southern Excursion, that SCRES issued the Standard Opinion (*Guifan yijian*), which might be better understood as the "Standardizing Opinion." This was the first systematic codification of the legal basis of an enterprise as a corporate form owning and operating productive assets.[4] The issuance of the Standard Opinion, plus a host of supporting regulations,[5] signaled the government's tentative affirmation of the shareholding experiment, as well as the start of its efforts to establish an appropriate legal and regulatory foundation.

The Standard Opinion set out the independent legal existence of companies limited by shares, defined the characteristics of equity shares, and, more importantly, allowed shareholders to benefit from and transfer interests in such enterprises. After two years of further experimentation, the Company Law was passed and became effective in 1994. The Company Law confirmed that the corporate form of organization for SOEs would be the basic instrument in China's economic development going forward. This represented a significant departure for China, given the premises on which the People's Republic of China (PRC) had been founded. But, in fact, the Company Law only recognized the reality of what the 1980s contract responsibility system and experiments with share issuance had brought into existence: highly autonomous enterprises and companies.[6]

The Company Law, however, was deficient in many aspects, so in practice it did not, and has not, superseded the Standard Opinion. Together these two documents plus a third, the Overseas Listing Rules,[7] provide the principal legal basis for the wide variety of shares to which China's share experiment has given rise. The Standard Opinion, however, remains the source law for China's categorization of share types. Both the Company Law and the later Securities Law shied away from this topic because it touches on the issue of the controlling state ownership of Chinese companies. No matter what China's experiment with stocks is, it is most certainly not designed to lead to privatization. A failure to uphold this point in the 1980s would have meant no stock exchanges and, despite the many changes over more than a decade, this topic remains highly sensitive.

Non-fungible shares, then, represent China's compromise with the Devil, and ever since then the forces of the market have tried to wriggle free. By defining different shares for different investor identities, the government has made it difficult in practice to exchange shares across categories. This, in turn, has made it difficult to supplant state control without first obtaining state approval.[8] If shares are not interchangeable, market forces will be distorted as, in fact, they have been distorted. But at the start, when markets were small and the experiment was still in its infancy, this possibility was not important or even a topic of consideration. It was more important to set up markets and move on.

SHARES OF WHAT?

There is no question that, by the end of the 1980s, a national effort to standardize the corporatization process was needed if "experimentation" was to develop in a healthy manner. For one thing, what were these newly restructured companies limited by shares offering to investors in the form of a piece of paper called a "share"? Putting aside the issue of a legal foundation, a company limited by shares quite obviously presupposes an operating objective quite different than an SOE: the maximization of shareholder value, rather than output units of a product. Underpinning this objective must be a fundamental reworking of a company's operations and, most importantly, its financial reporting and account-ing practices.[9] It wasn't until mid-1993 that the MOF enacted an accounting revolution for SOEs by requiring the adoption of general accounting principles based largely on International Accounting Standards (IAS). Until that date, SOEs did not even have an equity capital account available on their balance sheets.

Prior to the 1994 Company Law, Chinese SOEs had functioned as production units in a relatively centralized planned economy, and accounting practices were oriented to suit the needs of compiling the national plan. In fact, in the centrally planned economy, accounting practices developed by the MOF differed between industries. So, what was being sold to investors? The answer to this question and to those about the emergence of investor-specific share types can be found in how the financial side of an enterprise's operations was portrayed using Chinese accounting practices.

The Significance of Accounting Practices

Chinese accounting practices, like those of the Soviet Union, were rule-based, as opposed to principle-based, and adopted the concepts of "fund," "fund source," and "fund use."[10] By "rule-based" is meant an entire code of extremely specific accounting treatments developed to meet nearly every situation. Rather than proceeding from principles, accountants had only to determine in which specific "box" an item should be placed. In fund accounting, "fund use" means the use of designated funds to acquire property or supplies, and fund source is the specifically identified channel for obtaining such funds. There were three categories of funds: fixed, current, and special. These three fund categories were actually separate and independent balance sheets representing different aspects of one enterprise's operations. There was no integrated balance sheet as Western accounting understands it.[11] "Fixed funds" were those used for what the West would understand as investment in fixed assets. "Current funds" can be understood as working capital, while "special funds" are similar to depreciation and refer to monies set aside for purposes such as major renovations of fixed assets. The special funds derived largely from an enterprise's cost of production. Certain types of special funds, such as the employees' incentive fund and product development fund, were funded by a portion of the enterprise's profits.

Enterprises were required to comply with the principle of a specific fund for a specific purpose, and there could be no flexibility (in theory, at least) in transferring funds from one specific use to another. At specific periods, the enterprise had to provide its supervising ministry or bureau with copies of its fund balance sheets based on this principle of "Fund Use = Fund Source," as shown in Table 4.1. This accounting practice has had a deep and lasting effect on the development of China's stock markets.

Accounting Aspects of Early Shareholding Companies

Given the absence of any relevant regulations on the topic in the 1980s, how did enterprises transformed into shareholding companies show this in their accounting? Even more important, if the company sold shares to outsiders, whether state entities, other enterprises, or individuals, how was this evidenced and what implications were there of the treatment used?

One common method simply saw the company allocate share capital according to its source to each of the fixed and current fund accounts, as shown in Table 4.2. But it should not be surprising that there was apparently no

TABLE 4.1   Summary SOE "Balance Sheet" Using Fund Accounting

Fund Application		Fund Source
Fixed Assets		*Fixed Fund Source*
Original Cost		■ State Fixed Fund – state budget grant
Less:	=	■ Enterprise Fixed Fund – enterprise funds
Depreciation		■ Fixed Fund Loan – state bank loan
= Net Book Value		
Total		*Total*
Current Assets		*Current Fund Source*
■ Inventory		■ State current fund – state budget grant
■ Accounts		■ Enterprise current fund – enterprise funds
■ Receivables	=	■ Current fund loans – PBOC loan
■ Cash		
Total		*Total*
Special Assets		*Special Fund Source*
■ Bank deposit		■ State special fund – state budget grant
■ Special fund assets		■ Enterprise special fund – enterprise funds
	=	■ Special fund loans – state bank loan
Total		*Total*

Source: Based on Tong, Chow, and Cooper, pp. 25 and 110.

TABLE 4.2   Representation of Early Shareholding Company "Balance Sheet Liabilities"

Original Fund Source	Equity Contribution	Post-equity Contributions
Fixed Fund Source		*Fixed Fund Source*
State Fixed Fund		"State share" Fixed Fund
Enterprise Fixed Fund	$\Longrightarrow$	"Enterprise share" Fixed Fund
Fixed Fund Loan		Enterprise Fixed Fund
Total		*Total*
Current Fund Source		*Current Fund*
State Current Fund		"State share" Current Fund
Enterprise Current Fund	$\Longrightarrow$	"Foreign share" Current Fund
Current Fund Loans		"Individual share" Current Fund
		Current fund loans
Total		*Total*
Special Fund Source		*Special Fund Source*
State special fund		State special fund
Enterprise special fund		Enterprise special fund
Special fund loans		Special fund loans
Total		*Total*

Source: Based on Tong, Chow, and Cooper, pp. 25 and 110.

dominant accounting treatment emerging among the many proto-shareholding companies, although some local governments were prescient enough to have shareholding enterprises adopt Western-style balance sheets. The effort to reconcile fund accounting, under which enterprises had no equity capital of their own, with shareholding companies with equity capital accounts sheds significant light on the regulations adopted in the early 1990s, the heyday of the effort to "standardize (*guifan*)" the reform effort.

As will be discussed in Chapter 5, the transformation of an enterprise into a shareholding company involves one or more "promoters (*faqiren*)" contributing physical assets to the new company and, in return, receiving shares. Thus, if a state agency – for example, the Bureau of Heavy Industry – contributed certain equipment it owned to the new company, it would receive in return shares representing the value of that equipment.

If the new company continued to use fund accounting, such shares would likely have been treated as "State share/Fixed Funds." If individuals – for example, employees – used cash to buy shares in the company, their shares would have been entered as "Individual share/Current Fund." Depending on what type of asset was contributed, the related shares would be carried in the old fund source location on the balance sheets of the company.

This treatment is, from a Western accounting viewpoint, entirely confusing. For example, under the Western system, the purchase or disposal of a fixed asset or the write-off of inventory does not directly impact a company's equity accounts. In contrast, fund accounting methodology would result in a direct addition to or subtraction from, for example, the State share/Fixed Funds account. This approach simply does not work: equity shares do not represent a certain chunk of a company; they represent a share of a company's total assets after deducting various obligations to arrive at equity. Under fund accounting, presumably, if the specific assets related to the shares were used up or destroyed, the investment would be lost entirely, even if the company as a whole continued in existence!

In short, fund accounting leads to a fragmented view of a company, whereas the Western approach views the company's operations as an integrated whole. This is the background for Premier Zhu Rongji's comment that there are no chief financial officers in China. How could there be, when the bottom line relates to three different balance sheets? This discussion, though somewhat convoluted, is important. It clearly illuminates the intent of Article 4 of the 1994 Company Law, which went into effect on the eve of the first NYSE listing of a Chinese company. This article states, "The ownership rights to the state-owned assets of a company belong to the state."[12] In the context of the law providing the legal basis for creating Western-style corporations with a view to listing internationally, how is such a claim to be understood? It is easily understood by reference to fund accounting. If the state contributes fixed assets to a new company, it gets back shares representing those fixed assets only! The corollary to this is that since it owns those assets, how could the shares representing them be traded without it losing possession?

Given this way of thinking, state shares and enterprise-invested (also state-owned) shares were obviously those related to a Fixed Fund Source and Fixed Assets and, therefore, could not be sold without threatening state ownership of its original investment. In contrast, individual or foreign shares, since they are purchased in exchange for cash, should be a Current Fund Source and can be traded for other, equally fungible cash without impacting either individual rights or state ownership. These concepts, then, are the basis of the strict categorization of share types in the Standard Opinion and the segmented share structure of Chinese companies.

Today, the primary significance of this segmented financial structure lies in how China's stock market should be viewed and understood. As Chapter 8 will show, the markets in China for company shares are segmented precisely along the principles of the fund accounting practices in state planning.

THE 1992 STANDARD OPINION

Under the Opinion, a shareholding company is established when a promoter exchanges his ownership of certain real assets for shares of a new company. In Article 10 the Opinion set out as a basic principle that corporatization was limited to the state sector exclusively. Promoters were required to be Chinese legal persons in the state sector. Private or non-state sector entities of any kind were excluded.[13] The Opinion then worked out its elaborate share system based on these fundamental principles.

Basic Share Types

Unlike the 1999 Securities Law, the Standard Opinion permits a company to issue both common (*putong gu*) and preferred shares (*youxian gu*), although there were almost no issues of the latter. At the same time, it clearly defines a number of different types of shares based on the ownership characteristic of the contributed assets (see Table 4.3).[14] This definition did not just formalize the status quo of how shareholding companies were created during the 1980s; it froze it in place along the lines shown in Figure 4.1. State shares are the consequence of a government agency – for example, a ministry or a local government – contributing its lawfully held assets to the formation of a company limited by shares and receiving shares in return. Legal person shares represent the contribution by state-owned enterprises of their legally owned assets.[15]

Over time, a multiplicity of legal persons evolved, so that LP shares come in a wide variety of different types, but all are non-tradable and presumably held by a part of the state. To clarify what the state owned directly, certain LP shares are called state-owned legal person shares since "… the entities holding this type of share are state-owned in nature…"[16] This is an effort to differentiate among LP shares, since non-state-controlled companies are also legal persons under Chinese law.[17]

These two basic share types are also considered public (that is, state) shares (*gongyou gu*) given the underlying ownership characteristic of the assets contributed – that is, ownership by the state on behalf of the people. By logical extension, this terminology means that shares held by the investing public – that

TABLE 4.3 Types of Shares of Non-listed Shareholding Companies

Type of Share	Legally Permitted Holder of Share	Assets Contributable
State share	State Council authorized representatives of the state's investment in the company, typically state agencies or organizations at either the central or local levels	Buildings, equipment, patents, technology, land-use rights, cash
Legal person shares	Enterprises, institutions, or authorized social groups with legal person status	Buildings, equipment, patents, technology, land-use rights, cash
Individual shares	Either public retail investors or employees of a company who have invested their own wealth in the company	Renminbi cash
Foreign shares	Foreign investors using foreign currency to acquire RMB shares	Foreign currency

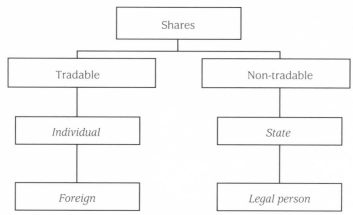

FIGURE 4.1 Standard Opinion: Basic Share Types

is, the "people" – are non-public shares (*feigongyou gu*). It seems odd that the people's direct ownership of shares in a company "owned by the whole people" is considered to be in some way at odds with the same people's interests as indirectly represented by the state.[18]

Elaboration of Share Types

These are the basic share types, but corporate developments since 1992 have resulted in some highly creative, if not wholly confused, elaborations on this theme, as shown in Table 4.4. These proliferating share types are the result of hair-splitting debates over precisely what relationship a given entity has with the state. Perhaps the logical conclusion of such negotiations is represented by the creation in 1998 of "individual shares of companies listed in the local OTC markets that have been acquired by a listed company but not yet listed."

The multiplication of share types has led to a variety of technical problems – for example, disclosure in annual reports and classification in the electronic data systems of the central settlement system and market data systems. The CSRC has repeatedly attempted to standardize the categories of shares (see Table 4.5),[19] but there has been no questioning of the basic validity of the approach.[20]

The simple fact is that China must address not just the technical issue of proliferation of share types, but the more important fact that they are not fungible across classes. See Table 4.7, later in the chapter, for samples of company share-holding structures.

Transfer of Ownership

On paper, state shares and legal person shares are legally transferable, but the purpose and scope of transfer is narrowly defined and the procedures drawn

TABLE 4.4 Pigeonholing Investors: Elaboration of Chinese Share Types

Year	Types of Share	Comment
1991	State share, "unit (*danwei*')" shares	Unit shares appear for first and last time
1992	State shares, legal person shares	Promoter shares, foreign capital promoter shares, overseas legal person shares, legal person shares, and individual shares become commonly used
1993	State shares, legal person shares, internal staff shares, and preferred shares	Internal staff shares and preferred shares come into usage
1994	State shares, Chinese promoter shares, foreign promoter shares, social legal person shares, leftover rights offering shares, and internal staff shares	Leftover rights offering shares (*zhuanpei yiliu gufen* or just *zhuanpeigu*) for disclosure purposes are entered as individual shares "High official" shares appear briefly in SZSE-listed companies
1995	State shares, domestic promoter shares, foreign capital promoter shares, social legal person shares, leftover rights offering shares, and internal staff shares	Types of shares gradually become a bit more defined and, taken as a whole, are considered as either non-tradable or tradable, each major category having a number of sub-types
1996	Promoter shares: • State-owned shares • Domestic legal person • Foreign legal persons • Other Social legal person shares Internal staff shares Preferred and other shares	The CSRC on January 1, 1997 makes a clarification of share types for first use in 1996 financial statements
1997	Same as 1996	State-owned legal person shares come into usage
1998	Same as 1996	Fund offering shares, strategic investor shares, general legal person shares, and individual shares of companies listed in the local OTC markets which have been acquired by a listed company but not yet listed themselves

Source: China Securities Daily, December 7, 1999, p. 4.

TABLE 4.5 CSRC Simplified Categorization of Principal Share Types

Principal Share Categories

1. *Promoter Shares: Shares held by original promoters but not yet listed and trading*
   i. State shares
   ii. Domestic promoter shares
   iii. Foreign promoter shares
   iv. Other promoter shares
   v. Social legal person shares
   vi. Internal staff shares
   vii. Preferred shares and Other

2. *Non-promoter shares: Shares held by non-promoters and not yet listed and trading*
   i. Pre-listing privately placed legal person shares
   ii. Shares left over from rights offerings
   iii. Internal employee shares
   iv. Other shares not yet listed and trading

3. *Shares already listed and trading*
   i. RMB-denominated, domestically listed shares (A shares)
   ii. Foreign currency-denominated, domestically listed shares (B shares)
   iii. Domestically listed company shares issued and listed overseas (H shares)

Source: CSRC, May 8, 2000, p. 179.

to make transfer of ownership difficult (see Table 4.6).[21] State shares, for all intents and purposes, are not transferable. Legal person shares are meant to be transferable only among legal persons and have in some cases been traded on STAQ, NETS, the auction houses, or now the newly established Third Board.[22]

As mentioned previously, the intent of the state at the time the Standard Opinion was formulated (1989–90) and enacted (1992) was to prevent loss of

TABLE 4.6 Rights of Ownership Transfer by Types of Shares

Type of Share	Legally Permitted Holder of Share
State share	Can be transferred subject to other state provisions
Legal person shares	Cannot be transferred for one year following establishment of company
	Cannot be transferred to employees of company in any manner
	Can only be transferred to other legal persons
Internal employee shares	Cannot be transferred for three years following establishment of company
	Can only be transferred among other employees of same company; the transfer or sale of these shares outside of the company is prohibited
Foreign shares	Can be transferred subject to other state provisions

TABLE 4.7 Illustrative Listed Company Shareholding Structures

Share Type (Mn)	Handan Steel	Double Crane	Hainan Airlines
State	996.6	0	17.3
State legal person	0	239.2	0
Domestic legal person including:			
Domestic promoter	0	16	117.5
Social legal person	0	0	124.5
General legal person	0	0	0
Internal employee	0	0	64.8
Foreign capital legal person	0	0	108
A shares	490	185.9	221.4
B shares	0	0	76.7
H shares	0	0	0
Total shares	1,486.6	441.1	730.3

control over state-owned enterprises, as well as the assets contributed to them.[23] An example from 1999 provides some insight into the kinds of situations the government must have considered when these share types were being formulated.

In the fall of 1997, the Chengdu Lianyi Group sought new funds by a negotiated sale of a portion of its LP shares equal to 40% to another legal person, the Guangdong Feilong Group, for RMB68 million consideration.[24] The two companies signed a "Legal Person Share Transfer Agreement," which specified the terms of Feilong's purchase, including the fact that it would be done on an installment basis. On formal signing, the shares were transferred and Feilong became Lianyi's largest shareholder. Unfortunately, relations between the two companies quickly degenerated, as Feilong was unable to make the installment payments for the shares it had received.

Consequently, a supplement to the original share transfer agreement was signed in late 1998. The agreement stated that the shares continued to belong to Lianyi Group and prohibited Feilong, in whose name the shares were now registered, from disposing of or otherwise using Lianyi's shares in any fashion until proper payment had been received. Shortly thereafter, Feilong informed Lianyi that it had more than sufficient funds and produced bank deposit books showing this. These later turned out to be counterfeit, but at the time Lianyi was satisfied. Then, in August 1999, Lianyi management received a notice from a bank in Guangdong that the RMB30 million loan it had borrowed had come due and must be repaid. Lianyi had made no such loan. An investigation began which showed that Feilong had used the Lianyi legal person shares as collateral to procure the RMB30 million loan. All attempts to locate the chairman of Feilong failed, the money was missing, and the Lianyi chairman was fired shortly after the case became public. In recent years, especially since 1999, many stories like this have been publicized in the financial press.

Regardless of the practical realities of business in China, the stringent, but locally approved, process for transfer explains in part how situations such as the Lianyi case can happen. What is interesting, however, is how little impact such transactions have on the public market, as discussed in Chapter 8.

THE 1994 COMPANY LAW

As previously noted, the Company Law makes no mention of the share types defined by the Standard Opinion.[25] By July 1994, when the Law was signed into effect by Vice Premier Zhu Rongji, thousands of companies limited by shares had been established across China. Of these, some 290 had actually listed A shares. In its only reference to the Standard Opinion, the Law required these companies "not completely satisfying" the requirements of the law to do so "within a specified time limit."[26]

In July 1995, a year after its becoming effective, the State Council initiated a national effort to conform Standard Opinion companies to the requirements of the Company Law with a completion date in late 1996.[27] This was a simple clean-up of government records for the most part, but it represented an opportunity to deal with share categories. The reality of the share types and corporate forms created by the Standard Opinion, however, was ignored. The government thus has allowed the Company Law in effect to call their legal basis into question. Market practice, however, ignores this and moves on. To this day, the Standard Opinion remains the foundation document of the securities industry.

In addition, the Company Law's failure to distinguish between common and preferred shares, or to provide for other share types or classes, virtually precludes the development of equity securities with different investment characteristics – for example, different voting rights. Since all shares enjoy on paper the same rights and the same benefits under the Company Law, it will be difficult without amendment to establish a basis on which minority shareholders or investors giving different value can be protected.[28] Financial sophistication, or even protection of the minority interests of domestic shareholders, was not, however, the principal priority of the government in the early 1990s. The acceptance of equity shares as a non-politicized financing instrument was sophisticated enough for the time.

Transfer of Ownership

The Law states that all shares possess the same characteristics of issue price, ownership rights, and benefits (tongjia, tongquan, tongli).[29] Similar to state-held shares under the Standard Opinion, shares held by "state-authorized investment organizations" can be legally "transferred" and such entities can purchase shares from other shareholders. However, the Law restricts shares held by the state from being transferred within three years of a given company's formation. The Law did not specify how the ownership of such

BOX 4   Selected History of State Share Transfers

1994	Provisional measures on the regulation of state-owned share rights issued by companies limited by shares.
Apr. 1994	Zhuhai Hengtong buys 12 million state shares of Shanghai Lengguang Industrial (600629) from Shanghai Construction Materials Group. This is the first case of a share transfer involving state shares.
Nov. 1994	Shanghai Lujiazui (600663 and 900932) buys back RMB200 million of state shares and issues same value of B shares.
Sept. 1995	State Council Office Notice transmits "Request for instructions from the SCSC regarding temporarily halting the transfer to foreign investors of state and legal person shares in listed companies."
Nov. 1999	Ten companies, including Jialing (600877) and Guizhou Tyre (0589), are selected to sell down part of their state shares through rights offers.
Dec. 1999	Shenergy (600642) buys back 1 billion state LP shares.
	Jialing offers investors the right to buy 0.361 state shares for every 10 shares held. Issue size is 100 million shares, subscription price of RMB4.5 per share. The shares become tradable on January 11, 2000. Undersubscribed.
	Guizhou Tyre offers the right to buy 1.59097 state shares for every 10 shares held. Issue size is 17.1053 million shares, subscription price of RMB4.8 per share. The shares become tradable on January 12, 2000. Undersubscribed.
Mar. 2000	Qinghai SAMB, the largest shareholder of Qinghai Digital Net Investment Group (000578), transfers 29.58 million state shares (26.88% of the total shares) to Shenzhen City Youyuan Investment Company.
Sept. 2000	Shanghai Highly Group (600619) buys back 42 million state shares at RMB2.28 per share.
Dec. 2000	Yuntianhua Company (600096) buys back 200 million state LP shares at RMB2.83 per share.
Dec. 2000	Changchun High and New Technology Industries Group (000661) buys back 70 million state shares at RMB3.44 per share.
Apr. 2001	Ningxia Hengli Steel Cable Co. (600165), the largest shareholder, publishes an advertisement soliciting buyers, domestic or foreign, for its state shareholding in Ningxia Hengli.
May 2001	Ningxia Hengli retracts the previous advertisement soliciting foreign investors and cancels its proposed meeting for prospective shareholders.

BOX 4 *continued*

June 2001	Tianyu Electric (000723) transfers 64 million state shares without first obtaining MOF approval or fulfilling CRSC requirements.
	State Council issues its provisional administrative measures for raising social security funds through the sale of state-owned shares. The move ended the bull market and the Shanghai index fell 40% over the next six months.
June–Oct. 2001	Numerous domestic companies sold a portion of their state shares, either through initial or secondary public offerings.
Oct. 2001	CSRC issues an order suspending the requirement of selling state-owned shares on the domestic securities market. Overseas listings continue to comply with the ruling.
Nov. 2001	CSRC solicits suggestions from the public on how to deal with the state share problem and receives over 4,300 replies.
Jan. 2002	CSRC issues a series of seven proposals designed to reduce the state share problem.
Apr. 2002	Yunnan Huayi Investment (000667) announces the proposed transfer of 72 million state shares from Yunnan SAMB to Beijing Mingliu Group, at RMB2 per share.
June 2002	Yunnan Huayi Investment (000667) announces the proposed transfer of 55 million state shares from Yunnan SAMB to Hainan Yangpu Group, at RMB2 per share.
June 2002	State Council announced its decision that, with immediate effect, the provisional measures providing for the sale of state-owned shares on the domestic securities market would cease to apply.
Sept. 2002	An SAC official announces that all the shares of Third Board companies will become freely tradable. The market fears that this is the first step in reintroducing the sale of state shares. The CSRC moves quickly to deny this suggestion.
Sept. 2002	Newbridge Capital is approved to buy a rumored 20% stake in Shenzhen Development Bank (000001) from existing shareholders in the form of state shares.
Nov. 2002	"Notice Regarding Transfer to Foreign Investors of State-owned Shares and Legal Person Shares of Listed Companies" is issued. The notice reverses the 1995 ban on foreign investors buying state shares.

shares should be transferred, like the Standard Opinion, noting that the issue will be dealt with separately in other laws or regulations.[30] Nearly 10 years and a certain amount of experimentation later, there has yet to be an unconditional clarification and none is expected in the medium-term future.

Shares defined as those not held by state organizations – for example, foreign LP shares – can be freely traded, but only after listing and only on legally constituted stock exchanges. On listing, the foreign LP shares become B shares and can freely trade. This particular "breakthrough" finally took place early in 2001 and was subject to a number of restrictions.[31] In short, state-held shares, and in practice, LP shares, do not possess the same characteristics and rights as those held by non-state investors. This problem has long been recognized and, in late 1999, public discussion began as to means of dealing with the issue. This problem is discussed in detail in Chapter 8.

LISTED COMPANY SHARES

The Standard Opinion was written in early 1992 when the only foreign or "special shares" available to foreign investors were B shares (or shares in a Sino-foreign JV which had transformed itself into a company limited by shares). These B shares were listed on the two domestic stock exchanges and, until February 2001, were legally available only to foreign investors.[32] The State Council issued further special regulations applicable only to B shares in 1995.[33] But all of this, as well as almost annual efforts by the Chinese government to "do" something (anything) to revive interest in the B-share markets, including opening them up to domestic investors legally, has been to no avail. B shares are an obsolete product category pushed aside by what the international market saw as the "real thing": H shares and Red Chips. The expectation is that, at some point, B shares will simply be swapped for A shares and that will be that.

This "real" effort to attract foreign equity capital began in October 1992 when the government announced that nine companies had been designated as listing candidates on the SEHK. On hearing this, investors said goodbye to B shares and hello to Hong Kong. These companies' shares quickly came to be called H shares, after Hong Kong. There followed not long after, in early 1994, a group of five companies designated to list on the NYSE and these, of course, came to be called N shares.[34] In late 1996, another two companies were designated to list on the Tokyo Stock Exchange, becoming potential T shares, and so on.[35] After 10 years, such experimentation has cooled off and companies list generally on the Hong Kong and New York exchanges. In any event, none of these alphabet shares, save the A shares, are anything except popular names (see Table 4.8).

As noted previously, the Company Law makes no provision at all for companies intending to offer shares or list on overseas stock exchanges. Therefore, the State Council passed the Overseas Listing Rules, sometimes called the Small Company Law, shortly after July 1994. The Rules define shares listed overseas as "foreign (capital) shares (*waizigu*)," whereas the shares of the same company listed domestically were called "domestic (capital) shares (*neizigu*)."[36]

Despite this alphabet soup of names of convenience (or satire), all such foreign or "special shares" by law enjoy the same rights and obligations as those enjoyed by domestic shares. The only notable exception is that, for

TABLE 4.8 Listed Companies Share Types

Type of Share	Legally Permitted Holder of Share
Foreign or "special shares" – also called B shares	Foreign and domestic investors who directly purchase RMB-denominated shares using foreign currency
RMB-denominated shares – also called A shares	Domestic investors only are allowed to purchase, hold, and trade
H shares or "special shares" – similar to B shares	Foreign investors who directly purchase RMB-denominated shares using foreign currency
N shares or "special shares" – similar to H shares	Foreign investors who directly purchase RMB-denominated shares using foreign currency

example, H shares are priced and traded in Hong Kong dollars and dividends are paid in Hong Kong dollars.[37]

In practice, however, there is a difference. It has been the Chinese custom to conclude Memorandums of Understanding with each separate regulator of the international stock exchange on which "special shares" may be listed.[38] These agreements are aimed at coordinating any differences between the listing and regulatory requirements of the particular overseas exchange and Chinese regulations and practices governing Chinese companies to be listed.[39] In certain instances, the arrangements reached provide holders of foreign shares' greater rights and protection than holders of domestic shares. For example, in the case of an SEHK-listed Chinese company, foreign shareholders are permitted to vote on certain matters of material import to the company's operations, while the majority shareholders are excluded. This right does not exist in the Chinese legal and regulatory context. The first time minority H-share investors succeeded in voting down a company action occurred in November 2002, almost 10 years after the first Hong Kong listing. Investors overturned a US$351 million acquisition of assets from its SOE parent by Angang New Steel.[40] No A-share investors attended the shareholders' meeting.

Should an individual overseas shareholder, however, wish to voice disagreement or claim damages from a listed company, the dispute would be settled under Chinese law. Hence, any extra rights foreign shareholders might have exist more on paper than in actual practice. Until consistently demonstrated otherwise, for all practical purposes their rights are equivalent to domestic Chinese non-state shareholders.

THE 1999 SECURITIES LAW

The promulgation of the Securities Law in 1999 had been anticipated for years in the hope that it would provide a solid foundation for the existing hodge-podge of laws and regulations. Indeed, the 1999 Securities Law, in

Article 1, states the objective of standardizing the issue and trading of securities as a general principle.[41] Unfortunately, however, the scope of the new law governs only the issue and trading within China of shares, corporate bonds, and such other securities as approved by the State Council. Government bonds are subject to separate laws and regulations. Insofar as equity securities go, the law seems to apply to both A and B shares; however, Article 213 notes that B shares are subject to other measures separately enacted by the State Council. This suggests that B shares continue to be subject to the 1995 Provisions.

The Securities Law, like the Company Law before it, makes absolutely no reference to state shares and LP shares. As a result, there is no clear legal treatment of how, or whether, such shares can be listed or traded. This is not an insignificant omission, since at present state and LP shares constitute 70% of the Shanghai and Shenzhen combined market capitalization. Based on existing laws, such shares can only be "transferred," but that did not stop experimental LP share trading the few times it was attempted in the 1990s.

Article 29 is the only part of the Securities Law directly applying to overseas-listed shares. The article imposes the condition that such companies as desire to list and trade their shares overseas must first obtain the approval of the CSRC. In this case, the catch-all general principle stated in Article 2 most certainly applies: "For matters not provided for in this Law, the provisions of the Company Law and other relevant laws and administrative regulations shall apply." This at least gives the market comfort that previous laws have not been superseded, but, given the confusing state of all such laws and regulations, it does little to develop the market in a positive manner.

In summary, the Securities Law does not relieve the uncertainty associated with the legal foundation of China's equity shares. State shares, LP shares, foreign shares, as well as "other" shares, have not been formally recognized by the two principal laws governing the establishment of shareholding companies and the equity securities evidencing ownership in such companies. Instead, the approach has been to patch up inadequacies, which further adds to confusion. The principal arbiter of such confusion, in the first instance, has been the CSRC, and then ultimately the State Council. This approach to matters can be expected to continue.[42]

CHAPTER 5

Packaging SOEs: Restructuring and Listing

Shares are not unique to capitalism only, they can also serve the modernization of socialism and will probably become a good way for us to raise capital.

Vice Premier Tian Jiyun, comments at the Shenzhen exchange,
April 1992[1]

W hat are companies in China, and how are they created and listed? This may seem a strange question, but before the 1992 Standard Opinion there was no legal basis for the creation of a company in China, nor was there even an awareness of the need. Under Soviet-style central planning, enterprises were a constituent part of the state, which owned everything. But they were not companies in any Western sense. Not until the shareholding experiment had proceeded too far for even Deng Xiaoping to stop it did it become obvious that enterprises needed a legal form.[2]

One of the authors once met the Minister of Finance of the Ukraine on an official visit to Beijing and was asked, "How do they do it?" He couldn't understand how unprofitable state-owned enterprises, of which his country had plenty, could ever actually raise money in Hong Kong, much less in New York. "How could you list *that*?" As the last 10 years have demonstrated, SOEs can be listed; moreover, they can raise a lot of capital. A large part of the answer to the Ukrainian minister's question lies in the packaging (*baozhuang*) work carried out by bankers and accountants.

From the very start in the early 1980s, the driving motivation behind the experiment with shareholding companies came from enterprise managers. This simply reflects the unquenchable thirst for capital throughout the Chinese economy. Even for major SOE groups, bank funding has never been enough and now is even more difficult to obtain. And this is the best case: collective and private enterprises do not enjoy such access, and informal means of funding are never sufficient. Meeting the requirements to list – it doesn't really matter where – is the easiest way to raise large chunks of money. Moreover, if management plays the game well, listing is a license to raise more. The entire enterprise cost of capital issue is a non-starter in the Chinese economic environment where demand is simply not elastic.

The government has, however, tilted the playing field in favor of its own companies. Even so, this has not been a guarantee. Enterprise management, given the opportunity, will seek any path to capital and take the consequences later. A CSRC official recently commented that there were 1,200 companies qualified to list and queued up ready to go.[3] With 100–200 companies listing a year domestically and a further half-dozen internationally, that is a long wait even after listing approval. It's a longer wait for the non-state sector.

This chapter reviews the legal building blocks which management must use to create a company, outlines the major issues confronting an SOE when taking on a restructuring with the goal of listing, and categorizes the evolution of listing structures.

EVOLUTION OF CHINESE CORPORATE LAW

The 1986 Shenzhen Corporatization Provisions

The Shenzhen government in 1986 was the first to create relatively comprehensive procedures for the restructuring of enterprises into companies that could sell shares.[4] These regulations empowered SOE management to take charge of the process with minimal state intervention. While the provisions were directed primarily at the restructuring of Shenzhen's own SOEs, the government welcomed all to use them as a guide: "other SOEs, cooperative enterprises implementing restructuring, and newly established internally capitalized companies limited by shares can also proceed based on these regulations."

The Shenzhen provisions defined SOE restructuring into a shareholding company as follows: "... transforming the net asset value of an SOE into shares representing the state's equity ownership, then transferring a portion of the state's ownership to other enterprises and individuals. OR taking in new shares from the state, other enterprises or individuals, then transforming the original enterprise into a company limited by shares in which the state, other enterprises and individuals participate in the shareholding."

This definition is notable for permitting two ways of raising capital through the sale of shares. Like overseas companies, the owners of the "original enterprise" could choose either to sell down their existing stake – that is, sell primary shares – or to sell new, or secondary, shares in the company. The economic result in both cases is the same: the original ownership interest is diluted. Once the central government took control of the process in 1992, however, the direct sale of state ownership interests was prohibited for ideological reasons: the state did not want to give even the impression that it was privatizing SOEs. In March 1992, Liu Hongru, a long-time supporter of stock markets, still found it necessary to state: "... I once again emphasize, the shareholding system is not privatization".[5] But key decision-makers had long since accommodated themselves to attracting capital via the equity joint venture path. For them, there now seemed little difference in selling shares that created a minority stake in what continued to be a state-controlled company. But for SOE management, there was a huge difference: greater autonomy.

There were a number of other areas in which the provisions broke ground. The provisions made it possible for foreign investors to acquire up to 25% of an SOE, but any larger share triggered the joint venture laws of the central government. Thus, the state, other enterprises and legal persons, foreigners, and individuals could all be shareholders. The newly formed company, with approval, was also allowed to raise money through the sale of shares overseas. Such measures were the forerunners to the B shares provisions. Investors, including banks and individuals, owed money by the potential shareholding company could carry out debt for equity swaps. Limits to how much the state, other enterprises, foreigners, and individuals could own of a given company's equity were to be set out in the company's articles of incorporation and not by the state. Shares could be sold, given as gifts, inherited, and used as collateral for bank loans. For all purposes, shares were the private property of the owner, or of the Shenzhen Finance Bureau as the state's designated trustee.

The Shenzhen government initiated the corporatization process by selecting the SOEs to be involved. Following selection, the Finance Bureau organized a work group including the PBOC branch and enterprise management. Much like the work done in the 1990s, this group was responsible for the "packaging" of the SOE, which was described as follows: "... non-productive assets and unused assets in general are not to be turned into shares. They can, through certain procedures, be transferred to the administrative body of other SOEs or institutions." Such packaging is designed to achieve enterprise profitability by "carving out (*boli*)" the productive part of an SOE. "Packaging" came to have a bad name in the mid-1990s when it was seen by investors (and the state as well) to be unsustainable in most cases.

In terms of actual practice, five different sorts of companies evolved under the Shenzhen regulations. The first included SOEs without significant state investment. These divided their net assets into both state and enterprise shareholdings and solicited investment by other enterprises as well as individuals. The second group included SOEs with significant state investment, which became companies with a single state shareholder and then solicited investment by other state enterprises. The third category included existing Sino-foreign JVs, which restructured as shareholding companies; the fourth, privately owned companies; and the fifth, limited liability companies with multiple shareholders, including state, collective, and private-sector investors.

In short, the liberal terms and implementation of the 1986 Shenzhen provisions show the influence of Hong Kong and Western capitalism, as well as the *zeitgeist* of the period.[6]

The 1988 Enterprise Law

This "law" has now been completely forgotten by all sides, and rightly so.[7] Although making one lasting contribution, the law is of a piece with the strict central planning era that was being rendered obsolete by events at the enterprise level. Like the Securities Law, it engendered significant debate, taking 10 years, 20 revisions, and six discussions by the NPC – and it shows it.[8] The debate circled around the issue of enterprise autonomy, which the law sought to define but in entirely administrative terms.

The key point, however, was that the law made all enterprises "legal persons" with civil responsibility for the property left by the state to their management and with independent budgets. Before this, "enterprise production, supply, marketing, personnel and materials [were] all controlled by the government. The enterprise remained only a producing unit that follows the government's orders."[9] But the Enterprise Law failed to include procedures marking the borders between the company and the state, so, in fact, little actually changed. SOEs remained so tightly intertwined with the state that it was hard to know where the enterprise left off and the state began. The close symbiotic relationship between the two continued in place wherein the state provided the SOE with raw materials and capital, and the SOE in return provided goods as well as social services, as shown in Figure 5.1.

The law applied to enterprises involved in both strands of experimentation – the contract responsibility system and the shareholding system. The Standard Opinion, therefore, at least had a basis on which to build. But the many local regulations for the restructuring of enterprises into shareholding companies provided far better guidance than the Enterprise Law. The Standard Opinion, rendering the final verdict, made no mention of it at all.

Overview of the Creation of a Shareholding Company, 1992 to the Present

The 1992 Standard Opinion and supporting legislation were aimed at "standardizing" the diverse local approaches to creating shareholding companies. The basic concepts were similar to the Shenzhen provisions, with the key exception being that the Opinion limited corporatization to the state sector exclusively. Promoters were required to be domestic Chinese legal persons in the state sector. Private-sector entities of any kind, including foreigners at the formative stage, were excluded. This, of course, had a major impact on the development of the stock markets, as well as the non-state sector, which lacked other means of financing. In general, however, many of the roots of the Standard Opinion can be found in the Shenzhen provisions. In fact, even after

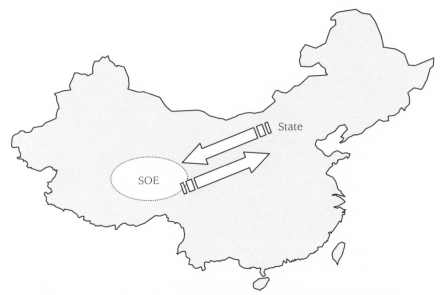

FIGURE 5.1   An Unrestructured State Enterprise Embedded in the State.

enactment of the Standard Opinion, Shenzhen was allowed to continue using its own regulations for the corporatization of its SOEs to the extent that there was no conflict with national regulations.

To preserve the state's investment, the critical part of enterprise restructuring lies in the determination of where the state ends and the corporation begins. Neither the Enterprise Law nor the contract responsibility system provided a clear, detailed process for boundary definition. Without a clear definition, who knew whose rights were what? This, of course, could and did lead to endless and wasteful argument.

The State Asset Management Bureau is now defunct (or at least out of sight in the MOF) but the boundary setting process is not.[10] The SAMB created a working team consisting of a licensed asset appraiser, a certified public accountant, and enterprise management. This group is held responsible by the state for defining the boundary between the original collection of assets – that is to say, the state enterprise – and the new company to be incorporated. This "boundary setting (*dingjie*)" naturally involves not a few disputes. In central planning, it was assumed that everything belongs to the state, so what is the need for documentation of ownership? The asset appraisal and audit work sorted this out once and for all. But it should not be surprising how, in an economy characterized by "ownership by the whole people," there can be so many claimants to any given article of value.

On completion of the appraisal and audit, the now certified NAV of the new company is set as its registered capital, transformed into shares (*zhegu*) with a par value of RMB1.00. The company is incorporated following a vote by a founding meeting of shareholders/promoters and approval by relevant company registration agencies.

The 1992 Standard Opinion

Under the Standard Opinion,[11] SOEs could be restructured into companies limited by shares in two principal ways: (1) the promoter method; and (2) the fund-raising method.

The Promoter Method

This approach requires the package of assets to restructure itself into a company limited by shares (see Figure 5.2). Whether there might be any packaging involved at this stage, as clearly addressed in the 1986 Shenzhen provisions, is not mentioned. These shares must then be placed in their entirety with the single promoter of the company. The promoter will normally be the original state agency which "invested" in and therefore "owned" the assets being restructured – for example, a local government or ministry. This path was used principally by the larger SOEs in preparation for public listings.

The Fund-raising Method

This approach takes two different forms: (1) the directed offering (*dingxiang muji*) method; and (2) the public offering (*shehui qunzhong muji* or *shehui muji*) method (see Figure 5.3). In a directed offering, the shares of the restructured company are acquired by the promoter as well as other legal persons in a manner not unlike a private placement. If additional approval is obtained,

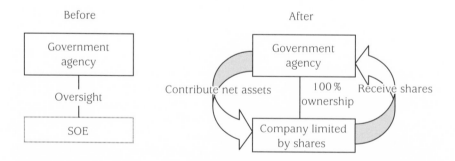

The state agency manages the SOE prior to corporatization, but does not "own" the SOE. As a result of the corporatization process, the state agency's original ownership of assets is identified and documented prior to their contribution to the new corporate entity. In return for the net assets, the state agency receives shares issued by the corporation and assumes an outright ownership relationship exercised through a shareholders' meeting and a board of directors.

FIGURE 5.2 The Promoter Method.

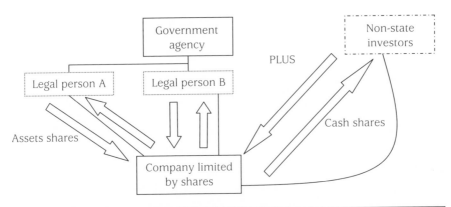

The state agency supervises a number of SOEs (A and B) each of which have held assets on behalf of the state in the enterprise being corporatized. Their original ownership of such assets is formalized, value appraised, and the assets contributed to the new corporation in exchange for shares. After a year, this new company receives approval for a public offering, receiving cash from the non-state investors in return for the issuance of new shares.

FIGURE 5.3 Directed versus Public Offering.

shares could be sold to employees of the given company as well. This is similar to the first approach noted in the Shenzhen provisions

In contrast, in a public offering shares can be sold to the public, in addition to being acquired by the promoter, in a two-step process. In the first step, the company is formed with the promoter holding the shares. On approval and after one year of operation, the company may apply to offer new, secondary shares to the public.

Approval Procedures

Once the promoters (*faqiren*) have decided to establish a company, the supervisory authority for the company's given industry, either a ministry for a centrally owned enterprise or a provincial industrial bureau for a locally owned one, acts as sponsor (*tuijianren*) and oversees the entire application process. The promoters must prepare a package of documents in support of their request.[12] This package is then reviewed and approved by a variety of government agencies with the process coordinated by SCRES or its local government counterpart. On approval the promoters have 30 days to complete preparatory registration procedures with the Bureau of Industry and Commerce. But this hardly marks the end of the process.

The promoters must next make their appropriate capital contribution. Once this has been fully paid into a pre-approved bank account or the ownership of specific assets has been transferred, they must call a shareholders' meeting within 40 days to establish the new company. Investors holding over two-thirds of the total shares must be present at the meeting.[13] Within 30 days of the shareholders' meeting, the board of directors must meet to approve the application to register the new company at the Bureau of Industry and Commerce. On completion of registration, which takes another month, the company commences its existence as a legal person.[14]

The 1994 Company Law

The Company Law narrowed the options for establishing a shareholding company to two methods: (1) the offer method; and (2) the promotion method.[15]

The Offer Method

Creation of a company via the offer method requires the promoters to subscribe to not less than 35% of the shares of the new company, with the remaining 65% to be issued in a public offering – all prior to formal legal establishment of the company. This is similar to the public offering method defined by the Standard Opinion. In reality, promoters have traditionally subscribed to approximately 75% of the original share capital, with the remaining 25% offered to the public. The reason for this was to absolutely ensure the unchallenged ownership and control of listed companies by the state.

The Law eliminated the directed offering option contained in the Standard Opinion. The directed offering allowed for the private placement of equity to other legal persons and, with approval, company employees. Nonetheless, the problem of how to address the ticklish reality of individual employee shares remained. Also, the problem of a public offering of a company not yet in legal existence remained. As noted before, such a procedure represents significant investor risk, particularly to minority shareholders, and for these reasons is not currently international practice in the world's major jurisdictions and so has not been attempted for overseas listings.

The Promotion Method

This method requires the promoters to purchase all shares in the company to be established, with subsequent capital raising restricted for one year (see Figure 5.4). The new shareholding company is legally established only after all promoters have fully made their capital contribution. Companies are required to have at least five promoters, by number, not economic interest, and more than half must reside in China. The intent of this requirement was to improve corporate governance by mandating multiple shareholders. In contrast, the Standard Opinion allowed "large-scale" SOEs to transform themselves into shareholding companies using themselves as the single promoter. Practice has been that the principal promoter generally satisfies this requirement by giving small, minority roles to entities owned by either the local government or other legal persons within its own group.

Relative to the provisions of the Standard Opinion, the combination of these requirements makes it difficult for enterprises to carry out the

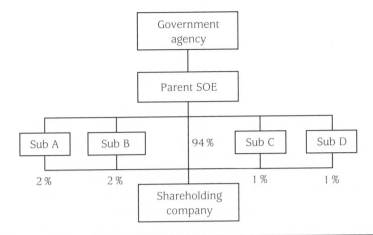

After restructuring, the newly corporatized shareholding company would have five shareholders, all members of the parent SOE group. This structure suits the letter of the Company Law but would hardly achieve the goal of improved corporate governance – all shareholders report to the same parent, and all directors on the board are under the control of the parent.

FIGURE 5.4 Corporatization Using the Promotion Method and before IPO.

establishment of a shareholding company aimed at completing an IPO: there must first be a one-year period of operation. This problem was resolved for those SOEs approved to undertake overseas public offerings by a special regulation passed by the State Council.[16] Overseas listing candidate enterprises must adopt the promotion method of establishment and may have fewer than five promoters. Moreover, on establishment the company may at once issue new shares. These, then, are the basic building blocks of listed Chinese companies. How companies actually come to restructure their operations and ownership to complete listings, however, is an entirely different matter.

HOW TO "PACKAGE" AN SOE

The legal building blocks are simple and straightforward. But to say that restructuring an SOE into a shareholding company with the hope of listing its shares internationally is a lot of work is an understatement. In this work, bankers are not alone in their effort to sort out what a company is going to be. There are lawyers (domestic and international) representing the "company," on the one hand, and the bankers on the other. Then there are the accountants, the asset appraisers (again, domestic and international), a public relations firm, a legal printer, and maybe a domestic financial advisor, all of whom are hired by the company, but orchestrated by the banker. The Chinese call this lot "intermediary organizations (*zhongjian jigou*)," which suggests that these professionals are viewed by the government as little more than shysters.

The Company Blueprint

The critical part of the work, as noted above, is to identify the assets that are meant to comprise the new company. To do this, enterprise management and the bankers sit down together to create the new company, starting by reference to what sort of operations a Western company in the same industry would own. A significant amount of research goes into creating this blueprint. The easy part is carving off schools, hospitals, police and fire departments, courts, tourism and hotel management operations, and dormitory areas for the workers and staff and any other entities which do not relate directly to the company's operations. Some of these functions can be directly passed over to the local government without objection, since they belong there in the first place. In addition, the responsibility for the pensions of retired workers, who with their dependents could number in the tens of thousands, is also largely left in what would become the parent company. The local government does not want this obligation. There are always surprises in this process. The final product of this packaging stage is illustrated in Figure 5.8, later in the chapter.

The Draft Audit

As soon as the banker and the company agree on a package, everyone else goes to work. A highly detailed and usually highly unrealistic time schedule coordinating everyone's work is put together by the banker. The touchstones of this schedule are the completion of a draft audit of the proposed company and an expected date of listing. The draft audit is the make or break event of a deal. The audit shows whether the assets chosen to be packaged were, in fact, productive and profitable, or whether they are like the rest of the company, not so productive and not so profitable. Despite the wiggle room for "creative" treatments which accounting principles provide, many deals blow up when the draft audit appears, unable to go forward due to irremediable lack of profitability or sufficient profitability.

The Asset Appraisal

The asset appraisal draft result is a critical part of the audit work as well, since it sets the accounting or book value of the fixed assets (property and equipment) and, therefore, depreciation, which can have a significant impact on profitability. Asset appraisal results are, therefore, the object of intense negotiation. The company always wants to hold down the adjustment, minimize depreciation, and so report higher net income and receive more IPO proceeds. But the SAMB must also be satisfied and, for it, assets can only appreciate.[17] The appraisal and the audit work go on simultaneously. Given the amount of money involved, it is not surprising that the asset appraisal industry has recently (and at last) come under a cloud.[18]

The identification and proper ownership documentation of assets is important for the formation of an independent company. However, from the point of view of achieving a public listing, the appraisal part of this work is completely unnecessary. An asset appraisal provides no useful information to investors on true asset value. The real question is not how much assets are worth on a company's books, but how the assets are used to produce products that can be sold at a profit. A company may have a beautiful plant which is poorly operated and creates no value at all. There are any number of these littered across the Chinese landscape. On the other hand, for the state, the asset appraisal is the key to sorting out issues of ownership and value of assets, which had previously simply been "given" to enterprises funded by budgetary grants (and, later on, bank loans). Without accurate appraisals and the associated work of formally documenting ownership, the result of the corporatization process is null and void. Whether the newly corporatized company is ultimately listed or not is a secondary matter.

The concept of value contained in an asset appraisal report is based on the principle of the replacement cost of the assets. This approach assumes that today's 10-year-old mostly depreciated machine is worth the price of a brand-new machine. In other words, if the company had to replace the machine by buying a new one, that is the replacement cost and that value is entered into the new company's book. The result of such an appraisal will always be to inflate the value of the company's fixed assets by definition with a similar increase in the company's capital account. This outcome is satisfying to the SAMB: through its dedication, the state's assets always show increases in value as a result of corporatization. Under its supervision, the write-down or write-off of the value of any machinery is nearly impossible in China. When creating a new company, asset values can only go up, never down.

Minimum Share Price

Aside from the impact on operations, the asset appraisal would be of little importance except for a related restriction on the price at which a company's shares can be sold. By regulation, shares must be priced at a level exceeding the company's NAV per share. This holds true for whether the deal is a public market offering or a private-market "M&A" transaction or asset transfer. The higher the appraised value of the fixed assets, the higher the NAV per share and, consequently, the higher the offering price must be set to sell the company's shares. If the company cannot be sold at this price after all share orders are received, the deal will not be approved by the CSRC. There is, therefore, great pressure on the company and its hired help to find a balance that satisfies the SAMB's objectives, while holding the increase in asset value to a level that allows the company to attempt the offering in the opinion of its bankers.

This outcome is largely the result of negotiation before the asset appraisal is submitted to the SAMB. There are a few legitimate actions, however, that can be taken to create an acceptable outcome. For example, no listed Chinese

---

BOX 5   Institutional Evolution of China's Asset Appraisal Sector

1989	First asset appraisal company established in Shenzhen.
Nov. 16, 1991	State Council set the regulatory basis for the asset appraisal sector.
1993	China Appraisal Society (CAS), an independent industry association, was established to specify qualifications for appraisal companies.
1996	A national examination certifying appraisers was introduced.
1997	107 appraisal companies had been qualified.
1998	SAMB eliminated by combining it into MOF, and State Council set up work teams to clean up the industry; two appraisal companies were required to sign each company appraisal report.
1999	MOF established new standards for asset appraisal institutions.
2000	CAS merged into Chinese Institute of Certified Public Accountants (CICPA); the former rural township enterprise asset appraisers were also merged into CICPA.
July 2001	First revised rules for asset appraisal passed by State Council.
Nov. 6, 2001	Legal representative of Guangdong United Dazheng Asset Valuation Company arrested for providing fraudulent reports for the September 2001 IPO of Macat Optics and Electronics.
Dec. 2001	MOF instituted a verification system for asset appraisal reports; regarded as the most significant revision to its original November 1991 decree.
Dec. 31, 2001	Persons involved in the fraudulent asset appraisal underlying the listing of Macat Optics and Electronics were formally sued in court. First time ever asset appraisers have been openly implicated in a fraudulent listing.
Jan. 22, 2002	CICPA institutes three warning system: after third warning, asset appraiser's certification will be revoked.
Nov. 2002	Sixteenth Party Congress announces the outline of a significantly decentralized asset management system.

Source: Caijing, June 5, 2002, p. 82; and November 20, 2002.

---

company ever owns (on behalf of the state) the land it sits on. It does not want to, since this would gross up the value of its assets so high that a listing would be impossible. In fact, no one in China has any idea of what land is really worth. In the absence of a real market for industrial property, there is no objective basis on which to value it. Land values are simply set by, what else, the State Land Management Bureau (SLMB) or its authorized representative at the local level. This issue is left behind with the parent company to deal with at some later date. The new company simply rents the "land-use rights (*tudi shiyongquan*)" from its parent based on a rent schedule which can be designed to boost bottom-line profits: little or no rent in the early years, increasing rent in the later years. Such arrangements are accepted by the SLMB and are perfectly legal. NAV can also be adjusted by altering company debt levels and running scenarios on fixed asset value. It is an understatement to say that domestic asset appraisal companies are extremely practical in their work. This is what got them into trouble.

Back to the Drawing Board

If the draft audit and asset appraisal reports still show the bottom line as insufficient to produce a successful listing, everything is up for grabs again in the company's design. Without going into excruciating detail, the bankers, company, and the accounting firm comb through the prospective balance sheet and income statement to identify items which might produce a large negative impact on profitability. This might include such things as a product line with low profitability, unproductive fixed assets creating large amounts of depreciation, too many employees, too much debt, excess taxes (taxes can sometimes be negotiated), and so on. Once such pieces are identified, the question arises of whether they can be got rid of. If the answer is yes, stuff them in the parent company.

Participants in this work cannot be accused of shortchanging the state (or even investors) since they seek ways to create value out of an SOE. With all due respect to the state, what is the value of an SOE? It most certainly is not what the balance sheet suggests before or after completion of a state-approved asset appraisal. And it is doubtful that any informed state leader believes that it is. The SOE's value is what the market places on it and nothing else. If the shares cannot be sold, then the company has no market value, only a book value which represents the results of a set of accounting decisions. This, unfortunately, is the status quo. The consequence is that the state, as ultimate owner, has no objective idea whether or not any given company is operating successfully and therefore is worthy of continued investment. For example, BaoSteel (*Baogang*) in Shanghai is China's most modern steel maker, as everyone knows. But on the eve of Baogang's Shanghai listing in 2000, even senior officials in the State Planning and Development Commission (SPDC) confessed to having no clear idea of what steel products the company made or if the company was truly profitable. Given the state of the asset appraisal, accounting, and the investment banking industries in China, this should not be a surprise.

This is the true problem of SOE reform in China: no one is sure of whether even the best companies are capable of reform if that means a rapid restructuring in preparation, whether for increased global competition or just an international IPO. And asset appraisal reports, no matter how rectified they may, are a poor guide in this process.

Approval Process

Each company, whether listed domestically or internationally, goes through a similar work process aimed at obtaining an extensive list of approvals.[19]

Approval documents for different aspects of the work constitute the bulk of the supporting documentation (which includes a Chinese copy of the draft prospectus for international offerings) to be sent to the CSRC for review and final listing approval.

The approval process in China rapidly escalates into a race, on the one hand, with time and market conditions and, on the other, with a bureaucratic process that is outside of both time and market conditions.[20] Every transaction has its stories of how domestic approvals were finally obtained. The general procedure involves a company representative literally camping out at the office of the particular approving agency, ingratiating himself with the official involved and ensuring that the application papers are not placed at the bottom of the official's in-box. More activist measures can also be taken to improve the speed of approval.

CORPORATE RESTRUCTURING FOR INTERNATIONAL LISTING

In early 1992, the government was just awakening to the great capital-raising potential of the shareholding system. The push for capital came from Chinese enterprise management as had been the case from the start, and they were about to see that the big money came from overseas listings.

The early 1990s continued to witness great creativity on the part of Chinese enterprises seeking, in particular, access to overseas capital. By the end of the 1980s, the Sino-foreign JVs had become a well-trodden path to gain access to technology and capital. But there were significant drawbacks to this approach: foreign partners who always wanted to do things their way. In addition, such JVs were generally not large in size.

On the other hand, if foreign capital could be acquired via overseas listings, the Chinese enterprise could receive the money directly from purely financial investors. Financial investors, as opposed to strategic investors, would not be involved in day-to-day operations. In addition, Chinese management could use the fact that their companies were listed overseas to improve their negotiating position with the government itself. Management, for example, could always argue that foreign regulators required them to act in certain ways. Then there was the money, larger amounts of it and all under company management control. In short, overseas financial capital had many positive aspects to Chinese firms.

The changing nature of China's experiment with listing can be seen clearly in the structures of the companies listed. There was a definite learning process on the part of company managers, as well as the government. The early tentative steps of discovery quickly led to the realization that a significant amount of capital could, in fact, be raised in the international markets. Failure of one model rapidly led to the development of new ideas and new models as investment bankers, responding to investor demand, pushed the experiment forward. At the same time, major international companies were experiencing a trend toward the globalization of their operations as trade barriers eased. China joined in this trend with its entry into the WTO in December 2001.

The changes in the international economic system posed a significant challenge to China. At the start of the 1990s, the central government embarked on its experiment with corporatization and listing in order to improve the productivity of individual enterprises. Enterprise management, for its part, wanted the additional capital. But by the beginning of the new century, the experiment had turned into a major government effort first to create and then to capitalize national champions, mammoth industry-wide companies seeking to compete with their global peers. Many previously independent enterprise managers suddenly found themselves a small part of a huge operation run by their previous ministerial overlords in Beijing. As China's economy grew increasingly open in the years following entry into the WTO, China would depend on its national champions to compete with other major multinational companies in the battle for global (and domestic) market share. In retrospect, the various experiments with listing during the 1990s provided the stepping stones to China's effort to challenge the world today.

The Brilliance China Case, 1992

At exactly the same time that Vice Premier Tian was speaking at the Shenzhen exchange, work had begun on China's first overseas listing, Brilliance China Automotive. In the history of all Chinese restructurings and listings, Brilliance set a speed record – six months – listing on the NYSE on October 7, 1992, on the eve of the establishment of the CSRC and the announcement of trial listings on the SEHK. The offering itself caused a furor domestically and internationally and, to say the least, demonstrated the great potential for overseas listings. To that point, the government did not truly believe that a Chinese company could be created that met the requirements of overseas regulators, especially the NYSE. Nor were there domestic regulations that took such listings into consideration. At the time, regulations only considered B-share listings and even these were in their infancy (and brief heyday): Shanghai Vacuum Tube had been completed only in November 1991. Consequently, the Brilliance IPO came as a shock to the many uninvolved parts of the government.[21]

The corporate structure that made Brilliance possible, in fact, took into consideration the incompleteness of Chinese corporate law, as well as the requirements of the U.S. Securities and Exchange Commission and the NYSE listing rules. It broke the ground that made possible a number of copycat NYSE listings, including China Ek-Chor Motorcycle (1993), China Tire Holdings (1993), and Yuchai Diesel (1994), and it was even adapted for the China Telecom IPO in 1997 (see Figure 5.5).[22] Today, this structure remains useful for offshore venture capital firms seeking to exit from their onshore investments.

By 1994, the direct listing of Chinese SOEs on overseas exchanges, whether New York or Hong Kong, had become the principal accepted path to onshore equity investment. As a result, the Brilliance structure fell out of use. This was

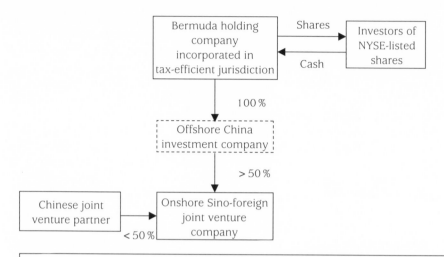

By the late 1980s, regulations on Sino-foreign joint venture companies had become quite transparent, making this offshore sale of an onshore investment possible. The listing structure requires that the offshore China investment company have management control over the China joint venture (equity ownership > 50%). The original offshore investor in the first step transfers the investment to the Bermuda holding company. This holding company is a specialized vehicle established to hold only the 100% of the original > 50% joint venture investment. From an accounting viewpoint, the holding company must consolidate the entirety of the Chinese joint venture due to ownership and management control. Thus, investors view a consolidated entity when the holding company issues new shares to the public, although they are actually only buying indirectly a piece of the holding company's equity interest in the Chinese joint venture.

FIGURE 5.5   The Basic Indirect Overseas Listing Structure.

largely because, at best, it gave offshore investors an indirect and somewhat complicated interest in Chinese companies. At worst, the CSRC did not like it: the structure provided an escape hatch from its scrutiny, since such transactions took place entirely offshore.

The Capital Iron and Steel Case (Shougang), 1993

The halcyon days for Shougang, at the time China's most politically correct steel mill, followed Deng Xiaoping's visit in the spring of 1992. Later on, visitors were always shown a massive oil painting of the legendary Shougang boss, Zhou Guanwu, in close discussion with Deng during a walk on the plant grounds. The point being made was clear and Zhou did get two things he wanted badly: his own bank – the Huaxia Bank – and an extension of terms for Shougang's contract responsibility system.[23] In 1992, he didn't think he needed an overseas listing: the contract responsibility system was more than enough to finance the company's needs. Instead, the listing went to the reputedly second-tier Maanshan Steel (*Magang*). In early 1993, when Zhou finally understood the clear advantages of a listing, he went for approval "by the shortest route possible" but he failed. So much for the timeless power of art.

But not giving up, he sent his son, Zhou Beifang, to Hong Kong. There, his son, in partnership with one of Deng's sons, proceeded to popularize "back door" listings (see Figure 5.6). Free of the political and bureaucratic constraints of the Chinese system, the two sons created a string of interlocking listed companies that issued shares in exchange for assets held by Shougang domestically. Shougang Concord Group became the prototype for China's 1997 Red Chips.[24]

This worked for a time, but was quickly judged as being ideologically untenable. The acquisition of "state assets" in return for paper shares in an overseas entity – that is, the transfer of the state-owned assets to an overseas non-state entity – was believed by certain parts of the government to be a great loss (*zichan liushi*). It was then only a matter of time before something was cooked up to stop Shougang. In this case, Zhou the Younger was arrested for corruption – he had allegedly lost a pile in the casinos of Macau. Shortly after his arrest, but after a suitable period, his father gracefully retired, attended the 1994 People's Congress as a delegate from Beijing, and dropped from sight. Shougang lost its political clout to the extent that now, on the verge of the Beijing Olympics, the polluting steel mill is being chased out of town.

The back door listing structure, however, has remained useful. It is especially popular in China's domestic markets, where reputedly private companies acquire listed SOEs on the verge, at last, of becoming a special treatment (ST) share. With this political cover, the private owners can at last get financing. It is ironic that Shougang had used private back doors to protect

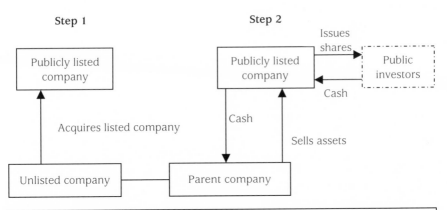

In Step 1, an unlisted Hong Kong company acquires control of a Hong Kong publicly listed company. This offer must be acceptable to shareholders and the regulators. Once management control is achieved, the listed company proceeds in Step 2 with a share offering. The attractiveness of the offering to public investors lies in how management portrays its business strategy and how the assets to be acquired will lead to increased profit (and presumably a higher share price). If the offer succeeds, the publicly listed company's management buys the disclosed onshore assets from its ultimate parent in China, which receives much-needed cash.

FIGURE 5.6 Back Door Listing with Share Offer.

itself, one of the great SOE groups, while these days companies make use of publicly owned back doors to protect privately owned companies.

Typical SOE Restructuring and Listing for International Listings

The problem confronting the investment banker[25] in China is to identify a non-corporatized SOE that has the potential to complete an international offering. The difficulty lies in the reality of an SOE, as described previously. Some potential transactions – for example, Wuhan Iron and Steel – were notable because in the end the enterprise and the state could not be pried apart without threatening the viability of the SOE itself. A more recent example of this problem is Petrochina, which, despite significant labor unrest in the Daqing oilfield, nevertheless proceeded to list in early 2000. To this day, Daqing workers excluded from the listed company continue to petition the central government for redress.[26]

Typical Early SOE Restructuring Methods

In the beginning of the overseas listing experiment, restructuring was relatively simple. Guided by the investment bank's view of the market, companies carved out the productive heart of the SOE and established it as a "company," leaving the uneconomic remainder to the "parent" SOE. This was a major issue for the first major H-share deal in 1993, Shanghai Petrochemical. Here the central government owned the company, but the Shanghai government was compelled under duress to assume responsibility for all social security-related liabilities associated with the company's retired worker population.

This approach worked once, but not twice. As a further example, in the Maanshan Steel transaction, also 1993, the bankers and company management created a lean steel company comparable in most respects to its Western peers. This was done, as is almost always the case, by excluding tens of thousands of redundant workers in preparation for the listing, leaving them in the parent holding company. But the parent, after the listing of the productive company, had limited cash flow with which to support the workers, causing significant difficulties. In contrast, before the listing, the cash flow of the "good" company was sufficient to support them all at a certain survival level, but of course at the expense of profitability by non-Chinese standards. Beginning just after the listing, these redundant workers began slowly migrating back to what by then had become the listed company. The results were predictable: the company's expenses bloated out and, combined with a poor market for steel products, drove the listed company into years of extremely poor profitability and losses. But at least the people had something to eat. This general problem, which is illustrated by Figures 5.7 and 5.8, quickly became evident to the people responsible for putting up the money to buy SOE shares: they didn't like it, since the value of their investments decreased. But it was also evident to the Chinese authorities themselves. They didn't like it either: it caused social problems.

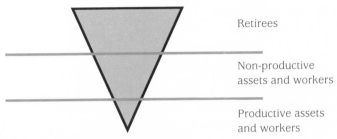

Retirees

Non-productive
assets and workers

Productive assets
and workers

FIGURE 5.7 An SOE Prior to Restructuring.

Consequently, the challenge became more complicated for the bankers suggesting a restructuring. Not only did bankers have to sift through an enterprise's business to find the most profitable part; they also had to ensure that the parent itself had sufficient cash flow to support what was left behind. This sort of balancing act was not easy and accounts in part for the high failure rates in the fourth group of listing candidates (see Chapter 6).

Second Wave of Restructuring Methods, mid-1990s

It is not surprising, therefore, that the so-called infrastructure companies became a fad during the mid-1990s. These "companies" satisfied the needs of both the Chinese government and investment bankers. First of all, the Chinese had few good stand-alone companies that increasingly sophisticated investors would put their money down for. Second, the bankers, for the same reason, had run out of deals: individual SOE restructurings didn't work. There had to be something new and there was: toll roads and then infrastructure companies – for example, ports.

Anywhere else in the world, such projects would have been financed by debt, whether from banks or the bond markets. But in China, the banks couldn't – or wouldn't – lend enough, and project financing was a non-starter for a variety of reasons, not least of which was the government's concern that

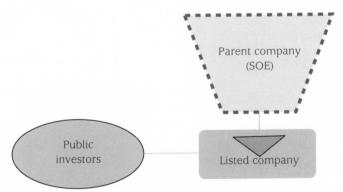

FIGURE 5.8 A Post-restructuring Listed SOE.

the loan or bond principal might not be repaid. Nor was the domestic bond market a viable alternative, for the same reason. The only financing alternative left was equity, whether from JV investors or from the public equity markets.

There were only two problems: there were no companies as such to start with, only the provincial Bureaus of Communications; and, in many instances, there was no profit either. But both problems were easy to solve: create a new company to hold a package of assets. These assets – for example, highways – could become tollways. Tollway revenues over a 10-year period could be easily projected, and investors sold a notional piece of it. What remained to be done was to concoct a tariff structure. This assumed, of course, that the roads were used and, if used, people actually paid (or collected) the tolls. Compared to the social engineering challenges of a real SOE, however, this was much easier work for the banker and all others involved in the process. These deals, illustrated by Figure 5.9, were similar to the power company transactions that were attempted in the early days of the listing experiment.

The key to making this collection of assets profitable was the tariff structure applied to it. This structure defined the fees associated with usage of the asset, whether it was a highway, a power plant, or a water treatment facility.

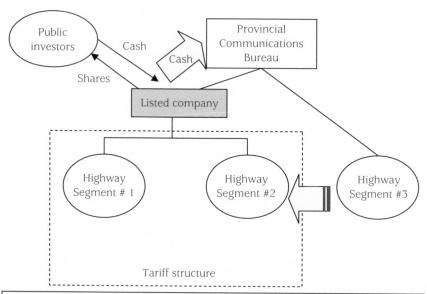

The Provincial Communications Bureau creates a subsidiary which becomes the listed company (ListCo). The Bureau contributes Highway Segments #1 and #2 to the new company in return for shares. At the same time, a tariff or toll structure is agreed to and put in place that covers all ListCo highways. To attract investors, the Bureau agrees to sell to the ListCo Highway Segment #3 and the ListCo agrees to buy at a fully disclosed price using the listing proceeds. On listing, the ListCo buys Highway Segment #3 and the Bureau injects it into the ListCo, thereby increasing revenue and profit.

FIGURE 5.9 The Typical Listed Infrastructure "Company".

The tariff was basically a contract between the "company" that was formed to manage and operate the assets and the governmental agency that had built the same assets and transferred them into the company. Once this tariff formula was agreed to, it became a simple matter of engaging a proper consultant who could develop credible volume projections, multiply by the tariff, and figure out how much revenue the new company would earn. No need for social engineering at all. The basic structure illustrated in Figure 5.9 was used by a number of companies, including Jiangsu Expressway (Nanjing to Shanghai), Chengyu Expressway (Chengdu to Chongqing), and Zhejiang Expressway (Shanghai to Hangzhou). All power company listings have used the same structure as well, including Shandong Huaneng, Beijing Datang, Huaneng International, and last and certainly least, the unfortunate Shandong International.

There were, however, a number of problems with this approach. First, since prices and costs change due to inflation, the tariff formula should also change to ensure profitability. But such changes, as well as the original tariff structure, were subject to the purview of the State Price Control Bureau. The Bureau's glorious role was to stand on the side of the "people" to ensure that the market economy did not gouge them. If the Price Control Bureau didn't agree to a proposed structure or increase, then there was no structure or increase. As an absolute rule, Price Control Bureaus did not like and did not accept anything resembling a set formula that could be used to calculate a tariff for anything beyond one year. Such formulas would have robbed the Bureau of its choke hold. This is what did so much damage to power company listings.

Prior to this equity financing experiment, tolls and costs were of course charged to users for water or power. But such prices were not calculated in relationship to the possibility of a defined set of assets generating a profit. Infrastructure projects for the most part were not even independent accounting units.[27] But with a formalized tariff structure in place and the company's shares offered to investors at a price reflecting a future projection of revenue, earnings, and return on capital, the Price Control Bureau could wreak havoc by refusing to adjust tariffs in accordance with unexpected increases in costs. This would have less impact on a bond price (as long as interest and principal was paid on time), but would kill share prices since they reflect expectations of earnings growth.

In short, the infrastructure company, with the exception perhaps of power companies, was nothing more than a tariff structure wrapped around a number of related or even non-related assets masquerading as a company. At the least, an SOE was a company even if undefined. Infrastructure equity financing was simply municipal bonds by another name (and without the principal payback). By the fifth group of listing candidates in late 1998, some municipal governments desperate for money and short on viable assets had thrown in everything but the kitchen sink – heating plants, ring roads, ports, water treatment facilities, breweries. They packed it up under a holding company owned by a government agency and called it "XYZ City Infrastructure

Development Co. Ltd." In fact, these so-called companies were little more than spun-off pieces of local governments. There was no true differentiation between the company and the state-planned economy.

Already, at this early stage in the mid-1990s, it was clear that the original policy motivation for international listings had not worked out. The idea that international markets could pressure the reform of SOEs might be true, but the restructuring of SOEs was a difficult social issue. The overseas listing process at this point was revealed for what it was: an opportunistic funding vehicle for state infrastructure projects.

The Red Chip Wave, 1996-97

The Red Chip structure represents a combination of Shougang's offshore company listing and the asset injection strategy of the infrastructure companies (see Figure 5.10). The structure had its heyday in the brief period before the retrocession of Hong Kong to China in late 1996 and the first half of 1997. Sponsorship by major municipal governments led investors to believe that the state would continuously inject choice assets, and therefore profitability, into what was, in

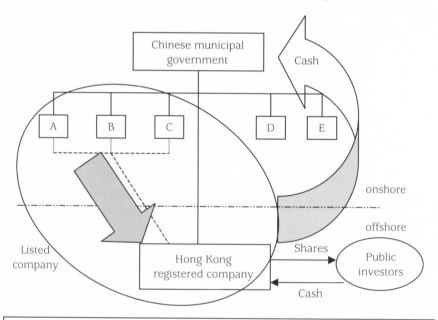

A municipal government will always have a Hong Kong registered company (or maybe a few). With the help of bankers and accountants, a proposed ListCo is created. The ListCo need not at the time of offering actually own a majority stake in the assets (A, B, and C) the government would contribute. But the proposed structure and *pro forma* financial statements must be judged attractive to investors before the Hong Kong company commences the offering. On completion of the offering, the cash payment and the injection of assets takes place simultaneously. Assets D and E remain for future secondary offerings and injections.

FIGURE 5.10   Red Chip Listed Company.

effect, the municipality's directly owned listed company. And the markets wildly welcomed listings by Shanghai Industrial, Beijing Enterprises, Tianjin Development, and others with oversubscription levels of over 100 times. It seemed for a time that China had found a sure-fire way to monetize its assets without all the dire social restructuring that individual enterprise listings necessitated.

But after the initial frenzy, things didn't develop as expected, for a variety of reasons. First, the Red Chips were collections of whatever assets the respective municipal government controlled that were profitable (after a real audit). For example, Tianjin Development included port facilities, a winery, and an Otis Elevator JV, among other assets. For that matter, Beijing Enterprises included the Badaling portion of the Great Wall. Investors ultimately could see little synergy to such conglomerates. Second, even China's best cities don't control an endless supply of profitable assets, no matter how restructured. So, the promise of endless profit growth through asset injection proved a pipedream. Finally, it is clear after modest reflection that these types of Red Chips, like the infrastructure companies, were an equity version of what in the United States are called municipal bonds.

Entire Industry Packaging and Listings, from 1997

The China Telecom (now named China Mobile) IPO in October 1997 changed the entire corporatization game in China. Raising over US$4 billion,

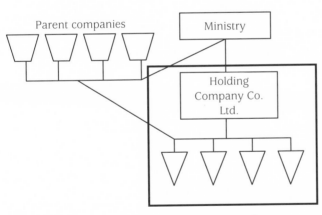

Bankers and accountants work with a ministry to select which enterprises under its supervision will be packaged under a holding company and listed. Each of the selected enterprises must be individually restructured and stripped of unproductive assets and people. The core operations are then individually audited and assets appraised. At the end of this stage, the financial books of each enterprise are consolidated into the books of the new company, the proposed ListCo. The process is repeated until the final financial statements appear attractive from a listing point of view.

FIGURE 5.11 Whole Industry Packaging.

China Telecom was the first listing of an entire industry, or at least a large part of it (see Figure 5.11). This was followed in 2000 by the listings of China Unicom, PetroChina, Sinopec, and, in 2001, China Aluminum. These were all huge companies encompassing most major enterprises in their respective industry. Their offerings raised huge amounts of capital – China Unicom, for example, raised US$5.1 billion. China's national champions began to take shape.

These restructurings incorporate ideas from the Red Chip and infrastructure transactions, but improve on them. Red Chips, as mentioned, were conglomerates of similarly owned assets, but the assets were in different industries. There seemed to be no synergy other than common ownership. The infrastructure companies were also packages of assets and in the same industry. But the key shared characteristic of these assets – steady income – was more supportive of a bond transaction than equity. This was overcome to some extent by asset injections, as was also the case with the Red Chips: new assets added revenue and profit and this could drive share prices upward. At the end of the day, however, a provincial transportation bureau has plans for only so many miles of tollways. The entire industry offerings comprised enterprises in the same industry, under the same supervisory organ (*zhuguan bumen*), and included further asset injections. These were true companies in concept at the time of their listings, even if further management efforts were required to consolidate and rationalize control after the offerings.

The attention given the major international listings and the fact that these have involved the state sector almost exclusively has obscured much of the activity in China's domestic listed and non-listed markets. These are the true locus in which the sorting out of the ownership of China's previously state-owned companies and assets takes place. This redistribution of ownership rights is negotiated in a process wholly compartmentalized from the public markets. As a result, there are significant consequences for the public stock market, as discussed in Chapter 8.

CHAPTER 6

The Fortunate Few: Listed Companies

Based on the Constitution, this law has been set to adapt to the needs of establishing a modern enterprise system, regularize corporate organization and actions, protect the legal rights of the company, its shareholders and creditors, maintain economic order, and advance the development of a socialist market economy.

Chapter 1, Article 1, Company Law, December 29, 1993

By the early years of the new century, over 1,400 Chinese companies have completed listings. Generally speaking, there are two broad categories of listed companies: the A and B shares listed domestically, and the H shares and the Red Chips listed internationally.[1] Domestically listed A-share companies have tended to be small and unfocused, with a variety of businesses under their corporate umbrella. Typical A-share IPOs have been in the US$50 million range, representing a 25% ownership interest. Disclosure, both at the time of listing and on an ongoing basis, tends to be extremely poor despite increasing CSRC efforts. The B-share companies – although restructured similarly to H-share companies – represent a continuing headache to the Chinese government. International investors have long since abandoned the market and, despite the market opening to them in 2001, even Chinese investors lack enthusiasm.

The H-share companies are SOEs which have gone through restructuring designed to complete an international IPO, one leg of which is always in Hong Kong. Transaction sizes generally have ranged between US$100 and US$600 million, with a handful of jumbo deals completed in recent years. In contrast to the A-share companies, H-share companies represent focused businesses which have (or have had) strong positions in China's domestic economy. The Red Chips are Chinese-controlled companies domiciled in Hong Kong, with the majority of their operating assets located in China. They tend to be conglomerates in which the Hong Kong entity acts as a funding vehicle for its Chinese operations or for the further acquisition of mainland assets.[2]

The listing process for international Chinese issues is similar to that of all internationally listed companies and depends on the regulator as to specific requirements. Success at listing also depends on the attractiveness of a company's prospects to investors. Back home, A shares are not subjected to the same quality of due diligence and restructuring. The domestic approval procedures an A-share company goes through prior to listing, however, are comparable to those of international Chinese issuers.[3] The primary market is the "hot" market in China. Because of an administrative pricing mechanism, Chinese investors expect huge trading profits in the first day or so after an IPO. Therefore, like the hi-tech craze in the West, investors pay little attention to the fundamentals of a particular company and treat most A-share companies as a commodity.

At the start of the listing experiment in 1992, there was a deliberate screening by the government. What it considered the best companies were offered on international markets, while smaller ones, or those that failed at an international listing, listed domestically. This has always been a bone of contention with the local exchanges, which complained of the government's failure to provide better product to domestic investors. Since 2000, this complaint has been resolved somewhat by allowing a few of China's major internationally listed companies to raise Renminbi by Shanghai listings. This has yet to change the nature of the markets.

A further complaint about the government's approach has come from international investment bankers who wanted to work as they did in other markets. The bankers wanted to select, rather than be told, which companies to list. From 1992 until December 1999, the government, acting through the CSRC, leaked, then formally announced, lists of overseas listing candidates. This led, of course, to marketing frenzies as bankers chased after the very limited number of permitted deals. Following the issuance of the Securities Law in 1999, however, bankers have gotten what they wanted. There are fewer, although larger, deals and, except for the top three to four firms, most bankers no longer have a place in the market.

Identifying Chinese companies that have listed in recent years has been made difficult since the brief hi-tech fad led to numerous overseas listings. Several hi-tech Chinese companies – for example, AsiaInfo – incorporated themselves offshore and listed on NASDAQ alone. It is nearly impossible, therefore, to identify their number. Also, in 2001 the SEHK revised its Hang Seng China-affiliated Corporations Index by excluding many illiquid shares. All in all, identifying overseas listed Chinese companies is no longer straight-forward. This attests to the fact that Chinese overseas listings have become more routine. At the same time, the Chinese corporate landscape over the past 10 years has become more complex. No such difficulty exists for China's domestic listings.

This chapter provides an historical review of how the listing process worked for companies listed in both the international and domestic markets. It then characterizes the companies that successfully listed in both markets, with a particular emphasis on A-share companies and their ownership structure. The data provided lead to the conclusion that the listing experiment has failed in its primary objective of effecting changes in corporate governance, a topic that the next two chapters develop in depth. It closes with examples illustrating how presumably private entrepreneurs have approached China's domestic markets.

WHO DECIDES WHO LISTS?

The 1999 Securities Law significantly changed the candidate selection process for public listing. The top-down quota system in place from the early 1990s was modified in 2000. By eliminating the distribution of quotas to ministries and local governments, securities firms now have broad scope to identify and develop listing candidates.[4] For its part, the CSRC plays a more passive role in reviewing listing application materials. For domestic applications, its focus now is to ensure they are in full compliance with all laws and regulations. For international offerings, however, the CSRC retains its full powers of approval. Once fully reviewed and approved, the candidate company must wait its turn to list. This can take some time unless, of course, the State Council provides the trump card permitting the company to jump the queue, as is normally the case for international offerings.[5]

Despite these changes, ministries and local governments continue to play a role in identifying and approving the selection of companies. Without doubt, the CSRC still works to conform the total amount of share financings with the numbers in the State Plan. It is worth reviewing the workings of the old system, since this is what has created the shape of the markets for Chinese companies today.

The "Big Book"

The listing process, as should already be clear, is highly bureaucratic and time consuming. Foreign bankers working in China look forward to at least a two-year gestation period before their babies face investors. Their domestic brothers and sisters fare little better. There is a one-year period following incorporation, a further approval, then a long wait in the queue. The process begins when the State Planning Commission (now the State Planning and Development Commission) lays out its annual financing plan for state enterprises in its "Big Book" (a.k.a. the State Plan). This ties into the overall enterprise production and sales plan. The proceeds from the sale of securities are also considered vis-à-vis commercial bank borrowing and foreign direct investment, on the one hand, and the state's monetary policy and foreign exchange reserve balances on the other. After the calculations and political balancing, a total figure representing capital to be raised by listings is entered into the State Plan. Once in the Plan, this figure becomes bureaucratic reality, market conditions or not.

Favored Industrial Sectors

In the old process, as with today's listings, the SPC considered which industrial sectors should be the beneficiaries of equity financing. It bases its considerations on such questions as which sectors are the current strategic focus of the state, which are open (or closed) to foreign investment, and so on. Until 1997, the SPC coordinated with SCRES for such decisions.[6] This top-down approach was balanced somewhat by the active lobbying of the SPC by ministries and provincial governments seeking to ensure financing for their favorite companies.

At this point, it becomes clear again that the non-state sector was never considered. It was never included in the Plan and was explicitly excluded by the 1992 Standard Opinion. How, then, could it be included in the deliberations about which enterprises should be able to finance through the sale of securities?[7] Equity financing in the primary market for Chinese companies, in either the domestic or the international markets, has been the domain of SOEs alone until very recently. This is the reality, notwithstanding the original 1992 lip service paid by the SPC and SCRES that "... the appropriate development of other economic entities should be permitted and encouraged ..."[8] Sino-foreign JV enterprises were outright forbidden in the beginning to establish shareholding companies. For those that had already succeeded in doing so before 1992, foreign shareholdings were either frozen as "overseas legal person" shares, which could not be listed or traded, or with approval could be issued as B shares. Such approval, however, did not come formally until 2000.[9]

The positive words spoken about the "non-state" sector at the recent 16th Party Congress suggest that this picture may change. In addition, the CSRC has said that domestically domiciled foreign companies may list on the Shanghai exchange, but none have yet taken up this offer.

Taking the Plan Apart: Listing Quotas

The second step in the former process involved the disaggregation of the national quota, a decision taken by the State Council, itself an indication of how political the process was. The CSRC then allocated the listing quotas among administrative agencies or regional governments across the country. For central government enterprises, quotas were distributed among the various industrial ministries. For locally owned enterprises, quotas were distributed to the provincial governments. Quotas were by regulation not allowed to be sold or traded.

Quotas for domestic and international listings in the past were defined in different ways. Quotas for A shares were distributed in terms of the number of shares to be issued. For example, a province might receive a quota for 200 million shares. The local government then allocated this out to one or more enterprises. This, in part, explains why the average IPO size on the A-share primary market has been so small. For H shares, the quota was defined in terms of the number of candidates. Thus, a ministry might be allocated one or two positions that it could fill from its system of enterprises across the country. In contrast to the A-share methodology, this did not limit the economic size of the potential transactions.

Once the CSRC had distributed the quotas, extremely active lobbying on the part of the enterprises and their respective government owners began. Here again, the State Plan had an impact. Investment funds are designated in the Plan for a five-year period and then divided into annual amounts. These amounts were further divided between the central and provincial-level governments. The central government has tended to invest large amounts in what, therefore, became large enterprises. Provincial governments have tended to spread their money more widely within their jurisdictions so that the size of local enterprises was somewhat smaller. Local governments, with less investable funds, established what became known by default as "small and medium-size" enterprises.

Who is the State "Owner"?

The success of an enterprise in obtaining a listing quota and, particularly, an H-share quota therefore depended on which part of the "state" its owner represented: the local, the provincial, or the central government. Stacking the odds against local enterprises was the fact that provincial governments held the approval authority for non-central government enterprises (of course, subject to CSRC and the regulating ministry review and agreement). Since provinces generally held only one quota for international listings and a limited number of A shares at one time, it was clear from the start which enterprises would be favored: the central and provincially owned enterprises. This again makes clear why non-state enterprises were extremely unlikely to have the opportunity to list. They do not belong to the state.

INTERNATIONAL PRICING

The issue of pricing involves a general explanation of how equity shares are valued. The value of a company's equity reflects the value of its future profit potential. If a company has exceptionally strong growth prospects, and therefore profitability, its shares should be worth more than a company with low growth prospects, all things being equal. The process of arriving at a judgment on future profit potential involves an understanding of the markets, the industry, the company, its management, and so on. Bankers build a financial model of the company incorporating this understanding, projecting its operations three to five years into the future.

Based on this and a comparison with similar companies whose shares are already listed and trading, a prospective price/earnings (P/E) ratio is arrived at.[10] Bankers then ask potential investors to consider an investment in the company based on this ratio (typically expressed in a narrow range of share price) and to place orders for the shares. The point is that the value of equity lies in how management directs the company's future performance and in how investors view the company's prospects. The past, while useful as a reference, is history. The approach, briefly described here, is the one used for overseas listings of Chinese companies. It is also the overwhelmingly predominant approach to equity valuation in use throughout the world's markets, the hi-tech fad notwithstanding. Until recently, Chinese practice was significantly different.

A-SHARE PRICING

In contrast to international practice, the Chinese used an administrative approach to pricing at the start. A-share pricing until 1997 was based on a for-mula which applied a 15 times P/E ratio to the average of the company's past three years' profit.[11] The intention was good: avoidance of excessive valuations based on over-optimistic projected earnings by overly optimistic (and greedy) bankers. There are many things wrong with this approach. First, reliance on past performance is obviously no guarantee of future performance. For exam-ple, earnings may have declined from a high to a low level during the three-year period, suggesting that the company was encountering difficulties. Second, a mandated multiple of 15 provides equal treatment for all companies, but companies are not equal. In the Chinese context of poorly trained and underregulated investment bankers, however, this approach made some sense. Due to the huge demand for new IPO shares, it is likely that secu-rities firms would have priced companies at much higher levels. This would have increased banking fees as well as proceeds to the issuer. It might, how-ever, have harmed retail investors and resulted in the party bugaboo of social unrest.

Beginning in late 1997, the CSRC experimented by adjusting the pricing mechanism to place a 70% weighting on the earnings of the most recent financial year and 30% on projected earnings.[12] Then, in late 1998, the CSRC encouraged domestic underwriters to use a P/E ratio higher than the figure resulting from the 1997 formula if the company's performance justified it. This was done for the first time in early 1999 with the IPO of China World Trade Center on the Shanghai exchange. Priced at nearly 20 times, the company's shares traded up only 15% in the days following the listing, in contrast to the typical 70–100% jumps in price of typical A-share listings (see Appendix 6). In short, in this case the issuer enjoyed a higher price and larger proceeds, while less was left on the table for investor profit. There were no complaints by investors.

Following this, on July 28, 1999, the CSRC announced the experimental adoption of the international approach to pricing domestic IPOs and selected the Konka Group Ltd. as the pilot issuer (see Box 6).[13] These new rules apply only to potential issuers with more than RMB400 million in total equity capital.

BOX 6   Konka: China's First Bookbuilding Experiment, 1999

The Konka Group is China's second-largest maker and exporter of color TVs and home appliances. It listed A and B shares in 1992 on the Shenzhen exchange. In order to raise funds for expansion, Konka planned to offer 80 million new shares in a secondary offering. Thus, investors were not limited to existing shareholders. China International Capital Corporation (CICC) was selected by the CSRC as the lead underwriter for this ground-breaking transaction. At the time, no firm had ever attempted to use international pricing methodologies in China's domestic market. It was highly uncertain how Chinese investors would respond.

In designing a bookbuilding offering structure, CICC had to consider the characteristics of potential investors. New share financings have a negative impact on the secondary market price of existing shares, as the new shares will dilute existing investor interest. This was typically dealt with by offering a deeply discounted price to existing investors. CICC and the CSRC, however, hoped that by directing efforts at new shareholders, the discount to the secondary market price could be reduced, benefiting Konka. At the same time, a reduced discount would benefit existing shareholders. Thus, the marketing focus was on new shareholders, particularly institutional and corporate shareholders, who might hold the shares for a relatively long time.

CICC arranged the first ever domestic roadshows in Beijing, Shanghai, and Shenzhen, including the traditional investor luncheon presentations and meetings with all 15 securities investment funds. Inexplicably, the State Council suddenly ordered a three-month lockup on investments by corporations. This greatly reduced corporate interest in the transaction. The roadshow, therefore, was turned into a purely media event to stimulate retail investors. CICC and the company were flooded with questions about the pricing process. The media was used extensively to educate investors on how bookbuilding worked, its merits, and, of course, why they should participate. Two hours before the close of the 10-day institutional offering period, CICC had received orders for only 10% of the offering. It appeared that the experiment might fail. Then orders poured in. At the end of the day, orders for just over 80 million shares, or more than 100%, had been received.

Compared to a typical A share, the subscription level was very low. The orders, however, provided sufficient support at an acceptable level of between a 4% and 7% discount to market. A satisfactory price range for the online retail offering could, therefore, be set. The online retail offering was a success: an oversubscription rate of 6.3 times the number of available shares. Adding in the institutional orders, there was a total demand of 7.3 times the 80 million available shares with upfront cash deposits of almost RMB9 billion. After discussion, CICC recommended that Konka accept, and it did, a per share price of RMB15.5. This represented a 5% discount from the previous 20 days' average daily closing price. In comparison, the average discount for similar offerings in 1999 was 34%. In short, the company left an estimated 29% less on the table, representing what had been the investors' upside potential.

BOX 6 *continued*

The strategy was judged a success based on the post-listing performance of Konka's shares. In the few days after the listing, Konka's price edged up slightly, while the overall market fell 1%. Also a positive sign, the volume of shares changing hands settled down after the first day to a range of 1.5 to 2.5 million per day. This method has now been used, with mixed success, for all large domestic listings – for example, BaoSteel (2000) and Sinopec (2001).

For issuers with less than this amount, the 1997 pricing method still applies. Like international practice, the 1999 regulations allow the underwriter to set a price range and seek investor bids based on it. The offering price is based on the results of an "offline (*wangxia*)" bookbuilding process directed at institutional and corporate investors, of which more later.[14] Bankers use the final negotiated price for the "online (*wangshang*)" retail offering.

In theory, this methodology should bring pricing in line with market demand, which, in turn, should reflect a more accurate valuation of the company's prospects. Given the Chinese situation, however, this may not be the result, at least in the near term. For this approach to work properly, investors need to be able to arrive at their own judgment of the company's value. At present, neither the few institutional investors, nor the corporate investors and certainly not the average retail investor, have this capability.[15] This new approach adopted for Konka and several companies thereafter dovetails with the CSRC's effort to make Chinese bankers, accountants, and legal advisors assume greater responsibility as required by the Securities Law. While in the past, it had, in effect, assumed all pricing responsibility based on its final approval authority, the CSRC now assumes a more passive role. What effect this will have on valuation and on how the market over time will react remains undetermined. In the case of Konka, however, the reaction was vivid – the underwriter received death threats and there was much criticism of the new pricing method in the press.[16]

ANALYSIS OF LISTED COMPANIES

As expected, a review of more than 10 years' listing experience indicates that the screening process has naturally had the effect of streaming Chinese companies (see Table 6.1). The larger and more prominent national or provincial companies have first listed shares internationally, while the smaller, locally owned companies have listed on domestic markets offering either A or B shares. To illustrate this point, through 2002 there were 128 H-share and Red Chip offerings, raising approximately US$43 billion or an average of more than US$336 million per offering. In contrast, there were 1,318 A-share

TABLE 6.1 Trends in Chinese Company IPOs, 1990–2002

	90	91	92	93	94	95	96	97	98	99	00	01	02	Total
H shares				6	9	2	6	16	2	3	6	8	14	72
Red Chip			5	8	12	2	4	12	1	5	2	3	2	56
Overseas	**0**	**0**	**5**	**14**	**21**	**4**	**10**	**28**	**3**	**8**	**8**	**11**	**16**	**128**
SH A	8		22	71	68	15	103	85	53	46	88	78	67	704
SH B	0		9	13	12	2	6	8	2	2	1	0	0	55
Sub-total	8		31	84	80	17	109	93	55	48	89	78	67	759
SZ A	2	4	18	52	42	9	100	121	52	50	49	0	1	500
SZ B			9	10	5	10	9	8	3	0	5	0	0	59
Sub-Total	2	4	27	62	47	19	109	129	55	50	54	0	1	559
Domestic	**10**	**4**	**58**	**146**	**127**	**36**	**218**	**222**	**110**	**98**	**143**	**78**	**68**	**1,318**
Total	10	4	63	160	148	40	228	250	113	106	151	89	84	1,446

Sources: Stock Exchange of Hong Kong and Wind Information.

offerings, raising US$81 billion or an average of US$61 million per offering. The scale is similar for B shares, for which there have been 114 offerings raising US$4.1 billion or an average of US$36 million per offering.

International Issuers

There have been two major groups of international issuers: (1) Chinese companies that have listed their shares directly on overseas markets – that is, H shares; and (2) the so-called Red Chips.[17] It is difficult to identify which Hong Kong-listed companies are, in fact, Red Chips other than by reliance on the Hong Kong Red Chip Index. As noted previously, however, the Red Chip Index has been reconfigured to exclude less liquid shares. Hence, this discussion on international issuers deals only with those Chinese companies that have directly listed on overseas exchanges, including in all cases Hong Kong. In addition, the discussion is divided into the pre- and post-Securities Law periods.

Pre-Securities Law Listings, 1992–99

Since 1992 there have been five formal groups of overseas listing candidates totaling 86 companies. Practitioners commonly referred to each group as a "batch." Candidates were selected based on the importance of certain sectors to the state. It is not surprising, therefore, that the largest number of candidates have come from the infrastructure and power sectors (25), followed by transportation (9), petrochemicals and chemicals (9), and steel (6), as shown in Table 6.2. Taken together, these names account for 57% of the total during this period. Of this group, 58%, or 44 companies, successfully completed their listings.

TABLE 6.2 H-share Listing Candidates by Industrial Sector, 1992–99

Industry	No. of Candidates	No. Listed	Success Rate (%)
Infrastructure	13	5	38
Power/Power Equipment	12	7	58
Transportation	9	5	56
Petrochemicals/Chemicals	9	6	67
Consumer Products	7	4	57
Steel	6	3	50
Building Materials	5	3	60
Agriculture/Foodstuffs	5	2	40
Pharmaceuticals	5	2	40
Machinery	5	3	60
Real Estate	2	1	50
Energy	2	1	50
Non-ferrous Metals	2	1	50
Other	4	1	25
Total	**86**	**44**	**51%**

The ownership of these entities reflects the planned investment environment described previously. Of the 86 entities, 28 were owned by the central government, 43 by provincial governments, and 15 by local governments, or about two for each provincial-level government. For the most part, the central government has invested in and, therefore, "owned" all the major power plants, steel companies, airlines, and automakers. Provincial governments have had a difficult time, especially at the end of the period, finding candidates of an economic scale sufficient to interest international investors. A visit to Sichuan, the richest inland province, in 1996 found the local securities authorities wringing their hands in frustration. They could not identify even a single suitable candidate to use their quota, although in the Fourth Batch the province put forth a highway, one steel company, and a chemical fertilizer plant.

Reviewing the composition of each batch by industrial sector and considering the element of time over which the batches came out brings out a number of interesting points (see Table 6.3). First, the power and transportation sector was heavily favored by government policy in the first two batches and most candidates successfully listed. This sector, however, completely failed to attract investors in later groups. This reflected a dearth of appropriate candidates in the case of transportation (trucks, planes, and railways) and a significant lack of investor interest in power. Even so, the government continued to push power companies in the Fourth Batch. Investor lack of interest

TABLE 6.3 Listing Candidate Batch Composition by Sector

Industry*/ Date of Batch	10/1992	1/1994	9/1994	12/1996	12/1998	Total
Petrochemicals/ Chemicals	3 (3)	2 (2)	0	4 (1)	0	9 (6)
Machinery	2 (2)	1 (1)	0	2 (0)	0	5 (3)
Steel	1 (1)	2 (0)	0	3 (2)	0	6 (3)
Consumer	0	1 (1)	3 (3)	3 (0)	0	7 (4)
Power/Power Equipment	1 (1)	6 (6)	0	5 (0)	0	12 (6)
Transportation	0	7 (5)	1 (0)	1 (0)	0	9 (5)
Building Materials	0	3 (2)	0	2 (1)	0	5 (3)
Pharmaceuticals	0	0	2 (2)	3 (0)	0	5 (2)
Infrastructure	0	0	1 (1)	5 (4)	7	13 (5)
Energy	0	0	0	2 (1)	0	2 (1)
Agriculture/ Foodstuffs	1 (1)	0	0	2 (1)	2	5 (2)
Real Estate	0	0	0	2 (1)	0	2 (1)
Non-ferrous Metals	0	0	0	2 (1)	0	2 (1)
Other	1 (1)	1 (0)	0	3 (0)	0	4 (1)
Totals	**9 (9)**	**22 (17)**	**7 (6)**	**39 (12)**	**9 (0)**	**86 (44)**

*Number of successful listings in parentheses.

reflected the unpredictability of government tariff policy regarding what should be a steady, predictable industry. Petrochemical and chemical companies were steadily represented, but the failure rate was significant in the later batches as investors became wary of the volatile regulatory environment of the sector. Consumer-related enterprises grew over time but experienced significant failure in the Fourth Batch as the government selected companies that were makers of commodity computer and TV components. Following the listing of the Shenzhen Expressway in 1995, local governments China-wide concluded that highways, ports, and whatever else a city or province might call "infrastructure" could be slung together in a "company" and listed. There was, thus, an explosion of follow-on deals, accounting for the high number of infrastructure candidates, most of which failed.

Given the process, candidate selection often failed to match market interest. Misinterpretation of what the market signaled, the momentum of the process itself, and a continuing feeling that anything could be sold combined to make possible the Fifth Batch. This was the last batch before the passage of the Securities Law and the emergence of the industry-wide, national champion restructurings. This last group of nine companies consisted of seven so-called infrastructure companies and two agriculture concepts, conceived after the unexpected success of First Tractor in early 1997. The abrupt failure in early 1999 of a group of farms in Heilongjiang Province, which were cobbled together, put a quick end to this "concept."

The monolithic character of Fifth Batch companies and its failure indicated the close of the first period of the overseas listing experiment. By the end of the decade, nearly all major companies in the favored policy sectors had been selected as candidates: there simply were no more "good ones" to choose from.[18] Moreover, international investors had been burned so often by listed companies failing to deliver on their promises that they had lost interest in what was, after all, an SOE reform effort. Finally, Chinese companies themselves had lost interest in the process: it was too difficult and frequently failed to deliver the expected money, while preparatory expenses ran into the millions of dollars. Instead, they were turning their sights to the domestic A-share markets where they could complete listings with far less difficulty and fewer questions asked.

The geographic origin of each candidate underscores the point just made. A quick review shows a preponderance of candidate enterprises from China's more prosperous coastal provinces and cities (see Table 6.4). It is not surprising that the country's capital, Beijing, accounted for 14% of the total number of candidates, followed by Guangdong with 12%. Beijing, though it is not heavily industrialized, is the home of the central government, while Guangdong is the most dynamic regional economy. Taking them all together, the coastal provinces (excluding Liaoning and Guangxi) accounted for 49% of total candidates. Contrariwise, the northeast accounted for only 12% despite its heavily industrialized character, leaving the interior provinces at only 39% (30% excluding Sichuan).

The skewed geographic breakdown only partly reflects the government's failed policy to reduce the economic gap between China's east and west.[19]

TABLE 6.4 Listing Candidates by Geographic Location of Incorporation

Province	No. of Candidates	No. Listed
Beijing	12	9
Guangdong	10	7
Shandong	7	5
Sichuan	7	5
Shanghai	4	3
Anhui	4	3
Liaoning	4	1
Zhejiang	3	1
Jiangsu	3	3
Henan	3	2
Tianjin	3	1
Jilin	3	1
Heilongjiang	3	1
Hebei	3	0
Hubei	3	0
Yunnan	2	1
Jiangxi	2	1
Other (one each)	12	0
Total	**86**	**44**

The rest is economic reality. Take the northeast, for example; although it is highly industrialized, most enterprises are in the heavy industrial sector, have outdated plant facilities, and would not make a profit even under Chinese accounting practices consistently applied. Jilin, for example, receives the majority of its tax revenues from First Auto Works (FAW). At the time FAW's name came up as a potential listing candidate, every investment bank in the world beat a path to its door. But no amount of work, even by the best investment banks (and everyone gave it a try, egged on by an anxious Ministry of Machinery), could come up with an idea that would lead to a successful listing of even a part of the company. There simply was nothing of interest to international equity investors. FAW later listed part of its operations on the A-share market. The northeast is China's Rust Belt, and until the economy in that region turns around or new industries emerge, it is simply impossible to use publicly raised international capital to finance such enterprises.

At least this was true on an enterprise-by-enterprise basis: the industry-wide restructurings solved this problem. But even for A- and B-share listings, which have lower standards, less than 11% of all companies listed on the Shanghai exchange come from the northeast. So, despite appearances, identifying appropriate listing candidates for the international market has been an extremely difficult task. If Shanghai could come up with only five candidates during this six-year period, the difficulties elsewhere are easy to imagine.

Post-Securities Law Listings, from 2000

The failure of the Fifth Batch is the consequence of going to the same group of international investors for too long with the same idea – a minority stake in a single SOE. The China Telecom (now known as China Mobile) IPO in October 1997, however, represented a break with the past. This wasn't just because the telecom sector globally was beginning to be viewed as highly attractive. An important feature of the listing was the national character of the company: China Mobile represented the first industry-wide restructuring in China's reform program. No longer were investors being asked to finance a chopped-up SOE operating in some distant and unknowable province. China Mobile offered a near monopoly situation to investors in the dynamic mobile telephone industry. The more than US$4 billion this IPO raised internationally woke up the State Council to a new possibility: list entire ministry systems. If listing was all about financing, then this was clearly the way to go.

Work began almost immediately on the oil and gas sector, the aluminum industry, and continued on the telecom sector, with the results shown in Table 6.5. Over the next three years, six centrally owned companies listed, raising nearly US$15 billion. This figure almost equals the US$15.7 billion that represents the total raised by all overseas IPOs completed through 1999. Moreover, this list does not include the more traditional listing of Bank of China's Hong Kong operations completed in July 2002, which raised US$2.1 billion. Nor does it include the huge secondary offering done by China Mobile in 2000, which alone raised US$6 billion. Vice Premier Tian Jiyun, who commented in 1991 that IPOs would be a good way to raise money, would have been proud, if not ecstatic.

While such blockbuster IPOs have been few in number, there remain in planning China Netcom, the competitor of China Telecom, portions of a recently restructured power industry, railways, insurance and, perhaps, media. Big companies make for potentially big capital and, the government hopes, national champions that can compete internationally. The failure of China

TABLE 6.5 Post-Securities Law National Champion IPOs, 2000–02

Company	Industry	Date	IPO Size (US$ Bn)
PetroChina	Oil and gas	4/7/00	2.9
China Unicom	Telecoms/mobile	6/22/00	5.1
Sinopec	Oil and gas	10/19/00	3.3
China National Offshore Oil	Oil and gas	2/28/01	1.4
China Aluminum	Mining and processing	12/12/01	0.5
China Telecom	Telecoms/fixed line	11/8/02	1.4
Total Capital Raised			**14.6**

Telecom to complete its IPO in late 2002 as originally structured, however, has cast a shadow, if only on the telecoms sector.

Domestic Issuers

There have been two periods of intense domestic market activity (see Table 6.1 earlier in the chapter). The 1992–early 1994 period was the first time China was really "hot" as far as world capital was concerned. The outburst of energy following Deng Xiaoping's Southern Excursion was the principal stimulus restoring China's confidence in the future after the dark days of 1989. The markets were next extremely quiet in the second half of 1994 and during all of 1995, due to high interest rates and various administrative measures aimed at controlling inflation. Such measures included a near halt in approvals for new IPOs, given their potentially inflationary impact. The markets rebounded in 1996, as the country emerged from the danger of hyperinflation, and in 1997, due to the enthusiasm generated by Hong Kong's restoration to China, with both years recording almost one IPO per day. Overall market performance is reviewed in Chapter 9.

Geographic Origin: The Coastal Provinces Dominate

Listed companies sorted by geographical area show a marked affinity for their local exchange (see Table 6.6). This is not surprising, since the exchanges originally served enterprises in their respective administrative regions only. On the Shenzhen exchange, 115 issues, or 22.4% of all listed companies, are from Shenzhen or Guangdong, while only 18 Guangdong companies have chosen or been apportioned to list in Shanghai. The contrast is even more

TABLE 6.6 Geographical Distribution of Domestic Listed Companies by Exchange

	Shenzhen	%	Shanghai	%
Guangdong	115	22.4	18	2.8
Shanghai	0	0.0	130	20.1
Beijing	23	4.5	41	6.3
Jiangsu	22	4.3	41	6.3
Shandong	27	5.3	34	5.3
Sichuan	30	5.8	31	4.8
Hubei	28	5.4	30	4.6
Liaoning	29	5.6	28	4.3
Zhejiang	10	1.9	43	6.7
Fujian	18	3.5	24	3.7
Others	212	41.2	226	35.0
Total	**514**	**100%**	**646**	**100%**

Source: *China Securities and Futures Statistical Yearbook 2002,* FY2001 data.

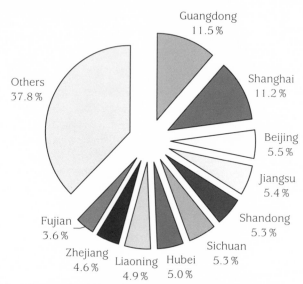

FIGURE 6.1 Geographical Distribution of Domestic Listed Companies.
Source: China Securities and Futures Statistical Yearbook 2002, FY2001 data.

marked in the case of Shanghai-based companies: 130 Shanghai companies are listed in Shanghai and none in Shenzhen. If Zhejiang and Jiangsu are included into a "Greater Shanghai" area, then the distribution is even more noticeable. Taken together with Shanghai, the East China region accounts for over 33% of all Shanghai listings, but only 6.2% of Shenzhen listings.

For the country as a whole, the top 10 provinces account for 62.2% of all listed firms, with Guangdong firms best represented, closely followed by Shanghai (see Figure 6.1). Even though these 10 provinces account for the bulk of all listed companies, all 31 provinces are represented on the stock exchanges: Tibet and Ningxia, two of the country's poorest provinces, have two and three listed companies, respectively. This result is similar to that of the H shares and reflects the reality of China's uneven development.

Industry Classification: Manufacturing Predominates

The published data on the breakdown of listed companies by industry is somewhat confusing, as many Chinese companies suffer from not having a clear core business (see Table 6.7). Management commonly expands into a variety of businesses, creating corporate structures that are described as "large and complete, small and complete." Similar to the Red Chips, such companies cannot be classified as conglomerates but more as "conglomerations."

As can be seen, "old industry" companies dominate the exchanges. While such companies may be more in favor after the collapse of the Internet

TABLE 6.7 Distribution of Listed Companies by Industrial Sector

Industry	% of Listed Companies
Agriculture	2.6
Mining	1.5
Manufacturing	57.8
– Food	4.7
– Textiles	5.2
– Wood Products	0.2
– Paper	2.1
– Chemicals	11.0
– Electrical	3.0
– Metals	9.1
– Machinery	15.6
– Medical	5.5
– Other	1.4
Energy and Water	3.8
Construction	1.7
Transport	4.1
IT	5.1
Wholesale and Retail	8.4
Banking and Finance	0.6
Real Estate	2.9
Social Services	3.4
Media	0.9
Conglomerate	7.2

Source: China Securities and Futures Statistical Yearbook 2002, FY2001 data.

bubble, in China, unfortunately, old industry really means "old, inefficient SOEs." It is worth noting that in 2001 the financial sector as a whole represented only 0.60 % of all listed companies. This figure changed somewhat in 2002 with the listing of China Minsheng Bank and China Merchants Bank, both large transactions.

Market Capitalization: Small Market Cap Stocks

Given the previous quota-based method of candidate selection, small market capitalization stocks dominate both exchanges (see Figure 6.2). The market capitalization calculation[20] used in this section is based on the total number of shares, A shares, and non-tradable shares at the A-share price.

The international calculation methodology in China gives a spurious result herein called "notional" market capitalization. Since approximately 70 % of the shares of a listed company are by regulation untradable, the market capitalization calculation is exaggerated. A quick and easily arrived at estimation simply assigns the market value of shares to the free float, or amount of listed and traded shares. For example, Shanghai has 307 companies each with a notional market

FIGURE 6.2 Listed Companies by Total Market Capitalization (1,190 companies). *Source:* Wind Information, November 30, 2002.

capitalization of US$200–400 million. It would be more accurate to say the range is US$70–130 million, or only 30% of the notional capitalization. Looked at this way, some 72% of listed companies have a capitalization of less than US$130 million. As will be discussed in Chapter 8, even this figure is too high.

The largest companies by market capitalization are listed on the Shanghai market (see Table 6.8). The government's deliberate policy has been to develop Shanghai in the expectation that the two exchanges will at some point merge. As part of this policy, since late 2000 there have been no IPOs on the Shenzhen exchange, while several jumbo issues have gone to

TABLE 6.8 Top 10 Companies by Notional Market Capitalization

Rank	Company	Listed Overseas	US$Bn
1	Sinopec	Yes	27.6
2	China Unicom*	Yes	7.0
3	China Merchants Bank	No	6.6
4	BaoSteel	No	6.4
5	Huaneng Power International	Yes	6.1
6	Jiangsu Expressway	Yes	5.4
7	Pudong Development Bank Co.	No	4.7
8	China Minsheng Banking Corp.	No	3.5
9	Shenzhen Development Bank Co.	No	3.0
10	Shanghai Lujiazui Finance and Trade Zone Development Co.	No	2.6

Source: Wind Information, September 27, 2002.
Note: *Represents China Unicom parent.

Shanghai. Of the top 10 companies, only one, Shenzhen Development Bank, is from Shenzhen.

Free Float: Typically Less than 50%

Since the limited amount of tradable shares is a critical issue in understanding the domestic market, it is worth breaking down the listed companies based on their free float. Free float is defined as the total number of all tradable shares – A, B, and H shares – expressed as a percentage of the total number of shares – that is, non-tradable plus tradable shares. As Figure 6.3 illustrates, the vast majority, some 82%, of listed companies have a free float lower than 50%. Out of the top 10 largest companies by market capitalization, only Shenzhen Development Bank has a free float greater than 50%; other major companies range between 20% and 30%.

This same information can be looked at from the top down. Figure 6.4 illustrates the share structure of both markets. In this view, listed A shares account for only 28–37% of the total number of shares outstanding. The limited free float has a significant impact on company as well as market valuations, as discussed in Chapter 8. This section aims only to define the structure of company shareholdings.

Tradable Share Ownership: Highly Concentrated

Free float and market structure information draw a broad picture that can be illuminated by looking into the actual number of shareholders per company. This data ties in with further information on the topic of investors included in the next chapter. It is worth an initial look here, however, since it says a lot

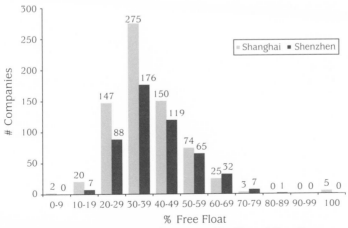

FIGURE 6.3 Listed Companies Categorized by Size of Free Float.
Source: Wind Information, November 30, 2002.

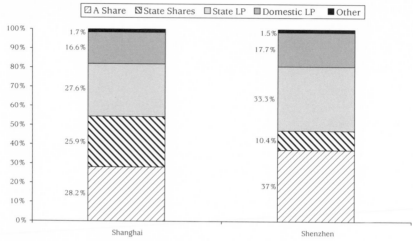

FIGURE 6.4 Share Structure of Shanghai and Shenzhen Exchanges.
Source: Wind Information, November 30, 2002.

about the nature of listed companies per se, but, more broadly, is a source of many of the problems with the market.

As previously discussed, Chinese listed companies have two broad categories of shareholders: (1) those who hold A shares; and (2) those who hold non-tradable state or legal person shares. These two categories may overlap, with legal person shareholders also participating in the A-share market. The average A-share investor, in contrast, is unaware of, and excluded from, much of the activity in the markets for LP shares.

In general, holders of A shares own only around 30% of the notional market capitalization of any given firm. This 30%, however, represents an aggregate number: at the company level, there is a very uneven distribution of listed share ownership. Figure 6.5 shows the distribution of companies on the combined markets by the total number of A-share shareholders. Of the 1,182 companies that provided data at the end of September 2002, 64% had fewer than 50,000 shareholders and fewer than 5% had more than 150,000 shareholders.

The Shenzhen exchange also provides exact shareholder information categorized by amount of shares held. The exchange defines six categories: shareholders holding less than 1,000 shares, from 1,000 to 5,000 shares, from 5,000 to 10,000 shares, from 10,000 to 50,000 shares, from 50,000 to 100,000 shares, and greater than 100,000 shares. In addition to the number of shareholders in each category, the Shenzhen exchange also provides the percentage of total A shares controlled by a given category.

The data for a sample company, Beijing Center Gate Technology, show that its 375 million A shares were held by nearly 351,000 different accounts

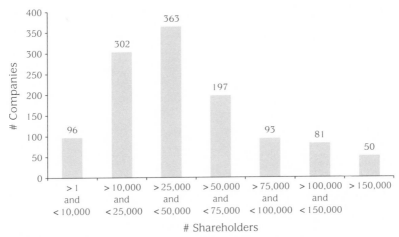

FIGURE 6.5 Distribution of Companies by Number of A-share Holders.
Source: Wind Information, September 27, 2002.

(see Table 6.9). So far so good; there appears to be a very broad distribution. But shareholders with less than 1,000 shares, the moms and pops the market is noted for, control only 24% of the A shares, even though they represent 70% of the total shareholders. In this example, less than 10,000 accounts control 33% of the outstanding A shares. As shown in the following chapter, the larger accounts may represent far, far fewer shareholders than the figure indicates. China's professional market players on an individual basis actually control hundreds, and perhaps thousands, of separate accounts.

The overall market is similar to the Center Gate picture. Over 58% of all A shares trading in Shenzhen are controlled by only 9% of the shareholders

TABLE 6.9 A-share Holdings and Company Control, Beijing Center Gate Technology

Total A Shares (000)	Total Holders	Category	No. of Holders	%	No. of Shares (000)	%	Avg. Holding (Shares)	Value of Avg. Hldg., (RMB)
374,840	350,650	<1,000	246,092	70	88,837	24	361	4,577
		1,000~5,000	95,090	27	159,307	43	1,675	21,243
		5,000~10,000	6,173	2	38,983	10	6,315	80,076
		10,000~50,000	3,012	1	48,729	13	16,178	205,142
		50,000~100,000	180	0	11,620	3	64,556	818,567
		>100,000	103	0	27,363	7	265,663	3,368,611

Source: Shenzhen Stock Exchange, FY2001.

TABLE 6.10 Shenzhen Market A-share Holdings and Company Control

Shareholder Categories		% Holders	% Control	Avg. Value (RMB)
1,000 shares		52.8	10.2	4,562
1,000–5,000		38.1	31.1	20,495
5,000–10,000	9%	4.3	11.3	73,932
10,000–50,000	controls	3.6	22.3	214,777
50,000–100,000	58%	0.7	8.7	770,220
>100,000		0.4	16.3	2,971,951

Source: Shenzhen Stock Exchange, FY2001.

(see Table 6.10). Although representing the vast majority, the small sharehold-ers control very little of the actual listed stock. It should be remembered that these figures are for the A-share component only, or 37% of Shenzhen capi-talization. Consequently, this 9% controls about 21.5% of the total notional market capitalization and 58% of the A-share free float.

Exchange data permit the shareholder structure to be further refined. The picture that develops out of Table 6.11 shows a direct relationship between company market capitalization and state control. The larger the market capitalization, the greater the state's holdings. As might be expected, the smaller companies with values less than US$200 million on the whole have 34.2% state ownership as compared to companies over US$800 million, where the state holds over 50%. This is not strange, as most of the large listed companies have come in the last three to four years and the diluting cycle of stock dividends and rights offerings has yet to begin. Moreover, the largest companies, those with a market capitalization over US$5 billion, have been listed since 2000, the year the Shenzhen exchange ceased doing IPOs. This explains why Shenzhen has no jumbo companies.

The table represents a snapshot of a single moment. For example, Unicom in October 2002 completed its domestic IPO. Of the 25% interest it sold, 14% remains locked up with "strategic" investors; the other 11% trades as A shares.

TABLE 6.11 State Control of Listed Companies by Market Capitalization

(US$ Mn)	Shanghai				Shenzhen			
	State %	LP %	Other %	A/B/H %	State %	LP %	Other %	A/B/H %
<200	34.2	23.4	2.0	40.4	33.7	24.4	0.8	41.1
200–400	38.4	20.8	2.0	38.8	40.7	17.0	1.2	41.1
400–600	38.7	19.9	3.7	37.8	39.8	16.5	2.4	41.3
600–800	45.6	15.7	1.9	36.7	40.1	20.0	1.2	38.6
800–1,000	55.5	9.4	4.6	30.6	52.9	10.4	3.8	32.9
1,000–5,000	56.0	11.1	0.0	32.9	56.4	9.2	0.0	34.3
>5,000	69.0	10.8	0.0	20.3	–	–	–	–

Source: Wind Information; "State" includes state and state LP shares.

At the end of the six-month lock-up period, the 14% LP shares magically become A shares in the central registry and can be sold. In the course of one day, the company will go from state ownership of 89% to 75%. Similarly, with the passage of time, rights issues and stock dividends slowly whittle down the state holding in relative terms, as can be seen by reading the table from the bottom up.

For simplicity's sake, the same six categories have been combined to form two, one showing holdings of less than 5,000 shares and the other showing holdings of greater than 5,000 shares (see Figure 6.6). In the figure, a small dot represents small shareholders as against their total percentage of ownership in a company. The figure shows at a glance that smaller shareholders typically control very little of any given company.

What does all this mean? An average company's listed A shares will generally be held by about 50,000 different accounts. More than 50% of accounts will hold less than 1,000 shares. These moms and pops control less than 30% of the company's A shares. On the other hand, the top 10% of accounts, or 5,000 accounts, will hold about the same 30% stake. Since many large investors control numerous accounts, it may be realistic to say that perhaps only a few hundred or a thousand distinct individuals control the public trading of many listed companies.

This situation has nurtured a market where insider trading, price manipulation, and off-market back-room deals have become an accepted part of the business. For the companies, on the other hand, even this high concentration of holdings provides limited leverage on management, unless it is combined with control of the non-tradable shares. Company ownership structures are segmented by market, so how can issues of corporate governance, for example, be

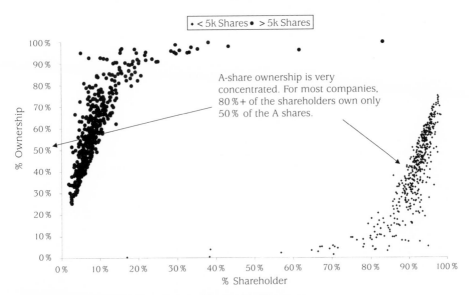

FIGURE 6.6 Shenzhen A-share Ownership Distribution.
Source: Shenzhen Stock Exchange, FY2001.

advanced? What goes on in the public market has little to do with or impact on what goes on in the OTC market, and vice versa. The simple conclusion from this is that the objective of SOE reform via corporatization and listing has yet to succeed.

Public Market Valuation Overview

How the market values companies is a critical topic introduced here and discussed more fully in Chapter 8. At the end of September 2002, some 1,129 companies had positive P/E ratios distributed as shown in Figure 6.7. It is obvious from the figure that Chinese companies have high P/E ratios – that is to say, the shares appear to be very valuable. The average market P/E is 40–50 times, but one in seven companies has a P/E over 100 times. High P/E valuations, however, do not necessarily signify successful, highly profitable companies. In fact, the reverse is far more likely. High demand for a limited amount of shares will result in a high price per share. If this is combined with low earnings per share, the calculation will show a very high P/E ratio.

In fact, listed companies do have low earnings per share, which have been declining for the past three years, as shown in Table 6.12. This information ties back into market capitalization values discussed previously, again indicating that the market is inaccurate in its primary role of assigning values to companies.

The CSRC has long been aware of this reality. At the start of the overseas listing effort, a few H-share companies were allowed subsequently to issue A shares domestically in order to raise local currency. Due to increasing disparities in valuation, as well as problems involved in diluting down international investors,

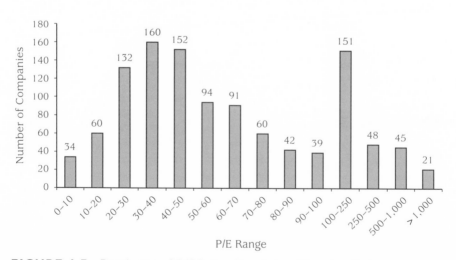

FIGURE 6.7 Distribution of P/E Ratios, Shanghai and Shenzhen Exchanges.
Source: Wind Information, September 27, 2002.

TABLE 6.12   Earnings per Share, Shanghai and Shenzhen

	12/31/99	12/31/00	12/31/01	6/30/02
Number of companies	1,158	1,186	1,199	1,191
Number with positive earnings	1,077	1,090	1,048	1,023
Number with negative earnings	81	96	151	168
Average positive EPS (RMB)	0.273	0.267	0.230	0.107
Average negative EPS (RMB)	−0.645	−0.544	−0.671	−0.108

Source: Wind Information.

dual listings halted in the mid-1990s. Since 2000, however, major overseas listed companies have again been permitted to list domestically. A major reason for this has been the CSRC's effort, first, to improve the quality of investment for domestic investors and, second, to list companies with a large float, making manipulation impossible. A problem has arisen, however, surrounding the fact that domestic investors pay a higher price for much the same rights as international investors. In this case of cross-border valuations, the market is again segmented, this time by the inconvertibility of the local currency.

A NOTE ON PRIVATE COMPANIES

As is well known, private companies have found it difficult not only to list, but also to raise funds from local banks. This is not to say that there are no private or family-owned listed companies. A recent study lists what are called the top 100 richest entrepreneurs in China, all of whom control listed companies.[21] Based on this study, the unlisted companies owned by these men control 10.7% of all listed firms in terms of notional market capitalization.[22] This seems fairly high but, in fact, it is the lowest percentage in non-Japan Asia and is significantly lower than other Chinese markets: for Hong Kong the percentage is 66.7% and for Taiwan, 48.2%.[23] Given the fundamental premise of market development over the past 10 years and the reality of China's economic system, this fact is not surprising.

The study analyzed some 1,033 listed companies, of which 134 were non-state-controlled. These 134 companies fell into two major categories: (1) those that have listed directly (54 firms); and (2) those that have become listed by buying an already listed company, which is then restructured (80 firms). Non-state or private control of both types of companies is typically concealed behind a number of non-listed legal entities. These are controlled either by an individual or family members or even management and employees (see the case of Dazhong Taxi in Chapter 8).

While many believe that private companies are the key to genuine growth in the economy and the stock market, the companies included in the sample still suffer from some of the same structural problems of the market. The 100 private owners in the study control 91 different listed firms in which the non-tradable shares account for 57.1% and employee shares for 2.5%. Only 21 of the 91 companies have more than a 50 % free float. The financial illiquidity due to the plethora of non-tradable shares plagues the private firms just as it does state holders of legal person shares. The segmentation of shares, on the other hand, creates the conditions by which private entrepreneurs can gain controlling ownership of a listed vehicle.

In summary, the selection process for both international and domestic listings has been, and largely continues to be, part and parcel of the state planning process. Consequently, the market is dominated by companies in which some part of the state holds the controlling, although over time diluted, stake evidenced by shares that are publicly untradable. The international market has seen two stages of development. In the first stage, 1992–99, restructured SOEs and offshore companies with domestic assets were the primary issuers. By 1999, this source was virtually exhausted and the experiment almost at a standstill. The 1997 IPO of China Mobile, however, broke new ground, showing that entire industries could be restructured and listed, raising huge amounts of new capital. The year 2000 witnessed a number of industry listings, including China Unicom, PetroChina, and Sinopec. There are, however, a limited number of industries that can be restructured in this way and this stage may now be coming to a close itself.

In the domestic markets, a Chinese listed company is likely to be an SOE from the Shanghai, Guangzhou, or other coastal region, operating in the manufacturing sector. It will likely have an estimated market capitalization of much less than US$200 million priced at a P/E ratio of 40–50 times. In reality, this market capitalization, no matter how calculated, is overestimated. Only 30 % of the company's shares will be freely tradable and they will be held by about 50,000 different accounts. However, one-third of its total A shares will be held by as few as several hundred individuals. Despite this concentration, A shares typically represent a minority stake in a company; how they are held or traded has very little impact on the company. A part of the company, or in some instances even a majority share, has been sold off, but control has not (yet) been affected. It is little wonder that corporate governance is a major issue in China. Listed companies receive no market discipline in terms of openness, integrity, and efficiency other than, as in some cases recently, at the direct administrative intervention of the CSRC. If the market cannot effect change in a company, then the objective of the reform effort of the past decade has failed.

It has failed because the quality of listed companies has remained low even for those with years of listing experience. The history of the quota system has allowed companies with the greatest need and best connections to dominate the market, rather than those with solid economic performance or the prospect of it. This is to be expected given the reality of how China has developed. On the other hand, Shanghai and Guangdong companies have received the bulk of the fund-raising opportunities. The fact that these are the most economically dynamic regions in China suggests that their companies should also be the best. This may well be true; however, the market has not provided the mechanism to make them even better. This comment extends to most, but not all, overseas listed companies as well.

CHAPTER 7

Where Have All the (Retail) Investors Gone?

To say that the Chinese stock market is a market for the masses with 60 million investors is not true.

Hu Shili, Chief Editor, *Caijing* magazine, October 2002

The truth is that investors in China's stock markets are very few but very rich. The analysis in this chapter suggests that as few as one million people control the A-share markets. And that may be an overestimate. This is not a market characterized by tens of millions of retail investors, as the often-repeated 66 million investor account figure suggests. The major players are individual professionals with the securities houses and gray market fund management companies stirring the soup. The government has sought to offset the power of such speculators by trying to build a base of "institutional investors," including fund managers, insurance companies, and pension funds. Following China's entry into the WTO, foreign participants are also being welcomed to play a part in the market either as joint venture partners in a brokerage or as Qualified Foreign Institutional Investors (QFIIs). Such investors are preferred, since they would seek out the best companies and hold shares for long-term gains, thereby promoting the market's development. Market participants may become somewhat more diverse in the near term, but they have yet to have the expected impact. Things will not change substantially until after full WTO implementation in 2007. At that time, foreign participants will presumably be able to enter without restriction.

On its surface, retail investors dominate the market, accounting for 99.6% of total A-share account holders. Domestic and foreign media continually cite the huge number of accounts as evidence of, first, the market's retail character; second, the Chinese public's widespread investment interest; and third, the danger of social unrest should the market collapse. It would appear that there is a day trader in almost every urban household and that the market is a great success. This image has played a large role in the popular view of the Chinese juggernaut. These numbers, however, are wholly misleading, as was partially shown in Chapter 6. Not only are they misleading, they are outright wrong.

This chapter is divided into two sections. In the first, a review of investor data seeks to determine just how many investors are truly active in China's A-share market. This further develops the data on company shareholders presented in the last chapter. The second section looks at the relative influence on the market of its various participants, from speculators to insurance companies.

HOW MANY INVESTORS?

China has recorded remarkable growth in stock-market participation judging by the number of open accounts (see Figure 7.1). There has been a 30-fold increase in open accounts over the past decade. In the past three years alone, accounts have increased by 50%. It appears, therefore, that there is a growing and broadening participation in China's markets by the Chinese people themselves. Nothing could be farther from the truth. The likelihood is that there are not more than five to 10 million actual holders of shares and less than one million active traders, and this is before adjusting for "ghost" accounts. The findings, summarized in Table 7.1, not only significantly alter the perception of the market, they also have serious policy implications.

First Cut: Double Counting

Existing regulations permit an individual to open only one account with a given exchange. It is, therefore, reasonable to assume that most investors, and certainly all active investors, open both Shanghai and Shenzhen accounts to allow stock

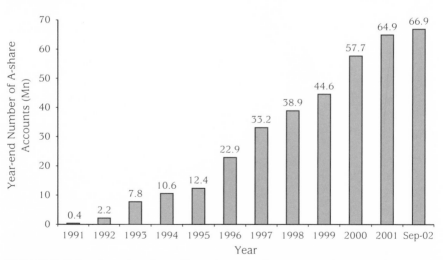

FIGURE 7.1 Growth in Open Share Accounts, Shanghai and Shenzhen Exchanges. *Sources*: Shanghai and Shenzhen stock exchange data, September 30, 2002.

TABLE 7.1　Investor Accounts, Summary Findings, Shanghai and Shenzhen Exchanges

Item	Estimated No. of Accounts (000)
Shanghai and Shenzhen open accounts	67,000
1. Discount for double counting	33,500
2. Active accounts	6,600–22,000
(assuming holding range of three and 10 shares)	
3. IPO participants	2,000
4. Open B-share accounts (before adjustment)	400–800
5. Widely held company shareholders	200–700
Average listed company shareholders (60% of companies)	50
Ghost account factor, assume 500 accounts per player	
▪ IPO participants adjusted	4
▪ Active accounts adjusted	13–44

trading on both exchanges. The number of accounts at both exchanges is very similar for any given year, supporting this assumption. This double counting immediately halves the number of investors to approximately 33 million distinct individuals with one Shanghai and one Shenzhen account apiece (see Table 7.2).[1]

This number still appears to be quite healthy, but other factors combine to decrease it dramatically. First of all, there are undoubtedly many dormant accounts set up by investors who took a punt, lost money, and withdrew from the market. This is particularly the case in Shenzhen, as discussed below. Other accounts are used only to invest in IPOs, after which the investor sells out the shares to lock in profit. Then there are the illegally opened multiple accounts, called "ghost (*guihu*)" accounts, used by major market players (*dakuan, dahu,*

TABLE 7.2　Accounts Opened at the Shanghai and Shenzhen Exchanges

Year	Shenzhen (000)	Shanghai (000)
1991	257	110
1992	1,051	1,112
1993	3,533	4,225
1994	4,830	5,730
1995	5,550	6,825
1996	10,896	12,033
1997	16,098	17,068
1998	19,011	19,916
1999	21,900	22,722
2000	28,300	29,433
2001	31,650	33,367
September 30, 2002	32,454	34,415

Sources: Shanghai and Shenzhen stock exchange data.

and *zhuangjia*), securities companies, and gray market investment consulting companies to manipulate share trading. It is well known that such players use false identification sourced by sending professional runners into the countryside to buy peasant identity cards in bulk (discussed further below).[2] In addition to these improperly used real ID cards, brokerage offices convenience major players by opening multiple accounts as well.

While difficult to verify or quantify, rumors circulate of large, active investors controlling thousands of different trading accounts. As a point of reference, the previously cited case of Lu Liang, or Mr. K, exposed his personal control of over 1,500 different accounts. Many market watchers estimate that taken together, these factors decrease the number of active investors to far below 10 million, as shown in the next section.

Second Cut: Active Accounts Number Around 10 million

Data relating to active accounts sheds further light on the investor question. Table 7.3 compares the total number of accounts opened at each exchange against the total number of accounts holding shares in companies listed at each exchange. Thus, if an account held shares of three companies, it was counted three times in these data. For the past three years, there have been more open accounts than shareholders – that is, many accounts are sitting empty. As at the end of June 2002, nearly seven million accounts held no share balances in Shenzhen.[3] Shanghai ran a positive balance, meaning that accounts held shares in multiple companies.

Since an investor can be expected to hold more than one stock at any given time, a relatively accurate estimate of the total number of shareholders can be arrived at. Ignore the problem of multiple accounts for the moment. Assuming, then, that the average active investor holds three different stocks, the calculation shown in Table 7.4 puts the number of investors at a bit more

TABLE 7.3 Shareholder Account Activity, Shanghai and Shenzhen Exchanges

(000)	12/31/99	12/31/00	12/31/01	6/30/02
Shenzhen total number of accounts	21,895	28,304	31,652	32,260
Shenzhen total number of shareholders	20,446	25,223	27,049	25,460
Difference: accounts > holders	**1,449**	**3,081**	**4,603**	**6,800**
Shanghai total number of accounts	22,722	29,433	33,269	34,162
Shanghai total number of shareholders	23,192	31,013	38,956	35,207
Difference: holders > accounts	**469**	**1,580**	**5,687**	**1,045**
Total number of shareholders	43,638	56,236	66,005	60,667
Total number of accounts	44,618	57,737	64,922	66,422
Difference: *	**−980**	**−1,501**	**1,083**	**−5,755**

*(−) = accounts > shareholders

Source: Wind Information System.

TABLE 7.4   Estimate of Active Shareholders, Shanghai and Shenzhen Exchanges

Data/Assumptions	Calculation (000)
Total Shenzhen shareholders	27,049
Total Shanghai shareholders	38,956
Total holders of shares	66,005
Assume:	
Each investor holds three different stocks, then investors =	**22,002**
Each investor holds five =	**13,201**
Each investor holds 10 =	**6,600**

Note: As of December 31, 2001.

than 22 million. If an account holds on average 10 shares, then active shareholders would number 6.6 million. Introducing the double count discount, the range would be from 3.3 to 11 million shareholders. No matter what assumptions are used, the only way there can be more than 66 million investors in China is if each investor account held shares in only one company. This is most certainly not the case.

Data available for 1995 from the Shenzhen exchange throw some light on this problem. The data include the Shenzhen SEZ geographic area only and not the entire Shenzhen market. Column A in Table 7.5 shows the number of stocks held in a given account – one stock, two stocks, and so on. Column B shows the number of accounts with that number of stocks – for example, 87,784 accounts hold one stock, and so on. The final column shows the

TABLE 7.5   Shenzhen SEZ, Number of Shareholders, 1995

No. of Stocks Held (A)	No. of Accounts (B)	%	Value of Stocks (RMB Mn)	%	A x B = No. of Shareholders
1	87,784	14.9	1,705	11.2	87,784
2	308,414	52.2	2,706	17.7	616,828
3	55,643	9.4	1,468	9.6	166,929
4	38,784	6.6	1,185	7.8	155,136
5	27,079	4.6	1,055	6.9	135,395
6	19,222	3.3	980	6.4	115,332
7	14,247	2.4	913	6.0	99,729
8	10,273	1.7	783	5.2	82,184
9	7,443	1.3	705	4.6	66,987
10	5,548	0.9	538	3.5	55,480
>10*	16,647	2.8	3,227	21.1	332,940
Totals	**591,084**	**100.0**	**15,265**	**100.0**	**1,914,724**

Source: Shenzhen Stock Exchange Fact Book 1995; *assume 15 stocks.

number of shareholders using the same methodology (A × B) used by the exchanges to calculate the number of shareholders, as shown in Table 7.3.

In short, in the Shenzhen SEZ the absolute number of accounts holding at least one stock in 1995 was 591,084. Based on the exchange methodology, the number of shareholders is estimated at 1,914,724. In contrast, the total number of open accounts in Shenzhen SEZ at that time was only 1,743,244. So, at the end of 1995, on the eve of the great 1996 bull market, only 33.9% of all accounts were actually invested in the market. What does this suggest about Shenzhen in 2002? Scaling the proportions up and assuming that shareholders numbered 25 million, then there would be roughly eight million actual accounts holding a portfolio of stock, in contrast to the 32 million accounts open.[4] This, of course, does not take into account the fact that professionals hold numerous accounts.

Third Cut: IPO Participation Shows Only Two Million Active Accounts

In 2001, there were 67 A-share IPOs all concentrated on the Shanghai exchange. The absolute number of lottery participants ranged from a high of 3.1 million to a low of 27,871.[5] Of the 67 companies, 29 had less than one million subscribers, 16 had between one and one-and-a-half million, 13 had between one-and-a-half and two million, and nine had over two million. IPOs with subscribers of two million or less accounted for nearly 87% of the year's offerings. For example, Tongling Sanjia Moulding (600520) recorded 2,087,181 investors on December 31, 2001 on subscription. The stock started trading on January 8, 2002, and as of June 30, had only 8,123 shareholders. The simple conclusion is that there are typically about two million active participants in the primary market, or only 6.7% of Shanghai's 30 million-plus open accounts.

Fourth Cut: The B-share Story Points to an Even Lower Number

In March 2001, domestic Chinese investors were legally permitted to open foreign currency B-share accounts. As B shares had traditionally traded at substantial discounts to A shares, the natural expectation was that this valuation gap would rapidly disappear. This was at the outset perceived by market commentators to be a guaranteed gold mine for Chinese investors, and everyone expected a rush to open B-share accounts at the start of the run up in prices. Allowing for the passage of one year to ensure an accurate count, the question becomes, how many accounts were opened as of March 2002? The answer is: only 800,000 in Shanghai and 430,000 in Shenzhen. Keep in mind that there is double counting, with single investors opening accounts on both exchanges. Disregarding this, however, at a maximum there were only 1.2 million people opening accounts for what was a sure-win investment. Where are the investors?

Fifth Cut: Widely Held Stocks Are, in Fact, Narrowly Held

Company shareholder data previously presented in Chapter 6 help to hone the estimate further. As of September 30, 2002, there were 1,182 listed companies providing shareholder data, of which only 50, or 4.2%, had more than 150,000 shareholders. The bulk of the companies, 60%, had fewer than 50,000 shareholders. Tables 7.6 and 7.7 break out those companies with the largest number of shareholders, the so-called widely held stocks.

As an example, take Sichuan Changhong, a leading television maker that has been the most widely held stock on the Shanghai exchange for three of the past four years. In that period, the number of Shanghai accounts

TABLE 7.6   Top 10 Most Widely Held Stocks in Shanghai

	1999 Year-end	2000 Year-end	2001 Year-end	Sept. 2002 Month-end
1	Changhong 706,369	Changhong 712,433	Changhong 707,202	Changhong 653,385
2	Shanghai Petro. 325,850	Shanghai Petro. 381,208	Sinopec 549,974	Sinopec 509,646
3	Guangdong MeiYan 266,966	Pudong Dev. Bank 309,541	BaoSteel 468,091	BaoSteel 400,432
4	Qingdao Haier 250,968	Shanghai Water 300,350	Anshan Construction 381,221	Shanghai Brilliance 327,618
5	North China Pharm. 249,050	Qingshan Paper 285,044	Shanghai Petro. 344,475	Shanghai Petro. 322,326
6	Maanshan Steel 246,189	Guangdong MeiYan 283,635	Guangdong MeiYan 326,606	Guangdong MeiYan 318,885
7	Qingqi Motorcycle 243,798	Shanghai Intl Airport 283,107	Shanghai Brilliance 305,141	Qingdao Haier 300,011
8	Shanghai Water 242,710	North China Pharm. 264,331	Shanghai Water 301,335	Qingqi Motorcycle 266,853
9	Gezhouba Co. 221,484	Shanghai Brilliance 261,120	Qingqi Motorcycle 283,620	Pudong Dev. Bank 252,957
10	Pudong Dev. Bank 221,309	Minsheng Bank 257,030	Qingdao Haier 281,626	Qingshan Paper 247,868

Source: Wind Information.

TABLE 7.7 Top 10 Most Widely Held Stocks in Shenzhen

	FY1999	FY2000	FY2001	9/30/02
1	Shenzhen Dev. Bank 705,443	Shenzhen Dev. Bank 810,000	Shenzhen Dev. Bank 778,568	Shenzhen Dev. Bank 642,229
2	China Baoan Group 338,435	Beijing Center Gate 356,683	Beijing Center Gate 350,650	Beijing Center Gate 327,308
3	FAW Car Co. 297,404	FAW Car Co. 318,214	Yantai Dongfang Elec. 294,873	China Baoan Group 285,958
4	Hainan Sundiro 232,752	China Baoan Group 256,628	China Baoan Group 286,013	Yantai Dongfang Elec. 276,279
5	Shenzhen Energy Inv. 226,777	Shenzhen Energy Inv. 246,242	FAW Car Co. 260,137	Angang New Steel 262,802
6	Beijing Center Gate 225,090	China Vanke 228,620	Angang New Steel 251,573	FAW Car Co. 222,543
7	China Vanke 217,717	Hainan Sundiro 221,210	Hainan Sundiro 225,551	Hainan Sundiro 212,563
8	Panzhihua New Steel 192,503	Shenzhen Hongkai 194,159	Shenzhen Energy Inv. 217,309	Shenzhen Energy Inv. 208,427
9	Chang Ling Group 165,359	Haikou Agriculture 189,993	Beijing Shougang 208,373	Haikou Agriculture 198,748
10	Dongguan Winnerway 163,142	Shanxi Taigang Stainless Steel 187,579	Huludao Zinc Industry 207,905	China Vanke 197,425

Source: Wind Information.

increased 51.4% to almost 33.4 million, yet the number of shareholders in this presumed Blue Chip actually fell by 7.5% to about 650,000. The data tell a similar story for other Blue Chips. Even the billion-dollar new issues by major companies such as Sinopec and BaoSteel have only 500,000 investors. This does not support the credibility of 33 million active investors.

The story is the same, if not worse, for Shenzhen. Beijing Center Gate Technologies is an excellent example here. This stock was the darling of the China Internet bubble and received enormous media and government attention, touted as Beijing's answer to Silicon Valley. The stock was as hot as stocks get. Center Gate ended 1999 with only 225,000 investors, increasing only to around 350,000 at the peak of the bubble in 2000.

Sixth Cut: Rate of Account Opening: Mass Account Openings in Remote Areas?

It is difficult to substantiate rumors of individuals holding multiple accounts with other than anecdotal evidence. Facts exist to support such rumors indirectly. The Shanghai exchange provides data for daily new account openings sorted by province.[6] The information used here is not conclusive, but it is highly suggestive. For example, Gansu Province is located in China's far west and, as one of the poorest regions, is hardly a hotbed of investor activity. In February 2001, only 4,332 accounts were opened in Gansu, not many by east coast standards. What is surprising, however, is that 2,751 accounts were opened on February 15 and 1,578 on February 27, together totaling 4,329. A similar picture is seen in March, when there were only four days when new accounts were opened: two accounts on each of March 13, 29, and 30, then suddenly 3,472 on March 23. The probability that 3,400 Gansu residents picked this one day, which was not an active one on either exchange, to open an account is non-existent. Moreover, in April 2001 only four accounts were opened and in the entire month of May, none.

In contrast, Tianjin, the port for Beijing, is a wealthier city with a more active investor population. In the month of January 2001, 5,681 accounts were opened, 5,659 on one day. During March, an average of 433 new accounts were opened each day. Then suddenly, on March 22, 14,346 accounts were opened.

Gansu and Tianjin are not the only regions where this anomaly can be seen. The data show that every province has days when the total number of accounts opened surges high above the average. While some days will be busier than others, even a cursory review of the data suggests that account opening is often organized, rather than the result of organic growth. Moreover, the activity in Gansu suggests that batch processing of account opening forms is unlikely; true investors would be quite dissatisfied if it took more than one to two days to open an account. Nor were there any new regulations or market-shaking news coming out on these few active days. The reasonable conclusion, therefore, is that these were instances of organized mass "ghost" account openings by one or a small group of investors at a small number of cooperative brokerage offices. The fact that 32 of 52 brokerages in Gansu were closed down for fraudulent activities during the same period by the CSRC suggests that such investors would have little trouble finding help there.[7]

Multiple accounts controlled by one or a small group of investors, therefore, seem to be a major factor in the recent rapid growth in new accounts. While new and legitimate investors are surely entering the market, they are not doing so in the numbers implied by the account opening data.

Final Cut: Physical Constraints: 26,000 People in a Brokerage Office?

CSRC figures state that there are 124 securities companies in China operating 2,566 brokerage offices. A number of firms also provide online trading facilities or off-site terminals for their larger accounts only; online investors in 2002 totaled only 400,000. Investors placing orders in person at a brokerage office carry out the vast bulk of trading. Assuming that the 2,566 offices service 66 million investors means that an average office handles about 26,000 accounts. Excluding the inherent double counting still leaves 13,000 investors per office. It is true that trading offices can be crammed at times, but 13,000 live accounts is a physical impossibility. China's brokerage industry does not have the physical capacity, nor is the technology pervasive enough yet, to service anything near 33 million investors.

The evidence cited above is summed up quite well by Hu Shili, *Caijing* chief editor: "There are more than 60 million accounts opened in Shanghai and Shenzhen, giving rise to the claim that there are 60 million stock investors. ... Experts estimate that truly active accounts trading at least once a week number no more than four million, and those 'professional investors' who operate every day no more than one million. This figure doesn't even include 'ghost' accounts, that is, those opened by one speculator who purchases thousands of ID cards to open those accounts."[8] What she has spelled out, but not said directly, is that the true number of active investors numbers from 500,000 to two million, after eliminating the double counting, but not considering the ghost accounts. This is at most 3% of the number cited all the time in the media and, taking everything into consideration, is optimistic after all.

Why Does it Matter?

Aside from legal and regulatory issues, does this rather shocking finding matter? The answer is quite obviously, "yes," for a number of reasons. The false 66 million investor figure has a negative impact on policy decisions taken by the government. For example, the recent halt in the sell-down of state shares was largely out of concern for social stability. Even the small dilution of their holdings seemingly had the small investor up in arms. The reality, however, is that there are not enough small investors that would be hurt to have such a large policy impact. The government would be better able to take decisive measures to improve the market if it faced up to reality. Instead, a rich minority and government-owned securities firms successfully duped the government into protecting their positions.

This highly inflated number, however, gives a false sense of security to those responsible for China's markets. Although there have been periods of "share fever," the vast majority of the urban populace has not gained from the stock market. In short, the market is simply not as successful (or as dangerous) as officials have portrayed. The great majority of the Chinese people are low-paid workers with little job security. They are saving and not playing the stock market, since the government has abandoned their jobs to the free market. This explains why bank savings have increased and not been deployed in the market. Moms and pops cannot afford to invest in stocks; it is simply too risky.

Finally, these account figures mislead businesses by grossly exaggerating the potential customer base for software, periodicals, books, Internet portals, and, for that matter, brokerages. In fact, some one-third of the 22 securities firms with underwriting licenses are reported to be losing money.[9] The revised investor numbers explain this situation, the decline in exchange membership, and, most certainly, the continued industry consolidation of the past few years. Who, then, are China's investors?

WHO ARE CHINA'S INVESTORS?

China has the same general categories of investors as seen in stock markets elsewhere. Their relative importance in the A-share markets, however, is somewhat different. At their inception, the markets were largely the domain of individual investors, whether pure retail or professional. With the creation of national securities companies in 1992, trading became more institutionalized and individual professionals became prominent. More recently, the government has sought to develop an institutional investor base (see Table 7.8). According to some reports, institutional investors now account for nearly 56% of secondary market trading.[10] This section reviews current market participants in order of their influence as measured by estimated investable capital. Table 7.9 summarizes the capital amounts estimated to be held by each of the major types of market participant. As should be expected, this total exceeds the value of the free float and is about twice the value of the primary market.

Gray Market Money Managers

Until 2001, everyone knew that there was a large gray investment funds market, but its size was unclear. Then information began to leak out. By conservative estimates, such privately managed funds were thought to total

TABLE 7.8 Recent Growth in Retail and Institutional A-share Accounts

| (000) | Shanghai | | | Shenzhen | | |
Date	Individual	Institution	% Inst.	Individual	Institution	% Inst.
Dec. 1998	19,860.5	55.6	0.28	18,924.7	86.2	0.45
Dec. 1999	22,646.7	75.6	0.33	21,788.1	107.2	0.49
Dec. 2000	29,312.0	121.2	0.41	28,164.7	139.2	0.49
Dec. 2001	33,110.7	158.7	0.48	31,497.6	154.6	0.49
Sept. 2002	–	–		32,287.9	166.3	0.51
Growth	**66.7%**	**185.4%**		**70.6%**	**92.9%**	

Sources: Shanghai and Shenzhen stock exchange data.

TABLE 7.9 Investor Capital versus Primary Market Size

	Amount/Capital (RMB Bn)
Size of Primary A-share Market[1]	**500–650**
Total bank deposits (09/2002)[2]	8,400
Insurance company assets[3]	596
Pension funds[4]	60
Gray market money managers[5]	700–900
Retail accounts[6]	500–600
Securities companies[7]	200
Securities investment funds[8]	53
Corporates[9]	25–30
Insurance company investment in SIFs[10]	27.9
Total Investable in A Shares	**1,506–1,811**
Expressed in US$	**US$180–220 billion**

Sources: (1) *Qianlong*, January 31, 2002; (2) www.pbc.gov.cn; (3) CIRC; (4) *AWSJ*, November 12, 2002, p. M5; (5) *Caijing* and PBOC estimates; (6) Author's estimate; (7) Funds under management, *Caijing*, July 2001, p. 69; (8) Table 7.16; (9) Total funds raised from corporates in 2001 Shanghai IPOs; (10) CIRC.

around RMB200 billion.[11] Then the PBOC surveyed 6,979 advisory companies only in Beijing, Shanghai, and Shenzhen in April 2001. Based on this, the bank estimated that managed funds nationally may be as much as RMB900 billion.[12] If true, this would be more than 10 times the amount managed in the legal funds sector and about half the value of all tradable shares. This is unlikely to prove too much of an exaggeration.

The PBOC surveyed 6,953 investment consultants, investment managers, investment advisors, financial advisors, and financial managers in Beijing, Shanghai, and Shenzhen. The account opening balance requirements for 3,626 such companies in Beijing only are shown in Table 7.10.

Some 50% of these companies were reluctant to reveal the number of accounts opened. Of the remaining 50%, 15.5% had five or fewer, 19.2% had five to ten, 3.8% had 10 to 20, and 11.5% had 20–50 accounts. Assume, then, that a slight majority of 52%, or 3,640, of the nearly 7,000 advisory companies in the three cities provide financial management services in addition to pure advice. If each company on average has RMB150 million under management, then total gray market funds would total around RMB546 billion.[13] If we add in a conservative estimate of funds managed by the brokerages, say RMB100 billion,[14] plus funds managed by advisory companies elsewhere in the country, then a total figure of RMB700 billion would hardly be an exaggeration.

Who holds accounts at these advisory companies? The PBOC survey found that companies opened 69.3% of all accounts in a company's name, individually controlled companies 3.8%, companies held by other companies and individuals 15.4%, and "other" companies 11.5%. Not all funds are directed

TABLE 7.10 Beijing Private Fund Manager Survey: Required Account Balance

Balance Required (RMB Mn)	Investment Consultant	Investment Manager	Investment Advisor	Financial Consultant	Financial Manager	Total
<1	1,021	60	1,504	26	5	2,616
<5	154	18	168	0	0	340
<10	37	220	121	0	0	378
<30	17	178	22	2	0	219
<50	1	38	5	1	0	45
<100	0	19	3	0	0	22
<200	0	4	1	0	0	5
<500	0	0	0	0	0	0
>500	0	1	0	0	0	0
Total	**1,230**	**538**	**1,824**	**29**	**5**	**3,626**

Source: Caijing, July 2001, p. 70.

at the stock markets; some 23.1% invest only in CGBs. Excluding those, all others invest in shares, with some 50% investing in the secondary markets.

Such extreme concentration of wealth in a small number of hands can move the markets. Based on primary market subscriptions in 2001, it is estimated that capital dedicated to IPOs totals around RMB500 billion and hardly ever exceeds RMB650 billion.[15] Against this background, the IPO of the famous maker of "white lightning," Guizhou Maotai, illustrates the financial power of major market players. On July 25, 2001, the Shanghai Index stood at 2,112. Over the next four trading days, the index rapidly dropped to 1,920. Just at this moment, there were four IPOs in the final stages of listing and a total of RMB662 billion in subscription funds was frozen in the central depository pending final settlement. In short, all funds normally tied up in subscribing to IPOs were already tied up. The bulk of this money was scheduled to be returned to investors on August 1.

Then on July 31, there were two IPOs: Guizhou Maotai was priced at a high RMB31.39 per share, while the other stock was a small issue of only 22 million shares priced at RMB5.69. The timing of the IPO raises questions given the exceptional circumstances of presumed market illiquidity. The subscription funds tied up by Guizhou Maotai totaled an additional RMB199 billion and the number of subscribers was only 200,713. The smaller offering tied up a further RMB68 billion. Together the funds for these two deals, RMB267 billion, were equivalent to almost 50% of the typical primary market subscription volume. Added to the already frozen funds, the amount reaches RMB929 billion, about 30% more than usual. Where did all this money come from? Who would or could invest at a time when the market had already fallen 10%? With more than the normal amount of money already frozen in other deals, a cheaper company competing for funds and Maotai so expensive, normal retail investors would be discouraged, if not wholly unable to come up with funds to subscribe. What was going on?

The answer seems obvious: this was a "special service" the securities companies provided for the gray market money managers and "big shots" (*dahu*). By listing the shares at such a time, the brokerages (and maybe even the exchange, since it schedules offerings) effectively excluded all but those with the most money, allowing them to achieve higher allocations in a favored company. These favored investors put down nearly RMB200 billion (US$25 billion) and numbered only 200,000, on average putting down RMB1 million each. And who can say but that these same investors didn't also subscribe to the other IPO offered that day?

Corporate Investors

As shown in Table 7.8, in late 2001 there were around 160,000 net non-retail accounts, which might be thought to fall largely into the corporate bracket. In the West, "corporates" refers to legal entities whose main business is not the management of capital. In China, the scope is similar but also includes gray market money managers or almost any legal person. It excludes pension funds, insurance companies, and FMCs; it includes SOEs, restructured or otherwise. The state has imposed restrictions from time to time on the participation of corporates, especially SOEs, in the markets. Beginning in 1999, CSRC regulations, however, have allowed them to subscribe to IPOs subject to holding restrictions (or a "lock-up") of a minimum of six months for a so-called strategic holding or three months for a common investment.[16] Listed companies have also been restricted from share trading, but often skirt these regulations by going through a related party. Smaller firms make use of an individual account to trade.

Of the top 10 largest listed stocks, shown in Table 6.8 in Chapter 6, five companies allocated shares to strategic and general investors (corporate) and fund investors during their IPO transaction. As Table 7.11 illustrates, corporate investors, a.k.a. SOEs, have played a significant part in the successful underwriting of the large stocks. Most of these issues approached or exceeded US$1 billion, and corporate support averaged 40–50% of funds raised.

TABLE 7.11   Corporate Investor Allotments, Jumbo Offerings

Stock (in Mn)	No. of Shares Strategic	No. of Shares General	No. of Shares Fund	Issue Size	IPO Price (RMB)	Size (RMB Bn)	Strategic + General (%)
Sinopec	570	0	0	2,800	4.22	12	20
China Merchants Bank	430	362	108	1,500	7.3	11	53
Huaneng International	100	0	3	250	7.95	2	40
BaoSteel	447	486	494	1,877	4.18	8	50
China Unicom	518	1,430	302	5,000	2.3	12	39

Source: Wind Information.

Beijing Capital Iron and Steel (*Shougang*) offers an early example of this practice. On December 16, 1999, Shougang completed its IPO on the Shenzhen exchange. Issuing 350 million shares at RMB5.15 per share, the transaction raised a total of RMB1.8 billion, a relatively small amount. Half of the 350 million shares were reserved for corporate buyers, with 92 million shares issued to 21 different strategic investors. The largest strategic investor was Shanghai BaoSteel. BaoSteel was allocated 12 million shares, three other companies 10 million, and the remaining 17 investors between two and six million shares each.[17] These strategic investors were subject to a six-month lock-up period.

How long did the "strategic" investors hold the shares at the end of the lock-up (see Table 7.12)? Post-IPO in mid-December 1999, Capital Steel's shareholding structure included the 175 million LP shares allocated to both strategic and general investors. By the end of March 2000, however, the general LP shares (*yiban farengu*), subject to a three-month lock-up period, had become tradable A shares. By the end of June, all 92 million "strategic" shares had also become freely tradable A shares. Of Shougang's original 21 strategic investors in late 1999, only one was still among the top 10 shareholders by October 2002. As a whole, all strategic investors had sold down more than 75% of their original stake within the first two years of the listing. The picture is similar at the other companies relying on corporate support at the IPO stage. The corporate investment mentality, thus, is similar to that of the individual – short-term gain rather than long-term investment results. At the end of the lock-up periods, corporates tend to sell out their

TABLE 7.12 Post-IPO Changes in Shareholding Structure, Capital Steel

Type of Share	June 30, 2000 (Mn)	March 31, 2000 (Mn)	December 31, 1999 (Mn)
Total Shares	**2,310**	**2,310**	**2,310**
A shares	350	258	175
B shares	–	–	–
H shares	–	–	–
State shares	1,960	1,960	1,960
State LP	–	–	–
Domestic LP	–	92	175
Domestic Promoter	–	–	–
Social LP	–	–	–
General LP	–	–	83
Strategic Investor	–	92	92
Fund Offering	–	–	–
Internal staff	–	–	–
Non-tradable foreign capital	–	–	–
Preferred shares	–	–	–
Natural person	–	–	–

Source: Wind Information. Shougang's shareholding structure has not changed from June 2000.

"strategic" holdings. It has been rumored, however, that some firms have entered into agreements to sell their shares to third parties (read securities companies) at an agreed price but with delayed share settlement.

China Unicom, a jumbo issue, is an example of just how far the word "strategic" has been stretched by this market practice. In its October 2002 domestic listing, Unicom issued five billion shares at a very low price of RMB2.30 (the lowest IPO price of any Chinese A share to date). Of these, 518 million shares were allocated to 15 strategic investors, 302 million shares to the 56 listed stock investment funds, and 1.429 billion shares to general LP investors. The three groups together underwrote 45% of the issued shares. Unfortunately, no public data exist detailing the general LP investors, but data are available for the fund buyers and strategic buyers.

The fund allocations varied in size from over 25 million shares (two funds) to less than 90,000 shares for one fund. Funds, while hardly "strategic," at least might be expected to hold their allocations for a slightly longer period than a typical retail investor. The so-called strategic investors each received 35 million shares, except one who received 28 million shares. These strategic investors included Beijing Capital Airport Group, Shanghai Auto, Sinochem, and COFCO and these are only the well-known ones. It is difficult to see how such companies might view their investment in China Unicom as strategic, unless the word is used in a much broader sense. This situation, however, was not unique to China Unicom.

From late 1999, when the CSRC opened the market to corporate investors, up to October 2002, a total of 66 companies issued shares via initial or secondary offerings which were supported by 1,116 strategic investor placements, raising over RMB25 billion. The number of strategic investors has varied from 1 to 139 per issue, although on average an offering is likely to have around 20 strategic investors. A total of 828 companies have acted as strategic investors. The vast majority, 660 firms, have been a strategic investor only once, while 113 firms have invested twice and the other 55 firms between three and nine times. As shown in Table 7.13, two companies, Jiangsu Meihua Scientific Industry and Shanghai Auto, have been strategic investors in nine different firms.

The diversity of companies and businesses in which these two companies invest is surprising, once again straining the meaning of "strategic." Bioengineering, energy, plastics, telecoms, conglomerates, and tourism (among others) hardly spring to mind as related businesses. The benefits that the companies can derive from one another seem limited: the strategic investor comes from a very different industry, and the holding period of their shares, again, is generally a matter of months, rather than years.

A cynical observer might suggest, therefore, that the authorities use strategic shareholders to ensure the successful sale of larger IPOs. In such an estimation, the A-share market does not safely have sufficient liquidity to soak up larger offerings. This seems hard to fathom, however, given that the primary markets in 2001 attracted on average around RMB600 billion (US$72 billion) in subscription money per IPO. So, there are a number of

TABLE 7.13   Strategic Holdings of Jiangsu Meihua and Shanghai Auto

Jiangsu Meihua		Shanghai Auto	
Code	**Company**	**Code**	**Company**
000402	Finance Street Holding Company	000078	Neptunus Bioengineering
000700	Jiangnan Mould and Plastic Technology	000301	Wujiang Silk Company
000787	Powerwise Information Technology	000973	Foshan Plastics Group
600091	Baotou Tomorrow Technology	000975	Chongqing Wujiang Electric Power
600600	Tsingtao Brewery	600008	Beijing Capital Company
600716	Yaohua Glass	600050	China Unicom
600827	Shanghai Friendship Group	600258	Beijing Capital Tourism
600887	Yili Industrial Group	600602	SVA Electron Company
900955	Shanghai Matsuoka	900955	Shanghai Matsuoka

Source: Wind Information, October 31, 2002.

questions left unanswered by this regulation. First of all, why allow SOEs to buy large blocks of cheap shares and not the retail public?[18] Since shares in the primary market are a sure thing, anyone stands to realize healthy profits once the stock starts trading given a good allocation of shares. Second, who decides to allocate how much to what corporate and at what price? Third, who decides whether a corporate is a strategic investor subject to a longer lock-up period or a general investor subject to a shorter lock-up? Finally, where do these usually cash-strapped corporates get the funds to finance their dabbling in the stock market? Even more to the point: what if the value of the shares declines before they can sell them? To a large extent, the answer to these questions is the securities firm, which undoubtedly shares a portion of the profit "earned" by the "strategic" investor.[19] The other part of the answer is the banks.

Aside from profiting from A-share trading, corporates are usually the largest shareholders of listed firms (see Table 7.14). This is so not due to any A-share holding, but through their control of non-tradable state and LP shares. For the majority of listed firms, the controlling and largest single shareholder continues to be the original promoter and founder of the company. Since nearly 70% of all shares are still non-tradable, corporate shareholders have a far greater stake in the stock market, or at least the listed companies, than the small number of corporate accounts would imply.

TABLE 7.14 Size of Holdings of Top Three Largest Shareholders of Listed Companies

	1st Largest	2nd Largest	3rd Largest	No. of Companies Top 3 > 50%	Total No. of Companies
Shanghai	45.0%	8.7%	3.3%	473	677
Shenzhen	43.0%	8.3%	3.4%	310	490

Source: Based on June 30, 2002, semi-annual company reports, in *Securities Market Weekly*, Issue 71/72, 2002.

Manipulators and Big Shots

At this point, the inclusion of "manipulators" and big shots in a list of market participants should not seem at all strange. In the Chinese markets, the stock manipulator has taken on almost superhuman qualities. Everyone always understood that the limited number of freely tradable shares and an unsophisticated retail base could produce easy pickings for such professionals. The confession of Lu Liang and the subsequent trial of his trading ring, however, have confirmed to the public that all the rumors were true (as usual). Manipulators are not just a handful of individuals with limited funds operating on the fringes of the market; to a significant extent, they *are* the market.

Hundreds of trading halls and nearly every securities firm were involved in some sort of illegal activity to support Lu's trading tactics. He was able to raise billions of Renminbi in illegal funding and even published false stories under his pseudonym, "Mr. K," in the respected *Securities Market Weekly*, to support his trading strategy. He was able to buy not only A shares, but LP shares as well, thereby ensuring absolute control of the companies he had "in play." Based on evidence presented to the court, Lu followed four basic steps to establish his trading empire.[20]

First, he created a position (*jiancan*) in the target company. From the end of 1998 to May 1999, Lu allied with Zhu Huanliang, a major player in Shenzhen, to put the shares of a company called China Venture Capital (*Zhongkechuang*, now called Shenzhen Kondarl (Group) Co.; 000048) into play. At a pre-agreed price of around RMB13 per share, Lu purchased 30 million shares of China Venture Capital from Zhu and transferred them over the course of one year into over 1,000 separate investor accounts all under Lu's control. Over 80% of these accounts had been "provided by brokerage offices." At the peak, Lu and Zhu together controlled more than 93% of the tradable shares of China Venture Capital.

Raising financing (*rongzi*) is the critical second step. According to Lu's chief dealer and fund coordinator, the initial capital Lu raised came from his original 2.8 million shares of China Venture Capital. Financing additional purchases was simple: Lu borrowed cash from various securities houses against the stock he held. This, too, is illegal. In January 1999, Lu had raised about RMB64 million, which he used to buy more China Venture Capital A shares from Zhu.

He again borrowed against these additional shares and so on, paying between 8% and 15% on the loans. Eventually, 125 brokerage offices supported his financing strategy. Lu was leveraged to the hilt.

In the third step, Lu acquired LP shares. He set up various shell companies under the common name of "Yanyuan," which began to acquire LP shares of China Venture Capital from its largest shareholder in May 1999. With the LP shares in hand, Lu and Zhu were now the largest shareholders of China Venture Capital and they took control of the board in early 2000. The acquisition of LP shares was funded solely from profits derived from driving up the share price of China Venture Capital, then selling out at the optimum moment. By May 1999, China Venture Capital's share price had doubled since November 1998.

Creating a favorable trading environment was the fourth step. To promote his trading in China Venture Capital A shares, Lu wrote favorable news stories about the company's reorganization, new investment projects, and new business strategy. He and his colleagues directed trading in the stock with the help of staff in over 100 brokerage offices churning shares in over 1,000 accounts to drive the stock price higher.[21] His public relations campaign was designed more to cover his activities, than to draw in huge numbers of new investors, although he needed them to eventually buy out his position. In fact, shareholder numbers in China Venture Capital during this period show that Lu Liang had driven away nearly everyone except himself and perhaps other players (see Table 7.15).

The more that Lu and his colleagues traded, the more they built a highly leveraged position.[22] They eventually raised a total of RMB5.4 billion, of which RMB4 billion had been used in building their position. Thanks to the bull market of 1999 and 2000 and Lu's concerted rumor mongering, the China Venture Capital stock price eventually reached over RMB80, as compared to his original buy-in price of RMB13 (as shown in Figure 7.2). The remaining RMB1.4 billion he used to expand his operations to include other stocks – for example, Maanshan Steel, Shanghai Zhongxi Pharmaceutical, Laiwu Steel, and Harbin Suibao Electric Heating.

Go back to the data in Chapter 6 showing that the average company has only 50,000 shareholders. Combine that with the fact that Lu Liang himself controlled over 1,500 accounts and that he had eight other colleagues working

TABLE 7.15 China Venture Capital, Number of Shareholders

Date	No. of Shareholders
December 1998	5,379
June 1999	6,575
December 1999	6,175
June 2000	7,018
December 2000	14,787
December 2001	63,286
June 2002	54,659

Source: Wind Information.

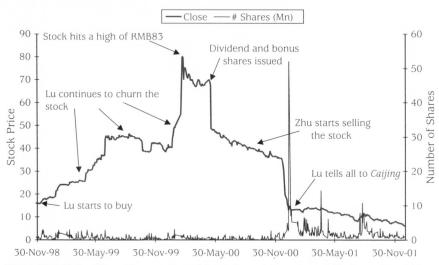

FIGURE 7.2 China Venture Capital Stock Price, November 1998–December 2001. *Source*: Wind Information.

with him and assume that they also controlled a similar number of accounts. His gang, therefore, might have controlled as many as 14,000 accounts, and certainly a group of such players will control this many. So, how many distinct shareholders might an average company actually have? The estimates shown in Table 7.1 at the start of this chapter do not appear exaggerated at all. Then consider the concentration of financial resources.

Securities Companies

There are currently 124 securities brokerages in China with a network of 2,566 brokerage offices and total regulatory capital of RMB104 billion. As firms struggle to meet the capital requirements of the Securities Law as well as the professional licensing requirements of the CSRC, they can be divided into four types.[23] There are 18 comprehensive (*zonghe quanshang*) firms with an average regulatory capital of RMB2.2 billion controlling 927 offices (see Table 7.16). Second, there are 28 brokerages (*jingji quanshang*) with an average capital of RMB155 million and 196 offices. The third category includes those firms making the transition from unrestructured firm to approved brokerage or comprehensive firm. Here there are 54 under the CSRC's guidance with average capital of nearly RMB1 billion and 1,084 offices. Finally, there are the "not-yet-standard (*weiguifan*)" securities companies, totaling 24 with 359 offices and average capital of RMB266 million. Most of the latter category will ultimately be closed, or perhaps some might be acquired by foreign securities firms which may now enter into ventures with local brokerages.[24]

The securities companies can also be divided into those controlled by central government entities and those by local governments. Information on current

TABLE 7.16   Top 20 Securities Firms by Regulatory Capital

	Name	Type	Regulatory Capital (RMB Mn)	Offices	Location
1	China Galaxy Securities	Comp.	4,500	178	Beijing
2	Shenyin Wanguo	Comp.	4,200	109	Shanghai
3	Haitong Securities	Comp.	4,006	95	Shanghai
4	Guotai Junan Securities	Comp.	3,700	118	Shanghai
5	Southern Securities	Comp.	3,450	85	Shenzhen
6	Everbright Securities	Comp.	2,600	46	Shanghai
7	Xiangcai Securities	Comp.	2,515	26	Changsha
8	China Merchants Securities	Comp.	2,400	31	Shenzhen
9	Bohai Securities	Pending	2,317	29	Tianjin
10	CITIC Securities	Comp.	2,082	41	Beijing
11	Tiantong Securities	Comp.	2,036	64	Jinan
12	Guoyuan Securities	Comp.	2,030	36	Hefei
13	Changjiang Securities	Comp.	2,000	26	Wuhan
14	Guangfa Securities	Comp.	2,000	72	Guangzhou
15	Guoxin Securities	Comp.	2,000	22	Shenzhen
16	Hua-an Securities	Comp.	1,705	24	Hefei
17	Zhongguancun Securities	Comp.	1,540	14	Beijing
18	Beijing Securities	Comp.	1,510	26	Beijing
19	Shanghai Securities	Comp.	1,500	34	Shanghai
20	BOCI Securities	Pending	1,500	0	Shanghai

Source: CSRC, October 25, 2002.

ownership is very difficult to come by.[25] The major state banks, however, were the principal promoters of the three national brokerages at their inception (Huaxia, Guotai, and Nanfang). Even more interesting, by mid-2002, 162 listed companies had invested RMB14.8 billion in 80 securities houses, according to data provided by Wind Information. It is no surprise that the brokerages, large and small, are at the heart of the money flows, as shown in Figure 7.3.

In all of the shenanigans described previously, the securities companies have played a central role.[26] They provide account services and finance margin trading as in the case of Lu Liang.[27] They advise issuers on size of offering, its timing, and its price. They allocate shares to strategic investors based on wholly non-transparent criteria and buy their resulting positions before lock-up periods expire. They collaborate with manipulators by talking up shares on inside information and taking parallel proprietary positions.[28] They liaise with the exchanges to ensure favorable treatment for their issues. They run their associated securities investment management companies as their second treasury. In addition, they augment their own funds with the deposits of the retail investor.[29] And they can always rely on the support of the banks, corporations, and ultimately local governments, which are their principal shareholders. That they do so is no surprise given the economics, weak regulation, and

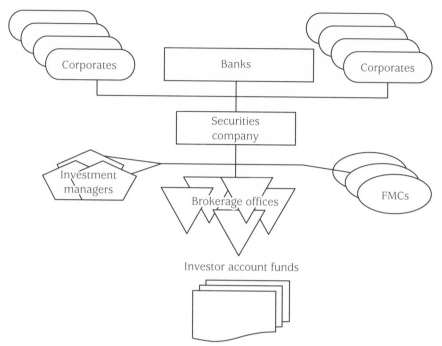

FIGURE 7.3 Securities Companies are at the Nexus of Money Flows.

overcapacity in an industry with few "real" investors and a commodity product. Is it any wonder that the CSRC must tread lightly in this area?

Given this combustible mix, it is no surprise that there have been two serious crises involving major firms. The first, the 327 bond futures blow-up in 1995 involving SISCO (Wanguo Securities), has been described previously. The second saw the chairman and CEO of Junan Securities, Zhang Guoqing, rescue the firm from bankruptcy by a hugely risky, but ultimately successful, trading squeeze on Shenzhen Development Bank shares in 1996 (see Chapter 9). Having won his bet, he was discovered transferring control of the company to himself in 1997.[30] This presumably took chutzpah, given that Junan was known to be backed by China's security apparatus. Or perhaps it was Zhang who had their backing. In any event, his source for the required RMB700 million to accomplish the takeover was never disclosed. In both cases, the government resolved the problem through merger, creating Shenyin Wanguo and Guotai Junan, two of China's largest brokerage houses.

To limit the potential harm to the larger economy, reform efforts have aimed at isolating brokerages from the banking sector à la Glass-Steagall in the United States. This was attempted during the course of the late 1990s as part of the banking reform initiated by Zhu Rongji in 1994.

The first step in this process was the separation of the PBOC branch system from its own investments in securities firms and trust companies.[31]

BOX 7   Major Points in the Development of China's Securities Companies

Sept. 1985   PBOC Shenzhen branch approves founding of Shenzhen SEZ Securities, China's first specialized securities firm. Ideological bickering prevents it from operating for two years.

Apr. 1988   PBOC sponsors the creation of 33 securities companies in all major cities to facilitate the distribution and trading of treasury bonds. By the end of 1988, there were 34 securities firms and over 100 trading counters across the country.

1990   PBOC releases "Administrative Measures for Securities Companies," the first regulations developed for the securities brokerage industry. At the end of 1990, there were 44 brokerages.

Oct. 1992   Following the founding of the two exchanges, the PBOC, together with MOF, the four major state banks, and a number of major corporates, established national securities firms in Beijing, Shanghai, and Shenzhen. Huaxia, Guotai, and Nanfang were born, with their major shareholders being the four state banks. At the end of 1992, there were 87 brokerage firms.

2nd-half 1992   As China's economy began to overheat, many brokerages began to invest in real estate and other industries. At the same time, many ministries and local governments began to set up financial institutions. This led to a nationwide financial frenzy. The clean-up of these illegal brokerages, leasing companies, trust companies, and so on, has yet to be completed a decade later.

Dec. 1993   The State Council's "Decision on Reform of the Financial System" initiated a clean-up of the financial sector and a division of banking and securities sectors à la Glass-Steagall. The PBOC also approved Guangfa, Haitong, Fujian Xingye, and China Merchants Securities as subsidiaries of Guangdong Development Bank, Bank of Communications, Fujian Xingye Bank, and China Merchants Bank. Total number of brokerage firms reached 91.

1995   PBOC begins separating banks from their own securities operations and using them as a basis to create new brokerages, including CITIC Securities, Everbright, Dapeng, Pingan, Weishen, Great Wall, and Xiangcai. There were now 97 brokerages.

July 1996   PBOC issues a decree ordering its branches to spin off their securities operations involving a total of 63 units. In October, it orders all banks, insurance companies, city credit cooperatives, corporate finance companies, and leasing companies to close or transfer some 763 securities outlets. By 2000 year-end, all but 20 had been dealt with.

BOX 7 *continued*

June 1998	PBOC handed over to the CSRC its licensing and supervisory authority for the securities industry. By year-end, the focus was on separating trust companies from the securities industry. This alone involved more than 960 securities units. At the same time, the Audit Bureau began a review of all brokerages, finding every kind of financial impropriety including misappropriation of customer funds. The bureau also found another 300 illegally operating brokerages which it began to close down. With the passage of the Securities Law, the CSRC began relicensing all brokerages.
Dec. 2001	China's commitment to the WTO calls for foreign participation in brokerages and fund management companies of up to 33%.
Aug. 2002	Anshan Securities shut down at last, the first such case.

Source: Based on *Caijing*, September 5, 2002, p. 37.

In December 1993, the State Council issued a decision aimed at separating the banking system, the securities industry, and insurance companies.[32] The State Council permitted banks and industrial enterprises to invest in financial institutions, including securities firms. But it prohibited securities firms from investing in any sector except the securities industry. This doesn't solve the problem.

In 1994, the PBOC in principle severed the MOF and local government finance bureaus from any ownership of securities firms. In 1995, the State Council prohibited the major banks from owning trust and investment corporations, which, in turn, usually either owned a securities firm or had their own internal securities department. Work then began on hiving off the securities operations of both banks and non-banks. In 2000, Galaxy Securities was created from several hundred of the remaining trust company brokerage operations; hence its huge office network that exceeded 400 at the time of its formation.

The Securities Law confirmed the 1993 style of segregation in Article 6. The same article also states that securities firms are to be established independently of the same three sectors. On passage of the law, the CSRC announced that it would review all securities firms and reissue their business licenses.[33] This was largely completed by July 1, 1999, but the CSRC continued to encounter practical difficulties as it sought to sever relationships conflicting with this article.[34] The extent of this difficulty can be seen in the 24 "irregular" firms, those "tough, hard to chew bones," still hanging on in late 2002.

It can be expected that the number of large securities firms will decrease significantly because of obvious overcapacity, lack of profitability, and improving regulatory enforcement. An indirect sign that this is happening will be that the volume of trading in the market will decline correspondingly.

Retail Investors

It is clear, then, that there are far fewer active retail investors than previously believed. Disregarding the ghost account problem, the greatest penetration of the markets is in the Shenzhen and Shanghai regions. Beyond these two regions, the 10 richest provinces account for 70% of all open A-share accounts, as shown in Table 7.17. There is a local preference for account opening – for example, Guangdong residents opened 18.9% of Shenzhen accounts, but that figure falls to 9.6% for Shanghai accounts. Before adjusting for double counting, nearly 29% of Guangdong residents have opened accounts, 23% for Shanghai and 18% for neighboring Jiangsu. "Stock fever", when retail investors drive the markets, has hit China from time to time and has affected primarily the richer, more developed parts of the country. These 10 provinces represent nearly 25% of China's population and half of the country's gross domestic product (GDP).

Recent efforts to enliven the markets have been based on the government's conclusion that the great bull market in the U.S. created a "wealth effect." Just see the famous June 15, 1999, *People's Daily* editorial for a sample of the government's "irrational exuberance." This wealth effect, it was believed, contributed to the heroic consumption binge U.S. citizens have gone on in recent years. In China, however, the analysis presented here suggests that those who get rich from playing the markets are those who are already more than well off. This portion of the populace may be the largest potential consumers, but they are a minority representing less than 0.06% of the population and that is based on the full 66 million accounts. Moreover, judging from the geographic distribution of accounts, it doesn't appear that boosting the markets will have a significant enriching effect on the interior provinces

TABLE 7.17 A-share Account Breakdown by Province

	Shenzhen Accounts (%)	Shanghai Accounts (%)
Jiangsu	8.6	9.5
Shanghai	8.5	14.4
Sichuan	7.6	7.3
Guangdong	18.9	9.6
Shandong	5.1	6.2
Liaoning	4.9	6.2
Beijing	4.5	4.4
Zhejiang	4.5	5.0
Hubei	4.2	3.4
Fujian	3.2	3.3
Top 10 Total	**70.1%**	**69.3%**
Other	29.9%	30.7%

Source: China Securities and Futures Statistical Yearbook, 2002 (as of FY 2001).

(except perhaps Sichuan).[35] Or, if the source of ghost account ID cards is the countryside, it will have no impact at all.

Securities Investment Funds

Although it has grown significantly, the funds industry is still a very small part of the A-share market, accounting for between 3% and 4% of the tradable market capitalization (see Table 7.18). On average, 66% of fund assets is invested in equity. Even if fully invested, holdings would still be only 5% or so of the tradable shares and not enough to move the market. However, with daily trading volume in, for example, Shanghai of around RMB7.3 billion, fund managers can have an impact on individual company shares. In contrast, the gray market money managers control capital equal to half the value of the free float. Thus, it is too early to imagine that a professionally managed fund industry can positively promote the market's development.

By mid-2002, there were 15 fund FMCs operating 54 funds, three open-ended, the rest being closed-end funds. The 54 funds held RMB53.6 billion worth of A shares in 989 different listed companies. Equity holdings per fund varied from RMB260 million to RMB2.6 billion.[36]

Securities investment funds *per se* are more properly a traded product than a market participant; however, by looking at these funds, the effort is to see through them to the strategies and performance of the fund managers behind. In the beginning, in the early 1990s, investment funds were a product uniquely created by the regional trading centers.[37] The first fund established, the Wuhan Securities Investment Fund, was approved by PBOC Wuhan Branch in October 1991 and raised RMB10 million. A year later, the first specialized fund management company in China was established in Shenzhen, the Shenzhen Investment Fund Management Company.

Through 1996, a total of 75 investment funds were established (see Table 7.19). Taken together, these funds had raised some RMB730 million (or US$88 million), an extremely small amount which, if averaged out, comes to only a little more than US$1.2 million per fund. Of these, 27 were listed on the two national exchanges (including 15 local funds that traded electronically in Shanghai and Shenzhen) and 48 were listed and traded on the various regional trading centers. In terms of approvals, only four funds had received approval from PBOC Beijing, while local PBOC branches had signed off on the remainder.

TABLE 7.18   Securities Investment Fund Size

(RMB Mn)	No. of Stocks	Value of Fund Holdings	Average Value	A-share Market Capitalization	Fund/Market Capitalization (%)
Shanghai	612	35,772	59	911,449	3.9
Shenzhen	377	17,876	47	602,963	3.0

Source: Wind Information, June 30, 2002.

TABLE 7.19   Trends in Fund Establishment

	93	94	95	96	97	98	99	00	01	Sept. 02
SZ SIF	0	0	0	0	0	I	9	17	25	29
SH SIF	0	0	0	0	0	4	11	16	23	25
Total SIF	**0**	**0**	**0**	**0**	**0**	**5**	**20**	**33**	**48**	**54**
SZ Other	0	8	10	10	10	9	7	I	0	0
SH Other	I	12	12	15	15	15	15	2	0	0
Total Other	**I**	**20**	**22**	**25**	**25**	**24**	**22**	**3**	**0**	**0**
Total Listed	I	20	22	25	25	29	42	36	48	54
Open Funds									3	17*

Sources: Shenzhen and Shanghai stock exchange data. *This figure includes funds that have been approved but yet to raise funds. Systematic data do not exist for the period before 1993.

The uncontrolled growth of fund establishment led to a halt in their approval in 1994. This control was not lifted until the end of 1996 on the eve of the enactment of standardized measures regulating the industry.

Prior to the 1997 restructuring of the industry, fund management companies generally managed only one fund and with poor results. Due to their limited available capital, the funds themselves had little impact on the markets, particularly since many also invested in real estate and the like. This reflects the fact that, aside from "oversight" by local governments and branches of the PBOC, funds were entirely unregulated. Table 7.20 illustrates the fact that the management structure for most of these original funds was entirely conflicted. Frequently, the fund promoter and manager were the same legal entity, or the promoter and custodian were the same. Clearly, there was a need for national regulation if the industry was to develop beyond this early stage.

Adopted in late 1997, the "Provisional Measures for Managing Securities Investment Funds" provided the industry with the foundation for a new start.[38] The 1997 Fund Measures affirmed the important contribution funds could make to the markets if they were managed properly. Together with

TABLE 7.20   Role Definition in the Management of Investment Funds, pre-1997

	Fund Promoter	Fund Manager	Custodian
Banks	9	I	18
Trust Companies	51	34	30
Securities Companies	20	13	3
Insurance Companies	3	0	I
Enterprises	17	17	0
Government	I	0	0
Totals	101	65	52

Source: Cao Fengqi, p. 233.

supplementary measures,[39] the provisions clarified and standardized the structure of funds, as well as the obligations of fund managers, trustee banks, and investors and placed all approval, regulatory, and supervisory authority with the CSRC.

Regulators have placed great hope in the standardized securities funds as a less dangerous path into the A-share market for such sensitive industries as insurance. A quick look, therefore, at the reality of their performance may provide a better understanding of things to come (see Table 7.21 for fund asset allocation). Analysis here focuses on NAV and closing price, since most funds are closed-end. This simply means that after the initial subscription period, the fund manager does not receive or redeem the fund units until maturity, typically 15 years. The units simply trade on the secondary market as shares, or units, of the fund itself.

The secondary market price of fund units can vary significantly from the actual value of the underlying funds assets. This price discrepancy is called

TABLE 7.21   Distribution of Fund Holdings across Industries[40]

Industry	Value of Holdings (RMB Mn)	%
Agriculture	693	1.2
Mining	1,828	3.3
Manufacturing	25,934	46.7
– Food	2,780	5.0
– Textiles	2,271	4.1
– Wood Products	98	0.2
– Paper	669	1.2
– Chemicals	3,898	7.0
– Electrical	1,848	3.3
– Metals	3,484	6.3
– Machinery	7,232	13.0
– Medical	3,507	6.3
– Other	147	0.3
Energy and Water	5,311	9.6
Construction	857	1.5
Transport	5,543	10.0
IT	3,401	6.1
Wholesale and Retail	2,977	5.4
Banking and Finance	3,795	6.8
Real Estate	1,645	3.0
Social Services	1,912	3.4
Media	352	0.6
Conglomerate	1,292	2.3
Total	55,539	

Source: Wind Information, September 30, 2002.

either the premium or discount to NAV. NAV performance, in part, drives the premium or discount – that is, how well the fund manager does his or her job selecting stocks. It is also, in part, driven by sentiment, and supply and demand considerations.

At the start, funds were characterized by high premiums based on little underlying share performance. Investors were excited about the new product and drove up the premiums. This tells more about the investor understanding of this new product class than about how the funds were managed. The first two funds opened at premiums of 100% above their NAV – incredibly expensive! It appears that investors did not fully understand how securities funds should be valued. It was an expensive lesson for those who bought in that first year and did not get out. There followed a year of continuous premium contraction as investors gained a better understanding of the linkage between NAV and closing prices. In addition, NAVs showed little change as the fund managers remained cautious and the stock market itself was stagnant.

As more funds were listed, few were able to distinguish themselves among the pack and all funds traded with similar premiums. By mid-May 1999, however, most funds were trading around NAV. This coincided with the late May rally in the stock market that the famous June 15, 1999, *People's Daily* editorial strongly supported. Propelled by the rally, the funds generally performed well, with a few outperforming the Shanghai A-share index. However, these NAV gains failed to correspond to equivalent gains in unit closing prices and the funds began to trade at a discount to NAV. This can probably be explained by the dominance of direct stock trading. When investors poured into the market, they directly bought up favorite names rather than securities funds. This is not to say that the funds were not oversubscribed upon issue or that their absolute returns were not good; many showed returns of over 20% in a three-month period. It merely shows the problems of closed-end funds as an investment vehicle. Or maybe there was more to it than that.

As it turns out, unfortunately, fund performance during this period seems in large part to have been the consequence of rank manipulation by fund managers. This became known as the "Black Fund Scandal." As mentioned in Chapter 3, a Shanghai Stock Exchange report on fund industry performance leaked out at the end of 2000, but rumors of its existence had hit the markets long before.[41] The exchange analyst had closely monitored fund trading during two periods, the first from August 9, 1999 to December 3, 1999, and the second from December 3, 1999 to April 28, 2000. The results were not encouraging. During the first period, two FMCs were singled out in particular. These two companies traded shares between existing funds and newly listed funds, using the latter to solve the performance problems of the former. Called "churning (*duidao*)," some 76 different stocks were involved in a series of transactions in which one fund dumped its shares into the other. This is considered manipulation, as it creates volume, and volume trading in a share attracts other investors into the market. Once the share price has been driven up, the manipulators cash out at a profit. The report noted that most FMCs were guilty of churning their accounts.

Activity in the second period under scrutiny was even broader, involving some 140 stocks. The report also detailed a variety of different methods of collusion between funds under the same FMC and between different FMCs. Since most FMCs are controlled by securities companies, there is also the strong likelihood of collusion between the proprietary trading operations of the securities companies and their related FMC. This relationship, which should be at a distant arm's length, raises the issue of FMC independence. The report cited a number of instances where there appeared to be common trading strategies. Compounding this is the fact that securities firms usually hold stakes in two, and sometimes three, different FMCs.[42]

None of this is particularly surprising; churning has been common in Western markets as well. Liu Hongru, the ex-chairman of the CSRC, expressed the optimistic viewpoint: "These funds are only two years old. As two-year olds they may wet their pants. You have to let them do this. … Grownups need to give a child of this age the most care."[43] Professor Liu is being ingenuous here. Surely the new funds were set up to avoid just these problems! In contrast, Professor Wang Lianzhou, the leading drafter of the Securities Law, strongly criticized the FMCs, concluding: "Fund managers never fail to collect their management fees no matter how poorly or how well their funds perform, which is abnormal."[44]

Following the scandal, the plan to sell state shares as part of all IPOs drove the markets down from June 2001. Since then, the funds have actually outperformed the underlying market, as shown in Figure 7.4. It is understandable why investors, and particularly insurance companies, and Professor Wang might not be satisfied, but they would be even unhappier had they bought A shares directly.[45] Combine

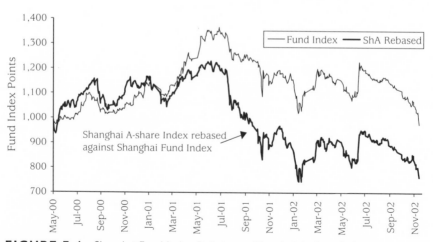

FIGURE 7.4 Shanghai Fund Index Relative to Shanghai A-share Index.
Source: Wind Information.

FMC manipulations with those of the other market participants and the result adds up to yet a further challenge to the CSRC and the government.[46]

Case Study: Hua-an Fund Management Co. and the Anxin Fund

The Hua-an Fund Management Company was one of the original five pilot fund management companies established under the 1997 Fund Measures. By all accounts, Hua-an is reputed to be one of the best-managed FMCs. Hua-an runs five funds, four closed-end – Anxin (500003), Anshun (500009), Anrui (500013), and Anjiu (184709, Shenzhen listed) – and one open-ended fund, Hua-an Innovation Fund. In 2001, Hua-an was the first to announce cooperation with a foreign fund manager, JP Morgan Fleming. In October 2002, Hua-an was again the first company to offer an index-linked open-ended fund tied to the Shanghai 180 index.

Details of the closed-end Anxin Fund, which was Hua-an's first, are given in Table 7.22. Of the two billion fund units, 1.94 billion were sold to the public; the remainder went to the fund sponsors. The public portion, like an IPO, was oversubscribed 52 times. Clearly, everyone was expecting a big run-up in the premium, not yet understanding that a fund unit is not an IPO share.

All funds provide a close of business Friday NAV figure which is widely distributed in the press, Internet, and exchange-based systems. The funds also provide a breakdown of their bond and stock holdings on a quarterly basis.

TABLE 7.22 Terms and Conditions, the Anxin Fund

Terms	Description
Fund Type	Closed-end
Offering Date	June 16, 1998
Placement	Two billion units
Face Value	RMB1 per unit
Investment Scope	Bonds and shares listed in China
Investment Objective	Long-term capital appreciation via investments in treasury bonds and stocks listed in China
Investment Restrictions	■ 20% net assets must be in CGBs ■ Not less than 80% of net assets in stocks and CGBs ■ Investment in one company must be less than 10% of net assets ■ Investment in one company not more than 10% of company's total capital
Maturity	15 years
Buyers	Natural persons residing in China
Management Fee	2.5% per annum
Distribution Policy	Not less than 90% of net earnings
Custodian	ICBC

TABLE 7.23 Asset Allocation, the Anxin Fund

Date	Fund NAV (RMB Mn)	% Equity	% CGBs and Cash
June 22, 1998	2,037	0.1	98.84
September 30, 1998	2,047	47.79	49.65
December 31, 1998	2,214	67.95	33.03
March 31, 1999	2,223	64.86	35.4
June 30, 1999	3,295	79.06	21.15
September 30, 1999	3,443	78.8	21.46
December 31, 1999	3,127	75.31	26.03
March 31, 2000	3,603	68.36	35.44
June 30, 2000	3,771	74.7	33.73
September 30, 2000	3,706	65.08	40.12
December 31, 2000	3,932	71.97	41.86
March 31, 2001	2,792	84.29	54.74
June 30, 2001	2,870	72.36	28.96
September 30, 2001	2,475	44.09	79.33
December 31, 2001	2,502	49.21	58.72
March 31, 2002	2,546	49.59	32.98
June 30, 2002	2,136	59.09	33.89
September 30, 2002	1,985	64.05	38.42

Source: Wind Information.

Table 7.23 illustrates how Hua-an has allocated funds between equities and bonds over a one-year period in the Anxin Fund and, with Figure 7.5, gives a feel for how this fund has fared.

Insurance Companies

The number of insurance companies has increased rapidly over the past several years. At the end of 2002, there were 52 insurance companies in China. Of these, 26 were foreign-invested, of which 17 were life insurance joint ventures and 11 were non-life. A further eight were in some stage of preparation.[47] As of September 2002, insurance companies held RMB596 billion in assets.[48] Given their role in developed markets, Chinese authorities view this group of investors as the key to the establishment of a strong institutional investor base. Through mid-1999, the bulk of their money was invested in CGBs, Policy Finance Bonds (RMB bonds issued by China Development Bank, China Ex-Im Bank, or China Agricultural Bank), or bank deposits. At this time, these were the only permitted types of investment product.

Regulatory changes in 1999 allowed insurance companies to invest up to 2% of their assets into "high credit quality" corporate bonds. The government has made efforts to enliven the corporate bond market beginning in 2002 by permitting major issues by China's best companies. It remains to be seen

FIGURE 7.5 Anxin Fund Closing Price versus NAV per Unit.
Source: Wind Information.

when such problems as poor secondary market liquidity, conflicting tax treatments, and unrealistic yields set by administrative means can be overcome.

The first word that insurance companies would be allowed to invest in shares leaked out during the 1999 summer rally. Rumor had it that up to 2% of their assets could be invested in shares. Then, in October 1999, regulators agreed to permit investments of up to 5% of their assets in A shares indirectly through the purchase of fund units (see Table 7.24).[49] This decision was received with varying degrees of enthusiasm even before the Black Fund Scandal of 2000, which, if nothing else, showed why investing directly might

TABLE 7.24 Insurance Investment in SIFs to Total Industry Assets

Date	Value of Fund Holdings (RMB Bn)	% of Total Assets
December 1999	1.48	0.6
March 2000	6.27	2.9
June 2000	8.36	2.8
September 2000	9.96	3.3
December 2000	13.35	4.0
March 2001	13.39	3.7
June 2001	14.34	3.7
September 2001	17.20	4.2
December 2001	20.90	4.6
March 2002	20.69	4.1
June 2002	21.63	3.9
September 2002	27.93	4.7

Source: China Insurance Regulatory Commission.

have been the better alternative. Nonetheless, with few other investment choices, insurance companies began to test the fund market in late 1999. Three years later they are approaching the 5% limit and have become a major supporter: their 5% investment is equivalent to approximately 30% of total funds value. Then, in November 2002, CIRC announced that it had removed the limits for investment in funds.[50] What remains to be seen is how much impact these presumably long-term investors will have on the performance of the FMCs.[51]

Pension Funds

Vastly underfunded in any event, the government has not permitted Chinese pension funds to invest in the stock markets either directly or indirectly. There are two broad categories of pension fund in China: social, which local governments operate; and corporate. Both types of funds are only allowed to invest in Chinese government bonds or cash deposits. Annual fund contributions at present are almost the equivalent of annual payments due to retirees, leaving the funds with little investable cash. In mid-2001, the government formally announced a plan to aid the pension funds through the sale of state shares as part of public offerings. This effort, though small, quickly failed in the face of a massive market selloff by supposedly retail investors.

The emerging problem is easy to see in Table 7.25. With a rapidly aging population and a tradition of generous support to retirees, the government will have to take action soon. First, it must find a way to fund its pension liabilities; then, it must liberalize regulations to enable the funds to invest in financial instruments with greater rates of return. Basing its decisions on the reality of the market and then cleaning it up would be a major first step.

Investor Base for Overseas Listed Chinese Shares and B Shares

The preceding discussion has dealt with the current investor base for China's A-share market. Obviously, the investor base for China's internationally listed

TABLE 7.25 China's Aging Population

	Population (Bn)	0–14	15–64	65+
1995	1.21	327	808	76
2000	1.26	328	845	87
2010	1.35	293	956	104
2020	1.43	287	989	153
2030	1.48	278	989	214
2040	1.49	287	950	252
2050	1.47	211	962	300

Source: World Bank figures, AWSJ, June 15–17, 2001, p. M1.

equity securities is significantly different. Looking into the investor base for international securities is the realm of the Equity Capital Markets (ECM) departments of the world's investment banks. ECM personnel are responsible for knowing all likely investors and tailoring an equity product that can suit investor taste – that is, be sold. Such information is extremely proprietary, although principal investors in listed companies can be sourced through the Bloomberg system. The intention, therefore, is simply to briefly touch on this topic.

Investors in the H-share market are easy to identify. Anyone with access to Bloomberg or Dow Jones can see who has invested in whom on a slightly time-lagged basis. When initially distributing H shares, the investment bank leading the underwriting typically reserves about 10–20% of the offering for the Hong Kong retail market. The remaining 80% is placed to a variety of professional investors in Asia, Europe, and the US. Such professional investors include specialists in emerging market equities, hedge funds, and specialist industry groups. The specialists may work at small hedge funds, major pension funds, and mutual fund companies. The major point is that all such institutional investors are professionals, are supported by large internal staffs, and have clearly defined investment parameters. In contrast, retail or individual investors generally make investment decisions based on current news, market fads, and so on, but without the sort of analysis a professional typically uses.

In contrast to H shares, Red Chips share great similarities with the B- and A-share companies and markets. They represent investment opportunities with a common characteristic: the issuing companies are long on sentiment and "concept," but, in the great majority of cases, are short on fundamentals. Having said this, there are distinctions in the investor base for each of these three types of equity securities, as well as between, for example, Shanghai and Shenzhen A shares.

As with the H shares, data are available from the major data services relating to the top 10 minority shareholders of a given Red Chip. This information does not really get at the question of which investors make the market in this type of stock. The definition of a Red Chip, however, sheds some light on the likely investor base. The SEHK has defined Red Chips very precisely as Hong Kong-listed companies with significant equity controlled by entities in mainland China.[52] The definition strongly suggests that Chinese government organizations, through their Hong Kong companies, are significant participants in Red Chip secondary trading. In addition, Hong Kong retail investors are unquestionably active. Finally, international investors have participated strongly in this market at times, particularly during its massive run-up in late 1997. Since then, it has largely fallen out of favor.

Since the March 2001 measures which lawfully opened the B-share markets to domestic investors, the investor base for Shanghai and Shenzhen B shares is wholly domestic, but it has been this way for the past decade. There is evidence to support this – for example, the *Shanghai Stock Exchange Fact Book 1998* data

TABLE 7.26   Ownership of Shanghai B-share Accounts by Country

Nationality of Account Holder	Shanghai No. of Accounts		Shenzhen No. of Accounts	
China Mainland	879,674	94.7%	455,648	82.0%
Hong Kong	15,285	1.6%	76,749	13.8%
United States	9,026	1.0%	5,506	1.0%
Macau	702	0.1%	3,571	0.6%
Taiwan	5,402	0.6%	2,822	0.5%
Canada	2,431	0.3%	1,865	0.3%
Australia	2,432	0.3%	1,659	0.3%
UK	1,614	0.2%	1,334	0.2%
Singapore	1,479	0.2%	938	0.2%
Japan	3,400	0.4%	785	0.1%
Other	7,637	0.8%	5,062	0.9%
Total	**929,082**	**100%**	**555,939**	**100%**

Sources: CSRC and Shanghai Stock Exchange, December 31, 2001.

show that over 66% of B-share account holders opened at brokerages in Shanghai were of Chinese nationality. Shanghai in 1998 was more of a true "mainland" market than Shenzhen (see Table 7.26). Therefore, it should be the case that there would be fewer Chinese-owned B-share accounts in Shanghai at the time. Shenzhen, although not reporting such data, should have had many more.

In conclusion, the first part of the experiment with equity markets was the easy part – restructure a few enterprises and list a minority interest. However, the market has now become the problem, but how to go about remedying years of regulatory inaction on this front? The government's focus is now changing to deal with the problem of market development. China's participation in the World Trade Organization may hasten this process, since the government has agreed to permit foreign involvement in the A-share markets through joint ventures in the asset management and securities industries. The success of this stage is critical if China's markets are to develop away from their current emerging market status.

CHAPTER 8

Sliced and Diced: China's Segmented Stock Markets

Share issuance is based on the principles of openness, fairness and equity. It must have the same rights for the same shares and the same benefits for the same shares. Each share issue must have the same issuing conditions and price. Any unit or individual buying shares should pay the same price for each share.

Article 130, Company Law

C hina's stock markets have evolved over more than a decade in channels set out by the 1992 Standard Opinion. With the primary objective of preserving the state's ownership of assets contributed to newly corporatized SOEs, the Opinion created two broad classes of shares, one tradable and the other non-tradable. Furthermore, the Opinion created sub-classes of non-tradable shares based on the distance of the entity contributing assets from the state. At least in the beginning, this approach succeeded in clearly defining certain rights of ownership, especially those of the state. In the planned economy, by contrast, such rights had been ambiguous except for the fact that the state in some sense owned everything. The unforeseen consequence of the Standard Opinion, however, was to create over time three (and then four) separate markets for different share classes. Contrary to the demand of the Company Law noted at the outset, in China, all shares are not treated equally. Nor do they enjoy the same price, nor are they traded fairly, and there is nothing transparent about the entire process.

The potential for separate markets was there from the start. In fact, it was realized almost at once when holders of LP shares sought to raise funds but were prohibited by regulation from selling their shares. Efforts to provide a market for such shares among other legal persons, of which STAQ and NETS were the earliest examples, failed.[1] They failed because it was a simple administrative procedure for private individuals, natural persons, to package themselves in the cloak of a company, a legal person. Consequently, shares associated with state assets could fall into the hands of the non-state sector. In short, such assets – and potentially entire companies – could become privatized. In the early 1990s, such an outcome was ideologically unacceptable.

But the problem remained: how to allow the owner of such shares to exercise his legal rights to sell them as defined in the Company Law? As the state sought a way out of the problem, practical realities – the unceasing demand for capital – asserted themselves and markets sprang up. For the most part, these were private markets where a buyer and seller negotiated between themselves. Where formal markets existed – for example, the auction houses – these became actively used until the state closed them off. In the meantime, the formal stock exchanges open to owners of tradable shares underwent rapid growth, listing hundreds of companies. This exacerbated the problem. Due to separate market development, a "segmentation mentality" has taken hold among market participants to the extent that it can be demonstrated that parallel stock markets operate within China.

By the start of the new century, such was China's demand for capital that the state found itself hard pressed to finance its own projects – for example, the much-needed pension reform. Like its companies, the state now wanted to exercise its own lawful rights to monetize its one potentially liquid asset: state shares. In taking a small step toward doing so, however, the state found that its actions strongly and negatively impacted the markets for tradable shares. Fearing the political consequences, the state backed off. How very ironic: the scheme it had created to solve one problem, unchallengable ownership, now placed heavy restrictions on its own freedom of action. Not only that, the scheme had also created a highly distorted market for the tradable shares. Fearing the outcome of thorough market reform, the state has been forced to pretend in public that its problems are limited to a small number of cases. Change, therefore, has come only at the margins and the status quo remains firmly in place.

The status quo, however, is no longer acceptable even to the state. This is not just a matter of the state needing capital. The strict segmentation of company shares prevents the state from realizing other critical goals as well. The long-sought-after benefits from the shareholding experiment – increased productivity, better corporate governance, greater competitiveness, and the creation, not destruction, of capital – remain unattainable for Chinese companies as long as the system is in place. Not only that, the emerging private sector, as well, is affected, and so on to the broader economy itself. Even worse, without broad and meaningful market reform, the state will find itself a blind and complaisant bystander in the spontaneous privatization of superficially state-owned companies – just what it had sought to avoid at the start.

This chapter, therefore, seeks to show that the Standard Opinion has created and then influenced the development of independent markets for the various tradable and non-tradable shares. By doing so, it seeks to set out the end result – privatization with Chinese characteristics. In fact, this style of privatization is a continuation of trends begun in the 1980s and interrupted by the political backlash of June 4.

SEGMENTED MARKETS

The principal function of any market is to price goods or services. In the case of stock markets, what is priced and sold are companies. Regulators and exchanges around the world specialize in creating the conditions in which information affecting the price of a company is equitably available to all buyers and sellers. The specific market condition they attempt to create is called transparency. With a sufficient degree of transparency, investors have a level playing field on which to make their investment decisions, whether the purchase of a few hundred shares or control of an entire company. These decisions in aggregate set the market value, or market capitalization, of listed companies. For Chinese companies, the markets do not play this function, for the simple reason that the different classes of stock trade in different and functionally independent markets, as illustrated in Figure 8.1.

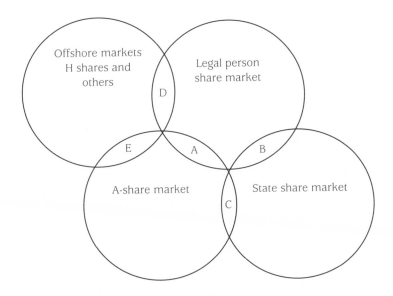

Based on the Standard Opinion, only one liquid market should exist, the A-share market. LP shares and state shares can be and are transferred within each class, but only with specific transaction approval by the state. Then there are the overseas listings. Over time, four parallel markets have evolved. The intersection of the A- and LP-share markets in Area A is open generally only to legal person entities on both a negotiated and, at times, a formal market basis. The typical A-share investor is excluded. The intersection of the LP and state share markets in Area B is also open only to legal person entities, but only on a negotiated basis. State shares sold in public offerings are found in Area C. Areas D and E indicate the expected participation of foreign investors through the QFII program (E) and acquisition of LP and state shares by negotiation. Separate and distinct, each market has little impact on the others.

FIGURE 8.1   Four Parallel Stock Markets.

A Shares versus H Shares

The existence of the first pair of markets is simple to demonstrate. A shares and H shares, in reality, are in fact both RMB shares. The only difference is that the H share is denominated in Hong Kong dollars and so is separated from its brother by China's foreign exchange control regime. For example, China Eastern Airlines (CEA) is a major airline based in Shanghai serving domestic and international markets. In 1995, CEA completed its IPO on the NYSE listing N shares, thereafter listing H shares on the SEHK and, subsequently, A shares on the Shanghai exchange. Taken together, these tradable shares account for 38% of the company's total shares. At what price do investors value CEA's operations? The values the market assigns to China Eastern's shares are shown in Figure 8.2. As can be seen, China's A-share investors (top black line) value the company far more – in fact, around four times more – than do investors in Hong Kong and New York. Furthermore, the company's H-share and N-share investors (bottom interwoven lines) are in complete agreement as to the company's value. So, which investor base is correct? Rather, what value do its investors assign China Eastern Airlines as a company? The question cannot be answered (see below).

The China Eastern example illustrates the problems associated with comparing domestic with overseas stock markets. Each market has a very different investor base; even more important, the financial environments are completely different. To begin with, because of currency controls, the A-share investor has few investment alternatives.[2] He can invest in A shares, B shares (if he has foreign currency), or CGBs, or put his money in the bank. Even if he owns foreign currency, he is restricted as to how much he can send abroad, assuming that he owns an overseas bank or securities account. China's investors, therefore, face extremely limited investment options. They cannot

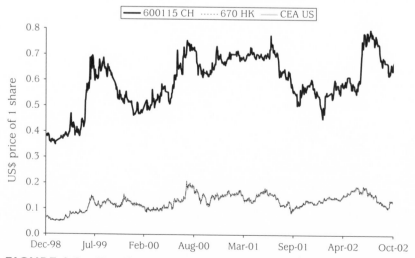

FIGURE 8.2 China Eastern Airlines, A-, H-, and N-share Prices.
Sources: Wind Information and Bloomberg.

give up on A shares, particularly of the larger, better companies: it's the only show in town. As long as prices are moving and there are opportunities to buy low and sell high, money will chase the A shares. This is, of course, the exact opposite of the overseas investor, who can freely convert his currency and trade any market and any type of security.

Nor are there arbitrage instruments that can keep the overseas and domestic shares trading in line, as do New York and Hong Kong.[3] There were 27 companies at the end of 2002 that have listed A and H shares. The H shares trade at discounts ranging from 50% to 90% of their respective A shares, as shown in Table 8.1.[4] The fact is that, because of currency control and regulatory measures, these two markets operate independently. At present, there is no way you can short the A shares of these companies and buy the H shares. Even if foreign exchange restrictions were lifted somehow, without the ability to at least short the A shares, the H- and A-share markets would still not become fully aligned. This is one lesson of the B-share market.

TABLE 8.1   Discounts of H Shares to A Shares, 27 Companies

HK Code	China Code	Name	A/H Discount (%)
902 HK	600011	Huaneng Power International	42.0
168 HK	600600	Tsingtao Beer	50.8
386 HK	600028	Sinopec	59.7
914 HK	600585	Anhui Conch	61.5
347 HK	000898	Angang New Steel	63.8
1171 HK	600188	Yanzhou Coal	64.7
338 HK	600688	Sinopec Shanghai Petrochemical	65.0
1138 HK	600026	China Shipping	69.7
1033 HK	600871	Sinopec Yizheng Chemical Fibre	76.3
1065 HK	600874	Tianjin Capital Environmental Protection	77.1
187 HK	600860	Beiren Printing	77.4
670 HK	600115	China Eastern Airlines	78.3
350 HK	000666	Jingwei Textile	79.6
323 HK	600808	Maanshan Iron & Steel	79.6
358 HK	600362	Jiangxi Copper	79.7
874 HK	600332	Guangzhou Pharmaceutical	80.2
300 HK	600806	Jiaoda High-Tech	80.5
719 HK	000756	Shandong Xinhua Pharmaceutical	80.7
177 HK	600377	Jiangsu Expressway	81.1
548 HK	600548	Shenzhen Expressway	81.5
553 HK	600775	Nanjing Panda	84.6
317 HK	600685	Guangzhou Shipyard	85.6
42 HK	000585	Northeast Electric	85.7
921 HK	000921	Guangdong Kelon	86.6
1072 HK	600875	Dongfang Electrical	86.7
368 HK	000618	Jilin Chemical	87.7
1108 HK	600876	Luoyang Glass	87.9

Sources: Quamnet and Wind Information, November 30, 2002.

A Shares versus B Shares

The B share has been a headache for the Chinese government for over a decade now. The market bloomed in the early 1990s, but it was left in the dust by overseas listings beginning in 1992. There have been few recent new offerings. In general, lack of interest, lack of quality companies, and lack of volume have plagued the market. Simply put, there are better Chinese investment opportunities elsewhere. H-share, Red Chip, and entire industry listings have all trumped the role the B-share market was supposed to play. The market has become the orphan of the Chinese securities world; even the mention of the name makes investors' eyes glaze over.

In Shanghai, 44 companies have issued both A and B shares; 43 have done so in Shenzhen. The exclusion of domestic investors, coupled with the total lack of foreign interest, meant that B shares have historically traded at an 80–90% discount to their respective A shares. All that changed in March 2001 when the CSRC announced the opening of the B-share market to domestic investors owning foreign currency deposits. As can be seen from Figure 8.3, prices in the two previously separate markets converged. The B-share price discount collapsed from around 75% to 30% and after 18 months of trading has leveled out at around 50%.

Domestic investors can now freely trade B shares and, together with Hong Kong residents, constitute about 96% of B-share accounts, as shown in Table 7.26 in Chapter 7. Foreign investors have not been enticed back into the

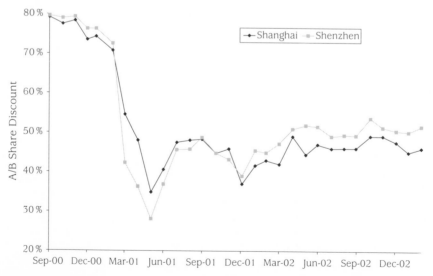

FIGURE 8.3 Discount of Shanghai and Shenzhen B Shares to their Equivalent A Shares.

Source: Wind Information.

Note: The data are averages of each of the stock discounts as at month-end.

B-share market by the CSRC's moves. Of the million or so accounts that were opened since the opening of the market, only a few thousand were foreign. There remains a general lack of interest: there is no primary market.[5] All new-issue activity is focused on the A-share market. As noted before, the CSRC does not allow either A or B shares to be borrowed and shorted. As a result, arbitraging the price differential is again not an option.[6] Since no arbitrage is possible, the markets remain unlinked and the discount remains (see Table 8.2).

Again, the question arises: which of the A-share price or B-share price is the correct price to value companies with both share classes? A shares can be valued at the A-share price and B shares at the B-share price, but what about the non-tradable LP shares? Even the exchanges, including the SEHK, are confused about this issue, seeking to avoid any questions by providing and using debatable definitions.[7]

In fact, companies with two classes of shares (but denominated in the same currency) were not uncommon in Asia prior to 1997. For many years, the Singapore, Philippine, Thai, and other markets defined a specific class of foreign shares in order to limit the impact of foreign capital on their markets. Consequently, such foreign stocks frequently traded at a premium to their local counterparts. The Asian financial crisis, however, put an end to such local/foreign splits and all these countries have now either done away with the dual share classes or at least opened formerly domestic shares to foreign participation. China's problems with its markets run deeper than just the local/foreign distinction, which, after all, can be resolved largely by a convertible RMB. The real share structure problem is to be found in the domestic, and not in the foreign, markets.

TABLE 8.2   Chinese Stock Markets' P/E Ratios

Year	Shanghai A	Shanghai B	Shenzhen A	Shenzhen B	H Share	Red Chips
1990	28.05	–	–	–	–	–
1991	81.83	–	26.71	–	–	–
1992	72.65	17.4	57.52	35.56	–	–
1993	42.48	–	44.21	20.11	–	–
1994	29.67	9.94	10.67	7.02	11.61	–
1995	16.32	8	9.8	6.01	10.05	–
1996	32.65	14.04	38.88	14.07	10.85	–
1997	43.43	11.99	42.66	10.67	14.84	–
1998	34.38	6.04	32.31	5.71	7.11	10.44
1999	38.14	10.05	37.56	10.38	–	–
2000	59.14	25.23	58.75	13.06	–	–
2001	37.59	43.39	40.76	25.3	6.41	18.72
2002	34.5	30.61	38.22	17.51	9.52	13.17

Sources: Shanghai and Shenzhen stock exchanges, and Stock Exchange of Hong Kong data. Blanks indicate unavailable data.

What Do A Shares Value?

Stock markets value companies, but this is usually the case when the total shares of a company are listed. Representing only 30% of company equity, what does the A-share market really value? For example, Beijing Center Gate takes its name from the locality in the city's university district that has become synonymous with hi-tech start-ups. The promoters of Center Gate did not include state agencies; only legal persons contributed to the company's formation. This was actually a takeover of a listed, but bankrupt company, although that is unimportant for this discussion. During the takeover and restructuring, the former company's shares had not traded.[8] The new company, Center Gate, had registered capital of 300 million LP shares. After restructuring on July 12, 1999, Center Gate's 187 million A shares priced at RMB5.78 began trading, and the stock closed sharply up at RMB31.95 on the first day. Three weeks later, in August 1999, the company announced a one-for-one rights offer priced again at RMB5.78. As the market was at RMB30, the rights issue was a guaranteed money-spinner for the company's existing shareholders. The cheap price for the rights offering was part of the takeover package agreed with the previous company's owners. The deal was, "Agree to a one-for-one share swap of your shares for Center Gate shares and we will throw in a cheap placement." After all, the shares were trading at RMB30 and the offer price was only 20% of this. Proper pricing for the rights issue, however, is not the point here. The question is: what price did the market assign the A shares once trading had begun again? As professionals in other markets will attest, the market is the final determinant of pricing. What the market decided here highlights the parallel universes of China's shares.

Before going ex-rights, Center Gate's A shares traded at RMB33.80. The next morning, as the offering proceeded, the Shenzhen exchange announced the new post-offering opening price. This price reflected the dilution caused by the new shares released into the market by the rights issue. *China Securities Daily*, the newspaper of record for the securities industry, carried the announcement. The calculation of the company's market capitalization, which was technically accurate, is shown in Table 8.3; its result was a price of RMB26.025 per share.

TABLE 8.3 Beijing Center Gate Rights Offering, Official Price

	No. of Shares (Mn)	Price per Share (RMB)	Total (RMB Mn)
Number of pre-rights shares	187 A shares + 300 LP shares	33.80	16,460
PLUS:			
Shares in rights offering	187	5.78	1,081
Sub-total	674		17,541
DIVIDE by:			
Total post-rights shares 17,541/674 =		**26.025**	

Unfortunately, the market did not agree with this calculation. The first day the shares traded following the offering, they opened at RMB23.42 down 10%, the daily mandated trading limit. The next day, the shares again dropped by the 10% limit to RMB21.08. Not until the third day did the shares resume normal trading, closing at RMB19.01, down almost 44% from the pre-rights share price. These events are illustrated in Figure 8.4.

After some thought as to why the RMB19 level, it becomes clear that the market had decided that the post-rights price should reflect *only* the tradable A shares in the company's capital base, and not the non-tradable LP shares. In other words, investors behave and price A shares as though non-tradable shares don't exist. Or if they do exist, they do so in an entirely different market that has no impact on their "own" A-share market. Though surprising, this finding is in line with how the state thinks, or at least once thought, about its own share contributions.

This interpretation is supported by a recalculation of the price with the result, shown in Table 8.4, of a price per share of RMB19.79. Thus, it seems clear that under current market conditions, Chinese A-share markets value A shares and nothing else. Investors do not attribute value to non-tradable shares; the two markets trade independently.

The "correct" answer to the Center Gate pricing problem is unclear. If one believes that the market is always right, then the market will ultimately determine the true value of a company. In that case, the impact of loosening restrictions on the sale of state and LP shares could be devastating, not only to the valuation of the company in question, but to market capitalization as well. This is the lesson of the 2001 effort to sell a small portion of state shares into the

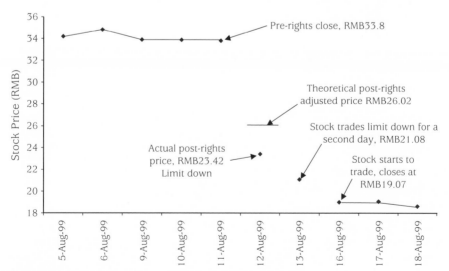

FIGURE 8.4 Beijing Center Gate Rights Offering History.
Source: Wind Information.

TABLE 8.4   Beijing Center Gate Rights Offering, Market Price

	No. of Shares (Mn)	Price per Share (RMB)	Total (RMB Mn)
Number of pre-rights A shares	187	33.80	6,321
PLUS:			
Shares in rights offering	187	5.78	1,081
Sub-total	374		7,402
Divide by:			
Total post-rights A shares	**7,402/374 =**	**19.79**	

public market. In contrast, as will be discussed later, the sale of state and LP shares in their own markets at drastic discounts to A-share prices has no impact at all on the A-share market.

How the market reacts in large part reflects investor expectations, so it is important to consider the element of investor psychology, including that of the state itself. It is likely that a part of the reason for the lower-than-expected trading price for the Center Gate shares is that it accurately reflects how investors understand what they are investing in. This goes back to the perspective of the state as embodied in Article 4 of the Company Law quoted earlier in Chapter 4, which can be summarized as: "The state assets contributed to a listed company belong to the state."

For its part, if the state contributes its own assets and receives non-tradable shares in return, it will not care how shares representing other assets trade except as a policy issue relating to social unrest. Moreover, it will not care how many shares are issued and at what price, as long as the company it owns and controls acquires financing. The A shares are some other investors' property and concern. In other words, the state's consideration of a company's cost of capital extends only to the cost of its original investment of equipment, land, or buildings.

Similarly, A-share investors who contribute cash seem to give no credit to any valuation that attempts to include the contributed state assets – they may be taken back! The retail investors, like the state, thus behave in an equally compartmentalized way. Their concern is only about their original cash investment. They may want to take their cash back, just as (in theory) the state can recoup its assets.

A Shares and LP Shares

In February 2001, the management of Guangdong Midea, a prominent white goods manufacturer, conducted an MBO.[9] Midea's largest shareholder, which was state-backed, sold a total of 72 million LP shares, representing a 14.9% stake, to the company's third-largest shareholder, Meituo Company. Meituo was established and controlled by a private individual, Midea's CEO. On completion of the sale, Meituo became Midea's largest shareholder. In short, Midea's CEO had effectively completed a management buy-out. The important point is not that the company had been effectively privatized, but that the shares were priced below Midea's NAV as well as its A-share trading price at the time. Meituo acquired the shares in two blocks priced at RMB2.95 and RMB3 per share. In contrast, the NAV at the time was RMB4.07 per share and the listed A-share price around RMB13.

Given the regulatory framework described elsewhere, this transaction and its pricing may appear surprising, if not illegal. To the contrary, below-NAV share sales have been the common practice for Chinese MBOs, which state agencies are routinely approving if not leading the auctions themselves. The comment on this deal made in the *China M&A Yearbook 2002* was that "qualified asset valuation intermediaries should be used to assess the value of these (legal person) shares to prevent the 'giveaway' of state assets."[10] The writer was perfectly serious. He makes no mention of the huge discount to the listed A-share price, much less of the role that the stock market should play in valuing a company. He seems to believe that the valuation of a company has no relationship to the value the stock exchange places on it. The whole focus of concern appears to be the discount to NAV and the potential loss to the state, not the role of market prices. And this from a publication sponsored by one of the earliest proponents of China's stock exchanges!

The Midea case is not unique. Once the reform current began flowing strongly in the direction of clarifying ownership relations, it was only a short jump into buying and selling the rights of ownership. Because freely tradable A shares constitute a minority stake in most companies' equity capital, changes in management control take place only through the "transfer" of non-tradable LP shares. It is a fact determined by the Standard Opinion that control of listed companies rests with the state and LP shares.

The auction houses played only a marginal role in changes of company control through the "transfer" of LP shares. This was also the case for STAQ and NETS. Auction house trades generally ranged from several thousand to a few hundreds of thousands of shares, far too small to affect overall ownership. Changes in ownership, therefore, are generally consummated in behind-the-scenes negotiated transfers, until recently receiving little scrutiny from either the regulatory authorities or stock-market investors. The *China M&A Yearbook 2002* is the only source of systematic information on this topic.[11] In 2001, the *Yearbook* listed over 400 M&A, MBO, or major corporate restructuring transactions. Of these deals, there were 56 transfers of LP shares of listed companies where full pricing details were available.[12] Shanghai-listed firms accounted for 31 of the transfers, with transaction sizes varying from as little as 3.95% of a company to as much as 56.8%. On average, 20.9% of total shares were sold. For these transactions, the transfer price of the LP shares ranged between a 54% to 91% discount to the company's prevailing A-share price, with the average discount being 81%.

Three of the 56 companies also had both A and B shares. As can be seen from Table 8.5, the LP share price has little to do with either listed share price. In general, it appears to be related to NAV, but in some cases, transfers were conducted at below NAV per share.

TABLE 8.5   Legal Person Share Transfers Market Impact

Date Company Code	11/29/01 Shanghai Zhenhua Port Machinery 600320	8/28/01 China Fangda Group 000055	3/23/01 Shanghai Lianhua Fibre 600617
A-share price (RMB)	14.86	14.17	20.6
B-share price (RMB)	8.09	6.03	8.26
NAV per share (RMB)	3.735	3.45	1.696
LP transfer price (RMB)	3.57	3.16	3.486
Discount to A-share price	76.0%	77.7%	83.1%
% of company transferred	21.1%	19.6%	6.0%

Sources: China M&A Yearbook 2002 and independent price research.

The disregard of the listed market prices does not bother the participants or, apparently, the state agencies approving the sale.[13] This is because the guardian of such transfer of ownership is not the CSRC, but local state asset management bureaus. For these bureaus, as long as the transfer price is at or above NAV per share, the state has not lost money. The bureaus are not charged with taking the A-share market into consideration. As for the buyer, he gains control of the company without having to deal with thousands of A-share investors – discussions can be conducted with a single or small number of sellers. The buyer also gets more bang for his buck by avoiding the higher A-share prices, gaining control for a fraction of the cost. The seller, often the original promoter of the company, is satisfied because he can realize cash for his shares. Both sides are happy, but what of the A-share investor in the company? The A-share investor is also content. The change of ownership has not affected his market in any negative way. In fact, the new owners will probably boost the stock price with promises of asset injections, greater revenues, and better profit.

It has been suggested that LP shares trade at a discount because they are illiquid and cannot be freely traded. This is certainly true, to a point. The shares cannot be traded on a day-to-day basis, but in many cases ownership control of the firm is being traded – 20%, 30%, 40%, and even 50% of all outstanding shares. What owner of a company is trading 20–50% of his company on a daily basis in the marketplace? The buying and selling of a small stake, as was seen in the auction houses, justifies a discount to the A shares given the illiquidity of LP shares. When the whole company is bought or sold, however, market valuation should play some role. If not, why have a market? Why not just trade at the NAV price?

State Share Buy-backs

State shares also are transferred among state entities, but in four cases in the late 1990s listed companies themselves actually bought back a portion of the state holdings from their parents, ostensibly to improve their overall shareholding structure.[14] Details of the companies and transactions are in Table 8.6. The four companies each bought a significant percentage of their existing share capital and then wrote off the shares, thereby reducing the total number of shares in existence. This should have resulted in a jump in the companies' A-share price, reflecting the greater stake that A-share investors now had in the company. Trading levels for each A share, however, remained unchanged.

The four buy-backs were completed at an 80% discount to the listed A-share price and valuation was based on NAV (not shown in table). The T + 1 and T−1 price entries shown in Table 8.6 are the trading prices of the A shares before and after the buy-back became effective. These show very little impact despite the formal market capitalization of each company showing a decrease similar in value to that of the canceled shares. Once again, this demonstrates that the A-share market is not aware of, or simply does not care about, the value of non-A shares. Only when the number of A shares increases or decreases does the secondary market respond.

The CSRC moved to halt these buy-backs, although they are permitted in Article 149 of the Company Law. The potential for misappropriation of company funds by the major shareholder is the problem. As a senior official at the CSRC bluntly put it, "… controlling shareholders often treat minority owners as ATMs when conducting connected transactions."[15] Buy-backs are impracticable for most listed companies, however, as they simply do not have the cash resources.

TABLE 8.6 State Share Buy-backs

Effective Date	September 7, 2000	December 5, 2000	December 28, 2000	December 27, 1999
Code	600619	600096	000661	600642
Name	Highly Group	Yuntianhua	Changchun Hi-Tech	Sheneng
Share Type	State	State LP	State	State LP
Shares before (Mn)	423	568	201	2,633
Shares after (Mn)	381	368	131	1,633
Repurchased (Mn)	42	200	70	1,000
Bought	9.95%	35.2%	34.8%	37.98%
Trade Price	2.28	2.83	3.44	2.51
Listed Price	12.73	13.75	15.71	11.98
Price Discount	82%	79%	78%	79%
T−1 Price	12.58	14	15.92	12.3
T+1 Price	12.63	13.42	16.41	12.06
Cap. Before (RMB Mn)	5,316	7,955	3,205	32,387
Cap. After (RMB Mn)	4,806	4,941	2,155	19,695
Change in Cap.	−9.6%	−37.9%	−32.8%	−39%

Sources: Shanghai and Shenzhen stock exchanges.

IS THERE A COMPANY VALUE?

In all the market activity in China, the company, purportedly the object of the entire reform effort, has itself remained wholly overlooked. It has been sliced and diced to assist changes in ownership of constituent parts (and to prevent them) and to raise capital. But separate share markets for different share classes fail to promote fundamental changes in performance. This can only come about if the stock markets, through valuing all the company's shares, directly influence management decision-making. This will only happen with greater shareholder interest in the company, rather than in its short-term stock price performance.

The importance of accurately valuing companies should be, but has only superficially been, a critical part of China's SOE reform program. This does not mean that the tools for technical valuation have not been popularized, but rather that such tools do not produce practical results in the Chinese context. The market's current inability to value listed companies properly is a direct consequence of the Standard Opinion and the state's perpetuation of illiquid classes of shares. The company, viewed through the prism of the stock markets, is a fragmented entity. In turn, this fragmentation traces its origins back to state planning and fund accounting. This earlier system also failed to treat an enterprise as an integrated whole, seeing it as three distinct parts that may, or may not, have represented a company from a financial viewpoint. In any event, sound financial management was not the goal of that system; production was, and largely still is, the principal objective.

What sense can be made from these kinds of markets? What do different prices mean for the market capitalization of companies and the market as a whole? It is tempting to simply say that the A shares are grossly overvalued and that H shares give a better indication of the "true" value of Chinese companies. H-share investors are presumably more experienced at valuing companies and certainly have dozens of other products in which to invest, in marked contrast to their mainland counterparts. Their valuation of Chinese companies, therefore, should arguably be better.

To get an idea, take as a case in point the Hong Kong-, New York-, and Shanghai-listed China Eastern Airlines, as shown in Table 8.7. The company's market capitalization – that is, its value as appraised by the market – is completely unclear, ranging from US$619 million to US$2.4 billion. The question, as before, is: what market sets the price standard? The Shanghai Stock Exchange ranks companies by their market capitalization (the "Shanghai method" in Table 8.7), but it ignores the existence of H shares; those shares are traded in Hong Kong, not Shanghai! A fuller calculation would be to add to this the H shares valued at the H-share price (point 2). A third way is to assume that the overseas investor valuation of H shares is really the "true" price of the stock (point 3). Following Chinese M&A practice (point 4), yet another calculation values the non-tradable state shares at NAV and throws in the A and H shares valued at their respective prices.[16] These four different

TABLE 8.7 China Eastern Airlines Market Capitalization

(in Mn)	A Shares (A)	Price (RMB) (Ap)	H Shares (H)	Price (HK$) (Hp)	State Shares (S)	NAV (RMB)	Market Cap (in US$)
Number/Price	300	5.52	1,567	0.99	3,000	1.286	
1. Shanghai Method $(A + S) \times Ap$			$(300 + 3,000) \times 5.52$			=	$2,200
2. Shanghai + H Shares $[(A + S) \times Ap)] + (H \times Hp)$			$[(300 + 3,000) \times 5.52] + (1,567 \times 0.99)$			=	$2,400
3. "True" Price $(A + H + S) \times Hp$			$(300 + 1,567 + 3,000) \times 0.99$			=	$619
4. Chinese M&A Price $(A \times Ap) + (S \times NAV) + (H \times Hp)$			$(300 \times 5.52) + (1,567 \times 0.99) + (3,000 \times 1.286)$			=	$865

Source: Wind Information, October 22, 2002.

approaches give dramatically different results. Which is the "correct" value is anyone's guess.

This approach can be extended to the stock market at large. Based on October 2002 figures, calculations using the official and the Chinese M&A methods again produce dramatically different results, as shown in Table 8.8. Looking at it in this way challenges the claim that the A-share market is the second-largest in Asia after Japan, as shown in Figure 8.5. The official definition of market size is based on a price that is the result of an imbalance in supply and demand coupled with manipulative practices in a small part of the market's share structure (the A shares). This price is then extrapolated on to the entire market. If the pricing of the H shares is truly a better indicator for Chinese companies, then even these figures may be overly optimistic, since many H shares trade below NAV. If the Chinese investor were able to invest freely in overseas markets and non-tradable shares were tradable, it may not be unrealistic to suppose that official market capitalization would fall to between US$100 and US$150 billion. This would put the combined A-share markets on a par with Malaysia or Singapore, but far behind Australia, Hong Kong, Taiwan, and Korea.

TABLE 8.8 Comparative Market Capitalization of Shanghai and Shenzhen

	Market Capitalization Official Figures (US$ Bn)	Market Capitalization M&A Valuation (US$ Bn)
Shanghai Exchange	330.68	173.74
Shenzhen Exchange	172.36	96.82
Total	**503.04**	**270.56**

Source: Wind Information, October 31, 2002.

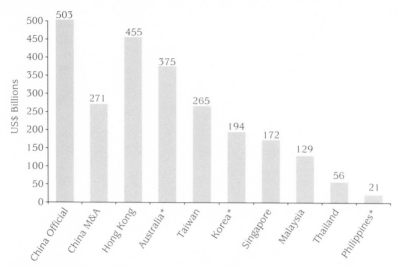

FIGURE 8.5   Comparative Market Capitalization, Non-Japan Asia.
Sources: Individual stock exchange websites, October 31, 2002; *Fy2001 data.

ECONOMIC INEFFICIENCIES OF SEGMENTED MARKETS

The Case of Zhengzhou Baiwen Department Store

The story of Zhengzhou Baiwen demonstrates the economic inefficiencies of a shareholding system without clear ownership risks (see Figure 8.6). Zhengzhou Baiwen Department Store (600898) listed on the Shanghai exchange on April 18, 1996.[17] The stock performed well over the next year, from RMB6.77 reaching as high as RMB28.4 by May 1997. The company posted strong profit growth through 1994–97 and was able to raise RMB155 million in July 1998 through a rights offering. Only one month later, the company announced that its first-half profits were significantly down on the previous year. The stock traded down to around RMB6.5 and continued to slide in the first half of 1999. On April 24, 1999, the company announced that it had lost over RMB500 million in FY 1998. Based on the auditors' report that the NAV of the stock was less than its face value, the exchange designated it a special treatment stock and restricted trading to a 5% up or down range. The fact that this came so soon after a large secondary offering would have triggered an investigation into the company, its underwriters, and auditors in the West, but not in China in 1998. The August release of the first-half 1999 results showed the company was still losing money and was technically bankrupt. So far, this was not an atypical case.

In December 1999, China Construction Bank announced it had transferred RMB1.9 billion of debt owed by Zhengzhou Baiwen to its Cinda Asset Management Company, making Cinda the largest creditor. The company, for its part, announced that they would set up a working group to devise a restructuring strategy and report back within six months. By late March 2000,

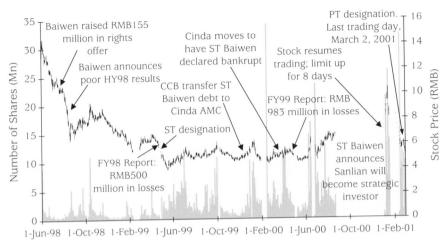

FIGURE 8.6 Zhengzhou Baiwen Trading History.
Source: Wind Information.

Cinda began to move to have Baiwen declared bankrupt. The company and its local government owner rejected the idea: it would spoil any hopes of a rescue plan, as well as cause a loss of face. Then, in April 2000, its 1999 financials came out showing that the company had lost an incredible RMB983 million.

After six months, the working group reported little progress on a restructuring plan but promised they would continue to look for a way out of the current difficulties. Shanghai suspended the stock from trading on August 21, 2000. Incredibly, help was just around the corner. In November 2000, the company announced that Shandong Sanlian Group would become a strategic shareholder in the firm. The exchange allowed the stock to resume trading on January 3, 2001, then suspended it again between March 5 and April 5, 2001, due to the restructuring. Because of its losses in 2000, the stock was eventually designated as a particular transfer (PT) stock, able to trade only on Fridays. March 2, 2001, was the last time that the stock traded, closing at RMB5.48.

Stocks in China often perform well even though the underlying company is bankrupt. Investors believe that the government will arrange some sort of rescue that will keep them happy. In this case, it was not to be. The rescue plan called for existing shareholders to transfer 50% of their shares to Sanlian. Those unwilling to do so could cash out at RMB1.84 for A shares and RMB0.18 for non-tradable shares. Sanlian would also settle RMB150 million owed to Cinda for a total of RMB30 million. Zhengzhou Baiwen Group, the parent and largest shareholder, agreed to the deal and transferred 14.4 million shares (half of its 15% stake) to Sanlian. Sanlian announced on June 25, 2002, that it had acquired 83.94 million shares from the other 67,610 shareholders of Baiwen.[18]

That, of course, was not the end of the story. Various accounting irregularities were discovered at Zhengzhou Baiwen in October 2000 and the CSRC started to investigate.[19] The CSRC inquiry exposed a long history of false

TABLE 8.9 Zhengzhou Baiwen False Profits

Year	Company Reported Net Profits/Losses (RMB Mn)	CSRC Figures: Net Profits/Losses (RMB Mn)	Overstatement
1994	25.13	22.29	2.84
1995	27.40	11.16	16.24
1996	49.89	38	11.89
1997	78.43	−19.53	97.96
1998	−502.41	−536.46	34.05
Total	**−321.56**	**−484.54**	**162.98**

Source: CSRC Punishment Verdict [2001] No. 19, September 27, 2001.

and misleading figures and information at the company (see Table 8.9). Zhengzhou Baiwen had overstated its net profits for 1994 through 1998. In short, the company had falsified its financial statements to gain a share listing. In addition to this, the company also used all the capital raised in its 1998 rights offer to pay off bank loans instead of the announced retail expansion. It was never reported what happened to the original IPO proceeds.

The CSRC found that Li Fuqian, the chairman, Lu Yide, the vice chairman and general manager, and 10 other directors were directly responsible for the fraud. It fined the company RMB2 million, Lu Fuqian RMB300,000, Lu Yide RMB200,000, and each of the other 10 directors RMB100,000.[20] In August 2002, Zhengzhou prosecutors brought charges of false accounting against Li Fuqian, Lu Yide, and Du Qunfu, the finance department head. On November 12, the Zhengzhou People's Intermediary Court found all three guilty and sentenced Lu Fuqian to a five-year prison sentence and a further three years of probation. The other two both received two-year prison terms followed by two years of probation. As for the company, Baiwen again showed a loss in 2000 but returned to profitability in 2001 and the first three quarters of 2002. As of late November 2002, six years after its IPO, the stock remains suspended from trading. In contrast, Enron, one of the largest companies in the US, failed, was declared bankrupt, its management were disgraced or indicted, and the NYSE had moved on, all within 12 months.

THE PATH NOT TAKEN

The experience of companies that carried out private placements in the 1980s and waited years to list suggests that the government could have taken a different approach to the shareholding experiment. The state is a minority investor in these companies, although it is the largest single shareholder.

There are 211 domestically listed companies whose combined A-, B-, and H-share free float exceeds 50% of their total equity capital.[21] Together they account for nearly 17.7% of the total number of domestically listed companies and for US$70 billion, or roughly 14%, of the total market capitalization of the two exchanges as of October 31, 2002. Among them, the shares of five companies are entirely listed and trading on the market – for example, Shanghai Feile Acoustics, the first enterprise to publicly offer shares. Is this situation simply an anomaly, have these companies really been privatized, and what, if anything, is their significance?

A review of their offering histories shows that of the 211 companies, 89 carried out private share placements prior to the full implementation of the 1994 Company Law, which prohibited this method of corporatization. Of these 89 companies, 23 completed placements during the 1980s, and a further 46 before 1994, while 22 more completed placements despite the Law's enactment (see Table 8.10). This record again underlines both the spontaneity of the shareholding experiment as well as the tremendous enterprise demand for capital.

The prohibition of placements was designed to give the state complete control over the corporatization process. With full CSRC approval now required, it would no longer be possible for companies to dilute state holdings to less than 50% before seeking state approval for listing. The 89 companies, therefore, are significant in that they used placements to raise capital freely without

TABLE 8.10 Subscription versus Listing for the 89 Companies versus All Others

	89 Companies Free Float > 50%			Other Companies Free Float < 50%		
Year	Placement	Listing	As Yet Unlisted	Placement	Listing	As Yet Unlisted
1984	3	0	3	0	0	0
1985	2	0	5	0	0	0
1986	4	0	9	0	0	0
1987	6	0	15	6	0	6
1988	4	0	19	31	0	37
1989	2	0	21	26	0	62
1990	2	6	17	11	2	71
1991	5	4	18	11	0	82
1992	16	8	26	74	32	124
1993	23	32	17	101	90	135
1994	5	16	6	33	94	74
1995	1	3	4	12	21	65
1996	8	11	1	164	192	37
1997	5	6	0	183	200	20
1998	1	1	0	102	105	17
1999	2	2	0	60	77	0
Total	89	89	0	814	814	0

Source: Wind Information.

regard for the potential impact on state control. In this, they were aided and abetted by the support of local governments.

These companies, as well as the 814 other companies that raised capital through placements, are among the "heritage problems (*lishi yiliu wenti*)" left over from the previous era of experimentation. As the data illustrate, once Deng added his support to the securities markets in early 1992, the number of placements surged as companies rushed to raise funds. This led to a rapid build-up in the queue to list that continued well after the enactment of the Company Law in 1994. By 1999 the state had succeeded in ending placements and had listed by way of introduction all such companies on the two exchanges. This brought all these companies and any future fundraising activity under the state's direct scrutiny. Thereafter, subscriptions to company shares and listing became more or less simultaneous, with both taking place only after full CSRC approval.[22]

The listing of the seemingly "privatized" shareholding companies marked the end of one potential outcome of the experiment: apparent privatization.[23] Even if this was not privatization, it suggests a path that might have avoided the share class proliferation that has created the illiquid overhang in China's stock markets. This point is illustrated by comparing Tables 8.11 and 8.12, which show the share composition of the Shanghai market in 1991 and 1999. Whereas in 1991 the overall market was evenly divided between tradable and non-tradable shares, by 1999 non-tradable shares accounted for nearly 72%.

This is the second point of significance of these companies. Had it adopted a more sophisticated approach in the early 1990s, the state would have been able to avoid the creation of today's massive overhang while maintaining control even with tradable shares. After all, in the preponderance of cases, the state remained the largest shareholder of these companies and controlled their boards. Given the times, the political sensitivity of the shareholding experiment, as well as China's heritage of central planning, such an outcome is probably beyond reasonable expectation. Nevertheless, with the passage

TABLE 8.11 Shanghai Market Capitalization Share Structure, 1991

| (Mn) | SSE Market Capitalization A-share Companies | | | |
	No. of Shares	RMB	US$	%
State Shares	1,778,841	977	118	33.2
Domestic Legal Person Shares	211,190	115	14	3.9
Individual Shares	692,359	380	46	12.9
Total Non-tradable	**2,682,390**	**1,472**	**178**	**50.0**
A Shares	2,682,390	1,472	178	50.0
Total Market Capitalization	5,364,780	160,228	356	100.0

Source: Annual Trading Statistics 1990–91; for comparability, US$1 = RMB8.28.

TABLE 8.12 Shanghai Market Capitalization Share Structure, 1999

| (Mn) | RMB | SSE Market Capitalization | | | |
| | | A Shares | | B Shares | |
		US$	%	US$	%
State Shares	426,311	51,487	27.3	2,836	38.2
Domestic Legal Person Shares	509,207	61,498	32.6	1,416	19.1
Overseas Legal Person Shares	19,762	2,387	1.3	132	1.8
Social Legal Person Shares	104,943	12,674	6.7	284	3.8
Internal Shares	19,927	2,407	1.3	103	1.4
Other	37,337	4,509	2.4	74	1.0
Total Non-tradable	**1,117,487**	**134,962**	**71.6**	**4,845**	**65.3**
A Shares	444,523	53,686	28.5		0.0
B Shares	0		0.0	2,574	34.7
Total Market Capitalization	1,562,010	188,648	100.0	7,418	100.0

Source: Wind Information.

of time, an additional 122 companies now have free floats greater than 50%. The state, for its part, has grown used to holding a controlling, although not necessarily a majority, stake in its companies. What this might suggest is discussed later in this chapter.

TRYING TO MERGE THE MARKETS

It is harder to fix something than to make the effort to get it right in the first place. Over the past few years, the government has begun to try to unify China's stock markets. This is being attempted for purely practical reasons: the state needs more capital. Unification in this context, therefore, means selling at least a part of the state's holdings into the A-share markets. There is no other efficient way for the state to monetize its own shareholdings in state-owned companies. Other factors driving the effort include a political willingness on the part of the government to divest itself from non-essential industries (*zhuada fangxiao*). Finally, there is a growing realization among policymakers that the current share system will have a growing negative impact on the future growth of the market and economy at large.

Size of the Problem

State-owned holdings are composed of state shares and state LP shares.[24] The two definitions should be treated as one categorization – state shares. By this definition, the state holds positions in 963 different listed A-share companies (Shanghai 551, Shenzhen 412).[25] If valued at A-share prices, the shares are worth US$252 billion, but at NAV they are worth far less, only US$89 billion.

The NAV standard is important, as noted previously, because the government prohibits the sale of state-owned assets below it. The recent highly problematic listing of China Telecom highlighted this restriction to the international audience.[26] As is obvious by now, the size of the government's holdings lies at the heart of the matter.

In 2000, a record year for domestic issuance, the Shanghai and Shenzhen markets raised just over US$18 billion, about 20% of the government's holdings valued at NAV. Any method aimed at relieving this huge position will either require a massive injection of fresh capital willing to buy the listed SOEs or will have a significant negative valuation impact on the prospects of new firms seeking to list. Given the magnitude of the problem, it is no surprise that there are many calls for China's savers to switch from bank deposits to stock investment. Or that foreign firms have been recently welcomed to buy state and LP shares.

Attempted Solutions

Since late 1999, the CSRC and the State Council have initiated a number of proposals and regulations, with limited success, designed to reduce the state's holdings. Each of these solutions, or a combination of them, would certainly be able to sell some of the shares, but none of them, or even all of them together, can solve the whole problem. The first attempt was to "auction off (*paimai*)" state shares in the A-share market. On November 29, 1999, the CSRC announced the selection of 10 listed companies chosen to auction off a portion of their state shares to current holders of A shares (see Table 8.13). Pricing was based on a range set above each company's NAV, but less than a

TABLE 8.13 CSRC-designated 10 Companies Auctioning State Shares

		Market Capitalization		Share Price		
Code	Name	RMB Bn	State %	11/26/99 (RMB)	3/12/99 (RMB)	% Rise
0667	Huayi Investment	2.23	74.0	8.51	8.58	0.8
0692	Huitian Power	3.06	62.4	13.04	13.23	1.5
0589	**Qianluntai A**	**1.87**	**61.8**	**7.13**	**8.87**	**24.4**
0426	Fulong Power	1.72	72.3	8.61	8.93	3.7
0401	Beidong Cement	5.29	74.5	6.30	6.29	-0.2
600663	Lujiazui	18.73	64.1	14.01	14.01	0.0
600877	**Jialing**	**3.47**	**74.8**	**7.29**	**8.19**	**12.3**
600129	Taiji Group	4.02	74.4	15.00	15.84	5.6
600717	Tianjin Port	3.40	72.9	9.73	9.82	0.9
600828	Chengshang Group	1.81	74.9	9.50	10.29	8.3

Source: Wind Information; state shares as of September 30, 1999; bold represents companies to offer before year-end 1999.

P/E ratio of 10 times earnings.[27] Given that the average P/E ratio for the market at the time was around 50, the CSRC's pricing reflects the thought that non-tradable shares are worth only 20% of tradable shares. In any event, it was done to make the state shares attractive propositions. As a CSRC official put it when announcing the plan, "The sale of state shares fully considers the actual situation of China's equity markets, the pricing is relatively reasonable and leaves a fairly large opportunity for profit. The reason why we are giving preference to original shareholders is because we want to fully care for the interests of current [A share] investors."[28]

In the days following the announcement, the shares of the two companies meant to complete their offerings before year-end 1999 traded up 24% and 12%. This surprising outcome reflected investor belief that acquiring shares now would enable them to acquire an equal number of cheap shares later so that, overall, they could book a nice gain. The only answer to this can be that it all depends on how high the initial buy-in cost is. In retrospect, this price movement was no doubt driven by market manipulators – the first company to attempt an auction failed miserably. The transaction, completed on December 28, 1999, was nearly 20% undersubscribed, forcing the underwriter to underwrite for a change! Market response to the second company was also cold: only 76% of the shares were subscribed. Following the second auction, the CSRC halted the entire effort. The failure of these two experimental deals reflected people's expectations of much lower pricing. Although based on a cheap 10 times P/E ratio, the calculation used the average of the past three years. The market felt that the consequent absolute price was still too high. The real problem is the absence of value creation and the market's knowledge that there were more state shares to come.

There is a further aspect as well. This is simply that even at a lower share price, insufficient demand from other, new investors exists to provide support in the secondary market. If the state truly believed that company shares were being offered to investors at an acceptable low price, there is nothing to prevent it from using international techniques to attempt to generate greater demand and higher prices. By treating a company's shares as a commodity, prices will naturally be lower and the entire market is unlikely to develop.

The 1999 first attempt to sell state shares thus received a cool, if not frosty, welcome. In June 2001, the State Council formally announced a second effort. The proposal required that 10% of new share issues consist of state shares. Funds raised in this way were to be allocated to the central government's social welfare fund. This was an exceptionally modest plan. As companies sell only new shares, assume that in an IPO the company sells shares equivalent to 25% of the post-offering combined capital. This means that the state share portion will represent less than 2.5% of total share capital.

What has been the result of this modest plan? It promptly put an end to the two-year-old bull market. Four months later, in late October 2001, the CSRC announced that domestic companies would no longer need to comply. Rumors have forced it to confirm repeatedly that all consideration of listing state shares had ended.[29] Overseas-listed companies such as China Aluminum and a number of GEM-listed companies continued to comply.[30] During the period the requirement was effective, 17 new domestic issues raised just over RMB2.31 billion (US$279 million) for the Social Welfare Fund, as shown in Table 8.14.

Since then, even the slightest whisper that state shares may be sold has caused the markets to tremble. In fact, investors have never recovered their confidence. It has now been amply demonstrated that state shares cannot trade freely – they can't even be spoken about freely! – without dramatically affecting stock prices.

This has led one of China's pre-eminent economists to suggest that the government should somehow compensate existing A-share investors for the losses that they will inevitably suffer.[31] This, of course, is nonsense. Any compensation scheme would need to treat all shareholders equally and would by definition reward the larger shareholders, which are without question among China's richest individuals or biggest SOEs. Here again, the government's refusal to acknowledge the limited investor population prevents it from taking the action it needs to take – broad market reform.

Concerning the economist's suggestion itself, if the government had the money to compensate A-share investors, it would not need to sell its shares to raise capital for the welfare fund in the first place. This is taking from the poor to give to the rich! The technical difficulties of such a scheme, such as finding

TABLE 8.14 Funds Raised through the Domestic Sale of State Shares

Code	Company	Date	No. of Shares (000)	Price (RMB)	Funds Raised (RMB Mn)
600498	Fiberhome Telecom.	7/24/01	8,000	21.00	168.0
600566	Hongcheng Machinery	7/28/01	4,000	7.80	31.2
600556	Beisheng Pharmaceutical	8/22/01	4,120	9.60	39.6
600569	Anyang Iron & Steel	8/15/01	25,000	6.80	170.0
600346	Bingshan Rubber	8/15/01	3,500	5.36	18.8
600539	Lionhead·Cement	8/18/01	8,000	6.98	55.8
600418	Jianghuai Chassis Co.	8/18/01	8,000	9.90	79.2
600519	Guizhou Maotai	8/22/01	6,500	31.39	204.0
600599	Liuyang Fireworks Co.	8/23/01	2,000	10.00	20.0
600508	Shanghai Datun Energy	8/24/01	10,000	9.00	90.0
600448	Huafang Limited	8/29/01	8,500	5.92	50.3
600596	Xinan Chemical	8/31/01	4,000	7.30	29.2
600322	Tianjin Realty Dev.	9/5/01	11,000	5.00	55.0
000756	Xinhua Pharmaceutical	9/14/01	3,000	13.00	39.0
600028	Sinopec	8/8/01	280,000	4.22	1,180.0
000836	Genius Co.	9/24/01	2,000	21.30	42.6
600779	Sichuan Quanxing	9/29/01	3,660	11.06	39.1

Source: Wind Information.

a fair price to compensate investors, are probably insoluble. Then there is the point that compensation assumes that investors were not aware of the risk of policy change or share sales, which simply is not true. In the event, this debate continues[32] without concrete results – it flies in the face of the long-time effort to develop markets.

Nonetheless, this type of thinking is representative of the "have your cake and eat it too" mentality that is pervasive in the market. There is a constant call in the state share sale debate that the value of existing A-share holdings must not be diminished. This is simply impossible. No market can maintain its current prices against a huge influx of new supply unless there is fresh capital entering. This, in part, explains the November 2002 policy change that allows foreigners to buy state and LP shares.[33] This change represents a significant shift in government thinking and should be welcomed. But it is unrealistic to expect foreign investors to be willing to invest significant amounts when the shares purchased will not be freely tradable. From another angle, evidence shows that H shares, by definition the best Chinese companies, are out of favor with investors even at prices below NAV. Paying NAV or above for illiquid shares of domestically listed firms, for all except the very best, is a remote possibility.

Given the success of the Hong Kong Tracker Fund, there have been calls for a fund to be set up to hold a part of the state shares and issue units to the public. Clearly, there is a variety of technical issues – for example, whether the fund can monetize its shares upon investor redemptions. The major problem, however, is that the entire fund industry in China, over 60 invested funds, at present controls only about US$10 billion in assets. This is only about 11 % of the NAV of state holdings and only 4 % if valued at market prices. Any state share fund would only be able to absorb a very small percentage of the state's holdings.

The conclusion from all this activity is that the domestic equity market is still not broad enough or deep enough to absorb even a part of the huge state sector. This explains the continued reliance on overseas offerings for major transactions. The recent QFII and state share sale initiatives designed to attract foreign investors and new capital are a response to the same problem. The way out will require time and the development of an investor base beyond the retail sector and market punters. As discussed in the last chapter, securities investment funds, insurance companies, pension funds, and other types of professional investors are only very recent market participants. Without such investors, it is very difficult to imagine how China's equity markets can develop further.

So the introduction of a QFII system on November 12, 2002, on the eve of the 16th CCP Congress, should be welcomed.[34] The measures closely follow the Taiwan model, where a similar QFII system has been in place for over 10 years, and have the express purpose of attracting long-term and beneficial investment into the domestic market. To this end, the regulations place certain restrictions on foreign investment. Qualified financial investors such as closed-end China funds are required to keep their money in China for a minimum of three years. Shares can be bought and sold freely within the period, but funds cannot easily be repatriated before that time. The QFII system is unlikely to attract major investment in the short term, due to the strict lock-up restrictions as well as the high valuation of domestic firms versus their overseas-listed cousins. This is the major point of contrast with Taiwan. China has over 100 (72 H shares and 72 Red Chips in Hong Kong alone) of its best companies listed internationally, so QFII is not the only channel through which to acquire China exposure. In Taiwan, it was the only avenue. Consequently, in China, QFII will probably become an end in itself, rather than a means to achieve a more market-driven stock market.

The QFII measures were announced the same week that the State Council reversed its ban on foreigners buying state or LP shares. These two measures should be seen in the same light as providing new channels for foreign capital into the domestic markets. Neither will have an impact on the market's structural problems. The QFII facility will no doubt change over the next few years, allowing a greater variety of foreign participants more flexible access. This does not solve the problem. The problem is that the *Chinese domestic investor* is the one starved for investment choices, not the foreign investor. China's stock markets will not play a meaningful role in the valuation and allocation of capital until Chinese investors can invest overseas or in a domestic market where all shares and shareholders are treated equally.[35]

Then there are the counterproductive initiatives. Throughout 2001, there was a debate in Hong Kong and Chinese investment banking circles about the possible issuance of Chinese Depository Receipts (CDRs).[36] The concept is based on the familiar American Depository Receipts listed on the NYSE or NASDAQ. An ADR is a US dollar-denominated security that represents a certain number of foreign shares held in trust and which are traded instead of the foreign share itself, for a variety of technical reasons. On request, the holder of ADRs can swap them into the underlying local currency shares. The CDR idea sprang from the desire to allow certain non-China-domiciled Chinese companies, such as China Unicom, access to the domestic A-share market.[37]

Eventually, the CDR plan came to nothing – and rightly so. The plan was merely a short-term funding exercise with a focus on the domestic market. There were very serious constraints on the ability of the idea to work – the non-convertibility of the currency would have made trading very difficult. The introduction of yet another class of securities into an already confused situation should have been a non-starter to begin with. The CDR idea, however, eventually failed due more to issues involved with the non-convertibility of the currency, rather than to the fact that it would have constituted yet another share class. In the end, the government avoided the CDR issue by letting China Unicom's domestic parent company list A shares, while the subsidiary company maintains its Hong Kong and New York listings. Even this situation is hardly transparent, since investors may think the companies are actually one and the same. Then, of course, there may be confusion about the different types of securities, just as there was in the early stages of the investment funds.

CIRCLES OF OWNERSHIP

With the advent of the shareholding system in the 1980s, China began what is perhaps the greatest reshuffle of asset ownership in history. In the early 1990s, it was one big grab with people claiming what they were already sitting on and then reaching for more. Overseas Chinese were flying into the country and buying hundreds of SOEs and flying in bankers to pick the good ones for IPOs. Companies, if they couldn't sell the shares, sold their assets – buildings, property, and equipment – leaving nothing but shells behind. Since then, things have quieted, but the spinoff of government holdings continues. Now this activity has been dignified by calling it M&A, but it is the same thing.

The stock markets provide a lens through which to view the action, which otherwise goes on unnoticed by the media unless there is a scandal or it is covered up by local governments. The markets, or a single company's capital structure, can be seen as a series of concentric rings or wheels, as shown in Figure 8.7. At its heart lies the state with its absolute control over market ownership exercised via state shares. Next, come the state's children holding LP shares. Then come the alphabet share holders. Over time, this group of wheels has grown in size due to new listings and other financings each year. In general, however, the state share of this system has remained largely the same in terms of relative size, at about 70%. But there is plenty of activity at the boundaries of each wheel as they grind against one another.

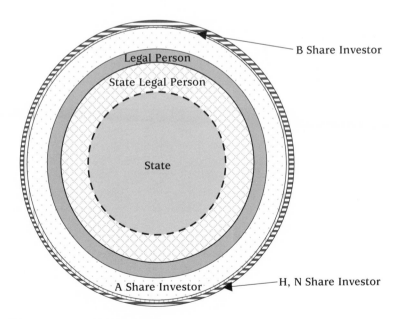

FIGURE 8.7 Circles of Ownership.
Source: 2001 CSRC data.
Note: Areas represent ownership percentage.

Looked at another way, the further out from the center, the greater the number and more diverse the nature of the investors … and the further you are from the state itself. For example, there is a big difference between holders of state-owned LP shares and those who picked up LP shares from an incomplete rights offering (*yiliu zhuanpeigu*). At the further reaches of the circles are the foreign investors. As this system spins, friction and centrifugal force gradually push the shares located in the center, the state shares, into the next layer, LP shares, and so on. Gradually, the current A-share holders, and even foreigners, would end up holding a much larger proportion of shares in companies and perhaps, in many cases, control. This process, driven by the centrifugal forces of greed and need, is happening now.

The key to achieving control, however, still lies on the non-tradable side of a company's shareholding structure. As shown in Figure 8.8, the proportion of tradable shares, including A, B, and H shares, has remained relatively constant over the past decade.[38]

This masks, however, the actual changes in ownership for those companies listed for a relatively long period. For these companies, state ownership has been diluted as a result of rights issues, the listing of internal employee shares, and for other reasons. At the same time, however, new companies come to the market. These companies naturally have a higher proportion of state and LP shares. The net consequence of these two trends is the relatively stable market breakdown between the two broad share classes.

The centrifugal force acting on the earlier listed companies, however, can be easily demonstrated (see Figure 8.9). At the end of 1995, there were 184 companies listed on the Shanghai exchange. Between 1995 and October 2002, 61 companies showed no change in the proportion of tradable A shares,

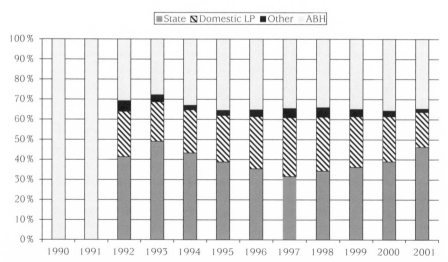

FIGURE 8.8 Trends in Shanghai and Shenzhen Market Share Structure, 1990–2001. *Source:* CSRC data.

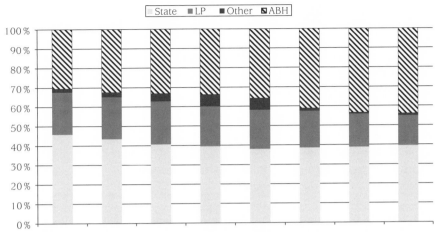

FIGURE 8.9 Change in Ownership Distribution for 123 Listed Companies.
Sources: Shanghai Stock Exchange and Wind Information.

whereas the remaining 123 did. For these 123 companies over that seven-year period, the ratio of tradable to non-tradable shares changed from 31:69, the same as the current market structure, to 44:56. This effectively means that their state ownership has been slowly diluted by subsequent secondary market sales.

As a second example, take a later and larger sample of 449 stocks for the 1999–2002 period. Of these, 121 stocks had no change in the ratio and 318 saw an increase in tradable shares. Ten companies actually showed an increase in non-tradable shares. For the 318 companies, in 1999 the ratio of the two share classes stood at 35:65. By 2002, tradable shares had increased to 41.2%. In addition, companies in this group with a free float greater than 50% increased from 44 to 97. In this second sample, dilution was the result of rights offerings (68%), the listing of employee shares (27%), and other reasons (4%). Overall, by early 2003, some 211 companies had a free float of over 50%.

So, over time, the state's ownership, if not control, is being significantly diluted, driven by the unending quest for more capital. While the A-share market may be larger in size, this does not necessarily mean that the state is losing control. From available information, the largest shareholder for most companies is the original state promoter.[39] This promoter usually has continued to be the largest and controlling shareholder unless, of course, holders of tradable shares were to unite.[40]

PRIVATIZATION WITH CHINESE CHARACTERISTICS?

Until accumulating A shares or other listed shares can create a controlling position and a challenge is mounted, changes in company ownership can come only through the OTC markets for non-tradable shares.[41] The attraction of owning a listed vehicle to raise funds has brought new players into the market. They buy out legal person stakes from cash-strapped state entities and change the management, like Mr. K, obscured behind a veil of LP shares. This is the Chinese M&A market, an area of the financial landscape that has been active for years. There have been thousands of LP share transfers and hundreds of companies restructured and sold. This is where LP and state shares are shaken loose and pushed into private hands. The M&A market, nevertheless, has generally been ignored or at least escaped meaningful scrutiny by the listed market or its regulators. The Securities Law and recently implemented regulations governing the acquisition of listed companies have been the first belated steps in trying to regulate this marketplace.[42]

The deals being conducted – exchange of ownership in listed firms, management buy-outs, and back-door listings – are all being done in parallel to the A-share market. As was shown previously, negotiations do not reference or look to the exchanges as a guide to pricing. The market structure and practical spirit of China's entrepreneurs have led to the development of this parallel market to suit their own needs. What else could they do? Control and majority ownership were vested with the original company promoters, by law always a direct part of the state. To gain control, it was necessary to start to transfer – that is, to buy and sell – these shares. This asset reshuffling may promote the spread and development of true private ownership in China. It is, however, far from solving the share structure problems and highlights in greater detail the limitations of the market. The proud new private owners face the same problems of illiquid shares as the old owner.

In the practical terms of the present, this is not all bad. In fact, from the point of view of M&A market participants, this situation is more than satisfactory. At this stage in the political and economic development of China, private property rights are nowhere guaranteed by due legal process, only by market practice. Best, then, to hide behind the curtain of LP shares. The market requires little disclosure to the public, much less the approval of public shareholders, even if, in an alternate universe, the A shares of the same company are listed. The last thing entrepreneurs (or the sellers of state assets) really want is transparency, and nor do certain portions of the state.

Shanghai Dazhong Taxi is a representative example of how a typical transaction aimed at gaining control is effected. Over a period of years, Dazhong gained control of a state-controlled company, completing a management/employee buy-out.[43] Dazhong management first spun off control of their Pudong subsidiary from the principal taxi company, Dazhong Taxi, as shown in Figure 8.10.

In the second step, Dazhong Taxi raised additional funds in a private placement of LP shares to its shareholders. Unfortunately, its principal state shareholder did not (probably, could not) participate. On the other hand, Pudong Dazhong took a large portion of the placement sufficient for it to replace the state as its former parent's largest and controlling shareholder (see Figure 8.11). A nice privatization two-step.

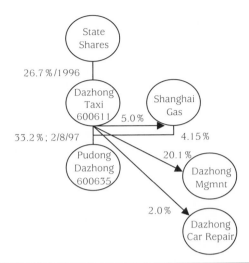

As of 1996, the state held a controlling interest of 26.7% in Dazhong Taxi. In February 1997, Dazhong Taxi acquired a 33.2% interest in a listed company called Pudong Dazhong. Three months later, Dazhong Taxi gave up its controlling stake by selling out portions to Shanghai Gas, Dazhong Management, and Dazhong Car Repair. At the end of this shuffle of shares, the Dazhong Group as a whole continued to own 28.2% of Pudong Dazhong, while the state continued to hold its original 26.7% interest in Dazhong Taxi.

FIGURE 8.10 Dazhong Taxi Gives up Controlling Stake in Pudong Dazhong, 1997.

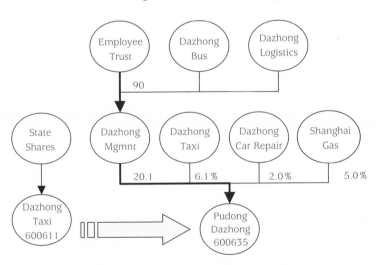

On December 24, 1999, Dazhong Taxi carried out a private placement of shares. Pudong Dazhong bought LP shares accounting for 24.7% of Dazhong Taxi's total post-offer shares. Since the state did not participate, its holding was diluted down to 20.1% from the previous 26.7%. Consequently, Pudong Dazhong became the controlling shareholder of Dazhong Taxi. The key point, however, is that Dazhong Management and employees had become the indirect controlling shareholder of Dazhong Taxi.

FIGURE 8.11 Pudong Dazhong Acquires a Controlling Stake in Dazhong Taxi, 1999.

It is impossible by looking only at the shareholding structure of Dazhong Taxi to know whether this is a state- or a privately owned company. All that can be seen is LP shares and A shares. The only way of knowing is by going company by company to identify shareholders. This can be done at the State Bureau of Industry and Commerce, the company registry. There are estimates that the private sector controls around 10.7%, or about 130 listed companies, which could be only the tip of the iceberg. If analysis could extend to unlisted shareholding companies,[44] which, together with the listed companies, total over 70,000, it would surely show a much higher proportion.[45]

The pressure to raise capital has forced the state's policy defining owner-ship rights in corporatized entities inevitably toward a sort of privatization. In the early 1990s, this possibility was well understood by the state, which defined shares in relationship to itself and then made state-owned shares untradable. Once ownership was evidenced in shares, however, the pressure to monetize them arose. A massive shifting around of corporate assets began as first one, then another company sought either to restructure its business or to raise funds. Over time, such LP share transfers have resulted in hidden pri-vatization. Since no law protects property rights beyond the shares them-selves, the true picture of corporate ownership and control has been obscured behind legal persons veiled as parts of the state. The inevitable existence of parallel markets for different share classes further complicates this reality. Ambiguous and legally tenuous, this is privatization with Chinese characteristics.

CHAPTER 9

The 10-year Bull Market

China's stock markets have developed quickly and their accomplishments are great, but they are very irregular. If they are to receive the people's trust, the investors' trust, then they have a lot of work to do.

Zhu Rongji, March 15, 2000[1]

C hinese commentators have described stock-market performance over the past decade as a "10-year bull market."[2] One glance at a chart of the two market indices shows why: they look like a roller coaster building up speed to that big hill (and then whirling down). There have been many crashes and slumps along the way, but, for all their flaws, investors have been attracted to stocks because they have all, at some point, produced bull markets. For quick money, Chinese investors have little other choice.

International investors, who are overwhelmingly huge fund managers, have alternately been enthusiastic and completely turned off. But they have always been interested: shares and stock exchanges in the world's largest communist country are simply too good a story. The quality and underlying performance of the companies may be dubious, but if a stock is trading up 5–15% a day, who cares? The bulls have roared for A shares in 1992, H shares in 1994, A shares again in 1996, Red Chips in 1997, and then A shares again from 1999 to 2001. Perhaps a better description would be to say that China doesn't have bull markets, only bubble markets.

This chapter focuses on the domestic markets, seeking to show how the many strands of the story in previous chapters come together in the actual marketplace. After a quick overview of how they traded and another juicy scandal, the chapter concludes with some measures of the market's character.

CHINA'S BULL MARKETS

The Early Years

The opening of the two stock exchanges signaled the end for the OTC and black-market trading of the 1980s. On its first day of trading, December 19,

1990, the Shanghai index closed at 99.98. Over the remaining six trading days in 1990, the index jumped 30%. From then on for the first full year, it rocketed up; by 1991 year-end, the index had closed at 292 points. The colorful curb markets outside the regional trading centers rapidly died out after the introduction of electronic book-entry trading in the summer of 1991. This single technical innovation got people off the streets and into (or, anyway, outside), brokerage offices, and went a long way to ensuring there were no outbreaks of riotous demonstrations. These were the years of the retail investor and trading was still a difficult process. Small investors would queue in their hundreds and thousands outside trading halls for hours, sometimes days, to place their orders. Larger investors could pay a monthly fee to use "Big Shot Rooms (*dahushi*)" where they could trade directly with the exchange and avoid the scrum of people outside.

The Shanghai exchange imposed strict ceiling and floor trading limits on the eight listed stocks,[3] initially set at a range of 5%, then 1%, and eventually as low as 0.5%.[4] Limits were designed to restrict price swings and ensure that investors faced less risk as demand for stocks far outweighed supply. The consequence, however, was that the *dahu* slowly pushed stock prices up by their daily limits day after day after day. Shenzhen showed a markedly different performance. The Shenzhen index made its debut on April 3, 1991, closing at 988.05 points. The market then fell for the next five months to a low of 402.5 as stocks came off their highs reached in the OTC and black markets. From its low, Shenzhen rallied strongly and recovered to over 900 points by 1991 year-end. Both markets, therefore, reflected the positions of their respective market before the exchanges opened. Shenzhen had just come off the speculative binge caused by "share fever," which Shanghai had avoided. Shanghai investors, excited by the exchange opening, were able to pick up and drive the markets in 1991, while Shenzhen recovered its footing.

Market conditions were very different in 1992 as investors in both Shanghai and Shenzhen passively reacted to decisions taken by the state (see Figure 9.1). For the first time, knowledge of the state's decision-making led to profit, and front running the state became a major pastime. Deng Xiaoping's Southern Excursion in February of that year energized market players, like everyone else in China at the time.[5] Together with a gradual relaxation of trading limits, shares started to take off. On May 21, all trading limits were lifted from the Shanghai exchange and the index doubled from 617 on May 20 to 1,267 on May 21. This was quick and easy money.

The vice mayor of Shanghai, alarmed by the extreme move, announced on June 2 that *dahu* were cornering the market. This started a readjustment that turned into a crash: people feared the exchanges might be closed. After falling 10% on the mayor's comment, shares continued to fall and by August 10, the day of the Shenzhen stock riots, the market was down more than 30% from its peak. Now the government intervened on the buy side to tidy things up before the 14th Party Congress. Such efforts failed and the market fell below 400 in mid-November.

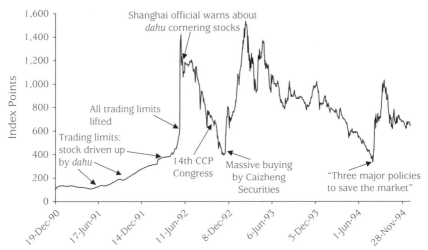

FIGURE 9.1 Shanghai Index Performance: December 1990–December 1994
Source: Wind Information.

The MOF-backed Caizheng Securities then went on a buying spree, which drew in other money to support the start of a rally. As trading volumes on both exchanges were extremely low in the early 1990s, it was easy to make a difference. The Shanghai exchange traded on average only RMB91 million in 1992 and RMB873 million in 1993, far below the RMB8 billion of 10 years later. Thanks to the MOF, share fever returned in late 1993. How it was touched off demonstrates that the retail sector was becoming less important. In October, the state announced the founding of three national securities companies – Guotai, Huaxia, and Nanfang – each sponsored by one of the major state banks. The age of institutionalized market making was in the offing.

As can be expected with Deng in its backyard early in the year, Shenzhen also recorded stellar gains in 1992. After a late April start, the market peaked the day of the famous stock riots at 2,884, up just short of 200% since January. The market fell 5% the day after the riots and continued to trade down through year-end, closing at just over 2,300 points. Average daily trading volume was RMB161 million, not bad with only six listed stocks.

From a peak in February 1993, Shenzhen traded down into what became a three-year bear market. From the second half of 1993, the Chinese economy had begun to show the effects of the wild excess loosed by Deng's enthusiasm for economics over ideology. Zhu Rongji, now the governor of the PBOC, raised interest rates twice in 1993 and embarked on a major restructuring of the financial system. Inflation, however, went soaring, peaking nationally at over 20% a year later.

On Saturday, July 30, the CSRC and the State Council announced the "Three Major Policies to Save the Market."[6] The policies included a freeze on all new issuance of shares, strict control over the size of rights issues, and measures to increase funds flow into the market. These psychological measures worked temporarily: on August 1, the market jumped over 33% and Shanghai briefly broke through 1,000 index points but ended the year at 647 points. The next year, with ever-increasing interest rates, saw very little activity on either exchange. Daily trading volumes were down, the number of new stocks issued was down, and the markets were down, 14% in Shanghai and 22% in Shenzhen. The securities industry was also hit by the "327" bond futures scandal, which effectively closed SISCO, one of the biggest players.

Shenzhen Development Bank Investment Performance

Shenzhen Development Bank was the catalyst for China's markets and, as shown previously, became one of the most widely held shares. A close look at how an investment in SDB actually performed underlines, from a micro-viewpoint, China's 10-year bull market. SDB's share performance is shown in Table 9.1. The table shows how an investment of RMB10,000 in the bank's shares would have grown in value, assuming that the investor subscribed for all the rights offerings.

This original investment, had it been sustained for 15 years, would have been worth over RMB14 million in late November 2002. At its peak in May 1997, the holding would have been valued at over RMB58 million. Certainly, with no capital gains tax, everyone would have gotten out then! Over the full period, although the lucky investor would have received over RMB1 million in

TABLE 9.1 Year-on-year Performance of Shenzhen Development Bank

Year	No. of Shares	Cash Invested (RMB)	Cash Received (RMB)	Value (RMB)
1987	500	10,000		10,000
1988	750	0	350	N/A
1989	1,500	15,000	0	N/A
1990	48,000	10,680	0	N/A
1991	81,600	172,800	0	2,394,960
1992	81,600	0	0	3,631,200
1993	159,120	130,560	24,480	3,556,332
1994	254,592	79,560	79,560	2,668,124
1995	305,510	0	76,378	1,964,432
1996	611,021	0	0	10,106,284
1997	916,531	0	122,204	20,805,258
1998	916,531	0	0	13,610,488
1999	916,531	0	549,919	15,993,469
2000	1,191,491	2,199,675	0	17,300,443
2001	1,191,491	0	0	14,595,759
11/02	1,191,491	0	178,724	14,417,036

Sources: Partly based on Hu Xuzhi, p. 168 and Wind Information.

dividends, he would also have been asked to contribute RMB2.6 million in rights offerings to avoid dilution. Had he not participated in rights offerings, the investor would still have earned over RMB500,000 in cash dividends. But his net worth at the end would have been only RMB5.7 million. The stunning performance of SDB in 1996 and 1997 was the driving force behind the 1996 and early 1997 bull market and this investor's fortune.

The 1996 Bull Market: Manipulator's Paradise

The end of 1995 and early 1996 saw the Shenzhen exchange and securities houses scratching their heads. There was little interest in shares, a near halt in list-ings, double-digit interest rates, and slowing economic growth. Market perform-ance was dreadful: the Shenzhen index had fallen 3.7% in 1993, 42.9% in 1994, and would close 1995, the year inflation peaked, down 22.3%. Something had to be done to attract money and interest back into stocks. SDB proved to be the answer, seized on most famously by Junan Securities. The next 16 months saw Shenzhen rise from 987 index points to over 6,000.

At the start of this play, the overall market was trading at a P/E of less than 10 times. SDB was trading at only seven times earnings, even though its 1995 net profits were expected to grow at over 23%. If this were true, the stock was cheap and there was only one way to go: up. In January 1996, a number of key players, including Junan, started quietly to build positions in SDB. The stock began to move a week before Spring Festival, trading up 20%. After the holidays, investors, now aware that SDB was "in play," were keen to trade (see Figure 9.2).

The bank's 1995 annual report came out in mid-March: operating income was up 49%, net profit was up 22%, and EPS was RMB0.84. Still the stock was valued at only 10 times earnings. Then the greater environment changed for

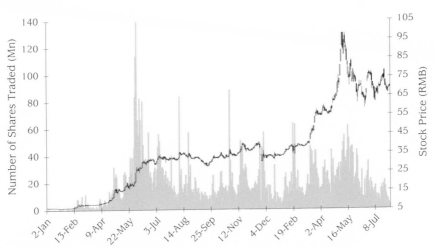

FIGURE 9.2 Shenzhen Development Bank, 1996–97 Performance.
Source: Wind Information; prices re-based for rights issues.

the better. Responding to a clear decline in inflation, on April 1 the PBOC announced that it would discontinue inflation-protected deposits and begin to liberalize interest rates. A month later, it would cut interest rates by about 100 basis points and again in August. SDB shares, hovering around the RMB8 level, popped. On April 4, the stock jumped 3.3% with 6.9 million shares traded. Trading ballooned to 31.7 million shares on April 26, a day that saw the stock climb 21%. SDB closed the month at RMB15.5, and its stellar April performance only encouraged the players to continue their manipulation and to set their sights even higher.

Share trading volume began to climb again when the bank conducted a 10-for-10 stock split on May 27. On May 31, the stock rose 22.3% on turnover of over 100 million shares; the next day, a record 139 million shares changed hands. This huge increase in volume heralded that a new player had entered, eager to repeat the success of earlier in the year.

By now a bull market was well under way in both Shenzhen and Shanghai. Concerned about the ultimate outcome, the Party finally intervened late in the year in the now famous *People's Daily* editorial by a "Special Correspondent" titled "On correctly understanding the current stock market." The editorial warned against the highly speculative nature of the current market. At the same time, trading limits were reintroduced for the first time since May 1992. In 1996, everyone still knew how to read the *People's Daily*. They ran for the doors. Over the next three days, SDB shares traded limit down and the Shenzhen market crashed, down 38% in eight trading days.

The markets were down but not out; within a few weeks they had recovered from their lows and were back to business as usual. Then, in March 1997, rumors began to circulate about possible government action against SDB. On April 19, the SDB board postponed the shareholder general meeting and announcement of its dividend distribution plan until late October, due to a fine of its Beijing securities department. Two days later, SDB issued its 1996 annual report: operating income was up 24%, net profits 81%, EPS of RMB0.7612, and a P/E of 40.8. The stock eventually traded as high as RMB54.49 and closed at an all-time high of RMB48.9 (unadjusted for rights).

It was obvious to all that the stock had been manipulated all through 1996 and 1997, but who was involved? Shenzhen-based Junan Securities was known to have traded heavily and reportedly made hundreds of millions, saving the company from bankruptcy.[7] On June 17, 1997, SDB's board admitted that from March 1996 to April 1997 it had used over RMB300 million to trade its own stock. It also disclosed that the bank had made over RMB90 million in profit from the trades. The board claimed that they had sold out all their holdings by April 17, 1997. With SDB out of the market and the other "smart money" cashed out as well, it was left to the retail investor to pick up the pieces. SDB's revenue and profit growth slowed to single digits in 1997 and the stock slowly traded down until the "519" rally in 1999.

This wild ride, of course, led the government to clamp down. Banks and SOEs were forbidden to use their own funds or borrowed funds to play the market. The CSRC was raised to a ministerial-level agency under the State Council, empowered by the Securities Law in December 1998. This gave the regulator the authority it needed to bring the markets into line.

The "519" Incident

The roots of China's own Internet bubble and the bull market beginning in 2000 extend back to May 1999. After the collapse of early 1997, trading slowed on limited volume, affected by slow domestic growth, deflation, and depressed sentiment after the onset of the Asian financial crisis. On May 13, 1999, a CSRC official announced the new listing approval system and elimination of the old quota system. He dismissed rumors of a closure or merger (with A shares) of the B-share market, supported foreign investment into the fund management industry, and expressed his hopes that the second board would be successful. Generally, all these points were seen as positive for the market, but it was not big news. And it certainly wasn't big enough to explain the share frenzy that was only a few days away.

On May 19, Shanghai opened near an intra-day low of 1,057, but from there climbed all day to close at 1,109, up 4.6% on the day. The same thing happened over the next three days, when the market climbed 3.5%, 1.8%, and 3.8%. Then the state sparked the tinder. In early June, stamp duty on B-share trades was cut and on June 10 the PBOC cut interest rates by 100 basis points. By this time, Shanghai was up over 28% since May 19, but it hadn't finished. Trading volumes that had been RMB2–4 billion per day before May 19 were now RMB10–20 billion for Shanghai alone.

Then, once again, the Party stepped in, this time to bless the rally. The famous June 15 editorial and its "Special Correspondent" claimed that "the recent stock market performance is reflecting the true macro-economy and market requirements, so it is normal for the market to rise."[8] Music to the ears. The next day saw the market rise 5.2% as people jumped in. On June 22, the Shanghai index broke the intra-day high of 1,558 dating back to February 1993. This was welcomed in trading halls nationwide with a 10,9,8… countdown and cheering. Three days later, Shanghai recorded over RMB44 billion in volume and found itself exhausted. The "519" Incident closing high was reached on June 29 with Shanghai at 1,739.21. One unfortunate investor in Chengdu found the record returns too much to take and collapsed dead of a heart attack in his local trading hall.[9]

The share frenzy was over, at least for the moment (see Figure 9.3). The July 1 implementation of the Securities Law kept the market apprehensive and cautious. The 50th anniversary of the founding of the republic on October 1 and its fabulous parade failed to spark enthusiasm. The CSRC's announcement in December that 10 companies would begin selling off their state shares as a trial only depressed things further. Little wonder no one wanted any part of this first attempt to unload the state's holdings. Shanghai ended 1999 down over 20% from its high, but still up 19.2% for the year.

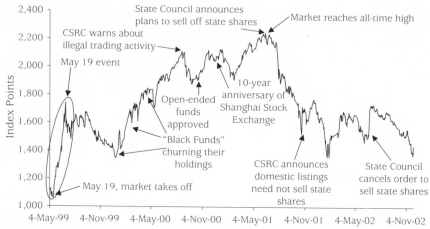

FIGURE 9.3 Recent Shanghai Market Performance: "519" and after.
Source: Wind Information.

But the bull was back with a vengeance in 2000, driven by the U.S. Internet bubble in the NASDAQ market. China bubbled, too, full of excitement, stories, rumors, and even some facts about the "new economy" and the Internet. As early as 1999, many companies had changed their businesses (at least in name) from "old economy" to "new economy" industries. Lu Liang, the stock manipulator, was one of the most famous examples, with his China Venture Capital Group, but others – such as Capital Steel – were making similar plans to enter the Internet- and "new economy"-related sectors.

Investors had learned the growth potential of Internet stocks from NASDAQ. The fast-growing Chinese Internet user base suggested that the prospects in China were bright as well. Then came a series of "new economy" listings. China.com had listed in July 1999 (but without its China piece). The listings of China's main Internet portals – Sohu (April 2000), Netease (June 2000), and Sina (July 2000) – fueled calls for a domestic Second Board. The CSRC obliged, posting draft regulations for the new market on its website and soliciting comments from the public. To date, there is still no Second Board.

The uneventful passing of the old millennium gave a psychological boost to the market. This, combined with the expected introduction of a Second Board and a generally supportive government attitude, sent investors and stocks off on an 18-month-long run. In early January 2000, the CSRC also allowed securities houses and investment funds access to the inter-bank market. This provided a new and deep source of funding. Then, during the Spring Festival holidays, the CSRC and PBOC issued new measures allowing comprehensive securities houses to borrow against their stock holdings. In March, Zhu Rongji, in response to reporters' questions, praised the stock-market development and its achievements, and emphasized its importance in the reform of SOEs.

In 2000, these seemed to be some of the positive reasons driving the market. With the passage of time, however, the true reasons behind this bull market have emerged. The start of the run in 2000 was, in part, catalyzed by the fund management companies churning their portfolios. Since the fund management companies are closely tied to securities houses, it would be realistic to assume they were also in there helping things along. If the securities firms were trading along, then their special clients would also have been in on it. The result when combined with Internet mania: a raging bull market, pulling along active and willing retail investors.

China's Internet Bubble

The domestic Internet bubble of early 2000 can best be seen in two stocks, Beijing Center Gate Technologies and Yi An Hi-Tech. As previously introduced in Chapter 8, Beijing Center Gate Technologies (000931) was one of the darlings of the bubble, although its bull market lasted only a few weeks. The company listed in July 1999 as an exit strategy for the beleaguered investors of failed Hainan Minyuan Modern Agriculture Group (000508). The new company then issued its controversial August rights issue. The new Center Gate was involved in a huge range of hi-tech businesses, from hi-tech investment, technical training, electrical products, construction and design to, of course, securities investment and venture capital. In short, the new company was a pure concept stock.

The stock began its bull market run after the 2000 Spring Festival holidays (see Figure 9.4). For two weeks in early February, the stock closed 10% limit up on nine out of 11 trading days. During this time, the stock was trading over 511 million shares daily, versus a total number of A shares of only 374 million. February 29 saw the stock hit an intra-day high of RMB44.8 and close at a high of RMB42.44. After that, the stock drifted lower and lower, and in late November

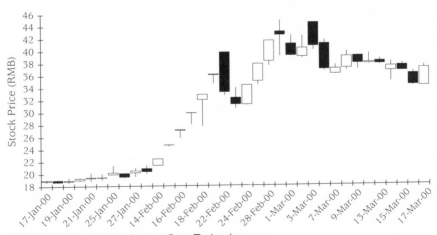

FIGURE 9.4 Beijing Center Gate Technology.
Source: Wind Information.

2002 it stood at just over RMB9. Earnings per share also fell in 2000 and again in 2001. Its third-quarter report for 2002 showed a loss of 5 cents per share.

All markets have psychological barriers. The Dow's 10,000 and the Shanghai index's 2,000 exist, even though they are nothing but a function of the decimal number system. One such barrier is the RMB100 price for a single share. Here the honors go to Shenzhen Yi An Hi-Tech Company (000008).[10]

Shenzhen Yi An was originally called Shenzhen Jinxing Development and Service Company. Not an attractive name and no longer an attractive business: property development and storage businesses. Jinxing had originally listed in May 1992 but had attracted little interest and its price traded around RMB10 for years. In short, it was a perfect takeover target. In June 1999, the Yi An Group became Jinxing's largest shareholder and "changed" its core business into a variety of hi-tech areas, including digital technology, electric cars, communication, nano-technology, and so on. It is almost as if Yi An management had picked up the latest hi-tech weekly and listed out likely products. The new company, Yi An, caught the wave of the "519" rally, reaching a high of RMB34.48, and closed the year at RMB42.3. At 1999 year-end, the company had only 2,878 shareholders; it was most definitely primed for a play by the very few people who held the shares: no doubt the Yi An Group management.

Trading resumed after the New Year holiday on January 4 and the stock climbed steadily all through January, although it never hit its "up limit" and attracted limited attention. By January 28, the final day before the two-week Spring Festival holiday, the stock closed at RMB91 (see Figure 9.5).

After the holiday, the stock continued its gains, closing at RMB97.39 on February 14, and breaking through RMB100 and eventually closing at RMB104.88 the next day. February 16 saw the stock hit its up limit of RMB114.83 and close there. On February 17, the stock hit an all-time intra-day high of RMB126.31, but its highest close came on the following day, RMB116.12. February 17 also

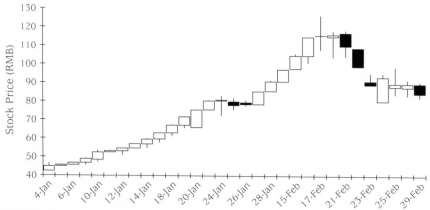

FIGURE 9.5 Shenzhen Yi An Hi-Tech: China's First RMB100 Share.
Source: Wind Information.

saw another stock break the RMB100 level, Tsinghua Unisplendour (000938). But what goes up must come down, and Yi An was no exception; from its highs of mid-February the stock steadily traded down to close at RMB50.31 by year-end, a return of 18.9% on the year.[11]

One 65-year-old woman reportedly had held her 11,800 shares of Shenzhen Jinxing since May 1992. Through stock splits her holding had increased to 25,396 shares by early 2000.[12] Her original holding of RMB318,000 (a substantial sum in 1992) peaked in value at over RMB3.2 million. Let us hope she sold out this time.

The year 2001 started well and with strong sentiment. The market continued to feed off new hi-tech stories and investments. All these stories were more or less the same; they are not stories of fundamental company performance, but of a group of players cornering a stock, then ramping it to death. The market reflected this. The Shanghai index rose over 50% in 2000 and confidence was high for 2001. As more new shares and investment funds were issued, the buying continued and the market continued to climb, testing the 2,100 level three times.

The fun certainly ended in mid-June 2001 when the State Council announced that 10% of any fund-raising should come from the sale of state shares. This led directly and immediately to the market's collapse, proving yet again that the A-share market is very sensitive to any measure that allows state and LP shares to trade freely. The markets fell, ending the year off more than 25%. The state attempted to stop the rout. In October 2001, the CSRC announced that domestic fund-raisings were no longer subject to the 10% policy, and again in June 2002, the State Council canceled the idea altogether.

As with all markets, when the bull market ends, the excesses of the "glory days" start to be exposed and become unraveled. Since June 2001, the market has reeled from a series of false accounting scandals at listed firms, further revelations of rampant stock manipulation, losses at investment funds and securities houses, and a worsening performance of listed companies. Even the early November 2002 announcement that foreign institutional investment would be permitted in the A-share markets failed to encourage investors. At the end of 2002, Chinese investors found themselves very much in a bear market. The problems of insider trading, destruction of shareholder value, and the sale of state shares are all out in the open and unlikely to go away quickly or quietly.

Despite the recent market decline, a comparison of the Shanghai A-share market and the Dow Jones Index shown in Figure 9.6 illustrates at a glance why Chinese speak about a 10-year bull market. These two markets at times show a somewhat similar performance, but there is no strong correlation between them. The figure has been "re-based" to late 1995 to eliminate the great market swings of Shanghai's early years. It shows what would have happened if an investor had placed US$100 (or its equivalent in RMB) in both markets on December 29, 1995, and held it until recently. On the

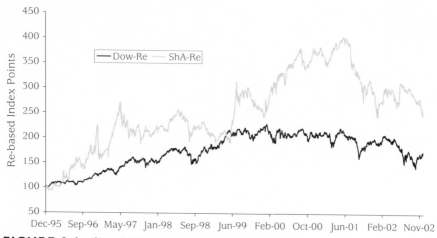

FIGURE 9.6 Shanghai A-share Index versus Dow Jones.
Sources: Wind Information and Bloomberg; re-based from December 29, 1995.

Dow he would be up at around US$175, but in Shanghai he would be holding US$250.

FUND INDEX PERFORMANCE

On May 9, 2000, the Shanghai exchange began publishing a securities invest-ment fund index.[13] The annual performance of the fund index, as compared to the return of the broader A-share index, can be seen in Table 9.2. Since funds invest mainly in A shares, with some CGBs and corporate bonds thrown into the mix, the index should generally be in line with the broader market. This certainly held true in 2000 and 2002. The funds, however, were managed well enough to avoid the worst of 2001 and to show positive returns in a falling market. As both the table and Figure 9.7 show, since the start of the index, funds have performed significantly better than the broader market. This is encouraging for the government's efforts to develop the fund management industry as a more reliable investment partner than their shareholders.

TABLE 9.2 Shanghai Fund Index versus Shanghai A-share Index: Annual Performance

Year	Fund Index Return (%)	Shanghai Index Return (%)
2000	13.2	14.8
2001	5.5	−20.6
2002*	−16.6	−12.9
From inception	−0.5	−20.6

* Return to November 2002.
Source: Wind Information.

FIGURE 9.7 Shanghai Fund Index versus Shanghai A-share Index Performance. *Source*: Wind Information.

THE FORGETTABLE B SHARE

In their 10-year history, B shares have seldom enjoyed the attention of their A shares siblings. There have been only three periods when they caught the attention of foreign and domestic investors (see Figure 9.8). Each time, the market has lacked staying power. This short summary of the B-share market will concentrate on Shenzhen, as it has shown the greatest market swings, although not necessarily greater volume than Shanghai. Shenzhen's volatility

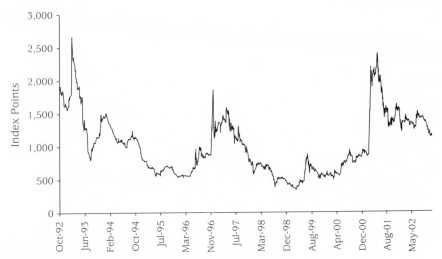

FIGURE 9.8 Shenzhen B-share Index Performance. *Source*: Wind Information.

is most likely a reflection of the participation of Hong Kong investors, who at times have been active.

The three periods of B-share market interest were January–February 1993, May 1996–May 1997, and March–May 2001. B shares began to be issued and listed on both exchanges in 1992. Shenzhen listed nine B-share companies in 1992, 13 in 1993, and another 12 in 1994. The B-share index initially fell upon launch, reflecting a weak A-share market. As the A-share market turned around, so did the B shares. Volumes during this time were very low, a fraction of what was seen in the A-share market. Consequently, the B-share market responded sharply to any significant buying or selling.

The second move in the market mirrored the A-share market's spectacular run-up in 1996–97. This time, the Hong Kong factor would no doubt have played some role, as Red Chips and H shares were also showing impressive returns. The last and most significant move of the market came as the state opened it to domestic A-share investors in March 2001. B shares closed before the 2001 Spring Festival holiday at 866 points. The new policy was announced during the holidays and, at their end, the market traded limit up for five days. By the end of March, the index stood at 1,978 points and reached a high on May 28, up 176% just since February. This performance, and the fact that the A-share markets were drifting lower, is what makes the small number of new investor accounts so interesting.

The problem, even today, is that the B-share market has always failed to attract and sustain interest and trading volume. For domestic investors, a principal reason is that there is no primary market. The inability to arbitrage shares of those companies with both A and B listings also creates a lack of interest.

TAKING THE MARKET'S MEASURE

Issuance

One of the confirmed successes of the Chinese markets is that they have been able to raise huge amounts of capital at home and abroad (see Table 9.3 and Figure 9.9). The markets reached a high point in 2000 when Chinese companies were able to raise about US$40 billion globally. The funds raised were more or less equally split between domestic and international markets, but typical issue size was noticeably different. Internationally, investors in 2000 supported the IPO issues of China Unicom (US$5.6 billion), Sinopec (US$3.4 billion), Petrochina (US$2.8 billion), and China Mobile's secondary offering, which raised a mighty US$7 billion. Domestically, it took 75 new issues to raise US$11.5 billion, on average about US$153 million. The remaining approximately US$8 billion was raised through secondary offerings.

As can clearly be seen, the international primary market is an important source of capital for Chinese companies, especially when trying to list the "industry-sized" deals. Together with the direct investment channel, this is the

TABLE 9.3 Issuance of A, B, H, and Red Chip Shares

	A Shares (US$ Mn)	B Shares (US$ Mn)	H Shares, Red Chips (US$ Mn)	Total (US$ Mn)
1991	87	–	–	87
1992	870	767	322	1,958
1993	3,267	451	1,159	4,877
1994	1,202	461	2,085	3,748
1995	1,030	402	306	1,738
1996	3,546	568	1,319	5,434
1997	10,278	973	9,186	20,436
1998	9,374	308	415	10,097
1999	10,792	46	909	11,747
2000	18,442	169	19,744	38,355
2001	14,277	–	2,434	16,711
2002	8,597	–	5,148	13,744
Totals	**81,762**	**4,144**	**43,027**	**128,934**

Sources: CSRC and SEHK websites.

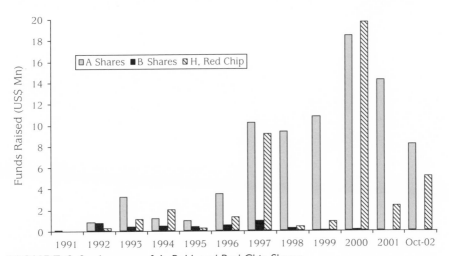

FIGURE 9.9 Issuance of A, B, H, and Red Chip Shares.
Sources: CSRC and SEHK websites.

only, for the most part, non-Chinese money that is coming into the market. As has been shown, many domestic IPOs, particularly the larger ones, simply recirculate the same money over and over. The domestic markets are hobbled by their inability to attract major amounts of fresh capital.

The ability of the domestic primary market to support larger offerings appears to have increased, as can be seen from the 10 largest domestic IPOs, nine of which were conducted in 2000 or later. To date, six Chinese companies have raised more than RMB4 billion through domestic listings: Shanghai

Pudong Development Bank (RMB4 billion), Minsheng Bank (RMB4.1 billion), BaoSteel (RMB7.8 billion), Sinopec (RMB11.8 billion), China Merchants Bank (RMB10.95 billion), and China Unicom (RMB11.5 billion). All of these except for Shanghai Pudong were achieved with significant support from corporate "strategic" investors, calling into question the market's true depth.

"Online" subscription funds in the past few years have commonly been in the US$50–70 billion range. It would seem, therefore, that US$500 million and larger offerings would have no difficulty in getting done without reliance on corporate investors. In addition, retail investors would probably welcome larger allocations, particularly of these better stocks. It is probable, however, that a significant portion of online subscription funds has been borrowed. Therefore, investors in this position would have a very short-term, one- to three-day time horizon, after which they need to flip their allocation and repay the loan. If major companies were sold into this situation, the market for their shares would collapse as all the "flippers" sell out their allocations. The problem is solved by locking up the strategic investors for three to six months. This gives time for the market in the new share to stabilize in trading and the locked-up shares to come into play gradually. It also provides a way for SOEs to profit a bit on the side.

Capitalization

Deng would have been proud: the markets have, in fact, been used in a most determined fashion since he spoke in 1992. The markets have been very successful in terms of the number of companies listed (see Table 9.4). Few would have thought that, out of the early chaotic, unregulated trading and issuance of the late 1980s and early 1990s, China would develop an efficient, standardized, and successful issuance process. Although problems abound in the quality of companies and their share structure, this should not detract from what has been a very successful past 12 years of growth for the exchanges. The notional capitalization of the market and the number of companies listed stands as testimony to the persistence of the reform effort.

Turnover

As the market has grown, so has trading volume, which has peaked twice, once in the bull market years of 1996 and 1997 and again in 2000 (see Table 9.5). Early in the new century, the market typically trades about RMB12 billion a day spread between the two exchanges, with Shanghai now accounting for about 60% of total A-share trading. The daily volume record was set on February 17, 2000, when Shanghai traded RMB47.1 billion in shares and Shenzhen RMB42.8 billion, a remarkable combined total of RMB89.9 billion (US$10.85 billion).

In addition to A and B shares, both exchanges trade a variety of investment funds, CGBs, CGB repos, and a selection of financial and corporate bonds (see Table 9.6). A shares dominate trading, especially in Shenzhen

TABLE 9.4   Shanghai and Shenzhen Market Summary

	Shenzhen				Shanghai			
Year	No. of A Cos. Listed	No. of B Cos. Listed	A Market Cap. (RMB Bn)	B Market Cap. (RMB Bn)	No of A Cos. Listed	No. of B Cos. Listed	A Market Cap. (RMB Bn)	B Market Cap. (RMB Bn)
1990	2	–	–	–	8	–	1	–
1991	6	–	8	–	8	–	3	–
1992	24	9	46	3	30	9	52	4
1993	76	19	125	8	101	22	208	13
1994	118	24	103	6	169	34	248	12
1995	127	34	88	7	184	36	243	9
1996	227	43	413	23	287	42	532	16
1997	348	51	812	19	372	50	903	19
1998	400	54	877	11	425	52	1,053	10
1999	450	54	1,173	16	471	54	1,444	14
2000	499	58	2,086	30	559	55	2,660	33
2001	494	56	1,531	62	636	54	2,693	66
2002	494	57	1,261	36	705	54	2,492	44

Sources: Shanghai and Shenzhen stock exchange statistics; market caps based on all shares at A-share price.

TABLE 9.5   Trading Volumes for A and B Shares: Annual Total and Daily Average

	A Total (RMB Mn)		B Total (RMB Mn)		A Daily (RMB Mn)		B Daily (RMB Mn)	
Year	SH	SZ	SH	SZ	SH	SZ	SH	SZ
1992	23,272	41,744	1,445	1,663	91	162	6	8
1993	226,168	126,087	7,886	2,579	873	487	30	11
1994	562,673	237,635	10,835	1,620	2,260	954	44	7
1995	304,263	91,596	6,083	1,704	1,247	375	25	7
1996	902,024	1,203,205	9,457	18,530	3,652	4,871	38	78
1997	1,355,024	1,674,497	21,293	21,369	5,576	6,891	88	91
1998	1,230,423	1,111,349	8,188	4,465	5,002	4,518	33	19
1999	1,682,620	1,422,336	13,959	13,046	7,040	5,951	58	56
2000	3,102,969	2,924,898	34,417	20,380	12,983	12,238	144	88
2001	1,987,684	1,336,520	283,254	223,059	8,282	5,569	1,180	953
2002	1,644,171	1,070,033	51,738	33,103	6,937	4,515	218	140

Sources: Shanghai and Shenzhen stock exchange statistics.

where only 6% of all CGB spot and repo business is conducted. In Shanghai, which has a long history of bond trading, CGB repos contribute a significant amount to the daily turnover. The short-term funding provided by repos, however, is often directed back into the A-share market for new IPO subscriptions or proprietary trading.

TABLE 9.6   Breakdown of Trading by Product: Shanghai and Shenzhen

	Nov. 2002 (%)		2001 (%)		2000 (%)		1999 (%)	
	SH	**SZ**	**SH**	**SZ**	**SH**	**SZ**	**SH**	**SZ**
A Shares	36.1	84.4	45.3	73.2	62.6	91.7	47.0	87.2
B Shares	1.2	2.7	6.5	12.2	0.7	0.6	0.4	0.8
Funds	1.2	5.0	3.1	6.6	2.7	4.6	3.8	6.9
CGB Spot	12.9	7.5	10.0	2.4	7.4	1.6	14.7	0.1
CGB Repo	48.4	0.0	35.0	5.3	26.5	1.1	33.9	4.7
Other Bond	0.2	0.4	0.2	0.3	0.2	0.4	0.1	0.3

Sources: Shanghai and Shenzhen stock exchange statistics; Shenzhen 2002 figures are for October 2002 month-end.

Dividends

Since 1989, the Chinese investor has focused on short-term gains, and is it any wonder? The high volatility of many stocks and the generally poor fundamental performance of the underlying companies have made long-term investing a risky and unrewarding business. Chinese companies have been very good at raising funds, but not so good at paying cash dividends back to investors.

As can be seen from Table 9.7, the dividend yield over the past six years has been below 1 %, although the number of companies paying has increased dramatically. The same picture is seen in Shanghai, where the dividend yield in 2001 was only 1.16 %.[14] Shanghai, like Shenzhen, also had a sharp rise in the number of companies paying dividends. In 2000, there were only 148 companies paying; in 2001, the number jumped to 407.

It is interesting to note as well the amounts of capital raised by the same companies in rights and other non-IPO offerings, shown in Table 9.7. Looking

TABLE 9.7   Dividends Summary: Shenzhen Exchange

Year	Dividends (RMB Mn)	% Yield	No. of Companies	Non-IPO Fund-raising (RMB Mn)
1994	1,555	1.24	75	–
1995	3,134	3.04	95	–
1996	2,304	2.63	76	3,073
1997	2,422	0.59	70	7,952
1998	4,564	0.56	109	19,308
1999	8,568	0.98	124	13,713
2000	8,731	0.74	153	38,403
2001	14,848	0.71	316	23,473
2002	12,004	0.81	264	12,528

Source: Shenzhen stock exchange statistics.

at 2001, for example, companies called on investors to put up RMB23.5 billion, while paying out as dividends RMB14.9 billion. Since holders of state and LP shares frequently do not participate in such offerings, but do receive a dividend, the comparison suggests that the market is being used, at least in part, to fund the dividends. At the same time, the state is diluting itself down, as discussed earlier.

Market Volatility

The A-share markets are commonly assumed to be particularly volatile. This impression is a remnant of the early 1990s, when the market could and did double in a day. Since then, they have become much less volatile and overall are not that much different from more familiar markets such as Hong Kong, at least from a stock index perspective.

This potentially surprising fact is substantiated in Table 9.8. The table shows the annual average of the 20-day historical volatility[15] for the Hong Kong Hang Seng Index, Red Chips, H shares, Dow Industrial, and the Shanghai and Shenzhen A-share indices. The volatility figures show that the markets, as already mentioned, are quite distinct in their movements and illustrate that there is little correlation between the mainland, Hong Kong, and U.S. markets.

Volatilities jumped sharply in Hong Kong in 1997, catalyzed by great expectations of the handover to China on July 1. They remained high throughout 1998 and beyond, only settling back below 30% in 2002. The Dow showed very low volatility up until 1997 and then started to climb, but really spiked in 2001 and 2002 as economic uncertainty increased and the Internet bubble

TABLE 9.8 Twenty-day Comparative Historical Volatility

Year	Hang Seng (%)	Red Chips (%)	H Shares (%)	Dow Industrial (%)	Shanghai A (%)	Shenzhen A (%)
1991	16.6	–	–	13.9	7.2	44.2
1992	20.1	–	–	10.5	64.1	41.5
1993	21.1	32.7	40.5	8.5	54.0	37.0
1994	28.7	29.5	39.5	10.6	60.5	50.5
1995	19.2	19.3	25.6	8.4	38.7	32.3
1996	15.6	19.3	24.9	11.5	38.2	39.3
1997	31.4	54.9	50.4	17.7	35.2	39.2
1998	41.7	62.7	57.5	18.3	19.3	21.2
1999	25.8	40.0	43.6	16.1	25.2	28.9
2000	30.8	46.4	41.9	19.6	19.6	21.6
2001	26.3	37.2	34.8	20.4	19.3	20.6
Nov. 2002	19.6	26.8	19.9	24.0	22.1	23.1

Source: Authors' calculations; 20-day volatility averaged for each calendar year.

burst. Shanghai and Shenzhen showed the incredible volatility they were known for from 1992 until 1997. Since then, both have settled down to more normal levels below 20–30%. Part of the decrease in volatility stems from the reimposition of daily trading limits. The limits have prevented the huge market swings seen previously. A further reason is that exchange indices include all listed stocks.[16] Consequently, no one or a handful of stocks dominate either trading or the index weightings. Other domestic indices represent a selection of around 30 or more and so are more influenced by the swings of the larger stocks.[17]

Figure 9.10 shows the rolling 20-day volatility for a one-year period from November 2001 to November 2002. As can be seen, Shanghai is not substantially more volatile than the Hang Seng or the Dow. The Hang Seng tends to move more with the Dow (see the last half of 2002), but during that time Shanghai's volatility dropped significantly, to as low as 10% at times.

Comparative Performance

Since the start of trading, the Chinese domestic markets have operated as a closed and isolated system due to the non-convertibility of the Chinese currency. The money invested into the A-share market is mainland Chinese money, and the A-share investor base does not have a significant presence outside of China. Until December 1, 2002, when the QFII system became effective, foreign money could not directly enter into the A-share market. This has insulated the A-share and bond markets from the "hot money" flows that

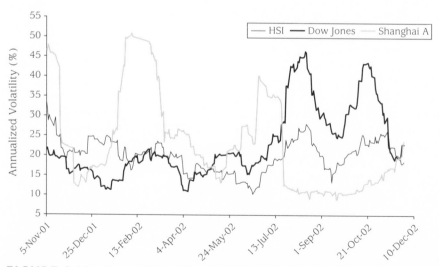

FIGURE 9.10 Average 20-day Historical Volatility for Hang Seng Index, Shanghai A, and Dow Jones.
Source: Authors' calculations; November 5, 2001–November 5, 2002.

TABLE 9.9   Year-on-year Performance of Shanghai, Shenzhen, Hong Kong, and the U.S. Indices

Return	Shanghai A (%)	Shenzhen A (%)	Hang Seng (%)	Dow Jones (%)
1991	129.4	–	42.1	20.3
1992	166.6	139.7	28.3	4.2
1993	6.8	–3.7	115.7	13.7
1994	–22.3	–42.9	–31.1	2.1
1995	–14.3	–22.3	23.0	33.5
1996	65.1	225.7	33.5	26.0
1997	30.2	30.1	–20.3	22.6
1998	–4.0	–29.5	–6.3	16.1
1999	19.2	14.3	68.8	24.7
2000	51.7	41.0	–11.0	–5.8
2001	–20.6	–30.0	–24.5	–7.1
2002	–17.5	–17.0	–18.2	–16.8
Dec. 90 to 2002	1,257.9	179.3	202.3	217.6

Sources: Wind Information and Bloomberg; return defined as % changes from year-end index close to year-end index close.

brought chaos to Asian markets in 1997 and later. Conversely, China has been unable to influence overseas markets except indirectly through H shares, Red Chips, or foreign currency-denominated bond offerings. A quick glance at the year-on-year returns of the leading indices in China, Hong Kong, and the U.S. highlights this isolation (see Table 9.9).

Not surprisingly, the performances of Shanghai and Shenzhen track one another quite closely. Only in 1996 does Shenzhen significantly diverge on the upside from Shanghai. Neither Shanghai nor Shenzhen follow Hong Kong or New York. At times, Hong Kong and Shanghai show a similar performance, but for quite different reasons (see Figure 9.11). Both the mainland and Hong Kong experienced bull markets in 1996 and 1997, but the factors behind such moves differed. The mainland case has been described above, but at that same time Hong Kong was booming. Its market was being driven by a hot property market, the Red Chip craze, back-door listings and asset injections, and a highly optimistic outlook about the return of sovereignty to China. After that party was over, the Hong Kong market felt the full force of the Asian financial crisis and the market plummeted. The government intervened directly to prop up blue chip names like the Hongkong and Shanghai Banking Corporation. The same crisis affected mainland market sentiment, but prices were already well down after their extraordinary bull market run. Consequently, the Asian crisis had very little real impact on Chinese stock prices.

Hong Kong started to recover from its lows of 1998 and showed strong returns in 1999. This was partly a bounce from extreme lows, but it also

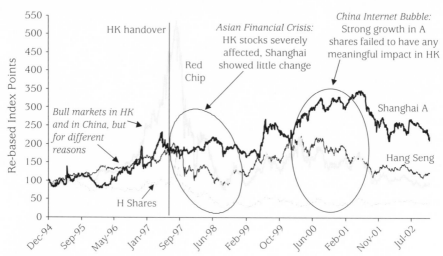

FIGURE 9.11 Comparative Performance, Hong Kong and Shanghai Shares. *Sources*: Wind Information and Bloomberg.

FIGURE 9.12 H-share and A-share Performance, 1993 and 1994. *Source*: Wind Information.

mirrored the Dow and NASDAQ telecom, IT, and Internet bubble. Both Hong Kong and the U.S. peaked in the first few months of 2000 at the time when the A shares were just getting into their stride.

The bursting of the Internet bubble and the global bear market knocked the Hang Seng sharply down in 2000, but it failed to make an impression on Shanghai. As Hong Kong suffered, the mainland markets carried on, peaking in June 2001. Although both Hong Kong and the mainland performed badly in 2001 and 2002, the reasons were very different. Hong Kong is fully exposed to the slowing global economy and still suffering from the hangover of the Asian financial crisis. The mainland, however, has been panicked by the possible sale of state shares, false accounting and fraud charges against listed firms, and a general loss of investor confidence in the market and the government's ability to support it. That is, until Shang Fulin, the new CSRC chairman, was appointed in late 2002.

The H shares, like their poor relative the B shares, boomed back in the early days before 1995. They represented the first chance for overseas investors to access a good-sized deal in what were supposed to be the best companies in China. Did this peak in H shares have any impact on the A-share market? Figure 9.12 tells the story. As can be seen, the first six months of the H-share index showed a near doubling in value while A shares followed along. There was a run-up of the A shares in November/December 1993, but that was a "technical" bounce from previous lows. Given this picture, the feelings of the Shanghai and Shenzhen exchange and city officials about the state policy of prioritizing overseas listings was not without foundation at the time.

CHAPTER 10

Looking Ahead 10 Years:
Divvying Things Up

Because the government controls the development of China's stock markets, the guiding ideology is very important. I want to emphasize that up until today the guiding ideology in developing the stock markets is still to "help state enterprises resolve their problems." But I think we should change this wording to say "help the state enterprises realize management by the people." ... There is a big difference here. Helping SOEs resolve their problems means how to let the people's money flow into the SOEs with the worst problems. But helping SOEs realize management by the people means how to let SOEs flow into the hands of those best able to manage them.

Professor Zhang Weiying, Beijing University, responding to Gao Xiqing,
January 3, 2000[1]

It is worth re-emphasizing how today's stock markets emerged out of changes in enterprises and local governments in the decade following the Cultural Revolution. Placing them in this larger context serves as a reminder that they remain a critical part of a much broader picture – how China's companies rise to meet the challenge of daily increasing foreign competition both internationally and domestically. The stock markets are not a narrow topic, nor is theirs a narrow history. They are the lens through which this struggle and its winners and losers can be seen most clearly.

China's companies and stock markets emerged in the 1980s out of an environment of extreme state planning and radical socialist ideology. Over the previous 30 years, this Chinese version of Leninism and Stalinism efficiently eliminated not only the private sector of the economy, but the institutions, words, and meanings associated with it. Limitations of technology and the vagaries of individual leadership at the local level, however, somewhat eased this severe environment. The emergence of Deng Xiaoping in 1978 meant an end to political extremism altogether. By the early 1980s, people could experiment with previously banned ways of solving enterprise problems, particularly financing problems, due to a significantly more relaxed political environment.

One line of experimentation was the contract responsibility system (*cheng-baozhi*). This was the politically mainstream attempt to address poor SOE performance, primarily by giving management greater autonomy. The system involved setting production (and therefore revenue) quotas for enterprises and letting them keep any profit in excess of the planned target. This policy began in 1979, but ran into difficulties because of the 1983–84 tax reforms. The MOF depended heavily on the collection of SOE profits to fund the state budget at this time. The new tax regime during its pilot implementation, however, had the effect of virtually eliminating the amount of funds the enterprise could retain. Enterprises, not surprisingly, fought against the new tax system and a compromise was reached whereby the SOEs guaranteed payment of a certain amount of tax to the MOF. Everything above this amount could be kept for their own use. The first contracts with enterprises were finalized in 1986 for a three-year period. The contracts were renewed in 1989 and 1992. The 1988 Enterprise Law exemplifies this approach. The Law gives a certain amount of autonomy to enterprises and enterprise management as an incentive to improved performance. The financial impact of this policy approach was significant and can be seen in the approximately 33% share taken by SOE legal persons in the capital structure of the Shanghai and Shenzhen exchanges.[2]

At the same time in the early 1980s, small rural and even urban enterprises began experimenting with things called "shares" to raise funds for new enterprises or projects. In contrast to the SOEs, which could mostly count on the state for financing, these small entities were forced to rely on themselves; they could not expect help from the banks. In 1979, the state affirmed their spontaneous financing experiments. This was important, since it provided the political cover needed to proceed. Over the course of the next five years, the number of enterprises using "shares" to raise capital increased significantly nationwide and by 1987 had produced the first relatively large and standardized share offering by Shenzhen Development Bank. By 1988, the shareholding experiment had become promising enough that Shanghai's new mayor, Zhu Rongji, would seize on it as the way out of the city's budgetary difficulties. The experiment now had a significant political sponsor and a channel to the very top – Deng himself.

In the late 1980s, however, there were still two groups of enterprises following these separate policy paths. The SOEs using the contract responsibility system had prospered and become increasingly independent-minded as, for example, Capital Steel's Zhou Guanwu. Their senior management began to pursue their own interests further through the issue of stock. Enterprises involved in the shareholding experiment had also been extremely creative. In 1988 there were already some 10,000 so-called shareholding enterprises whose stocks could be traded internally and, in some cases, on an OTC basis. The pressure from the enterprises, the self-interest of local governments, and the clamor of black-market crowds trading shares combined to force a very practical result.[3] Over the course of 1988 and 1989, the state determined to create an acceptable basis practically and ideologically for the shareholding system to continue its development. This effort was put on hold by the June 4 incident.

Events at the local level, oblivious of the mood in the capital, continued to push this process forward faster. Shenzhen Development Bank, by providing a rich dividend payout, catalyzed "share fever" in early 1989. Even June 4 could not put out the wild enthusiasm for shares that had suddenly taken hold. Given the party's overriding concern about social stability and the events of the preceding 12 months, the step to open stock exchanges was a short one, taken in the spring of 1990. Having done that, the next step – the idea of actually using the exchanges and the corporatization process in a positive fashion to raise money for SOEs – was also easy. The triumph of this policy line over the contract responsibility system came in July 1994 with Zhu Rongji's signing of the Company Law. By this time, there were 350 companies listed domestically and 23 overseas. Zhu's approval of the Company Law made possible the first direct listing of a Chinese enterprise on the NYSE – Shandong Huaneng.[4]

This is the big picture of events during those 15 years and it clearly shows how local events determined the final policy outcome. Why the shareholding system motivated local players can be shown more directly. As one enterprise boss (*laozong*) put it, "It's not who *owns* the money that's important, it's who gets to *use* the money." While it was true that in the early 1980s there was only a state and no private sector, by the end of the decade a non-state sector had begun to grow. Not only that, the state sector itself was on the verge of hollowing out due to the contract responsibility and shareholding systems. How did this work? As the *laozong* noted above, those who directly controlled and operated assets on behalf of the state in fact owned the assets, but they were not the true owners. In retrospect, however, they pushed in the direction that would clarify asset ownership.

In the absence of the requisite institutions, laws, and financial management systems, the shareholding system was tailor-made for this set of economic players and for the state itself. Why this was so can be seen by a comparison of the 1988 Enterprise Law and the 1994 Company Law. Briefly put, under the Company Law an enterprise underwent a restructuring to become an independent corporation with clear direct title to its own assets. In contrast, under the Enterprise Law, bosses got more autonomy and the enterprise was called a "legal person," but the issue of ownership was not in any way addressed. The enterprises remained a part of the traditional planned economy. From the viewpoint of enterprise management, this was not an ideal situation as their own positions remained undefined, even if powerful. From the state's viewpoint, this was not ideal, either. Under the contract system, enterprises shared a big chunk of what would otherwise have been 100% state tax revenues. This was not the case for the shareholding system, which had grown precisely because it attracted third party capital and not state budgetary contributions. With new capital, the companies would generate additional revenues the state could tax (and not share). How could the state not like this deal?

The transparency of the system was also a benefit to the state, but the local management team was even better off. In order to reorganize to become a company limited by shares, the actual ownership of assets funded by state funds or, like land, owned outright by the state, had to be systematically documented. After documentation, such assets were then deeded over to the new corporate legal entity in return for shares representing the same value. The shareholders of the new company now became the successors to the state, even if they were "acting" for the state. This process for the first time established a clear legal boundary between the company and the state. Such a boundary did not need to exist before under state planning, since the state encompassed everything and everyone. Now the state benefited by knowing exactly what it owned, while the local group, in fact, became the true owners.

At the end of the corporatization process, the previous enterprise management typically remained in place as the new corporate management. Under the new system, they reported to a board of directors and a board of supervisors, whose membership was set by a general shareholders' meeting – that is, the "state." But what was the state? The state was that particular entity – whether a ministry, its local bureau, or a local government – in charge of that particular type of company or sector. In short, nothing really had changed except the form of the arrangement. There was, however, a single critical difference: the company – that is, its management – now had outright legal possession of its own assets.[5]

What changes if the company sells shares representing an ownership interest? Majority shareholder approval for a sale is easy to arrange. The company's directors, its major shareholders, and the key local government approving agencies are the same group of people sharing similar interests who, in one way or another, represent the "state." Working together, this group can "arrange" things so that almost any company can meet listing requirements. With "state" approval, the company sells new shares and receives in return either additional assets or cash outright to do with what management, its directors, supervisors and (majority) shareholders wish.

The sale of new shares, rather than a portion of the company's existing shares, is a subtle but crucial point. While the result in either case is the dilution of the state's ownership, the sale of new shares increases total capital and leaves the existing state shares, which represent the underlying state assets contributed, in place and untouched. The "state" continues as the owner with an absolute majority of shares, as well as apparently unshakable control of its contributed assets. But this new self-financing capability allows the company (as well as its direct "state" owners) to cut a further and even more critical tie with the larger state, becoming less financially dependent. This works to the direct and personal benefit of all members of the company's broader "management team," which includes the supervising agency, the PBOC, and local government agencies.

The benefits (and beneficiaries) of this arrangement broadened as the experiment expanded beyond enterprise restructuring. The share fever that broke out in the late 1980s created more allies of the shareholding system. The banks established OTC counters, share transfers could be taxed, and banks and local government could earn transaction fees. Even social unrest worked to the advantage of this broadening interest group. Given its fear of social instability, the state with its planning and control mentality saw the wisdom of creating centralized and tightly managed securities exchanges. For local interests, this was a boon: the exchanges could be used for the benefit of each city's own companies. With significant company assets and an exchange, the city governments now possessed a self-financing tool on which the state initially imposed few controls. This perfect situation did not last long, largely due to the failure of local governments to manage the exchanges and their members properly. By 1996, the state had taken over control of both national exchanges and three years later closed down all regional exchanges.

As for the shares that were created by corporatization and listing, the state from the start was determined not to promote privatization. The resulting compromise created non-fungible share classes and, over the course of the 1990s, an increasingly lopsided public stock market. But this awkward approach did permit the listings to go forward. By this time in the early 1990s, the entire program had shifted its objective from improved production efficiencies to SOE recapitalization. Similar to share fever among retail investors, SOEs saw the financial benefits of selling at a multiple of NAV a new piece of paper valued on their books at NAV. They loudly clamored for listing quotas and approvals. As the decade progressed, the SOE holders of non-tradable shares also lobbied hard for the ability to sell: they, too, needed money. The state made sporadic attempts during the 1990s to create markets wherein these LP shares could trade, but these efforts failed. No matter. The local office of the SAMB held the authority to approve "transfers" of non-tradable shares in local companies, so there was, in fact, no problem. Chinese M&A was born. The same group of people at the local level, now including the SAMB, benefited from such sales. The SOEs received much-needed capital, and the local governments made sure that the transfer was made to a favored entity. Even for central government enterprises, such transfers were possible: the "state" is hardly unitary. Looking at television coverage of the 2,100 delegates to the 16th Congress of the CCP, someone commented, "*There* are the owners of China's economy."

The only problem from the "state" viewpoint was the lack of transparency: just who was down there buying up state assets? In the public markets, every trade and the new owner of the shares is clearly recorded in a central registry. For transfers of non-tradable shares between nominally state-owned entities, however, local approvals remained local and true ownership was, ultimately, obscured. This is one reason for the closure of the SAMB at the central government level in 1998: it did not (in fact, it could not) do its job, which was defined as preventing the loss of state assets. Of course, the elimination of a central government agency responsible to the "state" would make such "M&A" activity easier and, in fact, transactions have picked up substantially since that time.

In the public markets, the listed companies over time, whether through rights offerings or the listing of shares with "historical problems," have whittled down the weight of holders of state and LP shares. The analysis of two sample groups of listed companies showed that tradable shares in less than five years grew to account for over 40% of total company shares. In addition, the number of companies with a free float greater than 50% grew to be 216, or nearly 18% of all listed companies as of year-end 2002. Since the Company Law requires several promoters to establish a shareholding company, most listed companies have more than a single holder of state shares.

The conditions for the takeover of a listed SOE now become clear. This explains how Mr. K, by combining control of tradable shares and a portion of non-tradable shares, took over China Venture Capital. This, then, is the set of conditions making privatization of listed state-owned enterprises possible. Takeovers and buy-outs may be possible, but will still only result in a very obscure form of privatization. Without the guise of a typical state-owned or controlled company, how will the company obtain bank financing, how will welfare problems be addressed, and what will the company's legal status be? It is far more convenient and practical to leave such problems alone, use the assets (and the workers), and make money. This is the essence of "management by the people (*minying*)."

In 2000, the central government's strategic emphasis for SOE corporatization and listing changed for the third time. The state's first objective in the 1980s was to promote greater production efficiencies by increasing enterprise autonomy. When the state, thanks to Deng, finally saw what everyone else saw – the positive impact of the application of large amounts of capital – the objective changed again to SOE recapitalization in the 1990s. China's entrance into the WTO, combined with the success of industry-wide packaging and listing, has now shifted the focus to the creation and support of competitive national champions. Recapitalizing individual SOEs continues, but it is not going to create the companies that protect China's strategic industrial sectors from being dominated by foreign economic interests. With a policy emphasis focused on about 190 major companies, the central government is able to give less and less consideration to the nearly 170,000 other SOEs in China. Moreover, the state's growing financial needs – for example, the creation of a workable social security system – are forcing it to sell off unwanted stakes in unwanted companies. The indirect effect of the national champion strategy, therefore, will be to speed up the privatization of all such non-strategic SOEs. Some people believe this will be the last great chance to strike it rich in China.

How this will come about can be seen in the state's corollary strategy announced at the 16th Party Congress of November 2002.[6] In one of its major, if not *the* major, decisions, the Congress clarified how it intends to implement the long-existing concept of "seize the large and let go of the small (*zhuada fangxiao*)." The key sentence spoken by Jiang Zemin was: "Under the premise of upholding the principle of state ownership ... the state must set laws and regulations to build a management system for state-owned assets in which the center and the local governments separately represent the state in carrying out the role of investor, enjoying the combined rights of ownership, benefits, duties and responsibilities, managing assets and people together."[7] This sounds like so much hot air, but a new management system for state assets means speeding up Chinese-style privatization to those local governments that can read between the lines.

The current system of state asset management is based on the principle of "state-unified ownership, management by the different local levels (*guojia suoyou, fenji guanli*)." In theory, this has meant that all transfers of ownership of state interests in SOEs, whether evidenced by state and LP shares or not, had ultimately to be approved by the central government. Similarly, if an SOE decides to corporatize or, as in a few instances, to withdraw from state ownership, final approval rested with the central government. This will change under the new system, which is summarized by the principle of "state-unified ownership, with each level exercising property rights (*guojia suoyou, fenji xingshi chanquan*)."

In the planned economy, as has been mentioned, there was no concept of ownership; the state owned everything. It has only been in the past 20 years, and particularly during the 1990s, that ownership has been carefully defined through the process of corporatization, even if in most cases the state remains the controlling owner. Following the elimination of the SAMB in 1998, the MOF Enterprise Department (*qiye si*) became responsible for the approval of nearly all major corporate restructurings or transfers of property rights for the entire country. Obviously, this was simply not feasible: the approval process took too long – in some instances, years. First, the application was sent to the agency responsible for the specific industry. From that agency, the documents were sent to either the local government or the central SAMB, now the MOF, for final approval. For major companies, MOF approval was insufficient, so it became essentially a matter of getting the premier's approval. Under the new principle of local governments exercising their property rights, approvals can be made much more efficiently and quickly. The point is that this new policy will benefit the same local gang that this history of the shareholding system began with.

The new principle halts just on the verge of transferring direct ownership rights to local governments. In fact, explicitly transferring ownership rights over local companies to local governments was debated in the lead-up to the Congress. The argument against this expression, however, was simple: it would lead to outright privatization and, therefore, was politically unacceptable. "Exercising property rights" is different than "exercising ownership rights," since it signifies that the local government is acting as a representative of the state, not on its own behalf even if it, and not the center, was the primary investor. But the end result will be the same: local governments will be enabled to make decisions affecting the restructuring of local enterprises locally without referring to the center.

In fact, the likely outcome of this arrangement is well known. In late 1999, the Changsha municipal government enacted a very straightforward policy principle – "whoever invests has ownership, whoever accumulates capital has ownership." The practical application of this principle led to a major SOE "withdrawing from the state camp" to become a collective enterprise.[8] This caused a political shock up and down the country that finally reached Beijing. A central investigation team finally arrived to put a stop to such "unfair" transfers. In 2002, travelling through the eastern provinces of China, however, there were indications that such transfers of SOEs to private management have already taken place on a large scale and the results are impressive. But it is not true privatization.

Privatization with Chinese characteristics allows the state to spin off unwanted companies that are burdensome (for now). It is not true privatization, however, except perhaps in the sense that presumably non-state managers have the right to run the business, and the state no longer has to worry about the business and its workers (for the time being). As noted previously, there are as of yet no laws protecting private property rights. Within the "private" companies themselves, this reality is mirrored by the fact that "management by the people" is driven by individuals. Such companies have not really become independent as an institution with internal policies and procedures to handle management changes or other challenges. As another example, can the presumed "owners" of "privatized" companies sell them off to foreign companies without final state approval? Furthermore, the trend of the Communist Party to absorb so-called capitalist entrepreneurs illustrates the ability of the traditional Chinese system to co-opt outsiders, although there is a question just how "outside" such outsiders might be. In an ironic fashion, Jiang Zemin's "Three Representatives" may in practice mean a reversal of the state's effort to disengage itself from enterprise management.

While effective in the short term, the long-term economic benefits of this approach – whether the obscure transfers of listed companies or the shifting of their burden to entrepreneurs by local governments – remains unclear. How does the system move on once the initial burst of energy is gone? What can the next step be except full and true privatization? The idea that what is important is "who gets to use the money" suits a short-term and highly pragmatic mentality suited to the current situation. But people always will want more.

Of course, none of this directly addresses the problems of the stock markets, at least in the near term. Upon the transfer of a controlling block of shares in any shareholding company, the new owner will face the same problem of illiquid securities as the old owner. The overall market faces the same problem with its massive 70% state share overhang. For the company as well as for the country, the distorted capital structure prevents usable capital markets from forming and playing their role as ultimate arbiters of company value and success. As the experience of 2001 demonstrates, any announcement by the government of its intention to reduce the overhang by even a small share selldown will drive market valuations down. A major selloff might collapse the markets to as little as 20% of current levels. This will be politically unacceptable. Investors have rapidly learned that more shares means lower share valuations, all else remaining equal. There seems no easy way to address this problem head on.

Relating to this problem is the issue of Renminbi non-convertibility on the capital account. As the trading levels of the 27 companies with both overseas and domestic listings illustrate, there is a significant valuation differential between local and international shares, with domestic prices the higher. This differential amounts to more than five times for certain shares. What would be the impact of allowing full Renminbi convertibility? Full convertibility will come only when the Chinese government feels that it is dealing from a position of strength and, in any event, will come step by step. In this regard, the QFII system introduced at the end of 2002 is the first small step. This suggests that the country's economy and, indeed, its markets will be far more developed than they are at present. In such circumstances, predicting the Renminbi impact on Chinese shares is nearly impossible. First, will the overseas shares of the 27 companies at such a time still be cheaper than their domestic shares? Second, local investors worldwide tend to invest in their home markets in companies with which they are familiar. The same should be expected of Chinese retail investors at a minimum. A third point is that while Asian markets crashed during the recent financial crisis, this was in large part because foreign capital had been allowed in and then been suddenly withdrawn. China's case is the opposite. So, would shares fall? Perhaps if foreign capital can sell short the "expensive" China market if, indeed, it is expensive at that time.

Any way out of the market overhang will have to involve, as a first step, a substantial reworking of the current relationship between the state and investors. This relationship can be broadly described as follows: individuals buy shares of commodity-like SOEs in exchange for the state's unspoken promise to price such shares cheaply and to maintain relative market stability. Investors, consequently, have grown up with the perception of a state guarantee that the markets will operate in such a way as to ensure no one will lose money. Such reliance on the state means that if the markets do suffer for whatever reason, the government will most certainly take the blame. This explains the universal expectation that A-share investors should be compensated for any fall in the markets due to the floating of state shares. The state, on the one hand, should continue to distance itself from the market as it has been doing since 1999. On the other hand, listed companies should create true value and not false financial statements. At the least, the latter types of companies are now being cast under the media spotlight, exposed to fines and legal suits, and even being de-listed. Such actions have been long overdue, but must continue systematically.

The Securities Law has marked a surprisingly effective step forward in this regard. Under the Law, the CSRC, having given up power over the initial approval process, has gained it back on the enforcement side. As the plethora of scandals since 2000 indicates, the markets appear to be in for a well-over-due clean-up, although with a new CSRC chairman announced in December 2002 it is too soon to tell.[9] Underwriters are having to assume greater responsibility for the quality of the companies issuing shares; for the valuation, pricing, and trading of their shares; and, as sponsors, for their disclosure to investors on an ongoing basis. To date, however, only company auditors, who are less politically entrenched than the securities companies, have paid a high price for condoning outright underwriting fraud.

By the same token, investors will increasingly have to rely on their own judgment as to the merits of an investment, as well as to the standards of the particular underwriter. Given the large literature on market manipulation and almost daily exposures of company and management fraud, investors now have greater opportunities to educate themselves than before. In addition, they have the option of suing company management in court even on a quasi-class action basis.[10] This is a major breakthrough for minority investor rights. With the success of minority H-share investors in the 2002 Angang New Steel case, it should not be too long before local investors seek and get similar rights to prevent parent SOEs from using listed subsidiaries as "ATM machines."

Furthermore, companies, as well as IPOs, must be allowed to fail before markets can develop further, attracting the common investor back. In the U.S., Enron, the seventh-largest company in the country, went bankrupt; its management was publicly disgraced in the media and before Congress. The company's auditor, the venerable firm of Arthur Andersen, went bankrupt. There was a loss of confidence in CEOs, listed companies, and the character of the banking system. The market itself, however, kept trading and looking forward. A year later, normal market activity has resumed and the problem is beginning to recede into history. In China, a Zhengzhou Baiwen takes years to resolve. The company's shares remain listed but have not traded since March 2001. The state procrastinates, its roles as owner, regulator, and politician wholly in conflict.

The relative overemphasis on the primary market to the disregard of the secondary markets is also a problem that must be addressed. The state's historically cheap pricing of shares at issuance has guaranteed a quick return to investors in the primary market and, therefore, fixed people's minds on quick money. The current huge rates of oversubscription and hundreds of millions of Renminbi in cash deposits give the appearance of huge demand. In reality, such orders and monies represent no such thing. In the listing process, the company is largely of secondary importance – most important are the primary market shares and their quick profit potential. In spite of the use of international book-building and valuation techniques for larger deals to eliminate artificially cheap pricing, this psychology continues to be strong. A common saying is, "If you want to fry shares, fry fresh shares (*yao chaogu, chao xingu*)."

Related to this is the relative ease of borrowing and the use of multiple accounts, which together result in the huge amounts of subscription funds. Significant rates of oversubscription suggest that there should be substantial demand in the "after market" – that is, the post-offering two to three weeks. But because the majority of such funds are borrowed, the pressure to flip allocations in the first few days of trading is exceptionally strong. A direct consequence of this has been the inappropriate reliance on so-called strategic investors who are anything *but* strategic.

Having made this point, it is true that China's secondary markets are quite liquid and active, but they have not yet been used as an instrument to value companies efficiently. This is due to a number of factors, most especially the level of market participation. Market data show that some 60% of all listed companies have 50,000 or fewer investors. Even the most widely held companies have at most 500,000 investors. Other data make clear that this number itself is exaggerated by the number of ghost accounts held by professional players, including, no doubt, securities firms. A further factor here is the poor quality of listed companies themselves. When the MOF reports that 89% of a sample of listed companies falsified their financial reports to show improved performance, what else can markets trade on?[11] Then there is the problem of parallel markets. These factors severely hinder the development of a truly liquid secondary market that can value companies. A first step in solving this problem would be a public reassessment of what, in fact, constitutes the market. In this regard, most aspects are reasonably clear except the actual investor population. The massive effort required to re-register current investment accounts is not worth it even if it could be done effectively. Such an effort would turn into an end in itself, rather than a means to an end – in this case, an improved market environment. The exchanges, the depository company, and the CSRC now know how many active (and idle) accounts there are and can update this data each day.[12] The public acknowledgment of current reality would facilitate better business decisions throughout the securities industry as well as more transparent regulation by the government.

Additional measures would have the CSRC continue to beef up its market surveillance and corporate compliance functions to ensure greater market transparency. Greater transparency and systematic enforcement of existing regulations will over time eliminate such professionals as Mr. K. Strong, continued public support of minority shareholder interests would also be helpful. Insurance companies and pension funds should be allowed to participate directly in the markets – as AIG has quietly done for the past 10 years.[13] This would allow them to develop their own investment capabilities and would promote greater professionalism among institutional investors. The CSRC also must take care that the ambitions of the SAC do not make the Third Board anything other than a very small-time OTC market.[14] Finally, the state should allow non-state-sector enterprises of all ownership types, including private and foreign-invested, open access to the markets as long as they meet the publicly available legal criteria.

The Chinese markets will never play their full role in developing companies and the economy if these major structural challenges are not firmly addressed. Without a doubt, change will entail some very difficult days, as the past three years have demonstrated. Of course, if the status quo is maintained, the primary and secondary markets will grow but not mature. Funds will be raised and bull markets will come and go, but the longer the structural problems go unresolved, the more difficult any clean-up will be in the future. Having gotten this far, there is no guarantee of continued success for this first experiment with stock markets in an economy still managed by a state plan and with no protection of private property.

At the start of the 1990s, the combination of China and stock markets seemed to be a non-starter. It was something very few, if any, people outside China even thought about. Now, after over 10 years of at times wildly extravagant growth, China's markets face a critical moment. If their various participants have the will to meet and systematically address the challenges they face, the markets will throw off their emerging status to become the biggest and most vibrant in Asia. With the country a member of the WTO, entire new industries developing, and true privatization waiting in the wings, anything less should be seen as failure. Such failure would have a significant negative impact on China's continued blossoming as one of the world's major economic powers.

Appendix   I

Share Issuance and Listing on the Shanghai Exchange

RELEVANT LAWS AND REGULATIONS

1. Standard Opinion (May 15, 1992)
2. Securities Law (July 1, 1999)
3. Company Law (December 29, 1993)
4. Share Issuance and Trading Management Provisional Regulations (April 22, 1993)
5. Provisional Rules Concerning Share Issuance and Subscription Methods (December 26, 1996)
6. Notice about Questions Concerning the Placement of New Shares to Secondary Market Investors (February 14, 2000)
7. Supplementary Notice about Questions Concerning the Placement of New Shares to Secondary Market Investors (May 21, 2002)
8. Company Information Disclosure, Content and Style Standards for the Issuance of Securities (March 15, 2001)
9. Shanghai Stock Exchange Share Listing Regulations, Chapter 2 and Chapter 3, Part 1 (June 8, 2001)

LISTING REQUIREMENTS

According to the Securities Law and the Company Law, companies applying for the listing of shares must meet the following conditions:

1. The shares must be publicly issued following approval of the State Council Securities Management Department.
2. The company's total share capital must not be less than RMB50 million.
3. The company must have been in business for more than three years and have made profits over the last three consecutive years. In the case of former state-owned enterprises re-established according to the law or founded after implementation of the law, if the issuers are large

and medium state-owned enterprises, the period can be calculated consecutively.

4. The number of shareholders with holdings valued in excess of RMB1,000 must not be less than 1,000 persons. Publicly offered shares must be more than 25% of the company's total share capital. For companies whose total share capital exceeds RMB400 million, the ratio of publicly offered shares must be more than 15%.

5. The company must not have been guilty of any major illegal activities or false accounting records in the past three years before listing.

6. Other conditions stipulated by the State Council.

The conditions for application for the listing of shares by limited liability companies involved in high or new technology are set out separately by the State Council.

LISTING METHODS

I. Online Fixed Price Issuance Method

The lead underwriter offers shares for sale using the stock exchange's trading system (online). The shares can only be sold through this channel and can be subscribed for by any investor at any trading hall linked to the exchange. The price and size of the issuance are fixed. The exchange system calculates the total number and size of subscriptions and allocates the issued shares to the investors.

2. Online Price Range Issuance Method

In this case, the number of shares to be issued is fixed but the price is not. On issuance day, the lead underwriter will announce a price range and only bids within this range will be recognized. Subscription by investors is similar to Method 1; the investor may bid for shares through any exchange-linked trading hall. Once all bids have been received, the lead underwriter will announce the oversubscription ratio and fix the price. Only bids that were equal to or greater than the chosen price will receive shares. The exchange calculates the total number and size of subscriptions and allocates the issued shares to the investors.

3. Fixed Price Placement of Shares to Existing Secondary Market Investors Method

This placement method is based on the value of existing holdings of secondary market investors.

a. Value of Existing Holdings

Only investors holding at least RMB10,000 worth of either Shanghai or Shenzhen (not combined) listed A shares at the close of business on the publication date of the share issuance notice can take part in the placement.

b. Types of Shareholdings

Only A shares, including temporarily frozen senior management holdings and strategic and general legal person shares, count toward the value of the investors' holdings. Listed funds, convertible bonds, other listed securities or unlisted but tradable securities cannot be included, nor can internal staff shares, state shares, transferable rights shares, legal person shares, or B shares.

c. Subscription Ratio

Investors may subscribe for 1,000 new shares for each RMB10,000 value multiple of their A-share holdings. For example, an investor with RMB15,000 of Shanghai A shares may apply for 1,000 new shares; but an investor with RMB21,000 of Shanghai A shares may apply for 2,000 shares.

4. Online, Offline Accumulated Bidding Method

In this method, neither the price nor the number of shares to be issued is fixed. On issuance day, the lead underwriter announces a proposed price range and a suggested number of shares to be sold online and offline. Once online and offline orders have been received, the lead underwriter fixes an issue price. If the online portion is undersubscribed, the offline investors may subscribe for those shares, and vice versa. If both online and offline portions are undersubscribed, the lead underwriter will adjust the issue accordingly so as to ensure that the on- and offline sizes are the same.

ISSUANCE TIMETABLE

1. Online Fixed Price Issuance Method

Time	Actions
T-3	Issuance documents passed to SSE
	Contact designated publication, prepare share prospectus and share issuance announcement
	SSE prepares online issuance
T-2	Publication of share prospectus
	Publication of share issuance announcement (T-1 also acceptable)
	Relevant documents posted on SSE website
T	Online fixed price issuance date
T+1	Subscription funds frozen
T+2	Check funds, confirm subscriptions, allocate "lottery numbers"
T+3	Publish lottery success ratio
T+4	Clearing, registration, payments. Lottery result announced.
	Lead underwriter transfers raised funds to company. Prepares for listing.

Note: T = issuance date.

2. Online Price Range Issuance Method

Time	Actions
T-3	Issuance documents passed to SSE
	Contact designated publication, prepare share prospectus and share issuance announcement
	SSE prepares online issuance
T-2	Publication of share prospectus
	Publication of share issuance announcement (T-1 also acceptable)
	Relevant documents posted on SSE website
T	Online price range issuance date
T+1	Subscription funds frozen
T+2	Check funds, fix issue price, confirm subscriptions, allocate "lottery numbers"
T+3	Publish lottery success ratio
T+4	Clearing, registration, payments. Lottery result announced.
	Lead underwriter transfers raised funds to company. Prepares for listing.

3. Fixed Price Placement of Shares to Existing Secondary Market Investors Method

Time	Actions
T-4	Issuance documents passed to SSE
	Contact designated publication, prepare share prospectus and share issuance announcement
	SSE prepares online issuance
T-3	Publication of share prospectus
	Contact designated publication, prepare share issuance announcement
T-2	Publication of share issuance announcement
T	Fixed price private placement date
	SSE supplies the oversubscription ratio
	Contact designated publication, prepare oversubscription announcement
T+1	Publish oversubscription announcement
	Conduct lottery ceremony
	Contact designated publication, prepare lottery result announcement
T+2	Publish lottery result announcement. Subscription money paid
T+3	Subscription money received
T+4	Clearing, registration, payments. Lead underwriter transfers raised funds to company. Prepares for listing.

LISTING TIMETABLE

Time	Actions
L-7	Transfer all listed documents to SSE, contact designated publication about listing notice
L-5	Publish listing notice. Prepare listing ceremony.
L-1	Implement listing ceremony preparations
L	Share lists. Listing ceremony held.

Note: L = listing date.

LISTING PROCEDURES

The applications of limited liability companies for the listing of their shares are subject to the following procedures:

- CSRC approval.
- Submission of listing application documents. Only after gaining the approval of the CSRC can the company make an application for listing to the SSE and submit the listing application documents required by the SSE.
- Share custody. Before a company's shares can be listed and trading commenced, it must entrust its full register of shareholders to the Shanghai Branch of the China Securities Registration and Clearing Co. Ltd.
- Determination of the date of listing.
- Publish a listing notice. Following examination and verification by the SSE, the company must publish a listing notice five days prior to the listing and trading of its shares.
- Listing and trading.

APPLYING FOR LISTING

According to the provisions of the Securities Law, limited liability companies must submit the following documents when making an application for the listing of their shares:

- listing announcement;
- shareholders' general meeting resolution to apply for listing;
- company articles of incorporation;
- company business license;
- financial accounting materials for the last three years or since the founding of the company following legal verification;
- legal opinions in writing and a letter of recommendation from a securities company; and
- the most recent share prospectus.

In addition, companies must submit the following related documents according to the provisions of the exchange's rules for the listing of shares:

- listing application;
- documents from the CSRC approving its share issue, and issue and listing declarations approved by the CSRC;
- newly added financial materials as required following issue of the share;
- photocopy of its business license;
- personal particulars of the secretary of the board of directors and contact details of the secretary of the board of directors, securities representative, and legal representative;

- report regarding the shareholdings of the company directors, supervisors, and senior management of the company;
- circular determining the listing abbreviation of the company's stock;
- documentation showing the full custody of the company's stock;
- a written pledge of the company's largest shareholder pledging not to sell or repo its shareholding for a period of 12 months; and
- other documents required by the exchange.

LISTING AGREEMENT

The Listing Agreement is an agreement signed between the exchange and the listed company prior to the company's stock being listed and traded. It principally includes the following:

- The stock exchange provides trading facilities and convenient service for the trading of the company's securities.
- The listed company undertakes to abide by relevant state securities laws, rules and regulations, and related rules of the exchange.
- The listed company and its directors, supervisors, and officers undertake to accept the supervision of the stock exchange and be subject to sanctions by the stock exchange for any violations in accordance with the law.
- Listing fee and its method of payment.

The exchange can cease the trading of listed securities in accordance with the law. If the exchange determines that a company's securities no longer meet the conditions for listing, it can temporarily suspend or cease the listing of such securities.

Appendix 2

Listing Approval Inter-agency Coordination Process

Approval documents for each aspect of the corporatization work constitute the bulk of the supporting documentation provided to the CSRC for review and final listing approval.

Steps in the International Offering Approval Process

Item	Approving Entities	Comments
1. Corporatization proposal	Ministry/Prov. Govt	Preliminary approval
2. Corporatization plan	Ministry/Prov. Govt	Detailed plan showing: "company" designed for listing and rationale for listing
3. Overseas listing approval	1. Ministry 2. CSRC	Based on quota, if Ministry advances a given company, it will usually get CSRC okay
4. Project proposal	Ministry	The final packaging proposal developed by investment bankers
5. Initiate asset appraisal	1. Ministry 2. SAMB	The formal asset appraisal requires approval to begin
6. Initiate land appraisal	1. Ministry 2. SLMB	Only appraised if the land use rights remain in the packaged company
7. Approve asset appraisal	1. Ministry 2. SAMB	SAMB was required to give a formal response (but not necessarily approval) in three weeks
8. Approve land appraisal	1. Ministry 2. SLMB	SLMB is also meant to reply in three weeks
9. Tariff structure (if needed)	1. Ministry 2. SPCB	Formulas are not possible; the tariff is reviewed each year

Appendix 2 *continued*

Item	Approving Entities	Comments
10. State ownership interest plan	1. Ministry/Prov. Govt 2. SAMB	State ownership cannot be less than 51%
11. Corporatization plan	1. Ministry 2. SCRES	Corporate charter, shareholder breakdown, and issuance plan
12. Use of IPO proceeds	1. Ministry 2. SPC 3. State Council	To ensure that projects to be funded by IPO proceeds are included in State Plan
13. Valuation analysis	Ministry	Ministry knows the price it wants based on NAV analysis
14. Feasibility study	Ministry	Domestic financial advisor
15. Roadshow material review	1. Ministry 2. CSRC	To ensure roadshow materials conform with state policies
16. Incorporation of company	1. Ministry 2. SCRES	Actual formation of the designed company as a legal entity
17. FX account opening	Ministry	To receive IPO proceeds
18. Company registration	1. Ministry 2. SAIC	Business license
19. Prospectus review	1. Ministry 2. CSRC	To make sure "Risk Factor" section is not insulting
20. Offering and listing plan	1. Ministry 2. CSRC	Provides an opportunity to negotiate pricing range
21. Offering and listing plan	State Council	Ministry/CSRC joint submission
22. Transformation to company limited by shares	1. Ministry 2. SCRES 3. CSRC	The corporation becomes a company limited by shares and approved to issue new shares to foreign investors
23. Application for JV status	1. Ministry 2. MOFTEC	Gives the company a tax break for three years

Appendix 3

Top 20 Largest Companies by Market Capitalization November 30, 2002

Shanghai

Code	Stock	Market Cap (US$ Bn)	% Tradable
600028	Sinopec	27.4	22.6
600050	China Unicom	7.1	14.0
600036	China Merchants Bank Co.	6.3	13.8
600019	Baoshan Iron & Steel Co.	6.3	15.0
600011	Huaneng Power International,	6.2	29.2
600377	Jiangsu Expressway Company	5.5	27.2
600000	Shanghai Pudong Development Bank Co.	4.5	16.6
600016	China Minsheng Banking Corp.	3.4	20.2
600663	Shanghai Lujiazui Finance & Trade Zone Dev. Co.	2.4	35.9
600642	Sheneng Company	2.2	22.9

Shenzhen

Code	Stock	Market Cap (US$ Bn)	% Tradable
000001	Shenzhen Development Bank Co.	2.8	72.4
000539	Guangdong Electric Power Development Co.	2.3	39.7
000618	Jilin Chemical Industrial Company Limited	1.8	32.7
000959	Beijing Capital Iron and Steel Co.	1.7	15.2
000858	Wuliangye Yibin Co.	1.6	28.2
000549	Torch Investment Co.	1.4	63.9
000633	Shenyang Hejin Holding Co.	1.4	43.2
000866	Sinopec Yangzi Petrochemical Co.	1.4	15.0
000800	FAW Car Co.	1.2	33.5
000927	Tianjin Automotive Xiali Co.	1.2	15.0

Source: Wind Information; A shares only.

Appendix 4

Companies with Listed A Shares and H Shares November 30, 2002

A Share Code	H Share Code	Stock
000585	42	Northeast Electric
000618	368	Jilin Chemical
000666	350	Jingwei Textile
000756	719	Shandong Xinhua Pharmaceutical
000898	347	Angang New Steel
000921	921	Guangdong Kelon
600011	902	Huaneng Power International
600026	1138	China Shipping
600028	386	Sinopec
600115	670	China Eastern Airlines
600188	1171	Yanzhou Coal
600332	874	Guangzhou Pharmaceutical
600362	358	Jiangxi Copper
600377	177	Jiangsu Expressway
600548	548	Shenzhen Expressway
600585	914	Anhui Conch
600600	168	Tsingtao Beer
600685	317	Guangzhou Shipyard
600688	338	Sinopec Shanghai Petrochemical
600775	553	Nanjing Panda
600806	300	Jiaoda High-Tech
600808	323	Maanshan Iron and Steel
600860	187	Beiren Printing
600871	1033	Sinopec Yizheng Chemical Fibre
600874	1065	Tianjin Capital Environmental Protection
600875	1072	Dongfang Electrical
600876	1108	Luoyang Glass

Source: Wind Information.

Appendix 5

Companies with Listed
A Shares and B Shares
November 30, 2002

A Share Code	B Share Code	Stock
000002	200002	China Vanke Co.
000011	200011	Shenzhen Properties and Resources Dev. Group
000012	200012	CSG Technology Holding Co.
000013	200013	Shenzhen Petrochemical Industry (Group) Co.
000016	200016	Konka Group Co.
000017	200017	Shenzhen China Bicycle Co.
000018	200018	Shenzhen Victor Onward Textile Industrial Co.
000019	200019	Shenzhen Shenbao Industrial Co.
000020	200020	Shenzhen Huafa Electronics Co.
000022	200022	Shenzhen Chiwan Wharf Holdings Co.
000024	200024	China Merchants Shekou Holdings Co.
000025	200025	Shenzhen Tellus Holding Co.
000026	200026	Shenzhen Fiyta Holdings Co.
000028	200028	Shenzhen Accord Pharmaceutical Co.
000029	200029	Shenzhen SEZ Real Estate and Properties Group
000030	200030	Guangdong Sunrise Holdings Co.
000037	200037	Shenzhen Nanshan Power Station Co.
000039	200039	China International Marine Containers (Group) Co.
000045	200045	Shenzhen Textile (Holdings) Co.
000055	200055	China Fangda Group Co.
000056	200056	Shenzhen International Enterprise Co.
000058	200058	Shenzhen SEG Co.
000413	200413	Shijiazhuang Baoshi Electronic Glass Co.
000418	200418	Wuxi Little Swan Co.
000429	200429	Guangdong Provincial Expressway Dev. Co.
000488	200488	Shandong Chenming Paper Holdings Co.
000505	200505	Hainan Pearl River Holdings Co.
000513	200513	Livzon Pharmaceutical Group
000521	200521	Hefei Meiling Co.

Appendix 5 *continued*

A Share Code	B Share Code	Stock
000530	200530	Dalian Refrigeration Co.
000539	200539	Guangdong Electrical Power Development Co.
000541	200541	Foshan Electrical and Lighting Co.
000550	200550	Jiangling Motors Corporation.
000553	200553	Hubei Sanonda Co.
000570	200570	Changchai Company
000581	200581	Weifu High-Technology Co.
000596	200596	Anhui Gujing Distillery Company
000613	200613	Hainan Dadonghai Tourism Centre (Holdings) Co.
000625	200625	Chongqing Changan Automobile Company
000725	200725	BOE Technology Group Co.
000726	200726	Luthai Textile Co.
000761	200761	Bengang Steel Plates Co.
000869	200869	Yantai Changyu Pioneer Wine Co.
600054	900942	Huangshan Tourism Development Co.
600094	900940	Shanghai Worldbest Co.
600190	900952	Jinzhou Port Co.
600221	900945	Hainan Airlines Co.
600272	900943	Shangahi Kai Kai Industry Company
600295	900936	Inner Mongolia E'erduosi Cashmere Products Co.
600320	900947	Shanghai Zhenhua Port Machinery Co.
600555	900955	Shanghai Matsuoka Co.
600602	900901	SVA Electron co.
600604	900902	Shanghai Erfangji Co.
600610	900906	China Textile Machinery Co.
600611	900903	Dazhong Transportation (Group) Co.
600612	900905	China First Pencil Co.
600613	900904	Shanghai Wingsung Data Technology Co.
600614	900907	Shanghai Rubber Belt Co.
600617	900913	Shanghai Lian Hua Fibre Corporation
600618	900908	Shanghai Chlor-Alkali Chemical Co.
600619	900910	Shanghai Highly (Group) Co.
600623	900909	Shanghai Tyre and Rubber Co.
600639	900911	Shanghai Jinqiao Export Processing Zone Dev. Co.
600648	900912	Shanghai Wai Gaoqiao Free Trade Zone Dev. Co.
600650	900914	Shanghai Jinjiang Tower Co.
600663	900932	Shanghai Lujiazui Finance & Trade Zone Dev. Co.
600679	900916	Phoenix Co.
600680	900930	Shanghai Posts and Telecoms Equipment Co.
600689	900922	Shanghai Sanmao Textile Co.
600695	900919	Shanghai Dajiang (Group) Stock Co.
600698	900946	Jinan Qingqi Motorcycle Co.
600726	900937	Heilongjiang Electric Power Company
600751	900938	Tianjin Marine Shipping Co.
600754	900934	Shanghai New Asia (Group) Co.

Appendix 5 *continued*

A Share Code	B Share Code	Stock
600776	900941	Eastern Communications Co.
600801	900933	Huaxin Cement Co.
600818	900915	Shanghai Forever Co.
600819	900918	Shanghai Yaohua Pilkington Glass Co.
600822	900927	Shanghai Material Trading Center Co.
600827	900923	Shanghai Friendship Group Incorporated Co.
600835	900925	Shanghai Shangling Electric Appliances Co.
600841	900920	Shanghai Diesel Engine Co.
600843	900924	Shanggong Co.
600844	900921	Hero (Group) Co.
600845	900926	Shanghai Baosight Software Co.
600848	900928	Shanghai Automation Instrumentation Co.
600851	900917	Shanghai Haixin Group Co.

Appendix 6

China's Red-hot Primary Markets

China's IPO, or the primary, markets are the principal attraction to all domestic investors. The goal is to buy in at the IPO price and "flip" the shares out after a few days. Table 1 shows the average first-day jump of all IPOs for the past five years.

TABLE 1   Listing Day IPO Performance

Year	No. of IPOs	First-day Jump (%) High	First-day Jump (%) Close
2002	69	143	132
2001	73	153	141
2000	132	175	154
1999	97	127	113
1998	94	154	133
Average		152	136

Sources: Wind Information and authors' calculations.

As Table 2 shows, in 2000 and 2001 the number of IPO subscribers jumped significantly. This is likely to be the result of the jumbo IPOs, such as China Unicom, China Merchants Bank, and Sinopec, attracting greater than usual interest.

TABLE 2   Average Number of IPO Subscribers

Year	No. of IPOs	Average No. of Subscribers
2002	22	1,466,078
2001	73	1,123,075
2000	130	886,216
1999	97	605,122
1998	90	698,979
Average		852,066

Source: Wind Information.

Table 3 shows that the smaller IPOs are the most profitable in the primary market. The best-performing large IPOs are in the US$250–500 million range, as shown in Category F, but these are generally "special" IPOs – for example, Shanghai Pudong Development Bank. These are special in the sense that they are the first of an industry or are high-profile companies. The jumbo deals in Category G – for example, Sinopec, China Unicom, and so on – fail to perform.

TABLE 3   IPO Size versus First-day Price Increase

	IPO Size (RMB Mn)	No. of IPOs	First-day Jump (%) High	First-day Jump (%) Close
A	<250	94	232	207
B	250–500	217	158	143
C	500–750	78	123	108
D	750–1,000	33	74	64
E	1,000–2,500	36	65	53
F	2,500–5,000	6	91	79
G	> 5,000	4	43	30

Source: Authors' calculations.

Table 4 shows data for IPOs in terms of the average number of subscribers per IPO as measured by the number of *accounts* participating. In 2000, for example, 65% of all IPOs attracted less than one million subscriber accounts. In 1999, the situation was worse: 97% had less than one million subscriber accounts. Of course, this means the actual number of individual investors subscribing was much, much less.

TABLE 4   IPOs by Subscriber Account Numbers by Year and Size

No. of Subscriber Accounts (000)	2002	2001	2000	1999	1998
<250	0	4	2	6	5
250–500	0	9	17	30	24
500–1,000	4	24	65	58	51
1,000–1,500	9	17	37	3	8
1,500–2,000	4	11	9	0	1
2,000–2,500	4	6	0	0	1
>2,500	1	2	0	0	0
	22	73	130	97	90

Sources: Wind Information and authors' calculations.

Appendix 7

Glossary of English/Chinese Securities Terminology

English	Pinyin	Chinese
A shares	A-gu	A 股
Agency Stock Transfer System	daiban gufen zhuanrang xitong	代办股份转让系统
account churning	duidao	对倒
approval	pizhun	批准
asset appraisal	zichan pinggu	资产评估
asset carve out	zichan buoli	资产剥离
asset management bureau	zichan guanli ju	资产管理局
auction	zichan paimai	资产拍卖
auction house	chanquan jiaoyi zhongxin	产权交易中心
audit	shenji	审计
B shares	B-gu	B 股
banking (sector)	jinrong (ye)	金融(业)
bear market	xiong shi	熊市
Big Shot	dahu	大户
Blue Chips	lanchougu	蓝筹股
boundary setting	dingjie	定界
broker	jingjiren	经纪人
brokerage company	jingji quanshang	经纪券商
brokerage office	yingyebu	营业部
bull market	niu shichang	牛市
legal person shares	farengu	法人股
closed-end fund	fengbishi jijin	封闭式基金
commission	yongjin	佣金
Company Law	gongsifa	公司法
company limited by shares	gufen youxian gongsi	股份有限公司
comprehensive brokerage	zonghe quanshang	综合券商
conglomerate	jituan gongsi	集团公司
contract responsibility system	chengbaozhi	承包制
convertible bond	kezhuan zhaiquan	可转债券
create a (trading) position	jiancang	建仓
cyclicality	zhouqixing	周期性
de-listed company	tuishi gongsi	退市公司
directed offering method	dingxiang muji fangshi	定向募集方式

Appendix 7   *continued*

dividend	*guxi, hongli*	股息，红利
domestic legal person shares	*jingnei farengu*	境内法人股
dual listing	*liangdi shangshi*	两地上市
earnings per share	*meigu shouyi*	每股收益
Enterprise Law	*qiyefa*	企业法
equity share	*gupiao*	股票
examine and approve	*shenpi*	审批
exchange member	*jiaoyisuo huiyuan*	交易所会员
factory	*gongchang*	工厂
financial (sector)	*caiwu (or caizheng)*	财务 (财政)
fixed income security	*zhaiquan*	债券
follow-on or secondary offering	*zengfa*	增发
foreign capital LP shares	*waizi farengu*	外资法人股
foreign (overseas) shares	*haiwai gu*	海外股
fund	*jijin*	基金
fund management company	*jijin guanli gongsi*	基金管理公司
general LP shares	*yiban farengu*	一般法人股
government bonds	*guozhai or guokuquan*	国债 (国库券)
(Shenzhen) Growth Market	*chuangyeban*	(深圳)创业板
H shares	*H-gu*	H 股
hedge fund	*duichong jijin*	对冲基金
IPO	*shouci gupiao faxing*	首次股票发行
independent accounting unit	*duli hesuan danwei*	独立核算单位
index	*zhishu*	指数
(internal) employee shares	*(neibu) zhigonggu*	(内部) 职工股
institutional investor	*jigou touzizhe*	机构投资者
intermediary	*zhongjian jigou*	中间机构
investor	*touzizhe*	投资者
invisible seat	*wuxing xiwei*	无形席位
issuance quota	*faxing e-du*	发行额度
leftover rights offering shares	*zhuanpei yiliugu*	转配遗留股
legal person (shares)	*faren (gu)*	法人(股)
limited liability company	*youxian zeren gongsi*	有限责任公司
liquid (tradable) shares	*liutonggu*	流通股
liquidity	*liutongxing*	流通性
listed company	*shangshi gongsi*	上市公司
loss of (state) assets	*zichan liushi*	(国有)资产流失
M&A	*shougou jianbin*	收购兼并
management by the people	*minyinghua guanli*	民营化管理
manipulate	*caozong, caozuo*	操纵，操作
manipulated share	*zhuanggu*	庄股
manipulator	*zhuangjia*	庄家
market capitalization	*shichang jiazhi (shizhi)*	市场价值 (市值)
market index	*shichang zhishu*	市场指数
net asset value	*qingzichan jiazhi*	净资产价值
non-tradable shares	*feiliutong*	非流通股
NYSE-listed shares	*N-gu*	N 股

Appendix 7 *continued*

online offering	shangwang faxing	上网发行
offline offering	wangxia faxing	网下发行
open-end fund	kaifangshi jijin	开放式基金
ordinary shares	putonggu	普通股
OTC trading	guitai jiaoyi	柜台交易
ownership rights	suoyouquan	所有权
packaging (a company)	baozhuang	包装
parent company	mugongsi	母公司
Particular Treatment shares	PT-gu	PT股
pension fund	yanglao jijin	养老基金
pilot enterprise	shidian qiye	试点企业
preferred shares	youxuangu	优先股
price/earnings ratio	shiyinglu	市盈率
primary market	yiji shichang	一级市场
principal supervisory agency	zhuguan bumen	主管部门
private shares	feigongyougu	非公有股
private placement	simu	私募
privatization	siyouhua	私有化
promoter	faqiren	发起人
promoter method	faqi fangshi	发起方式
public (i.e. state) shares	gongyougu	公有股
public offering method	shehui muji fangshi	社会募集方式
quota	edu	额度
raise finances	rongzi	融资
Red Chips	hongqiugu	红筹股
restructuring (of assets)	chungzu	(资产)重组
retail investor	geren (or sanhu) touzizhe	个人(散户)投资者
rights offering	peigu	配股
roadshow	luyan	路演
trading seat on exchange floor	jiaoyi xiwei, youxing xiwei	交易席位，有形席位
secondary market	erji shichang	二级市场
secondary (follow-on) offering	zengfa gupiao, zengfa	增发股票，增发
securities exchange	zhengquan jiaoyisuo	证券交易所
securities investment fund	zhengquantouzi jijin	证券投资基金
Securities Law	zhengquanfa	证券法
securities repo	zhengquan huigou	证券回购
SEEC	lianban	联办
sell off (usually LP shares)	peishou	配售
share fever	gupiao re	股票热
share price	gujia	股价
shareholding cooperative system	gufen hezuozhi	股份合作制
shell company	kongke gongsi	空壳公司
social LP share	shehui farengu	社会法人股
special shares (e.g. B shares)	tezhonggu	特种股
Special Treatment shares	ST-gu	ST股
speculate (in stocks)	chao(gu)	炒股
sponsor	tuijianren	推荐人

Appendix 7   *continued*

Standard Opinion	*guifan yijian*	规范意见
(state) asset loss	*(guoyou) zichan liushi*	(国有)资产流失
state shares	*guoyougu*	国有股
state-owned LP shares	*guoyou farengu*	国有法人股
subscription	*muji*	募集
subsidiary company	*zigongsi*	子公司
supervise and administer	*jiandu guanli*	监督管理
suspension from trading	*tingpai*	停牌
technical analysis	*jishu fenxi*	技术分析
Third Board	*sanban shichang*	三板市场
township and village enterprises	*xiangzhen qiye*	乡镇企业
trading volume	*jiaoyiliang*	交易量
transfer (of ownership)	*zhuanrang*	(股权)转让
transform into shares	*zhegu*	折股
treasury bonds	*guozhai*	国债
two-way trading collusion	*daocang*	倒仓
tycoon	*dakuan*	大款
verify and approve	*hezhun*	核准
volatility	*bodongxing*	波动性
work unit shares	*danweigu*	单位股

Endnotes

Chapter 1

1 The date, place, time of day, and who Deng was speaking to are in Li Zhangzhe, *Zhongyu chenggong: Zhongguo gushi fazhan baogao* (Beijing: Shijie zhishi chubanshe, 2001), p. 522. See also Wang Lianzhou and Li Cheng (eds), *Fengfeng yuyu zhengquanfa* (Shanghai: Shanghai Sanlian shudian, 2000), p. 12. Li Zhangzhe's book is outstanding; virtually a blow-by-blow history of how the markets came to be. In China, this is the only systematic attempt at this known to the authors.

2 This story is frequently told in publications about the market's early years. See Li Zhangzhe, pp. 72–75; and Wang An, *Guye nishangzuo* (Beijing: Huayi chubanshe, 2000), pp. 69–70.

3 Li Zhangzhe, p. 74.

4 Jinbei actually was the domestic Chinese company owned by Brilliance China Automotive, an offshore holding company. Brilliance issued shares and was listed on the NYSE (CBA). Brilliance, in turn, was controlled indirectly by the PBOC. Brilliance continued through the decade of the 1990s to make news, and Jinbei actually turned into a successful mini-bus maker. Its shares have performed relatively well over the years. Then its mysterious chairman, Yang Rong, fell foul of the state in the early fall of 2002. He fled to his home in Los Angeles (not palatial) and is suing to recover (at least) his face. See, for example, "Province issues warrant for Yang Rong's arrest," *South China Morning Post* (*SCMP*), October 23, 2002, Business section, p. 1. Jinbei, in fact, had been working hard to list shares since the mid-1980s as well, and finally carried out a placement in 1988, receiving great publicity at the time by selling shares in a courtyard of the State Council! See Li Zhangzhe, pp. 104–10.

5 Hu Xuzhi, *The Evolution of China's Stock Markets and Its Institutions* (Beijing: Jinji kexue chunbanshe, 1999), pp. 82–84.

6 Even if the PBOC did not include them in its annual compilation of laws and regulations, these records have been preserved and can be found in Jiang Ping (advisor), *Jinrong falu fagui quanshu* (Beijing: Sanxia chubanshe, 1997), two volumes.

7 See, for example, Li Changjiang, *The History and Development of China's Securities Markets* (Beijing: Zhongguo wuzi chubanshe, 1998), p. 86.

8 For the full comment, particularly the last sentence, see the lead-off quote to Chapter 2.

9 The authors have been chided for not providing a citation linking this slogan to Deng Xiaoping. We have asked everyone in Beijing we know, except folks at the Central Party School. Everyone says this is Deng's creation. It most certainly does NOT belong to Mike Wallace who interviewed Deng for *60 Minutes* sometime in the 1980s. The idea that it might is risible. Relying on a search by *GOOGLE*, we have managed to trace it to a photograph in an obituary published at the top of the front page of *People's Daily* on April 12, 1983. The photograph shows 11 scientists parading behind a large red banner with the slogan on it, "*Songkexuejia xiaxiang yougong, bang nongmin* **zhifu guangrong**." The photograph is at www.cz165.co9m/travel/lcrw/syjr/2002913/0000000753.asp for those who have an interest.

10 Hu Shili, "The 16th Party Congress and China's stock index," *Caijing*, November 20, 2002, p. 6.

11 The primary market represents the value of all securities issued in a given year. The secondary market represents the value of all securities that can be traded based on their respective market prices at a given time. Market capitalization represents the total market value of all securities, listed or otherwise, of all listed companies.

12 Li Zhangzhe, p. 61.

13 Li Zhangzhe, pp. 63–66.

14 Li Zhangzhe, p. 91.

15 Li Zhangzhe, p. 80.

16 Hu Xuzhi, pp. 80–81; and Cai Jianwen (ed.), *Zhongguo gushi* (Beijing: Zhonghua gongshang lianhe chubanshe, 2000), pp. 205–6.

17 Shanghai was selected as a pilot location for the shareholding system experiment at the Beidaihe Meeting in the summer of 1986, being added to Shenzhen. See Cai Jianwen, pp. 17–19; for the situation surrounding the decision to establish exchanges, see Li Zhangzhe, pp. 128–39.

18 Of course, which exchange really opened first has been a matter of dispute ever since. See Box 2, in Chapter 2, for the details.

19 Gao Shangquan and Ye Sen (eds), *China Economic Systems Reform Yearbook 1990* (Beijing: China Reform Publishing House, 1990), p. 81.

20 In this regard, China has never sold what are called primary shares in any of its companies, only secondary shares. This means, simply put, that the corporatized entity sold only new shares, thereby expanding the company's capital base and diluting down the original shareholder's holding by proportion of total capital, but not in absolute terms. Privatization involves the state selling out the shares that it owns, the primary shares, to non-state investors and thereby diluting its holdings down, both proportionally and in absolute terms.

21 *Xincaifu*, August 2002, pp. 27–79.

22 CSRC, MOF, SETC, "Notice Regarding Transfer to Foreign Investors of State-owned Shares and Legal Person Shares of Listed Companies," November 4, 2002, www.csrc.gov.cn. This notice reverses a 1995 decision to cease transfer of such shares to foreign investors and also provides the required procedures for the transfer. As such, it signals greater state scrutiny of all such transactions.

23 The texts of both the December 19, 1996 and the June 15, 1999 *People's Daily* editorials are in Wang An, pp. 238–46. For a full commentary on the circumstances surrounding the December 16, 1996, editorial, see Yuan Fang (ed.), *Shinian gushi fengyun* (Beijing: Jingji kexue chubanshe, 2001), pp. 159–201.

24 Following the November 2002 16th Party Congress, Zhou Xiaochuan, the CSRC chairman since 2000, moved to head the PBOC. The new chairman, Shang Fulin, former head of the Agricultural Bank of China, in an unprecedented move, visited the major Chinese securities companies in January 2003. What he said shortly became clear – the market is on the way up again. The days of strict regulation appear to be over.

Chapter 2

1 Gao Shangquan and Ye Sen, *China Economic Systems Reform Yearbook 1990*, p. 81.

2 For an excellent treatment of pre-1949 stock exchanges in China, see W. A. Thomas, *Western Capitalism in China: A History of the Shanghai Stock Exchange* (Aldershot, England: Ashgate Publishing Ltd., 2001), pp. 187–208. For a Chinese view, see Cai Jianwen, *Zhongguo Gushi*, pp. 8–9.

3 The last of the three, the Tianjin exchange, was closed in July 1952, marking the start of China's experimentation with a Soviet-style planned economy.

4 On July 3, 1979, the State Council issued "Decision on Several Problems on the Development of Brigade Enterprises." This document stated that "In order to solve their financing needs, brigade enterprises can use an appropriate amount of brigade and production brigade accumulated funds and enter it into project equity (*tiqu shidang shuliang de [jileijin] ru guzijin*)." See Xue Weihong, *Gupiao yunzuo falu shiwu* (Beijing: Zhongguo chengshi chubanshe, 2001), p. 4; and Li Zhangzhe, pp. 61 ff.

5 Wang An, p. 72. These shares – legal person shares and internal employee shares – were deemed untradable. Gradually, in the latter part of the 1990s, internal employee shares

were listed and traded. The sale of LP shares remains an object of ideological dispute even to this day.

6 Li Zhangzhe, p. 74.

7 Wang An, pp. 70–71.

8 Despite being the pioneers of the shareholding experiment, all that Shanghainese will talk about of this period is the fact that in November 1986 a fake share of Feile was given to the visiting president of the NYSE who had participated in a Beijing conference on the financial markets. The nervous atmosphere of the time is illustrated by the fact that while there were over 20 speakers from the U.S., only Liu Hongru, then a vice governor of the PBOC, spoke for the Chinese side. Wang An, pp. 73–74.

9 This awkwardly named entity was established on a "trial" basis in September 1985. *Caijing*, September 5, 2002, p. 37.

10 Shenzhen Municipal People's Government, "Provisional Regulations on the Pilot Program for the Transformation of State-owned Enterprises into Shareholding Companies," October 15, 1986, *Jinrong falu fagui quanshu*, Vol. 2, pp. 2815–18.

11 Li Changjiang, p. 55.

12 Shenzhen Municipal People's Government, "Provisional Regulations on the Pilot Program for the Transformation of State-owned Enterprises into Shareholding Companies," October 15, 1986, *Jinrong falu fagui quanshu*, Vol. 2, pp. 2815–18.

13 Li Changjiang, p. 64; and PBOC Shenzhen SEZ Branch, "Notice on Several Issues Regarding the Administration of the Transfer of Securities between Accounts in Shenzhen," July 25, 1989, *Jinrong falu fagui quanshu*, Vol. 2, p. 2635.

14 The discussion of "stock fever" derives from Cao Er-jie, pp. 140 ff. Cai Jianwen cites this as the first case of market manipulation. See Cai Jianwen, pp. 205–6.

15 See Cai Jianwen, p. 21.

16 Complete and systematic market statistics exist only from the founding of the Shanghai and Shenzhen markets. There are differing accounts of Shenzhen market performance during the "share fever" period. Cai Jianwen states that the relevant jumps for the five Shenzhen shares for the same one-month period were:

Shenzhen Development Bank	100%
Vanke	38%
Yuanye	210%
Jintian	140%
Anda	380%

See Cai Jianwen, p. 32.

17 Li Changjiang, p. 64.

18 Shenzhen Municipal People's Government, "Notice on Strengthening the Administration of the Securities Market and Banning Illegal Trading," May 28, 1990, p. 2640; and Shenzhen Municipal People's Government, "Notice on Strictly Prohibiting Share or Debt Securities Financing without Authorization," September 15, 1990, p. 2641; both documents in *Jinrong falu fagui quanshu*, Vol. 2.

19 There were only seven publicly traded shares circulating in Shanghai at this time with a total of only 63 million shares (one quarter of the volume available in Shenzhen) with a population of around 13 million. Demand and supply got totally out of whack. See Cai Jianwen, pp. 35 ff.

20 PBOC, "Specialized Banks Must Not Directly Carry out Securities Trading Operations," August 11, 1990, *Jinrong falu fagui quanshu*, Vol. 2, pp. 2640–1. The PBOC hereafter permitted the banks to carry out securities-related business through their subsidiary trust and investment companies. This created other problems, which became all too clear at the end of the decade.

21 Li Zhangzhe, pp. 120–8.

22 On the eve of Deng Xiaoping's early 1992 Southern Tour, Liu Hongru, then the senior vice governor of the PBOC, put the number of pilot SOE-derived shareholding companies at 3,220, a figure which excluded rural TVE figures. Of these, 380 companies represented cases in which other SOEs had invested, 2,781 represented cases in which employees had invested in the shares of their own company, and 89 companies had issued shares to the public. The

consolidated shareholding structure of these 89 companies, as presented by Liu, is shown in Table 2.3 based on the share types codified in the Standard Opinion and compared to a sample of 20 Shenzhen companies reported by SCRES as of 1989. Liu Hongru, "Several Issues Regarding China's Experiments with the Shareholding Structure," *Renmin Ribao*, June 23, 1992, p. 5. Statistics for this period are few and far between and are suggestive at best. Upon SCRES's disbandment in 1998 as part of Zhu Rongji's attempt to streamline the bureaucracy, all old SCRES libraries and files were packed away somewhere, discarded, or lost.

23 A good overview of Shanghai's experience in the 1980s can be found in Gao Shangquan and Ye Sen, *China Economic Systems Reform Yearbook 1991*, pp. 66–73; and Zhu Huayou, "Retrospect and Policies for Future Development of the Shanghai Stock Exchange," in Gao Shangquan and Chi Fulin (eds), *The Chinese Securities Market* (Beijing: Foreign Languages Press, 1996), pp. 30–50.

24 Wang An, p. 134.

25 Beginning in 1988, the PBOC initiated an effort to bring such infringements on its authority under the control of its local branches. But, as will be discussed in greater detail in Chapter 5, the local branches of the PBOC have always been close partners of local governments, rather than part of a strong centralized organization. PBOC, "Notice on the Requirement of Approval by the PBOC for the Establishment of Securities Companies or Similar Institutions', July 15, 1988, *Jinrong falu fagui quanshu*, Vol. 2, p. 2751.

26 This story is taken from Wang An, pp. 82–83.

27 Li Zhangzhe, p. 130.

28 Of course, the governor was absolutely correct in his judgment. This caution continues through today and explains a good deal about the fits and starts of the market's development. Wang An, p. 83.

29 See "Some Preliminary Suggestions in Preparation For the Establishment of the Shanghai Securities Exchange (Summary)," March 1989, in Wang An, pp. 99–105.

30 Wang An, p. 84.

31 To this day, Shanghai dominates listed Chinese government bond trading, while Shenzhen is nearly dormant in this area.

32 SCRES, "Opinion on Strengthening the Management of Enterprises Undergoing Restructuring," May 1990, cited in Gao Shangquan, Ye Sen, Compilers, *China Economic Systems Reform Yearbook 1991*, p. 71; and discussed in detail in Li Zhangzhe, pp. 128–9.

33 Li Zhangzhe, pp. 129–30.

34 Fortunately, a Chinese-speaking Western anthropologist was in Shanghai during this period. She has produced a colorful piece of research about market participants in the early 1990s. Ellen Hertz, *The Trading Crowd: An Ethnography of the Shanghai Stock Market* (Cambridge: Cambridge University Press, 1998).

35 Cai Jianwen, pp. 45–50.

36 "Shenzhen, Shanghai stock exchanges to merge next year, Shanghai mayor says," *Chinaonline*, November 8, 2000, www.chinaonline.com. Not only has there been no merger, Shenzhen will again begin to list new companies in 2003. Reuters News Services, March 20, 2003.

37 The Shanghai and Shenzhen settlement centers were to become promoters of the new central settlement company. CSRC, "Notice on Establishing the China Securities Registration and Settlement Co. Ltd.," January 20, 2001, *Zhengquan qihuo fagui huibian* (2001), pp. 57–58.

38 Draft regulations for the Second Board were made available for comment in September 2000, and are still available for comment online. See CSRC, "Second Board Regulations (Consultation Documents)," September 2000, www.csrc.gov.cn.

39 "Shanghai Stock Exchange to List Abroad, Insider Says," *Chinaonline*, July 6, 2000, www.chinaonline.com.

40 PBOC Shanghai Branch, "Shanghai Securities Exchange Articles of Incorporation," August 1990, *Jinrong falu fagui quanshu*, Vol. 2, pp. 2756–8; and PBOC Shenzhen Branch, "Shenzhen Securities Exchange Articles of Incorporation," January 1, 1991, *Jinrong falu fagui quanshu*, Vol. 2, pp. 2746.

41 The earliest form of these commissions was seen in Shenzhen. Shenzhen Municipal People's Government, Chap. 6, "Shenzhen SEZ Provisional Regulations on the Restructuring of SOEs into Companies Limited by Shares," October 15, 1986, *Jinrong falu fagui quanshu*, Vol. 2, p. 2818.

42 CGBs must be bought and owned outright, as no securities borrowing facilities are permitted. Each individual CGB issue has a conversion ratio indicating the amount of the loan which can be borrowed against it. For example, CGB 9905 has a conversion ratio of 100, meaning that RMB100 can be borrowed against it. Other bonds have different ratios. Repos have standard maturities of one, three, four, seven, 14, 28, 91, or 182 days, but the market is deepest for the three- and seven-day repos. The minimum market trade is 100 *shou* or RMB100,000.

43 After a very brief stint in the CSRC in 1992, Wang Boming became one of China's original venture capitalists. Gao Xiqing is now a vice chairman of the CSRC but is about to be transferred to head up the national social security fund, and Wang Wei, who also became rich, is the author and publisher of the *China M&A Annual Report* and chairman and CEO of the consulting firm, China M&A Management Co.

44 Wang An, p. 92.

45 Wang An, pp. 20–27.

46 The conference was held at the Beijing Grace Hotel, now called the Harbour Plaza. Wang An, pp. 32–33.

47 The eight group members were: Gong Zhuming, director, Comprehensive Planning Dept., PBOC; Zhou Xiaochuan, assistant minister, MOFERT; Zhang Xiaobin, general manager, China Venturetech; Cai Zhongzhi, graduate student, PBOC; Wang Boming, ex-NYSE; Gao Xiqing, assistant professor, Foreign Trade University; Chen Dagang, Law Department, Beijing University; and Xu Xiaosheng, China Venturetech. The continuing influence of many of these staff members is significant.

48 Wang An, pp. 45–46.

49 Wang An, p. 49. Li Qingyuan following SCRES became Goldman Sachs' chief representative in Beijing during the 1990s, thereafter returning to the CSRC.

50 Wang An, pp. 93–94.

51 See SEEC, "The National Security Trading Automated Quotation System," in Gao Shangquan and Ye Sen, *China Economic Systems Reform Yearbook 1991*, pp. 106–10.

52 Wang An, p. 253.

53 Yao Chengxi, *Stock Market and Futures Market in the PRC* (Hong Kong: Oxford University Press, 1998), pp. 103–6.

54 Internal transfer of LP shares means transfers between existing LP shareholders of a given company. See Wang An, p. 255.

55 STAQ worked by simply doing listing by way of introduction of LP shares on its exchange. The selling shareholder sold out his portion for cash, then the shares traded back and forth between legal person investors. These were not IPOs; these were original promoters selling out their holdings in companies.

56 Gao Shangquan and Ye Sen, *China Economic Systems Reform Yearbook 1993*, p. 63.

57 Wang An, pp. 256–8.

58 PBOC, "China Securities Trading System Corp. Ltd. Operating Regulations," January 1, 1991, *Jinrong falu fagui quanshu*, Vol. 2, pp. 2764–74.

59 PBOC, "Articles of Incorporation of China Securities Trading System Co. Ltd.," March 8, 1993, *Jinrong falu fagui quanshu*, Vol. 2, pp. 2800–2.

60 Wang An, p. 73. Shenyang was also the home of the first overseas-listed Chinese company, Jinbei Passenger Vehicle. The success of these centers explains why the proportion of investors from these areas, which are not considered wealthy, continues to be so large on both the SSE and SZSE.

61 The invisible seat refers to seats that are located outside of the exchange building, as opposed to the visible seats, which are located on the exchange trading floor. All brokers have both types of seat.

62 The Shanghai and Shenzhen exchange statistics fully capture the trading volume conducted through the trading centers.

63 CSRC, "Notice on Several Problems on Further Restructuring the Securities Trading Centers," December 8, 1998, in CSRC, *Zhengquan qihuo fagui huibian* (1998), p. 95.

64 See the Mergers China website at www.bprsc.com.cn, which carries the detailed regulations for all 22 auction houses. The site also provides up-to-date auction transactions. After the dissolution of SAMB in 1998, local asset management bureaus remained in operation.

65 In the case of Shanghai, for example, the permitted category of assets includes: (1) the entire or partial assets – tangible, intangible, and financial – of unincorporated enterprises; (2) equity rights of limited liability companies and companies limited by shares; (3) assets of institutions; and (4) other legally approved property rights. See Article 13, "Detailed Implementation Rules, Measures for Managing Shanghai Property Rights Trading," SAMB, Document no. 165, 1999, carried in the Mergers China website, www.bprsc.com.cn. The detailed regulations for the other 22 auction houses can also be found on this website.

66 CSRC, "Notice on the Standardized Management of the Float of Non-tradable Shares of Listed Companies," September 30, 2001, www.csrc.gov.cn.

67 For details, see "How Investors of De-listed Companies Can Transfer Shares in the Agency Share Transfer System," September 11, 2002, Wind Information, www.wind.com.cn.

68 Although five companies have de-listed from the Shanghai and Shenzhen stock exchanges, only two have listed on the Third Board. De-listed companies are not automatically allowed to list, but are subject to a number of listing requirements; first, complete all legal de-listing procedures and then, with the support of one of the six sponsoring brokerages, make a formal application to list on the Third Board.

69 "The Third Board is not a garbage can," August 1, 2002, *Zhongguo jingyingbao*, cited on www.wind.com.cn.

Chapter 3

1 Wang An, p. 211.

2 Brilliance China Automotive listed on the NYSE on October 7, 1992, about one week before the announcement of the CSRC's formation.

3 The word *"jinrong,"* which can be translated as "finance," connotes matters relating to the banking sector. The word *"caiwu"* also can mean "finance," but more in the way of financial accounting (*caiwu kuaiji*). The securities sector is always referred to using the word *"zhengquan,"* which means securities. There is no way that *"jinrong"* and *"zhengquan"* can refer to the same or even similar things.

4 State Council, "PRC Provisional Regulations on the Administration of Banks," January 7, 1986, *Jinrong falu fagui quanshu*, Vol. 2, pp. 2085–9.

5 "Major events in the development of China's securities companies," *Caijing*, September 5, 2002, p. 37.

6 PBOC, "Notice that the Establishment of Securities Companies or Similar Financial Entities Must be Approved by the PBOC," July 15, 1988, *Jinrong falu fagui quanshu*, Vol. 2, p. 2751; and the State Council document is quoted in PBOC, "The PBOC Forwards the State Council's 'Minutes of the meeting on researching problems associated with cleaning up and restructuring government securities intermediary organizations'," August 10, 1990, *Jinrong falu fagui quanshu*, Vol. 2, p. 2754.

7 State Council, "Notice on Strengthening the Administration of Share and Debt Securities," March 28, 1987, *Jinrong falu fagui quanshu*, Vol. 2, p. 2633.

8 PBOC Shenzhen SEZ Branch, "Principles for the Review and Approval of the Issuance of Enterprise Shares (1989)," *Jinrong falu fagui quanshu*, Vol. 2, pp. 2467–8.

9 It is interesting to note the lack of importance assigned by the PBOC to the regulation of share issuance and trading: none of the various regulations enacted by local branches of the central bank were included in the PBOC's annual compilation of laws and regulations until 1990. Apparently, the PBOC did not consider such local events of national importance.

10 Cai Jianwen, pp. 13–14.

11 SCRES, "Opinion on Strengthening the Management of Enterprises Undergoing Restructuring," May 1990; Gao Shangquan and Ye Sen (eds), *China Economic Systems Reform Yearbook 1991*, p. 71.

12 PBOC, "Specialized Banks Must Not Manage Directly or Carry out Securities Trading Operations," August 11, 1990, *Jinrong falu fagui quanshu*, Vol. 2, p. 2640.

13 The banks were still working on this two years later. See China Construction Bank's response to a late 1991 PBOC circular requiring work groups and progress reports, "Notice on the 'Proposal on inspecting securities cleaning up work'," June 11, 1992, *Jinrong falu fagui quanshu*, Vol. 2, pp. 2711–13.

14 The mess was still being cleaned up in 2000. For example, see CSRC, "Implementing Details for the Approval Work of MOF Treasury Securities Intermediaries Being Relicensed as Brokerages," *Zhengquan qihuo fagui huibian* (2000), pp. 214–15.

15 PBOC, "Provisional Methods for the Administration of Securities Companies," October 12, 1990, pp. 2758–60; "Notice on Several Problems Relating to the Establishment of Securities Trading Agency Arrangements," October 19, 1990, p. 2761; and "Provisional Methods on the Administration of Securities Trading Business Offices," November 22, 1990, pp. 2761–4, all in *Jinrong falu fagui quanshu*, Vol. 2.

16 PBOC, "Provisional Measures for the Administration of Inter-regional Securities Trading," October 19, 1990, *Jinrong guizhang zhidu xuanbian 1990*, Vol. 1 (Beijing: Jinrong chubanshe, 1991), pp. 115–18.

17 But like the regional markets, both Shanghai and Shenzhen were geographically restricted to listing their own companies and trading within their own respective regions.

18 State Council, "Notice on the Problem of Shareholding System Pilot Points Publicly Issuing Shares," December 26, 1990, *Jinrong falu fagui quanshu*, Vol. 2, p. 2472. The first five companies listed on the Shanghai exchange were listings by way of introduction. This means that the shares were already traded over the counter and their listing on the exchange was purely an administrative affair involving the raising of no new funds.

19 As referenced in SCRES, PBOC, SAMB, "Notice on the Resubmission for Review and Approval by Pilot Shareholding Enterprises Issuing Shares to the Public," May 9, 1991, *Jinrong guizhang zhidu xuanbian 1991*, Vol. 1, pp. 40–42.

20 Song Guoliang, "The Provisional Divisions of Function in China's Securities Administration System and Their Characteristics," unpublished paper, Beijing, undated.

21 State Council, "Circular on the Establishment of the SCSC ('Establishment Circular')," October 12, 1992, CSRC, *Zhengquan qihuo fagui huibian* (1992–93), p. 15.

22 Of course, local PBOC officials were not alone in the effort to corner the market. All along, the various notices and bulletins put out by the State Council and others warned against party cadres, securities personnel, and bankers taking advantage of their positions to play the markets.

23 The issue of the role and structure of the industry regulator was one of the most disputed points of the draft Securities Law. The entire process leading up to the formal adoption of the Securities Law is described in great detail by one of the participants in Wang Lianzhou and Li Cheng, pp. 49–50.

24 Agencies assume their place in the bureaucratic hierarchy based on the position of their most senior leader. Thus, the SCSC was a ministerial-level (*zheng buji*) commission due to Vice Premier Zhu Rongji, while Liu Hongru's personal vice-minister position rendered the CSRC a *fubuji danwei*. In 1999, with Zhou Xiaochuan's assumption of the CSRC chairmanship, the CSRC became a full ministerial-level entity. Zhou, in turn, was named chairman as a result of the passage of the Securities Law in December 1998 which accorded the CSRC full responsibility for China's securities industry.

25 The functions of the SCSC and the CSRC were clarified in the famous State Council Document 68, "Notice on Further Strengthening the Macro-administration of the Securities Markets (No. 68)," December 17, 1992, CSRC, *Zhengquan qihuo fagui huibian* (1992–93), pp. 61–64.

26 The CSRC was non-governmental in order to insulate the state from any potential market scandals. The positive aspect of its status, however, was that the CSRC could pay its senior staff relatively higher wages and benefits and therefore attract well-qualified people.

27 Key staff members included Gao Xiqing and Chen Dagang as director and deputy director of the Legal Department (Gao holds a JD from Duke and Chen from Harvard Law School), Wang Jianxi as director of the Listing and Accounting Departments (several years at the NASD and a certified public accountant (CPA)), and, later on, Li Xiaoxue from SCRES. All except Li left on Liu Hongru's resignation in December 1995 and returned on the appointment of Zhou Xiaochuan in April 2000.

28 State Council, "Notice on Further Strengthening the Macro-administration of the Securities Markets," December 17, 1992, CSRC, *Zhengquan qihuo fagui huibian* (1992–93), pp. 61–64.

29 See Wang Lianzhou and Li Cheng, p. 35.

30 To get a flavor for how these local securities administration offices worked, read a selection of work reports in Chinese Securities Yearbook Editorial Board, *China Securities Yearbook 1998* (Beijing: Zhongguo jingji chubanshe, 1998), pp. 164–98.

31 For full details of this incident see Yao, Chapter 4.

32 Liu Hongru has written extensively about this and was the chief editor for an important book on the topic of overseas listings: Liu Hongru (chief ed.), *A Review of and the Prospects for Overseas Listings by Chinese Enterprises* (Beijing: Zhongguo caizheng jingji chubanshe, 1998).

33 For example, see "Power struggle blocks HK listings," *Window*, January 8, 1993, p. 59, which describes the CSRC's fight with the PBOC.

34 This section is based on an extended article by Liu Hongru, the first chairman of the CSRC, "Capital Markets and the Use of Foreign Capital," *Capital Markets*, March 1997. A version of this can also be found in Liu Hongru (chief ed.), *A Review of and the Prospects for Overseas Listings by Chinese Enterprises*, pp. 25–29.

35 SCSC, "Provisional Regulations for the Management of Securities Exchanges," July 7, 1993; Shanghai Municipal Securities Administration Office (ed.), *Zhengquan fagui huibian*, pp. 204–14.

36 "Shenzhen Securities Exchange Articles of Incorporation (Revised)," May 20, 1993; Chun Hong, Zhou Shengye and Wu Shaoqiu (eds), *Zhongguo zhengquan fagui zonghui*, Vol. 8 (Beijing: Zhongguo renmin daxue chubanshe, 1998), pp. 866–73.

37 The Shanghai articles referred to its operating scope and the CSRC only as follows: "... or any other capacity as permitted and entrusted by the national securities supervisory organ." In Article 7.4, "Shanghai Securities Exchange Articles of Incorporation," Revised March 1993; Chun et al. (eds), *Zhongguo zhengquan fagui zonghui*, Vol. 8, pp. 858–63. The SSE's operating regulations, however, specified the SCSC and the CSRC as its "supervisory organization"; Article 5, "Shanghai Securities Exchange Market Operating Regulations," January 1993; Chun et al. (eds), *Zhongguo zhengquan fagui zonghui*, Vol. 8, p. 840.

38 Zhu Huayou, "Retrospective and Policies for the Future Development of the Shanghai Stock Exchange," in Gao Shangquan and Chi Fulin (eds), *The Chinese Securities Market*, pp. 45–47.

39 SCSC, "Notice on the Authorization of the CSRC to Investigate and Enforce Violations of Securities Laws and Statutes," in CSRC, *Zhengquan qihuo fagui huibian* (1992–93), p. 212. The SCSC was authorized by the State Council to enforce securities laws in State Council, "Provisional Measures for Share Issuance and Trading," April 22, 1993, in CSRC, *Zhengquan qihuo fagui huibian* (1992–93), pp. 39–55.

40 Ministry of Justice, CSRC, "Provisional Measures for Determining the Qualifications for Lawyers and Law Offices Conducting Securities Business," January 12, 1993, pp. 251–2; MOF, CSRC, "Regulation on Determining the Qualifications of CPAs and Accounting Firms Conducting Securities Business," February 23, 1993, pp. 253–6; SAMB, CSRC, "Regulations on Determining the Qualifications of Asset Appraisal Companies Conducting Securities Business," March 20, 1993, pp. 257–9; Audit Office, CSRC, "Notice on Several Problems Regarding Determining the Qualifications of Auditing Companies Conducting Securities Business," March 23, 1993, p. 260, all in CSRC, *Zhengquan qihuo fagui huibian* (1992–93).

41 State Council, "Notice on Resolutely Prohibiting the Blind Development of the Futures Markets," November 4, 1993, in CSRC, *Zhengquan qihuo fagui huibian* (1992–93), pp. 70–71. Chairman Liu might have wished that futures had not been given the CSRC, since the SISCO fiasco in 1995 was the presumed reason for his removal from office.

42 SCSC, "Regulations on the Administration of Stock Exchanges," August 21, 1996; CSRC, *Zhengquan qihuo fagui huibian* (1996), pp. 50–66; Li Zhangzhe, pp. 506–7.

43 Among the problems were: (1) banks using IPO subscription funds to lend to securities companies for shares purchases of the same IPO; (2) listed companies speculating in their own shares; (3) securities companies using bank loans to drive the market up, and so on. Each market scandal in the end created more regulatory centralization. See Wang Lianzhou and Li Cheng, pp. 81–93.

44 Wang An, p. 211.

45 For example, the following issues required the final approval of the CSRC after being passed on by the exchange itself:

- listing of new securities products;
- provision of new services;
- revision of operating regulations;
- revision of articles of incorporation (SCSC approval required);
- any change in an exchange's number of seats; and
- revisions in the operating regulations of the settlement company.

On top of this, the CSRC was delegated the unilateral authority to:

- nominate the director and the deputy director of the stock exchange council;
- nominate the general manager of the exchange;
- propose the dismissal of the director and deputy director of the exchange council and the general and deputy general manager of the exchange;
- request the exchanges and their settlement companies to revise their articles of incorporation and operating regulations; and
- send personnel to investigate the operations, finances, or other matters of the exchanges and their settlement companies.

46 The self-interest of local governments, however, is still a living force. As described in Chapter 2, the decision to merge the two exchanges into one with Shanghai as the survivor has caused Shenzhen, the cradle of China's markets, to fight back. Tax revenues and civic "face" are the obvious key factors driving Shenzhen's refusal to go along.

47 The PBOC notice on this divestiture is not carried in its 1997 compilation of laws and regulations, nor is it noted in the CSRC compilation. See Yu Ning and Ling Huawei, "The life and death of Anshan Securities," *Caijing*, September 5, 2002, pp. 47–48.

48 See PBOC, MOF, Public Security Bureau, CSRC, "Opinion on Completing the Tail End of the National Securities Buy Back and Debt Clean up Work," July 11, 2000, in CSRC, *Zhengquan qihuo fagui huibian* (2000), pp. 180–1.

49 Securities Law, Chapter 10.

50 The topic of management of the markets using quotas was also a major philosophical dispute during the drafting of the Securities Law. See Wang Lianzhou and Li Cheng, p. 34.

51 Securities Law, Article 19.

52 CSRC, "CSRC Verification and Approval Procedures for Share Issuance," March 16, 2000, www.csrc.gov.cn.

53 See CSRC, "Notice on Issuing 'CSRC share offering verification and approval procedures'," March 16, 2000, www.csrc.gov.cn.

54 For a thorough discussion of the Listing Committee, see CSRC, *Securities Issuance and Underwriting* (Beijing: Shanghai caijing daxue chubanshe, 1999), pp. 125–7.

55 *Asian Wall Street Journal (AWSJ)*, Money & Investing, July 23, 1999, p. 1.

56 Janet Ong, "Chinese shareholders seize chance to sue," *International Herald Tribune*, July 27–28, 2002, p. 13. Subsequently, in January 2003, the court in a ruling determined to permit joint action suits. Implementing measures became effective on February 1, 2003.

57 Laura Cha was an executive director of Hong Kong's Securities Finance Commission before joining the CSRC in mid-2001.

58 CSRC, "Chairman Zhou Xiaochuan's Speech before the International Conference on Investor Protection," June 21, 2002, www.csrc.gov.cn.

59 "Firm pays out for misleading listing," *China Business Information Network*, November 27, 2002.

60 Bei Hu, "China urged to adopt class-action suits," *SCMP*, November 21, 2002, www.scmp.com.

61 Hu Shili and Wei Puhua, "Talking about regulation with Laura Cha," *Caijing*, January 20, 2002, pp. 34–51.

62 CSRC, "Guiding Opinion on Listed Companies Establishing an Independent Director System," August 16, 2001, www.csrc.gov.cn.

63 CSRC, "Implementation Procedures for Delisting and Provisional Listing of Loss-making Listed Companies," February 22, 2001, www.csrc.gov.cn.

64 The issue is: how can a state company be bankrupt? As discussed in Chapter 5, these companies, regardless of all the corporate laws China has on the books, are psychologically still regarded by large parts of the government as a constituent part of the state. The state as the sovereign cannot be bankrupt.

65 This claim to fame should be qualified since one of the five original Shenzhen listed companies, Yuanye, was actually de-listed, or more precisely, its shares stopped trading, on July 7, 1992, following the first major listed company market fraud. See Wang Lianzhou and Li Cheng, pp. 13–15.

66 CSRC, "Notice on the Establishment of Inspection Bureaus in CSRC Regions," September 6, 2000, www.csrc.gov.cn.

67 CSRC, "Notice on the Public Criticism of Triple Nine Pharmaceuticals and Related Staff," August 27, 2001, www.csrc.gov.cn. Triple Nine was approved to seek an overseas listing in 1996, but was unable to do so for both structural and due diligence reasons. The CSRC website carries numerous such examples.

68 Jane Lanhee Lee, "China orders tech company to return its IPO proceeds," *AWSJ*, September 10, 2002, p. M8.

69 Ling Huawei and Wang Le, "Yinguangxia falls into the trough," *Caijing*, August 2001, pp. 18–37.

70 Qin Liping, "Zhong Tian Qin's destruction," *Caijing*, December 20, 2001, pp. 34–54.

71 See Chapter 7 for further details. Ping Hu and Li Qing, "The inside story of funds," *Caijing*, October 2000, pp. 23–35. The article popularized the story of the "sauna" business style: two fund managers from different companies meet in a sauna – there are no recording devices or other records – to discuss unloading a particular stock position. "For each share you take off my position, I pay you one RMB." All in cash.

72 Of course, the fund managers implicated all cried out "Untrue!" And, also of course, the poor exchange analyst had a hard time for a period and eventually was forced to quit. See October 29, 2000, CCTV interview with Wu Jinglian, Premier Zhu Rongji's favorite economist, in Wu Jinglian, *Wu Jinglian: Shinian fenyun huagushi* (Shanghai: Yuandong chubanshe, 2001), pp. 186–91.

73 Hu Shuli, Li Qiaoning, and Li Qing, "The market manipulator Lu Liang," *Caijing*, February 2001, pp. 19–31.

74 Qin Liping, Kang Weiping, and Yu Ning, "Manipulator's paradise," *Caijing*, June 20, 2002, pp. 50–63.

75 See Chapter 7 for details of Mr. K's operations.

76 Wang Lianzhou and Li Cheng, p. 5. Its articles of incorporation, dated June 12, 1991, can be found in *Jinrong falu fagui quanshu*, Vol. 2, pp. 2781–3.

77 Chapter 9, National People's Congress, "Securities Law," December 29, 1998, in CSRC, *Zhengquan qihuo fagui huibian* (1998), pp. 5–32.

Chapter 4

1 Wang Lianzhou and Li Cheng, p. 12.

2 The Enterprise Law is discussed in Chapter 5.

3 Fujian Provincial People's Government, Article 16, "Provisional Decree on Fujian Province Shareholding System Enterprises," November 12, 1988, *Jinrong falu fagui quanshu*, Vol. 2, p. 2822.

4 SCRES, "Standard Opinion for Companies Limited by Shares," May 15, 1992, in CSRC, *Zhengquan qihuo fagui huibian* (1992–93), pp. 79–101. There was later a very brief and to the point clarification of the character of the Standard Opinion, since it was unclear whether an "opinion" was a "law" or a temporary measure. State Council, "On the Implementation of the Standard Opinion," in CSRC, *Zhengquan qihuo fagui huibian* (1992–93), p. 69.

5 Other key regulations released simultaneously with the Standard Opinion included SCRES, SPC, MOF, PBOC, State Council Production Office Joint Release, "Pilot Method for Shareholding Enterprises," May 15, 1992, pp. 75–78; SCRES, "Standard Opinion for Companies Limited by Shares," May 15, 1992, pp. 102–13; SPC and SCRES, "Provisional Regulations for the Macro-administration of Shareholding System Pilot Enterprises," June 15, 1992, pp. 114–18; and MOF and SCRES, "Accounting System for Shareholding System Pilot Enterprises," May 23, 1992, pp. 119–36, all in CSRC, *Zhengquan qihuo fagui huibian* (1992–93).

6 For extremely interesting case studies on the transformation of SOEs, see Peter Nolan, *China and the Global Economy* (New York: Palgrave, 2001).

7 State Council, "Special Decree on Companies Limited by Shares Offering Shares and Listing Overseas," August 4, 1994, in CSRC, *Zhengquan qihuo fagui huibian* (1994), pp. 34–37.

8 It is all about money: if a company needs to raise capital but is precluded from selling LP shares because it lacks the "state's" approval, then it is going to pay the state to get the approval. In other words, this compromise is a major factor leading to the corruption of the state from the inside.

9 This whole problem of the financial management and accounting system and confusion as to what should be done was noted by SCRES in its 1990 summary report. See Gao Shangquan and Ye Sen, *China Economic Systems Reform Yearbook 1990*, p. 86.

10 Tang Yun Wei, Lynne Chow, and Barry J. Cooper, *Accounting and Finance in China* (Hong Kong: Longman Group (Far East) Ltd., 1992), pp. 25 ff.

11 Although private schools and other organizations in the West funded through donations also use fund accounting, as donations often have different terms and conditions specifying their use.

12 Company Law, Chapter 1, Article 4, in Shanghai Securities Administration Office (ed.), *Zhengquan fagui huibian* (Shanghai: Xuexi dushu chuban gongsi, 1996), p. 4.

13 Standard Opinion, Article 10, excludes Chinese private enterprises, 100% foreign-invested Chinese enterprises, and Chinese natural persons from acting as a promoter. Sino-foreign JVs, however, can be a promoter, but can only represent less than one-third of the total number of promoters of a new company, in CSRC, *Zhengquan qihuo fagui huibian* (1992–93), p. 80.

14 The Standard Opinion in this regard closely followed regulations developed by the Fujian provincial government which defined five share types: (1) state asset shares; (2) collective asset shares; (3) foreign enterprise asset shares; (4) individual asset shares; and (5) enterprise own asset shares. Each share type was based on the ownership identity of the asset contributed. See Fujian Province People's Government, "Provisional Decree on Fujian Province Shareholding Enterprises," November 12, 1988, *Jinrong falu fagui quanshu*, Vol. 2, p. 2822.

15 The fact that SOEs own assets which the state itself does not directly own is a consequence of the contract responsibility system, widely implemented during the 1980s, which allowed SOEs to retain profits over a certain guaranteed level. These profits were then used to invest in assets that later became the basis for LP shares of various types.

16 SAMB, Article 4.1, "Implementing Opinion on the Administration of State Equity in Trial Shareholding Companies," March 3, 1994, in CSRC, *Zhengquan qihuo fagui huibian* (1994), pp. 170–1.

17 At the same time, in 1992, the government was probably not aware that a non-state legal person actually owned substantial assets. This seems to be borne out by the overwhelmed reaction of Deng Xiaoping during his Southern Excursion to Guangdong in early 1992. In early 1999, discussion began on permitting non-state-sector companies to make use of China's capital

markets, and a very few Sino-foreign JVs have been permitted to list shares domestically – for example, the China World Trade Center. This is the start of a trend that should grow in strength.

18 Just how anomalous this has been can be seen in the long-drawn-out effort to prevent individual shares owned by a company's own employees from being freely traded. See Yao Chengxi, pp. 10–11.

19 CSRC, "Notice on Several Problems Relating to the Production of the 1996 Listed Companies Annual Reports," January 22, 1997, in CSRC, *Zhengquan qihuo fagui huibian* (1997), pp. 164–6; and, more recently, CSRC, "Notice on the Operational Handling of Issues Related to Categories of Listed Company Shares," May 8, 2000, in CSRC, *Zhengquan qihuo fagui huibian* (2000), pp. 177–9.

20 Guo Qun, "The classification of non-tradable share equity accounts is in dire need of standardization," *China Securities Daily*, December 7, 1999, p. 4.

21 Standard Opinion, Article 30, in CSRC, *Zhengquan qihuo fagui huibian* (1992–93), p. 86.

22 It is relatively straightforward for an individual to become a legal person by setting up a company and registering at the SAIC.

23 For a discussion of this point, see Cao Fengqi, *Zhongguo zhengquan shichang: Shichang de fazhan, guifan yu guojihua* (Beijing: Zhongguo jinrong chubanshe, 1998), pp. 118–20.

24 "Lianyi Group discloses the inside story of its share transfer," *China Securities Daily*, November 5, 1999, p. 1.

25 See Howson, pp. 158 ff. Convertible bonds were also left out. The CSRC in early 2001 began seeking industry feedback on various pieces of draft regulation which would re-establish this product in the China market. The final regulation had yet to appear two years later. See CSRC, "Consultation Documents on Listed Companies Issuing Convertible Bonds," January 2001, www.csrc.gov.cn.

26 Company Law, Article 229, in Shanghai Securities Administration Office (ed.), *Zhengquan fagui huibian*, p. 45.

27 In July 1995, the State Council issued a circular which permitted companies, and listed companies in particular, established prior to the Company Law to re-register in order to comply with the Law. The work involved in bringing the older companies into conformity with the Company Law did not address the issue of share types. Rather, it was designed to obtain complete corporate documentation of existing limited liability companies, as well as companies limited by shares, using the threat of revoking their business licenses. The re-application work involved called for full disclosure of a company's shareholders or promoters, its registered capital, its articles of incorporation, its management structure, its financial accounting system, a new asset appraisal and a verification of the documents entitling the company to ownership of its assets. This was a simple clean-up of spotty government records. See State Council, "Circular on Initiating the Standardization of Original Limited Liability Companies and Companies Limited by Shares in Accordance with the Company Law," July 3, 1995, in CSRC, *Zhengquan qihuo fagui huibian* (1995), pp. 92–93; State Council Office of Trade and the Economy, "Notice on Several Problems Relating to 'The State Council Notice on conforming the original limited liability and shareholding companies with the Company Law'," December 29, 1995, in CSRC, *Zhengquan qihuo fagui huibian* (1995), pp. 235–7.

28 Howson, p. 160.

29 Company Law, Article 130, in Shanghai Securities Administration Office (ed.), *Zhengquan fagui huibian*, p. 27.

30 Company Law, Articles 147–8, in Shanghai Securities Administration Office (ed.), *Zhengquan fagui huibian*, p. 30.

31 CSRC, "Procedures for the Listing and Trading of Unlisted Foreign Shares of Domestically Listed Foreign Share (B Shares) Companies," February 22, 2001, www.csrc.gov.cn.

32 On February 19, 2001, the State Council approved domestic investors to participate in the B-share markets. CSRC, "Domestic Citizens Can Invest in the B Share Market," www.csrc.gov.cn.

33 State Council, "Provisions on the Listing of Foreign Investment Shares inside China by a Company Limited by Shares," No. 189, December 25, 1995, in CSRC, *Zhengquan qihuo fagui huibian* (1995), pp. 83–87.

34 In fact, they are really "N" American Depository Receipts (ADRs), since the ADRs are what is listed and trade in the U.S.

35 A securities industry joke at the time was what would shares listed in Paris be called? "P" shares or, in Mandarin, "*P-gu*," a homonym for the human posterior. That's investment banking.

36 The Overseas Listing Rules, like the Company Law, do not make mention of state and LP shares. In 2000, a major debate began over the reduction of the state's holding of state shares, and the CSRC required that IPO companies sell state shares as at least 10% of the total number of shares in the offering. The market collapsed. LP shares continue to be sold on a negotiated basis and, for a short time, through the local auction houses.

37 B shares are similar in that those B shares listed on the Shenzhen Stock Exchange are denominated in Hong Kong dollars and pay dividends in Hong Kong dollars, while those listed on the Shanghai Stock Exchange are denominated in U.S. dollars and pay dividends in U.S. dollars.

38 This practice was incorporated in Article 4, Overseas Listing Rules, in CSRC, *Zhengquan qihuo fagui huibian* (1992–93), p. 34.

39 See SCRES, "Supplementary Regulations for the Implementation of the 'Standard Opinion' by Companies Listing in Hong Kong," May 25, 1993, in CSRC, *Zhengquan qihuo fagui huibian* (1992–93), pp. 270–4.

40 Samuel Yeung and Bei Hu, "Activists block Angang proposal to buy assets from parent," *SCMP*, November 22, 2002, www.scmp.com.

41 National People's Congress, "Securities Law," December 29, 1998, in CSRC, *Zhengquan qihuo fagui huibian* (1998), pp. 5–32. The Securities Law came into effect on July 1, 1999. For a commentary, see Jackie Lo, "New PRC Securities Law Fails to Fully Unify Regulation of Securities Issues in China," *China Law & Practice*, February 1999, pp. 21–24.

42 Revisions to the Securities Law were being discussed during the 16th Party Congress and some may be passed by the National People's Congress (NPC) in 2003. To date, such changes are technical in nature alone – for example, adjusting the Law to current practice, as in SOE trading of A shares. See "Zhengquanfa xiugaigao yunniang duoxiang biange," *Guoji jinrongbao*, December 9, 2002.

Chapter 5

1 Wang Lianzhou and Li Cheng, p. 12.

2 Enterprises operating under the contract responsibility system did not need any additional legal basis other than, perhaps, the Enterprise Law. Once an enterprise starts selling parts of itself to outsiders, however, the whole issue of ownership and what it constitutes comes up.

3 "China says local firms want to raise capital in Hong Kong," *Wall Street Journal*, October 7, 2002, www.wsj.com.

4 The earliest regulations were the 1984 Shanghai "Eight Articles" discussed elsewhere. In 1986, Xiamen, Zhejiang, and Guangdong issued "provisional" regulations on enterprise shares and debt, but the 1986 Shenzhen provisions were more systematic. See Wang Lianzhou and Li Cheng, p. 17; and Shenzhen Municipal People's Government, "Provisional Regulations on the Pilot Program for the Transformation of State-owned Enterprises into Shareholding Companies," October 15, 1986, *Jinrong falu fagui quanshu*, Vol. 2, pp. 2815–18.

5 Wang Lianzhou and Li Cheng, p. 12.

6 To see just how liberal these were, compare the Shenzhen provisions with those developed by Fujian Province just up the road. The Fujian regulations represent the full statist view. Fujian Provincial People's Government, "Trial Decision on Fujian Province Shareholding Enterprises," *Jinrong falu fagui quanshu*, Vol. 2, pp. 2820–6.

7 "The People's Republic of China Law for Industrial Enterprises Owned by the Whole People," *Xinfagui suti dianzi zazhi,* www.law-lib.com/law.

8 Policy and Law Department, SCRES, "The Chief Contents of 'The Enterprise Law for public-owned enterprises of the People's Republic of China'," Gao Shangquan and Ye Sen (eds), *China Economic Systems Reform Yearbook 1990,* pp. 26–31.

9 Gao Shangquan and Ye Sen (eds), *China Economic Systems Reform Yearbook 1990,* p. 30.

10 The 16th Party Congress noted that a new system for the management of state assets was being worked on. See Chapter 10 for a discussion.

11 Just reading the Standard Opinion and comparing it to the Enterprise Law indicates how far China had come in terms of reform during what was admittedly a difficult four-year period. The Opinion is all about definition and process, the Law all about ideology.

12 It is a very thick package and includes the promoters' agreement, application, feasibility study, corporate articles of incorporation, asset appraisal report, verification report (by which a lawyer attests that all the facts are validly documented), draft prospectus, and the approval of the supervising ministry or bureau.

13 The purpose of the meeting is to: (1) review and comment on the promoters' plan to establish the company; (2) approve the draft corporate articles of incorporation; (3) elect the company's directors; and (4) elect the company's supervisors.

14 There is obviously a significant degree of risk in this process for potential shareholders. Public investors are particularly at risk, since their capital is being contributed to an entity which is not yet in legal existence and won't be for perhaps two to three months after they have put up their capital. The promoters are, as a result, made jointly liable for all costs associated with the effort, as well as for the return of any public funds with interest in the event that the new company is not established as expected. This requirement is likely to have been poor solace to those investors stuck with an investment in a potential deal that never went through. Of course, these were early days, so the whole issue of shareholder rights and obligations was not spelled out in either the Shenzhen provisions or the Standard Opinion.

15 Company Law, Article 74, Shanghai Securities Administration Office, *Zhengquan fagui huibian,* p. 9.

16 State Council, "Special Regulation on Companies Limited by Shares Offering Shares and Listing Overseas ('Overseas Listing Rules')," August 4, 1994, in CSRC, *Zhengquan qihuo fagui huibian* (1994), pp. 34–37.

17 The SAMB was eliminated in late 1998, and over the next two years asset appraisal companies were reviewed and required to terminate all shareholder or investor relations with state agencies. By 2000, the regulatory body for the appraisal industry became the Chinese Institute for Certified Public Accountants. This direction is correct; however, Chinese CPAs are not any better reputed than their colleague asset appraisers. Finding a replacement for the SAMB, however, was a tougher job. For comments on asset appraisals on a group of recently listed companies, see *Caijing,* June 5, 2002, pp. 84–89. The 16th Party Congress has established a new direction for the management of state assets – see Chapter 10.

18 Ling Huawei and Yu Ning, "Asset Appraisal Manipulation," pp. 74–82; and "The secrets of asset appraisal," *Caijing,* June 5, 2002, pp. 90–91.

19 See Appendix 1 for details of required materials.

20 See Appendix 2 for a sample of the entire approval process from the start of a project to its completion after the listing.

21 Liu Hongru, in particular, was incensed at what was in effect a blind shot administered by the PBOC. Since the 810 Incident, major work was going on behind the scenes to (1) establish the CSRC to replace the PBOC as the industry regulator; and (2) develop the SEHK as a listing venue for nine Chinese enterprises. Liu, as the first chairman of the yet to be formed CSRC, was of course furious. But this is not the place for the full story behind Brilliance, which has remained topical despite the passage of time.

22 In addition, there were a number of smaller transactions listing on the Toronto and Australian exchanges during the early 1990s. These, however, were truly rogue listings, at least in the eyes of the CSRC.

23 Shougang was the socialist enterprise model of its time, its success based on the contract responsibility system. After Zhou's fall, the company had to cough up the bank as well.
24 See www.hsi.com.hk for the official SEHK definition of a "Red Chip."
25 "Investment banker" in the Chinese context can only refer to a banker working for a foreign bank. Chinese securities firms do not have a comparable function.
26 For a detailed case study of the Daqing conflict with Petrochina, as well as a number of other significant companies, see Peter Nolan, pp. 50–52.
27 If a unit was not treated as an independent accounting unit (*duli hesuan danwei*), it did not have its own budget nor did it keep a full set of accounting records. With input from the producer or service provider and in reference to the Plan, the State Planning Commission would estimate the costs for the coming year. Based on this calculation, it would set a price that would allow the entity to cover its costs. There was never even a notion that there would be profit somewhere in the system – this would have been ideologically unacceptable!

Chapter 6

1 There are also a handful of NASDAQ shares, Hong Kong GEM shares, and British Virgin Island holding companies for issuers such as China Mobile. For the sake of completeness, a few Toronto, Singapore, and Australian listed companies "got away" from the state's grasp and are known today only by their shareholders.
2 The most successful Chinese IPO of all time, China Telecom (HK) Ltd., now known as China Mobile, raised US$4.3 billion in October 1997.
3 See Appendix 2 for an actual example of procedures for CSRC listing applications.
4 See CSRC, "Notice on the Announcement of 'CSRC approval procedures for share issuance'," March 6, 2000, www.csrc.gov.cn.
5 In fact, once an international offering is technically ready to go, the State Council usually pushes hard to get it done. This can result in disasters such as the China Telecom (yes, another China Telecom) IPO of November 2002. This was truly a disaster, as the market clearly did not want to buy into the company. The State Council pushed, and the deal got done at half the original size at the bottom of the pricing range and with heavy support by Chinese institutions. The government has yet to learn that the international markets are not the domestic markets.
6 The sectors are included and excluded in various state policy proclamations. For example, SCRES, SPC, MOF, PBOC, and SC, Article 1, "Trial Measures on the Shareholding System," May 15, 1992, in CSRC, *Zhengquan qihuo fagui huibian* (1992–93), p. 75; and CSRC, Article 1, "Circular on Certain Issues Relating to Share Issuance," December 26, 1996, in CSRC, *Zhengquan qihuo fagui huibian* (1996), p. 166; and, more recently, SC, "Notice on the Issue of 'Several policies on encouraging the development of the software and semi-conductor industries'," June 24, 2000, in CSRC, *Zhengquan qihuo fagui huibian* (2000), pp. 37–44. The trend has been to broaden the scope open to investors for a variety of reasons, including greater government familiarity with the implications of public listings, as well as the need to raise project funding.
7 At the National People's Congress in March 1999, China's Constitution was revised to give the non-state sector the same legal recognition as the state sector. Following this, there has been much talk of providing bank financing as well as opening the capital markets to the non-state sector. One trial balloon, which boosted the B-share markets briefly, was to allow private companies to issue B shares. On the other hand, what happens to a company's shareholding structure after listing is a different story, as noted in previous chapters. Direct listings of private companies, however, are rare. Those that have been done – for example, Yongyou Software – seem more to be window dressing. The company's owner is a member of the NPC and, very likely, the Chinese Communist Party (CCP). See *Xincaifu*, August 2002, pp. 38–59.

8 See SPC and SCRES, "Regulations on the Macro-administration of Pilot Shareholding Enterprises," June 15, 1992, CSRC, *Zhengquan qihuo fagui huibian* (1992–93), pp. 114–16.

9 CSRC, "Notice on the Issue of the Listing and Trading of the Unlisted Foreign Capital Shares of Domestically Listed Foreign Capital (B Share) Companies," September 1, 2000, in CSRC, *Zhengquan qihuo fagui huibian* (2000), p. 166.

10 There are a number of valuation methodologies in addition to the P/E ratio analysis mentioned here. Most involve projecting a company's performance a few years into the future. The P/E methodology prevails in China, so there is no reason to delve into what are very technical issues.

11 For a discussion of this practice, see Cao Fengqi, pp. 120 ff.

12 CSRC, "Notice on Doing a Good Job Carrying out Equity Issuance in 1997," September 10, 1997, www.csrc.gov.cn.

13 CSRC, "Circular on Further Improving the Method of Issuing Shares," July 28, 1999, *China Securities Daily*, July 29, 1999, p. 1.

14 As described in Appendix 1, Chinese IPOs until this innovation were conducted entirely via the central settlement company's electronic network or "online." The institutional and corporate order taking are organized entirely by the underwriters directly "offline." The institutional order book is used as the basis to set a price for the "online" retail offering.

15 International comparisons are not helpful given the huge secondary market differences in price levels. See Chapter 8 for more details.

16 *Focus*, No. 89, November 6, 1999, pp. 12–13.

17 Since 1999 there have also been a handful of listings on the Hong Kong GEM, which was designed to fulfill the NASDAQ role of providing capital for more speculative investments. Such listings typically raise less than US$10 million and are excluded in this discussion.

18 As a practitioner, the author searched such books as *China's 500 Companies* to identify potential listing candidates. Such books are divided into industrial sectors, with companies ranked by sales. By 1996, the top three or four companies in each sector had all been visited by a banker, or had failed at a listing or had listed. Things looked mighty bleak.

19 Up to 1999, the oil and gas industry located in the northeast and far west was not yet permitted to seek listings. In any event, the industry is centrally owned, but further capital would aid local development. On the other hand, as in the case of Daqing, restructurings can cause massive layoffs.

20 The calculation of market capitalization is the total number of a company's shares multiplied by the market price for the listed shares as of a fixed date. In the United States, this yields an accurate result since the free float includes all of a company's shares.

21 *Xincaifu*, August 2002, pp. 27–79. It is impossible to tell from exchange data alone which companies may be privately controlled.

22 This group of so-called private companies may be entirely different than the 97 companies referenced as having a free float greater than 50% in the previous section.

23 *Xincaifu*, August 2002, p. 29.

Chapter 7

1 To open an account, a person must present his or her official individual identity card (*shenfenzheng*). However, there is most definitely a market for such cards, which have been presented in bulk to willing brokerage offices to open accounts. These accounts are then funded and controlled by an individual manipulator.

2 Cai Jianwen, pp. 45–46.

3 Since IPOs are no longer carried out on the Shenzhen exchange, the trend of increasing numbers of empty accounts could also reflect a decrease in those who play only the primary markets. The corollary to this would be the large number of shareholders on the Shanghai exchange.

4 The calculation, which is extremely rough, would be as follows:

No. of Stocks	No. of Shareholders	No. of Accounts	%
1	1,198,260	1,198,260	14.9
2	8,419,761	4,209,881	52.2
3	2,278,597	759,532	9.4
4	2,117,621	529,405	6.6
5	1,848,155	369,631	4.6
6	1,574,293	262,382	3.3
7	1,361,310	194,473	2.4
8	1,121,819	140,227	1.7
9	914,379	101,598	1.3
10	757,307	75,731	0.9
>10 (15)	3,408,497	227,233	2.8
Totals	**25,000,000**	**8,068,353**	**100.0**

Source: Author's calculation.

5 "200,000 accounts with RMB200 billion control secretly the primary markets," *Qianlong News*, January 31, 2002, excerpted from *Zhengquan shibao* (undated).

6 Given the pure volume of information, this analysis looked only at January–March 2001. These data were originally available on the exchange's website. A recent upgrade of the site format, however, has removed it. A call to the exchange uncovered the fact that this function had been transferred to the central clearing company, which makes sense from a division of labor viewpoint. However, the clearing company's website is no match for the exchange's and these kind of data are not yet posted.

7 Instead of operating real brokerages, these organizations actively defrauded would-be investors. Their operations fleeced the public by faking securities sales through so-called simulated operations. Such operations include such things as running computer programs that appear to display market activity, but are actually random numbers on a screen. Simulated operations are not connected to a stock exchange and therefore can neither transmit orders nor register the transfer of sales. See "35 of 52 Gansu securities brokerages shut down," *Chinaonline*, February 26, 2001, www.chinaonline.com.

8 Hu Shili, "Disadvantaged groups should stay far from the stock market," October 20, 2002, *Caijing*, p. 6.

9 "One-third of stock brokerage outlets lose money," *Chinaonline*, October 1, 2001, www.chinaonline.com.

10 "Institutional investors become major participants of market," *International Financial News*, November 6, 2002, *Chinaonline*, www.chinaonline.com.

11 For the RMB200 billion estimate, see *Homeway Financial News*, January 23, 2001, www.homeway.com.cn; for the PBOC report, see Richard MacGregor, "New figures for China's unofficial funds sector," *Financial Times*, July 1, 2001, www.ft.com.

12 Xia Bin, "China's 'private funds' report," *Caijing*, July 2001, p. 70. Xia Bin was the director of the PBOC department responsible for supervising non-bank financial institutions. He was kind enough to provide his report to *Caijing*. Xia was later transferred to another department at the PBOC.

13 Xia Bin, p. 69.

14 Southern Securities alone is widely believed to manage half of this amount. *Caijing*, July 2001, p. 69.

15 "200,000 accounts with RMB200 billion control secretly the primary markets," *Qianlong News*, January 31, 2002.

16 This measure was designed to ensure that the jumbo domestic listings could be successfully completed. Apparently, the CSRC believed that at US$1 billion equivalent, the retail investor was not enough. It would seem, therefore, that the CSRC also understands the nature of the so-called retail market.

17 Shares were allocated to strategic investors based on the actual orders they placed. In the Konka case, corporate investors were divided into five different categories based largely on financial capacity, with investors in each category receiving the same amount of shares once the deal had been priced.

18 Admittedly, strategic investors are subject to a lock-up period, assuming, of course, there is no forward sale.

19 Zhang Jing, *Zhongguo gushi de wuqu: feishichanghua de gupiao shichang* (Beijing: Zhongguo zhengquan chubanshe, 2001), p. 236.

20 This section is excerpted from Qin Liping and Kang Weiping, "Manipulator's paradise," June 20, 2002, *Caijing*, pp. 50–68. This major report takes the Lu Liang story up through his first days of court hearings in which evidence was presented.

21 For a detailed description of his churning methodology, see Yu Ning, "Manipulating techniques in the secondary market for China Venture Capital," *Caijing*, June 20, 2002, pp. 62–63.

22 Given his financing method – the use of shares as collateral to raise money to buy more shares – Lu would have failed miserably had he not kept the value of the shares rising. Any decrease of, say, greater than 10% would have triggered default clauses and unwound the arrangement. Ironically, there was no honor among thieves: a falling out with his partner led to the collapse of his paper fortune.

23 The Securities Law established two categories of securities firm: (1) comprehensive securities firms; and (2) brokerage firms. The two are subject to different regulations and receive different licenses. The principal difference between the two is their scope of business and minimum registered capital. A comprehensive firm must have a minimum of RMB500 million in capital, whereas a brokerage needs only RMB50 million. In terms of business scope, the less capitalized firms can only carry out brokerage business. In contrast, comprehensive firms may broker securities, conduct proprietary trading, act as securities underwriters, and seek approval for other securities business from the CSRC.

24 Since foreign firms are limited to a 33% minority holding in a limited liability company (not a joint venture), this opening may not prove that attractive.

25 Since they are unlisted, the securities companies do not provide a complete list of their shareholders on their websites; nor does the CSRC site provide this.

26 For an impassioned indictment of the brokerages (as well as the entire market, for that matter), see Zhang Jing, pp. 150–79.

27 See the fines levied against the former head of a brokerage office; CSRC, "Decision on Fining Lu Hong for Actions Violating the Securities Regulations," December 19, 2001, www.csrc.gov.cn. Lu Hong, the general manager of Gansu Securities, provided illegal margin financing and traded clients' accounts without their knowledge. Lu was fined RMB500,000.

28 During the 1996 bull market, Haitong, Shenyin Wanguo, and Guangfa Securities all made use of access to bank funding and manipulated the shares of Shanghai Petrochemical, Lujiazui Development, and other shares making significant profits. The CEOs of these three brokers were dismissed and sentenced to terms in prison. Wang Lianzhou and Li Cheng, p. 84.

29 CSRC, "Decision on Fining [Six Senior Managers] of Zhejiang Securities for Violating Securities Regulations," December 10, 2001, www.csrc.gov.cn.

30 Zhang Jing, pp. 170–1.

31 Zhu's 1994 efforts were slow to have an impact. At the end of 1998, just prior to the passage and implementation of the Securities Law, it was estimated that there were 237 securities trading entities controlled by trust and investment companies with average capital of RMB30 million. See *Da Gong Bao*, January 18, 1999. PBOC, MOF, "Circular Mandating Severance of PBOC Local Branches from Economic Entities Managed by Them," September 4, 1993, *Jinrong falu fagui quanshu*, Vol. 2, p. 2060.

32 State Council, "Decision on Financial System Reform," December 25, 1993, *Jinrong falu fagui quanshu*, Vol. 2, pp. 2098–102. "The securities industry shall be operated and managed as a separate industry, independent of the banking, trust and the insurance industries. Securities companies shall be established independent of banks, trust institutions and insurance companies."

33 Applications were initiated early in 1999 and largely followed the rules set out in PBOC, "Provisional Regulations Relating to the Administration of Securities Firms," October 12, 1990, *Jinrong falu fagui quanshu*, Vol. 2, pp. 2758–60. The procedure should be the same, since that part of the PBOC Financial Institutions Department dealing with securities firms was transferred *en masse* to the CSRC in early 1999.

34 By mid-August, the CSRC had initiated the process based on a July 5 document, with completion expected before the end of September.

35 This assumes that anyone actually makes money. A recent survey of 3,750 retail investors in China's urban areas found that 70% had lost money. See Shenzhen *Shangbao*, October 5, 2001, p. 1.

36 The continued growth of the funds market is quite incredible. By mid-October 2002, the number of funds had increased to over 70, with 16 approved open-ended funds and 55 closed-end funds.

37 An excellent discussion of investment funds and the problems associated with them in the years prior to the standardizing legislation of 1997 can be found in Cao Fengqi, Chapter 7.

38 CSRC, "Provisional Measures for Administering Securities Investment Funds," November 5, 1997, CSRC, *Zhengquan qihuo fagui huibian* (1997), pp. 89–97.

39 See CSRC, "Notice on Problems Related to the Establishment of Fund Management Companies," December 12, 1997, pp. 200–2; and CSRC, "Notice on the Standards for Implementing 'Provisional measures for administering securities investment funds'," December 12, 1997, pp. 206–43, in CSRC, *Zhengquan qihuo fagui huibian* (1997).

40 Data shown are as of September 30, 2002. At this time, there were 24 Shanghai-listed funds and 29 Shenzhen-listed closed-end funds, plus five listed open-ended funds managed by 18 fund management companies.

41 Ping Hu and Li Qing, "The black inside story of funds," *Caijing*, October 2000, pp. 23–35. The research analyst at the exchange, Zhao Yuwang, was severely reprimanded for the leak and later on resigned; see Li Qing, "Zhao Yuwang's next step," *Caijing*, August 2001, pp. 52–54.

42 "Ten fund companies deny stock manipulation," *Chinaonline*, February 23, 2001, www.chinaonline.com.

43 "Former CSRC chief says fund scandal is all part of growing up," *Chinaonline*, November 29, 2000, www.chinaonline.com. Liu's comments were originally carried in *Zhongguo jingji shibao*, November 28, 2000.

44 "Scholar criticizes fund management system," *Chinaonline*, November 1, 2002, www.chinaonline.com.

45 The Fund Index does not begin until May 2000, so it is impossible to rebase it to the beginning of the year when "alleged" fund churning was going on.

46 Not much came of the CSRC's subsequent investigation of the fund scandals. See "Boshi Fund Management stands out in CSRC stock-manipulation report," *Chinaonline*, March 27, 2001, www.chinaonline.com. On the other hand, the public was educated and perhaps the tigers were for a time frightened.

47 Li Shufeng, "Foreign-invested insurers China map," *Caijing*, November 5, 2002, pp. 44 and 47. Interestingly, CIRC does not include on its website data on the total number of insurance institutions in China.

48 As carried in the Chinese Insurance Regulatory Commission's website, www.circ.gov.cn.

49 *China Securities Daily*, October 27, 1999, p. 1.

50 CIRC, "Quxiaode diyipi xingzheng shenpi xiangmu mulu," No. 58, November 12, 2002, www.circ.gov.org.

51 FMCs are, in early 2003, under strong pressure from insurers to convert closed-end funds into open-ended funds. See "China's fund managers under pressure from insurers," *Reuters News Service*, November 12, 2002.

52 See Hang Seng Services Ltd. at www.hsi.com.hk for the formal definition. The Hang Seng China-Affiliated Corporations Index (HSCCI) is created after thorough analysis and consultation with the investment community.

Chapter 8

1 Some have even gone so far as to suggest creating a "G-share" market for government ("G") – that is, state shares. It surpasses all understanding. See Han Zhiguo and Duan Qiang (eds), *Guoyougu jianchi: lishijiyu haishi xianshi fengxian* (Beijing: Jingji kexue chubanshe, 2002), p. 50.

2 In June 2001, Chinaonline reported a CSRC crackdown on the illegal trading of H shares by domestic Chinese. A large number of Chinese had taken tourist trips to Hong Kong, arriving with millions of RMB ready to invest in H shares and Red Chips.

3 Even the recent introduction of a QFII system is unlikely to bring the markets closer, since A shares are not permitted to be shorted. Moreover, a privately arranged short position will fail to impact the market, simply because the market won't know about it.

4 No company has A-, B-, and H-share listings.

5 To test this proposition, the government announced on November 18, 2002, that China Shanggong had been approved to carry out a secondary offering on the market, the first offering of any kind for over two years. *Dow Jones International News*, November 18, 2002.

6 Having said that, it would be surprising if some innovative trader at one of the Chinese securities houses has not entered into some illegal stock borrowing agreement to do the trade.

7 The domestic exchanges have adopted the following methodology for valuing listed companies' market capitalization. For companies with an A-share listing only, the exchange's value all shares, including the non-tradable shares, at the current secondary market price of the A share. This is, most obviously, incorrect, but the confusion grows. For companies with B, H, and other foreign currency shares, and A shares, the exchanges value each share class independently, but will NOT assign any value to the non-tradable shares. For companies with B shares only, only these are valued, while all non-tradable shares are ignored. Finally, for companies with H shares only, the SEHK follows Chinese market practice and ignores the value of all other share classes.

8 Center Gate's 1999 offering was not the entity's IPO. The predecessor firm, Hainan Minyuan, had come a cropper, been bought and restructured with a new asset injection. Brought back to life, it listed a second time under new management as Center Gate. This is not important to the argument at hand, which focuses on pricing. For the full (and all too common) story, see Yuan Dong (ed.), *Shinian gushi fengyun* (Beijing: Jingji kexue chubanshe, 2001), pp. 201–48.

9 Wang Wei, p. 358.

10 Wang Wei, p. 358.

11 See Wang Wei, pp. 34–120 and 340–405.

12 Not all the deals have been completed, as regulatory approval can take months or years, but they do get done.

13 It bothers the CSRC, however; see CSRC, "Zhongguo zhengquanhui yaoqiu jiachang dui shangshi gongsi feiliutonggu xieyi zhuanrang huodong de guifan guanli," October 8, 2001, www.csrc.gov.org.

14 In the case of Sheneng, an energy company belonging to the Shanghai municipal government, only 3.5% of all shareholders showed up to vote on the buy-back, and they passed it. The restructuring of the company's equity structure provided an excellent opportunity to assist the parent to monetize its state shares. See Zhang Jing, pp. 43–44.

15 Bei Hu, "China urged to adopt class-action suits," *SCMP*, November 21, 2002, www.scmp.com.

16 The usefulness of the NAV method is debatable. Of the 27 companies with A and H shares, in only four cases was the H-share price higher than the NAV.

17 A detailed history of Zheng zhon Baiwen from 1996 to 2000 can be found in Yuan Fang, pp. 239–44.

18 "Sanlian takes key stake in ailing Zhengzhou Baiwen," *SCMP*, July 1, 2002. As of September 2002, Sanlian was the largest shareholder with 98.3 million shares, Zhengzhou Baiwen Group next with 14.4 million shares, and the ubiquitous Southern Securities third with 3.73 million shares.

19 "Top execs of listed Zhengzhou company prosecuted for false accounting," *Chinaonline*, August 8, 2002, www.chinaonline.com.

20 One of the directors, 71-year-old Lu Jiahao, appealed the ruling twice, but the case was dismissed both times on a technicality. Lu claimed his role was as an "honorary consultant, putting me outside the responsibilities of independent directors as prescribed by current laws," *Beijing Today* (English-language newspaper), November 22, 2002.

21 Wind Information, October 30, 2002.

22 SCRES, "Notice on the Immediate Halt to the Approval of Shareholding Companies Formed through Private Placements and a Reiteration of a Halt to Approval and Issuance of Internal Employee Shares," June 19, 1994, CSRC, *Zhengquan qihuo fagui huibian* (1994), p. 184.

23 "Apparent" privatization, since the authors were unable to detect by analyzing the trading and dividend performance of these shares any difference from typical state-controlled A-share companies. This would suggest that other variables might be more important in Chinese-listed company performance than the shareholding structure *per se* — for example, the failure of A-share investors to unite a shareholders' meeting to toss out ineffective management.

24 As a reminder, state LP shares are those representing the investment of corporatized SOEs which have contributed their own legally owned assets to the restructuring of themselves into shareholding companies. This category of SOE is owned directly by a state agency.

25 Wind Information, www.wind.com.cn.

26 "China Telecom forced to delay public offering," *SCMP*, November 1, 2002, www.scmp.com.

27 *China Securities Daily*, November 29, 1999, p. 1. Shares left unsold will be made available to the securities investment funds, which will then enjoy a two-year lock-up.

28 *China Securities Daily*, December 2, 1999, p. 1.

29 See CSRC's announcement that it has no intention of even considering floating all shares of de-listed companies after they had completed restructuring and could re-list. Given there are only a few de-listed companies, just how sensitive this topic is becomes clear. CSRC, "The Main Markets Are Not Considering Floating All Shares," undated, www.csrc.gov.cn.

30 "Welfare fund still gains from share sales," *SCMP*, April 29, 2002.

31 Wu Jinglian, "An alternate proposal to reduce state-owned shares," *Caijing*, January 21, 2002.

32 "China's Xiangcai mulls special A-share rights," *Dow Jones International News*, November 27, 2002. A local brokerage suggests the government should give A-share holders "special rights," but fails to disclose a workable solution.

33 CSRC, MOF, and SETC, "Notice Regarding Transfer to Foreign Investors of State-owned Shares and Legal Person Shares of Listed Companies," *Securities Daily*, November 4, 2002.

34 CSRC, PBOC, "Provisional Measures for the Management of Qualified Foreign Financial Institutions," November 12, 2002, www.csrc.gov.cn.

35 There has been talk of implementing a Qualified Domestic Institutional Investor (QDII) program. This program would provide flexibility to licensed domestic institutions to invest in international markets. Due to exchange control, this will be a long time coming. This is confirmed by Zhou Xiaochuan, "China securities chief says no timetable on QDII," *Reuters News Service*, November 21, 2002.

36 "Beijing sees no big hurdles to CDR plan," *SCMP*, December 4, 2001, www.scmp.com.

37 China Unicom is a foreign-registered company with shares trading in Hong Kong and New York. Most other Chinese companies are China domiciled and so face no legal obstructions to listing A shares. Had Unicom listed A shares, it would technically have been the first "foreign" company to access the domestic markets, setting an unwanted precedent.

38 Share classifications by the various data providers in China are remarkably messy. Some information systems will define state shares as state LP shares; others may classify state LP shares as domestic LP shares and omit the state legal person class entirely. For example, the Shanghai exchange at FY2001 breaks out state and state LP shares as 40% and 13% of the market, respectively, while Wind Information Company calls it 30% and 24%. The reality is that such share classes are quite similar in nature, but there is a difference.

39 An early 2002 CSRC study showed that major shareholders on average held 44.6% of domestically listed companies. *SCMP*, November 22, 2002, www.scmp.com.

40 The CSRC, however, is urging that minority investors institute class action suits. "China urged to adopt class-action suits," *Chinaonline*, November 21, 2002, www.chinaonline.com.

41 This day may not be far away. The Newbridge Group acquisition of a controlling stake in the justly famous Shenzhen Development Bank might indicate what can be done in the post-WTO environment. However, this is a bankrupt financial institution and the negotiated outcome is a long distance away from accumulating a stake in the public markets.

42 CSRC, "Measures for Administration of the Acquisition of Listed Companies," September 28, 2002, www.csrc.gov.cn.

43 See "Minying ziben qibing," *Xincaifu*, August 2002, pp. 77–78.

44 Zhang Xindong, "Jiazugu," August 2002, *Xincaifu*, p. 28; see also in the same edition, "Jiazu kongshi shangshi gongsi licheng," pp. 32–33. This provides a history of the earliest privately controlled listed companies.

45 Numbers provided by private source but based on State Statistical Bureau materials. The figures for shareholding companies are significantly higher than those provided in the annual statistical yearbooks. These place the total at slightly less than 6,000, which is most certainly too low.

Chapter 9

1 Li Zhangzhe, pp. 649–50.

2 In fact, they have written entire books about it. See Tao Chunsheng and Guo Hong (eds), *Shi nian niugu* (Beijing: Jingji kexue chubanshe, 2001).

3 For the stories of the *Laobagu* (the good old eight shares), see Tao Chunsheng and Guo Hong, pp. 7–35.

4 Yuan Fang, pp. 1–34.

5 Hewitt, pp. 88–89.

6 Yuan Fang, pp. 67–93.

7 Zhang Jing, p. 170.

8 Li Zhangzhe, pp. 625–36; the full text of the December 16, 1996 and June 15, 1999 editorials can be found in Wang An, pp. 239–50.

9 Li Zhangzhe, p. 635.

10 Li Zhangzhe, pp. 699–702.

11 A final note on Shenzhen Yi An. The stock recorded profits in 1999 and 2000, but currently is an ST stock after posting losses of RMB1.692 per share in 2001 and RMB0.066 for the first three quarters of 2002. If it continues to lose money, it could well face de-listing.

12 Li Zhangzhe, p. 701.

13 The index represents the performance of all listed funds on the Shanghai market valued at the market, not NAV, price.

14 *Shanghai Stock Exchange Statistics Annual 2002* [authors' calculation].

15 Historical volatility is seldom used as a market measure in China. This is because there are no stock or index options in China and the quality of risk management is low.

16 The number of listed stocks has grown considerably, therefore dampening the index and the influence of the larger stocks.

17 The Shanghai 30 Index (which is now the Shanghai 180 Index, reconstituted on July 1, 2001) shows higher volatility but only 1 or 2 percentage points at most and is only 0.1% higher in 2002.

18 In this example, Shanghai will be used to represent Shenzhen as well.

Chapter 10

1 Wang An, pp. 364–5.

2 Cao Er-jie, pp. 240–50. SOEs retained profit and reinvested it in capital goods. These were later contributed to corporatizing entities in return for shares.

3 Hu Xuzhi, pp. 35–40.

4 Procedurally speaking, Li Peng, the premier, should have signed the Company Law. Li, however, was in Germany suffering badly the demonstrations of human rights activists. He left in a huff. Zhu, in the meantime, took the document from Li's desk and signed it. Li didn't like that either: his son was running a direct competitor of Shandong Huaneng. Had Zhu not signed when he did, the project would have missed its chance to list.

5 Rather, the new parent of the corporatized entity owns the assets through holding the company's shares on behalf of the state. Since parent and company management are coterminus in all cases, this makes no difference.

6 Shi Dong and Zhao Xiaojian, "Shiwanyi guozi zouxiang," *Caijing*, November 20, 2002, pp. 22–34.

7 Jiang Zeming, *Shiliuda baogao: xinsixiang, xinlunduan, xinjucuo* (Beijing: Yanjiu chubanshe, 2002), pp. 23–24.

8 "Changsha huibie guoqi," *Caijing*, September 2000, pp. 31–42.

9 It is too early to tell whether Shang Fulin, the new CSRC chairman, will continue down the path created by Zhou Xiaochuan. Initial indications are negative. The dismissal of Gao Xiqing, Shang's January 2003 visit to the major market players in Shanghai, and their response as shown by the market's substantial rise since, suggest a much more "Chinese" approach. In which case, the next bull market is beginning. Within one week of his trip to Shanghai, unprecedented for a CSRC chairman, trading volumes ballooned, the index was up 10%, and CITIC Securities, which had failed as an IPO, was up more than 20%. Once again, the markets are driven by individuals, not by institutionalized procedures and fundamental performance.

10 China's Supreme Court announced that joint (as opposed to class) action suits would be accepted and set out the procedures for filing on January 9, 2003. *Dow Jones International*, January 9, 2003.

11 *China Securities Daily*, December 23, 1999, p. 1. More recently it was announced that only 10% reported false numbers, but this rapid improvement strains credulity.

12 Such information does, in fact, already appear from time to time but not in a meaningful way. For example, the *Shanghai Securities Daily* on January 6, 2003, carried a one-sentence article noting that at the end of November 2002 only 14.7 million of 34.5 million accounts held shares of which more than 90% were valued at less than RMB100,000; accounts with a value greater than RMB1 million numbered only 53,293. *Shanghai Securities Daily*, January 6, 2003, p. 2.

13 Ramoncito dela Cruz, "China AIG unit denies wrongdoing in A share investment," *Dow Jones Newswires*, December 13, 2002.

14 Even the CSRC's magazine is putting out articles on how to "develop" the Third Board – see Qiu Bingqing, "*Sanban wuweiping*," *Zhengquan shichang zhoukan*, October 26, 2002, pp. 14–21.

Select Bibliography

Newspapers and Periodicals

Asian Wall Street Journal
Caijing
China Securities Daily
Financial Times
People's Daily (Renmin Ribao)
South China Morning Post
Xincaifu (New Fortune)

Electronic Information Systems

Bloomberg
Qianlong Data System
Wind (*Wande*) Information System

Websites

Bloomberg — www.bloomberg.com
Caijing magazine — www.caijing.com.cn
China M&A — www.mergers-china.com
Chinaonline — www.chinaonline.com
China Securities Daily — www.cs.com.cn
Chinese bonds — www.chinabond.com.cn
Chinese Foreign Exchange — www.chinamoney.com.cn
CIRC — www.circ.gov.cn
CN Information Co. — www.cninfo.com.cn
CSRC — www.csrc.gov.cn
Hang Seng Services Ltd. — www.hsi.com.hk
Homeway — www.homeway.com.cn
HK Securities and Futures Commission — www.hksfc.org
Mergers China — www.bprsc.com.cn
PBOC — www.pbc.gov.cn
Quamnet — www.quamnet.com
Securities Association of China — www.s-a-c.org.cn
Shanghai Futures Exchange — www.shfe.com.cn
Shanghai Securities Daily — www.stocknews.com.cn
Shanghai Stock Exchange — www.sse.com.cn
Shenzhen Stock Exchange — www.sse.org.cn
South China Morning Post — www.scmp.com
SSCCRC — www.ssccrc.com

State Administration of Foreign Exchange   www.safe.gov.cn
State Statistical Bureau   www.stats.gov.cn
Stock Exchange of Hong Kong   www.hkex.com.hk
Third Board   www.siita.org.cn
Wind Information System   www.wind.com.cn
World Federation of Exchanges   www.world-exchanges.com

Publications

Yearbooks or Annuals

China Securities Regulatory Commission (ed.), *Zhengquan qihuo fagui huibian* (1992–2001) (Beijing: Falu chubanshe, undated), annual.

Gao Shangquan and Ye Sen (eds), *China Economic Systems Reform Yearbook* (1989–93) (Beijing: China Reform Publishing House), annual.

People's Bank of China, *Jinrong guizhang zhidu xuanbian* (1989–91) (Beijing: Jinrong chubanshe, 1991), annual.

Shanghai Stock Exchange (ed.), *Shanghai Stock Exchange Statistics Annual 2002* (Shanghai: Renmin chubanshe 2002), annual.

Shenzhen Stock Exchange (ed.), *Shenzhen Stock Exchange Fact Book 2001* (Beijing: Zhongguo jinrong chubanshe, 2002), annual.

Wang Wei (ed.), *China Mergers and Acquisitions Yearbook 2002* (Beijing: Huaxia chubanshe, 2002), annual.

Books, Articles and Monographs

Cai Jianwen, *Zhongguo gushi* (Beijing: China Commercial United Press, 2000).

Cao Er-jie, *Research and Prospects for the Chinese Securities Markets* (Beijing: Zhongguo caizheng jingji chubanshe, 1994).

Cao Fengqi, *Zhongguo zhengquan shichang: Shichang fazhan, guifan yu guojihua* (Beijing: Zhongguo jinrong chubanshe, 1998).

Chinese Securities Regulatory Commission, *Securities Issuance and Underwriting* (Beijing: Shanghai caijing daxue chubanshe, 1999).

Chen Zhiwu and Peng Xiong, "Discounts on Illiquid Stocks: Evidence from China," Yale International Center for Finance, Yale ICF Working Paper No. 00-56, September 2001.

Chun Hong, Zhou Shengye, and Wu Shaoqiu (eds), *Zhongguo zhengquan fagui zonghui*, Vol. 8 (Beijing: Zhongguo renmin daxue chubanshe, 1998).

Gao Shangquan and Chi Fulin (eds), *The Chinese Securities Market* (Beijing: Foreign Languages Press, 1996).

Han Zhiguo and Duan Qiang (eds), *Guoyougu jianchi: lishi jiyu haishi xianshi fengxian* (Beijing: Jingji kexue chubanshe, 2002).

Hertz, Ellen, *The Trading Crowd: An Ethnography of the Shanghai Stock Market* (Cambridge: Cambridge University Press, 1998).

Howson, Nicholas C., "China's Company Law: One Step Forward, Two Steps Back," *Columbia Journal of Asian Law*, 11(1), 1997, pp. 127–73.

Hu Shili, Li Qiaoning, and Li Qing, "The market manipulator Lu Liang," *Caijing*, February 2001, pp. 19–31.

Hu Xuzhi, *The Evolution of China's Stock Markets and Its Institutions* (Beijing: Jinji kexue chunbanshe, 1999).

Jiang Ping (advisor), *Jinrong falu fagui quanshu* (Beijing: Sanxia chubanshe, 1997), two volumes.

Jiang Xinwen (ed.), *Guide to Shareholding Enterprise Restructuring and Actual Examples* (Beijing: Zhongguo jingji chubanshe, 1997).

Li Changjiang, *The History and Development of China's Securities Markets* (Beijing: Zhongguo wuzi chubanshe, 1998).

Li Zhangzhe, *Zhongyu chenggong: Zhongguo gushi fazhan baogao* (Beijing: Shijie zhishi chubanshe, 2001) with CD ROM.

Ling Huawei and Yu Ning, "Asset appraisal manipulation," *Caijing*, June 5, 2002, pp. 84–89.

Ling Huawei and Wang Le, "Yinguangxia falls into the trough," *Caijing*, August 2001, pp. 18–37.

Liu Hongru (ed.), *A Review of and the Prospects for Overseas Listings by Chinese Enterprises* (Beijing: Zhongguo caizheng jingji chubanshe, 1998).

Liu Hongru, "Several issues regarding China's experiments with shareholding structure," *Renmin Ribao*, June 23, 1992, p. 5.

Nolan, Peter, *China and the Global Economy* (New York: Palgrave, 2001).

Ping Hu and Li Qing, "The black inside story of funds," *Caijing*, October 2000, pp. 23–35.

Qin Liping, Kang Weiping, and Yu Ning, "Manipulator's paradise," *Caijing*, June 20, 2002, pp. 50–63.

Shi Dong and Zhao Xiaojian, "Shiwanyi guozi zouxiang," *Caijing*, November 20, 2002, pp. 22–34.

Tang Yun Wei, Lynne Chow, and Barry J. Cooper, *Accounting and Finance in China* (Hong Kong: Longman Group (Far East) Ltd., 1992).

Tao Chunsheng and Guo Hong (ed.), *Shinian niugu* (Beijing: Jingji kexue chubanshe, 2001).

Tenev, Stoyan and Zhang Chunlin, *Corporate Governance and Enterprise Reform in China* (USA: World Bank/IFC, 2002).

Thomas, W. A., *Western Capitalism in China: A History of the Shanghai Stock Exchange* (Aldershot, England: Ashgate Publishing Ltd., 2001).

Walter, C. E. and Howie, F. J. T., *"To Get Rich is Glorious": China's Stock Markets in the 80s and 90s* (UK: Palgrave, 2001).

Wang An, *Guye nishangzuo* (Beijing: Huayi chubanshe, 2000).

Wang Lianzhou and Li Cheng (eds), *Fengfeng yuyu zhengquanfa* (Shanghai: Shanghai Sanlian shudian, 2000).

Wang Wei and Ouyang Xiaomin (eds), *M&A Handbook* (Beijing: Zhongguo shidai jingji chubanshe, 2002).

Wu Jinglian, *Wu Jinglian: Shinian fenyun huagushi* (Shanghai: Yuandong chubanshe, 2001).

Xia Bin, "Report on China's private funds," *Caijing*, July 2001, pp. 66–75.

Xue Weihong, *Gupiao yunzuo falu shiwu* (Beijing: Zhongguo chengshi chubanshe, 2001).

Yao Chengxi, *Stock Market and Futures Market in the People's Republic of China* (Oxford: Oxford University Press, 1998).

Yu Ning and Ling Huawei, "The life and death of Anshan Securities," *Caijing*, September 5, 2002, pp. 34–48.

Yu Tian, Wu Yigang, and Lei Fen, *Guoyougu jianchi yu gushi touzi celue* (Beijing: Zhongyang minzu daxue chubanshe, 2001).

Yuan Fang (ed.), *Shinian gushi fengyun* (Beijing: Jingji kexue chubanshe, 2001).

Zhang Jing, *Zhongguo gushi de wuqu: feishichanghua de gupiao shichang* (Beijing: Zhongguo zhengquan chubanshe, 2001).

Zhang Xindong (chief writer), "*Xincaifu*: 100 jiazu," *Xincaifu*, August 2002, pp. 27–79.

Index